ISBN 978-0-266-94515-4
PIBN 11114508

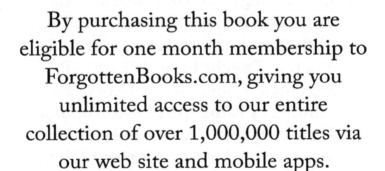

C E R E A L   C O U R I E R

Official Messenger of the Office of Cereal Crops and Diseases
Bureau of Plant Industry, U. S. Department of Agriculture
(NOT FOR PUBLICATION)

Vol. 21   No. 1

January 15, 1929
Personnel (Jan. 1-15) and Field Station (Dec. 16-31) Issue

PERSONNEL ITEMS

Dr. A. M. Brunson, agronomist in the cooperative corn investigations
at Manhattan, Kans., who came to Washington in November, left for his
headquarters at Manhattan on January 3.

Dr. J. G. Dickson, agent in the cooperative cereal disease investigations that are being conducted at Madison, Wis., spent a few days in Washington after his return from the scientific meetings in New York. He left
for his headquarters at Madison on January 5.

Chester N. DuBois, junior scientific aid in cereal experiments at the
Arlington Experiment Farm, resigned his position on January 15 to enter
another line of work outside of Washington.

Dr. Hurley Fellows, associate pathologist in charge of the cooperative
investigations with wheat foot rots at Manhattan, Kans., spent about four
weeks in Washington, leaving for his headquarters on January 3.

Dr. J. R. Holbert, agronomist in charge of the cereal-disease investigations conducted in cooperation with Funk Bros. Seed Co., Bloomington, Ill.,
and the Illinois Agricultural Experiment Station, spent about 10 days in
Washington and left for his headquarters at Bloomington on January 5.

Dr. H. B. Humphrey, principal pathologist in charge of cereal-rust
investigations, was made Editor-in-Chief of Phytopathology by the Council
of the American Phytopathological Society at the meetings of the Society
in New York in December.

Dr. M. T. Jenkins, associate agronomist in charge of cooperative corn
investigations at Ames, Iowa, who came to Washington in November left for
his headquarters on January 3.

C. O. Johnston, assistant pathologist in charge of the cooperative leaf-rust investigations at Manhattan, Kans., who spent a few weeks in th Washington Office, left for his headquarters on January 5.

Dr. E. B. Mains, agent in the cereal-disease investigations that are being conducted in cooperation with the Purdue University Agricultural Ex periment Station at La Fayette, Ind., came to Washington on January 2 for conferences with members of the Office staff. He left for La Fayette on January 5.

Hickman C. Murphy, agent in the cereal-rust investigations conducted in cooperation with the Iowa Agricultural Experiment Station, who spent four weeks in the Washington Office, left for his headquarters at Ames on January 5.

Dr. J. D. Sayre, of the department of botany, Ohio State University, came to Washington on January 2 to attend the Third Annual Corn Borer Research Conference and to confer with members of the Office regarding the progress of cooperative corn borer research in Ohio.

D. E. Stephens, superintendent of the Sherman County Branch Station, Moro, Oreg., will come to Washington about January 20 to confer with members of the Office of Dry Land Agriculture and other officials of the Department.

VISITORS

Among the visitors in the Office in the period from January 2 to 15 were the following:

Dr. R. A. Brink, associate professor and assistant in genetics, Col of Agriculture and the Agricultural Experiment Station, University of W sin.

C. R. Burnham, assistant in genetics, Agricultural Experiment Stat University of Wisconsin.

R. M. Caldwell, State Leader of barberry eradication, Madison, Wis

L. E. Call, dean of the division of agriculture and director of th experiment station of the Kansas State College of Agriculture.

J. J. Davis, head of the department of entomology, Purdue Univers

P. L. Errington, a former barberry scout in South Dakota.

C. B. Hutchison, director of the Giannini Foundation of Agricultural Economics, and associate director of research at the Agricultural Experiment Station, University of California.

M. B. McKay, plant pathologist in the department of botany and plant pathology, Oregon Agricultural Experiment Station.

Dr. C. F. Noll, department of agronomy, Pennsylvania State College.

Dr. George Stewart, professor of agronomy, Agricultural College of Utah and the Agricultural Experiment Station, Logan, Utah.

Miss L. M. Venable, formerly assistant in flax investigations of this Office, and now connected with the extension service of the University of North Carolina.

MANUSCRIPTS AND PUBLICATIONS

1 An article entitled "Effects of Temperature on Leaf Acidity and Moisture of Certain Spring and Winter Wheats," by Annie M. Hurd-Karrer, was submitted on January 4 for publication in the Journal of Agricultural Research.

2 A brief manuscript entitled "Hetero-Fertilization in Maize," by George F. Sprague, was approved on January 7 for publication in Science.

3 An article entitled "A Composite Hybrid Mixture," by Harry V. Harlan and Mary L. Martini, was approved on January 9 for publication in the Journal of the American Society of Agronomy.

4 An article entitled "Barley Variety Tests at a High-Altitude Ranch near Obsidian, Idaho," by Harry V. Harlan and F. W. Shaw, was approved on January 9 for publication in the Journal of the American Society of Agronomy.

N. Y. Cornell Agr. Expt. Sta. Mem. 117, entitled "Chromosome Numbers in Zea mays L.," by L. F. Randolph, was received in December, 1928, bearing date of publication of June, 1928. (pp. 3-44, pls. i-iii) (Office of Cereal Crops and Diseases, B. P. I., U. S. Dept. Agr., in cooperation with the N. Y. State Coll. Agr., Ithaca, N. Y.)

The article entitled "Seed-Coat Structure and Inheritance of Seed Color in Sorghums," by Arthur F. Swanson, appears in the Journal of Agricultural Research 37 (10): 577-588, fig. 1. Nov. 15, 1928. (Received January 8.)

Yearbook Articles

Slight changes have been made in the titles for Yearbook papers submitted for the 1928 Yearbook of the Department of Agriculture since they were noted in the Cereal Courier 20 (25): 306. Oct. 10, 1928.

The titles as approved on January 7, 1929, are as follows:

48 Flaxes Resistant to Wilt Developed at Experiment Stations. A. C. Dillman.

49 Corn Breeding for Resistance to Cold Yields Good Results. J. R. Holbert and W. L. Burlison.

50 Corn Smut Reduces Yields and Lowers Sugar in the Stalks. A. M. Hurd-Karrer and H. Hasselbring.

FIELD STATION CONDITION AND PROGRESS

HUMID ATLANTIC COAST AREA (South to North)

GEORGIA

State College of Agriculture, Athens (Cereal Agronomy, R. R. Childs)
(December 21)

At the Georgia Coastal Plain Experiment Station, Tifton, where Mr. Childs conferred with W. J. Davis, agronomist, from December 18 to 20, a good stand of all varieties of small grain had been obtained; all are making excellent growth. Mr. Childs and Mr. Davis checked the results of the 1928 experiments.

It was noted that the fall acreage of oats in the southern part of the State was above normal; this probably is due to the fact that there is a shortage of feed stuff in that section caused by the tropical storms that damaged the corn crop in August and September.

All of the grain here at the College is coming along in good shape. Most of it was seeded fairly early, and the season has been favorable so far.

VIRGINIA

Arlington Experiment Farm, Rosslyn (Small Grain Agronomy, J. W. Taylor)
(January 14)

No temperatures sufficiently low to injure fall-sown grains have been experienced. The lowest temperature for the winter thus far recorded was 13 degrees on January 8. The aphids so prevalent and destructive to fall grains during the past fall are still at work though their numbers appear to have been reduced.

Greenhouse activities of the agronomic section for the winter of 1928-1929 have increased somewhat. Plants of spring wheat crosses and oat hybrid grown under electric lights are now heading. So far the wheat plants have shown fewer abnormalities under greenhouse conditions than in previous years

Arlington Experiment Farm, Rosslyn (Corn Breeding, F. D. Richey)

Arlington Experiment Farm, Rosslyn (Cereal Smuts, V. F. Tapke, Acting in Charge)

Arlington Experiment Farm, Rosslyn (Virus Diseases, H. H. McKinney)

NEW YORK

Cornell University Agricultural Experiment Station, Ithaca (Cereal Breeding, H. H. Love)

HUMID MISSISSIPPI VALLEY AREA (South to North)

LOUISIANA

Rice Experiment Station, Crowley (Rice Agronomy, J. M. Jenkins) (January 9)

Excellent weather in December permitted farm operations to proceed with few interruptions. The temperature was much the same as of December of last year. The precipitation was much less, however. Rain occurred on 11 days, with only one heavy rain, making a total of 3.89 inches. Last year rain fell on 15 days, with three heavy rains, the total being 7.86 inches. The 18-year average precipitation is 6.25 inches.

A temperature of freezing or below was recorded on 15 days during the year: 7 days in January, 2 days in February, and 7 days in December. In 1927 freezing temperatures were recorded on 12 days: 5 days in January and 7 days in December.

Work on the station was farther advanced by the end of December than in any previous year. Plowing was completed on the 20th. The greater portion of the rice crop was fanned during the month. Ditches have been cleaned and roads repaired.

Agricultural Experiment Station, Baton Rouge (Corn Breeding. H. F. Stoneberg)

MISSOURI

Agricultural Experiment Station, Columbia (Cereal Agronomy, L. J. Stadler)

TENNESSEE

Agricultural Ecperiment Station, Knoxville (Corn Breeding, L. S. Mayer)

IOWA

Agricultural Experiment Station, Ames (Oat Breeding, L. C. Burnett)

Agricultural Experiment Station, Ames (Corn Breeding, M. T. Jenkins)

Agricultural Experiment Station, Ames (Crown Rust of Oats, S. M. Dietz)

ILLINOIS

Funk Bros. Seed Co., Bloomington (Corn Root, Stalk and Ear Rots, J. R. Holbert)

INDIANA

Purdue University Agricultural Experiment Station, La Fayette (Corn Rots and Metallic Poisoning, G. N. Hoffer)

Purdue University Agricultural Experiment Station, La Fayette (Leaf Rusts, E. B. Mains)

WISCONSIN

Agricultural Experiment Station, Madison (Wheat Scab, J. G. Dickson)

MINNESOTA

Agricultural Experiment Station, University Farm, St. Paul (Wheat Breeding, K. S. Quisenberry, Acting in Charge)

Agricultural Experiment Station, University Farm, St. Paul (Stem Rust, E. C. Stakman)

Agricultural Experiment Station, University Farm, St. Paul (Flax Rust, H. A. Rodenhiser)

GREAT PLAINS AREA (South to North)

OKLAHOMA

Woodward Field Station, Woodward (Grain Sorghum and Broomcorn, J. B. Sieglinger)

KANSAS

Agricultural Experiment Station, Manhattan (Cereal Breeding, J.H.Parke

Agricultural Experiment Station, Manhattan (Corn Breeding, A.M.Brunso

Agricultural Experiment Station, Manhattan (Wheat Foot Rots, Hurley Fellows)

Agricultural Experiment Station, Manhattan (Wheat Leaf Rust, C. O. Johnston) (January 12)

The writer returned from a month's stay in Washington on January 7, to find the coldest weather of the winter in the southern Great Plains. Considerable snow fell on January 5, but it was accompanied by a high wind which swept it from the fields and drifted it in the roads. More snow has fallen since, however, and most fields have a fairly good snow cover. Winter wheat seems to be in excellent condition, with little winterkilling thus far and plenty of winter moisture.

Reports from cooperators at the leaf-rust nurseries in Texas, Oklahoma, and Kansas indicate that very little fall infection of leaf rust occurred in that area this fall. A small amount of rust was present at College Station, Texas, on December 5, and a moderate amount was collected by Dr. T. A. Kiesselbach at Lincoln, Nebr., on December 28. Considerable rust was present in the Manhattan nursery on November 28, but very few fresh uredinia could be found at that time.

The leaf-rust studies in the greenhouse are well under way. More than 100 F_1 plants and about 600 F_2 plants representing 6 crosses are being grown to maturity. These have been inoculated with leaf rust in the seedling stage and the rust readings have been taken. Sixty-six cultures of leaf rust from various sources are being carried in the greenhouse. Most of these have been transferred to lantern globe chambers to prevent mixtures. Thirty of them have been tested on differential varieties of wheat and the physiologic forms have been identified.

Some of the F_1 hybrids which have Chinese (C. I. No. 6223) for one parent are beginning to head. This is the earliest heading we have ever recorded in our greenhouse studies at Manhattan.

Hays Branch Experiment Station, Hays (Cereal Agronomy, A. F. Swanson)

NEBRASKA

North Platte Substation, North Platte (Cereal Agronomy, G. F. Sprague)

NORTH DAKOTA

Agricultural Experiment Station, State College Station, Fargo (Flax Diseases, --------)

Dickinson Substation, Dickinson (Cereal Agronomy, R. W. Smith) (December 18)

The dry weather that prevailed during the fall has continued until the present time. About an inch of snow fell during the first week of December but the ground is now bare again. Temperatures have been slightly above normal except for one brief cold spell when the temperature dropped to 19 below zero on December 4.

The dry condition of the roads has favored the marketing of grain and a considerable quantity of wheat is marketed in Dickinson daily.

Grain from increase fields of wheat, oats, and barley grown on the Substation last summer is being cleaned and stored. Samples of wheat varieties grown in the replicated plots have been sent to Washington and to Fargo for milling and baking tests.

Supt. Leroy Moomaw is expected to return from Washington next week.

(January 3)

The total precipitation for the past year at the Substation was 15.32 inches which is about 0.22 of an inch below normal. However, cereal crops produced the highest yield obtained during the past five years. This was due to the favorable distribution of rainfall, the months of June, July, and August having more than the usual amount of rain. The May precipitation was more than an inch below normal, making drought conditions that affected the yield of early cereal varieties. The heavy snowfall of the previous winter, especially in November and December, helped to offset the lack of rainfall in the spring.

Low mean temperatures occurred every month of the growing season with the exception of May and aided in producing good yields of small grain but retarded the development of the corn crop. The temperatures were above normal in January, February, March, November, and December, as well as in May, making the wintry portion of 1927 mild and pleasant.

During the present winter the ground has been practically bare of snow all the time until New Year's Day when a light snow began that has supplied about 3 inches of snow.

Supt. Leroy Moomaw returned December 20 from a trip to Washington, D.C.

Northern Great Plains Field Station, Mandan (Flax Breeding, J. C. Brinsmade, Jr.) (January 2)

The weather in December was generally mild for this time of year, really more like autumn than winter. Maximum temperature, 47 degrees December 27; minimum, -15 degrees December 3. Total precipitation, 0.17 of an inch.

Observation of the flax still standing in the field indicates that there was very little loss of bolls or seed in December. A photograph was taken on December 11 of the flax standing up straight in a snow drift. The entire absence of bolls on top of the snow indicated that there had been no loss since the snowfall of December 4.

Northern Great Plains Field Station, Mandan (Cereal Agronomy, E. R. Ausemus)

MONTANA

Judith Basin Substation, Moccasin (Cereal Agronomy, B. B. Bayles)
Joe L. Sutherland) [January 2]

(Summary of Climatic and Crop Conditions for the Past Season)

Fields of winter wheat were injured severely by a combination of
blight (Helminthosporium) and weather conditions in the fall and spring.
It was necessary to reseed many fields while others were summer fallowed
because of poor stands of winter wheat.

A large part of the winter wheat was seeded early in August, 1927.
The long, warm fall weakened these early sown fields to such an extent
that many were attacked by blight and entered the winter in a diseased
condition. Except for a short period during the first part of January,
1928, a fair amount of snow covered the winter-wheat fields from November 1 to March 1. A killing temperature of -5 degrees on April 13, after
warm weather in March and the first part of April had brought the wheat
out of dormancy, probably was the main factor in the large amount of
winterkilling.

The season was very favorable for spring grains except for a drought
period in May and the first part of June which caused some delayed germination. However, there was enough rainfall from June 14 until harvest to
produce good yields.

The fall was exceptionally favorable and all grains were stored in
good condition.

A summary of the precipitation records for the crop year (Sept. 1 to
August 31) gives an annual precipitation of 13.46 inches which is more than
3 inches below the 20-year normal of 16.64 inches. The precipitation for
May (0.53 of an inch) is the lowest on record for this month at the Substation and all months, but November, from September, 1927, to June, 1928,
are far below average in this respect. The precipitation for the calendar
year of 1928 was 12.21, the 20-year average being 16.35 inches.

The seasonal precipitation (April 1 to August 31) was 8.93 inches,
while the average over a 20-year period is 10.29 inches.

Montana Agricultural Experiment Station, Bozeman (Le Roy Powers)
(January 2) (J. A. Clark)

The following yields were obtained from 17 varieties of winter wheat
grown in triplicate plots. Blackhull and Superhard were the highest yielding varieties, the new smut resistant Oro variety ranking fourth.

Table 1. Yields of winter-wheat varieties grown in 3 systematically replicated plots at the Montana Agricultural Experiment Station, Bozeman, Mont., in 1928

Class and Variety	Mont. No.	Yield (Bu. per Acre)
Hard Red Winter		
Blackhull	9	57.1
Superhard	45	55.3
Nebraska No. 60	5	54.3
Oro	68	53.5
Karmont	7	53.3
Turkey	4	53.3
Regal	69	53.2
Montana No. 36	36	52.5
Kanred	2	51.9
Ridit	38	50.3
Kharkof	3	49.3
Newturk	33	46.7
Minturki	10	44.8
Iowa 1946	8	44.7
Soft Red Winter		
Jones Fife	16	47.9
Berkeley Rock	25	39.8
White		
Albit	44	45.5

The more important standard varieties of spring wheat were grown in triplicate 1/40-acre plots, and the yields obtained are presented in Table 2. Reliance and a selection from it were the highest yielding hard red spring varieties, and Baart was the highest yielding white wheat.

Table 2. Yield of spring-wheat varieties grown in 3 systematically replicated 1/40-acre plots at the Montana Agricultural Experiment Station, Bozeman, Mont., in 1928

Class and Variety	Mont. No.	Yield (Bu. per acre)
Hard Red Spring		
Reliance	582	77.1
Reliance Sel. 40	---	70.6
Supreme	531	70.1
Marquis 10B	511	69.2
Kitchener	525	66.8
Marquis (Average 2 strains)	---	65.1
Ceres	578	62.5
Marquis (Langs)	513	61.0
White		
Baart	---	75.2
Federation	---	72.7

The less important standard varieties and a number of hybrid selections increased from the nursery were grown in triplicate 1/120-acre plots.
The results obtained from these trials are presented in Table 3. Additional selections of Reliance and other Kanred x Marquis hybrid selections
produced the highest yields.

Table.3. Yield of spring-wheat varieties and hybrids grown in 3 systematically replicated 1/120-acre.plots at the Montana Agricultural Experiment Station, Bozeman, Mont., in 1928

Variety or Cross	Hybrid No.	Nursery No.	Mont. No.	Yield (Bu.per A.)
Reliance Sel. 16	B-8-11-16	14	---	90.7
Reliance Sel. 64	B-8-11-64	22A	---	89.7
Kanred x Marquis	B-9-11-27	28	---	86.3
Kanred x Marquis	B-9-14-42	41	---	83.3
Federation x Dicklow	(Hybrid J)	--	---	81.7
Champlain	--------	--	583	80.7
Kanred x Marquis	B-2-14-20	11	---	79.3
Renfrew	--------	--	576	78.3
University 222	--------	--	577	77.7
Marquis[1]	--------	--	---	73.1
Kanred x Marquis	B-9-14-24	37	---	72.7
Triumph	--------	--	530	69.7
Kota x Marquis	1656.81		---	69.0
Dicklow	--------	--	506	61.0

[1] Average of six different lots.

Judith Basin Substation, Moccasin (Cereal Agronomy, Joe L. Sutherland
for B. B. Bayles) (January 2) (J. A. Clark)

The yields in bushels per acre, together with percentage of protein
and protein in pounds per acre of the spring wheat varieties grown in the
nursery at Moccasin are presented in the following table.

Crude protein content, pounds of protein per acre, and yield in bushels
per acre of spring wheat varieties and hybrid selections grown in triple rod
rows, replicated three times at the Judith Basin Substation, Moccasin, Mont.,
in 1928

Variety or Cross	C. I. No..	Nursery. No.	Protein (per cent)	Protein (Lbs.per A.)	Yield (Bu.per A.)
Reliance Sel. 22	----	17	13.7	249	30.3
Hard Federation x Marquis	----	456	14.4	257	29.7
Marquis x Hard Federation	----	666	12.8	227	29.5
Do	----	657	13.3	234	29.3
Kanred x Marquis	----	33	14.7	251	28.5
Marquis x Hard Federation	----	729	13.2	225	28.4
Do	----	674	13.2	224	28.3
Baart	1697	---	14.6	247	28.3
Ceres (2 tests)	6900	---	14.0	236	28.2

Continued

Variety or Cross	C. I. No.	Nursery No.	Protein (Per cent)	Protein (Lbs. per A.)	Yield (Bu. per A.)
Hard Federation x Marquis	----	678	13.8	233	28.1
Hussar x Hard Federation	----	1018	13.4	225	28.0
Marquis x Hard Federation	----	659	13.8	229	27.6
Mindum	5296	---	15.9	261	27.4
Marquis x Hard Federation	----	663	12.9	211	27.3
Do	----	673	12.4	202	27.1
Kota x Marquis	8004	1656.84	13.8	224	27.0
Hard Federation x Marquis	----	453	14.9	240	26.8
Supreme Sel. 22	----	---	13.3	238	26.7
Marquis x Hard Federation	----	706	13.8	219	26.5
Marquis 10B (2 tests)	----	---	14.8	233	26.4
Marquis x Hard Federation	----	708	13.5	214	26.4
Akrona	6381	---	15.2	240	26.3
Marquis x Hard Federation	----	727	13.2	208	26.3
Peliss Sel. 14	----	---	16.1	253	26.2
Hard Federation Sel. 31	----	---	14.4	226	26.1
Marquis x Hard Federation	----	378	14.6	228	26.0
Marquis III	8023	---	14.4	225	26.0
Kanred x Marquis	----	35	14.0	218	26.0
Red Bobs Sel. 25	----	---	12.8	199	25.9
Marquis x Hard Federation	----	651	13.9	214	25.6
Vermillion	----	---	15.1	231	25.5
Hard Federation Sel. 79	----	---	14.2	217	25.5
Marquis x Hard Federation	----	398	13.7	210	25.5
Hard Federation Sel. 60	----	---	15.1	229	25.3
Marquis x Hard Federation	----	672	14.4	219	25.3
Red Bobs Sel. 51	----	---	13.6	206	25.3
Hard Federation x Marquis	----	745	13.8	209	25.2
Marquis x Hard Federation	----	656	13.6	206	25.2
Supreme Sel. 13	----	---	13.1	198	25.2
Marquis x Hard Federation	----	736	13.0	196	25.1
Reliance Sel. 16	----	14	14.5	219	25.0
Kitchener (2 tests)	4800	---	14.0	210	25.0
Marquis x Hard Federation	----	409	13.9	208	24.9
Hard Federation Sel. 82	----	---	14.5	216	24.8
Kanred x Marquis	----	41	13.9	207	24.8
Marquis x Hard Federation	----	433	13.7	204	24.8
Axminster	8196	---	14.7	218	24.7
Reliance Sel. 64	----	22A	13.9	206	24.7
Marquis x Hard Federation	----	413	13.6	202	24.7
Do	----	670	13.3	197	24.7
Kota x Hard Federation	----	299	14.6	215	24.6
Red Bobs (2 tests)	6255	---	14.2	210	24.6
Marquis x Hard Federation	----	675	13.9	205	24.6
Kanred x Marquis	8018	---	14.6	215	24.5
Marquis x Hard Federation	----	400	14.3	210	24.5
Do	----	710	13.7	201	24.4
Do	----	395	13.4	196	24.4
Nodak	6519	---	15.4	225	24.3
Red Bobs Sel. 32	----	---	14.3	208	24.3

Continued

Variety or Cross	C. I. No.	Nursery No.	Protein (Per cent)	Protein (Lbs. per A.)	Yield (Bu. per A.)
Marquis x Hard Federation	----	427	13.9	203	24.3
Hard Federation x Marquis	----	676	12.2	178	24.3
University 222 (2 tests)	----	---	14.1	204	24.1
Kanred x Marquis	----	39	13.6	196	24.0
Marquis x Hard Federation	----	399	14.9	214	23.9
Montana King	----	---	14.8	212	23.9
Supreme (2 tests)	8026	---	14.1	202	23.9
Marquis x Hard Federation	----	734	13.9	199	23.9
Reliance	7370	---	13.7	197	23.9
Marquis x Hard Federation	----	668	13.1	188	23.9
Red Bobs Sel. 32	----	---	13.0	186	23.9
Marquis x Hard Federation	----	402	13.4	190	23.7
Hard Federation x Marquis	----	677	13.6	193	23.7
Kanred x Marquis	----	37	13.5	192	23.7
Marquis x Hard Federation	----	661	13.5	192	23.7
Do	----	421	13.3	189	23.7
Kota (2 tests)	5878	---	14.8	210	23.6
Kanred x Marquis	----	11	13.7	194	23.6
Hard Federation x Marquis	----	680	14.8	208	23.4
Hard Federation x Prelude	----	256	14.7	206	23.3
Hard Federation Sel. 90	----	---	14.5	203	23.3
Marquis x Hard Federation	----	671	13.4	187	23.3
Hussar x Hard Federation	----	1020	13.9	193	23.2
Kota x Hard Federation	----	317	14.4	200	23.1
Do	----	295	13.7	190	23.1
Marquis x Hard Federation	----	393	13.2	183	23.1
Supreme Sel. 8	----	---	13.1	182	23.1
Kubanka	1440	---	15.5	213	22.9
Hard Federation x Marquis	----	747	14.6	201	22.9
Marquis x Hard Federation	----	719	13.4	184	22.9
Marquis (16 checks)	3641	---	14.4	194	22.7
Power	3697	---	16.9	229	22.6
Marquis x Hard Federation	----	649	13.7	186	22.6
Kota x Marquis 1656.81	8185	---	14.9	201	22.5
Marquis x Hard Federation	----	381	14.1	190	22.5
Do	----	418	14.1	190	22.5
Kanred x Marquis	----	28	15.1	203	22.4
Kota x Kanred	----	619	13.6	182	22.3
Kota x Hd. Fed. x Kanred-Marquis	----	700	13.4	179	22.3
Renfrew (2 tests)	8194	---	14.4	177	22.3
Marquis x Hard Federation	----	723	13.2	176	22.3
Do	----	716	13.7	182	22.2
Supreme Sel. 14	----	---	13.3	177	22.2
Reliance (Pure for Form 17 rust)	----	---	15.2	202	22.1
Marquis x Hard Federation	----	705	13.3	176	22.1
Kota x Marquis 1656.125	----	---	15.6	203	21.7
Garnet (2 tests)	8181	---	14.8	192	21.6
Kanred x Marquis	----	471	14.5	187	21.5
Hard Federation (5 tests)	4733	---	14.1	131	21.5
Supreme Sel. 11	----	---	12.9	166	21.4

Continued

Variety or Cross	C. I. No.	Nursery No.	Protein (Per cent)	Protein (Lbs. per A.)	Yiel (Bu. per
Hard Federation Sel. 71	----	---	15.0	192	21.3
Kanred x Marquis	----	38	14.2	181	21.3
Supreme Sel. 1	----	---	13.1	167	21.3
Peliss Sel. 100	----	---	16.4	209	21.2
Marquis x Hard Federation	----	653	14.3	182	21.2
Do	----	377	13.8	176	21.2
Red Bobs Sel. 26	----	---	14.1	179	21.1
Hard Federation x Prelude	----	256	15.5	193	20.7
Federation	4734	---	14.1	175	20.7
Mondak	7287	---	16.0	196	20.4
Kota x Hard Federation	----	301	14.4	171	19.8
Kota x Galgalos	----	482	15.2	180	19.7
Peliss	1584	---	16.6	195	19.6
Supreme Sel. 4	----	---	13.2	154	19.5
Red Bobs Sel. 30	----	---	13.5	152	18.8
Quality	6607	---	17.6	197	18.7
Kota x Hard Federation	----	345	15.0	168	18.7
Marquis x Erivan	----	240	14.6	163	18.6
Hope	8178	---	14.6	162	18.5
Kota x Hard Federation	----	290	15.4	170	18.4
Marquis x Hard Federation	----	709	14.0	152	18.1
Reward	8182	---	17.2	186	18.0
Marquis x Sunset	----	346	14.6	157	17.9
Hard Federation x Prelude	----	273	15.3	154	16.8
Ruby	6047	---	15.3	153	16.6
H-44	8177	---	15.0	147	16.1
Kota x Hard Federation	----	285	14.8	143	16.
Peliss Sel. 98	----	---	17.9	168	15.(
Erivan	2397	---	14.2	133	15.
Peliss Sel. 89	----	---	17.1	159	15.
Red Chaff (club)	4241	---	17.1	153	14.
Kota x Hard Federation	----	284	14.4	122	14.

WESTERN BASIN AND COAST AREAS (North to West and South)

IDAHO

Aberdeen Substation, Aberdeen (Cereal Agronomy, G. A. Wiebe)

Agricultural Experiment Station, Moscow (Stripe Rust, C. W. Hungerfor

WASHINGTON

Agricultural Experiment Station, Pullman (Cereal Breeding, E. F. Gaines)

OREGON

Sherman County Branch Station, Moro (Cereal Agronomy, D. E. Stephens)

CALIFORNIA

Biggs Rice Field Station, Biggs (Rice Agronomy, J. W. Jones)

University Farm, Davis (Cereal Agronomy, V. H. Florell)

Agricultural Experiment Station, Berkeley (Cereal Smuts, F. N. Briggs)

BARBERRY ERADICATION PROGRESS

OHIO

Ohio State University, College of Agriculture, Columbus, J. W. Baringer

INDIANA

Purdue University College of Agriculture, La Fayette, W. E. Leer

MICHIGAN

Agricultural College, East Lansing, W. F. Reddy

WISCONSIN

Department of Agriculture, State Capitol Annex, Madison, R. M. Caldwell

ILLINOIS

Box 72, Post Office Building, Urbana, R. W. Bills

IOWA

Iowa State College, Ames, P. W. Rohrbaugh

MINNESOTA

Agricultural Experiment Station, University Farm, St. Paul, L. W. Melander

NEBRASKA

College of Agriculture, University Farm, Lincoln, A. F. Thiel

SOUTH DAKOTA

College of Agriculture, Brookings, R. O. Bulger

NORTH DAKOTA

Agricultural Experiment Station, State College Station, Fargo, G. C. Mayoue

MONTANA

State College of Agriculture, Bozeman, W. L. Popham

WYOMING

College of Agriculture, University of Wyoming, Laramie, E. A. Lungren

COLORADO

Agricultural College, Ft. Collins, E. A. Lungren

C E R E A L   C O U R I E R

Official Messenger of the Office of Cereal Crops and Diseases
Bureau of Plant Industry, U. S. Department of Agriculture
(NOT FOR PUBLICATION)

Vol. 21   No. 2

January 31, 1929
Personnel (Jan. 16-31) and Project Issue

PERSONNEL ITEMS

R. O. Bulger, State Leader of barberry eradication in South Dakota, came to Washington on January 28 to assist the associate pathologist in charge of barberry eradication in summarizing progress and cost data of the barberry eradication campaign for the past calendar year and determining field policies for the current year. Mr. Bulger will remain in Washington about three weeks.

Loren L. Davis, agent in the cooperative cereal investigations conducted at Manhattan, Kans., under the direction of Dr. John H. Parker, came to Washington about the middle of January for conferences with Office officials and to use the Department library.

Mr. Davis left Washington on January 25 to return to Manhattan, from which place he will proceed to Aberdeen, Idaho, to succeed G. A. Wiebe in charge of the cereal experiments at the Aberdeen Substation, which are being conducted in cooperation with the Idaho Agricultural Experiment Station.

Dr. H. V. Harlan, principal agronomist in charge of barley investigations, left Washington, D. C., on January 30 for Sacaton, Ariz., where he will conduct breeding and selection experiments in the cooperative barley nurseries at the U. S. Field Station. He also will take notes on and harvest barley varieties. Similar work will be done at the Aberdeen Substation, Aberdeen, Idaho, and at points in California, Oregon, Washington, and Utah. Upon completion of this detail Dr. Harlan will return to Washington, D. C.

Dr. George N. Hoffer, agent in charge of corn root rots and metallic-poisoning investigations in cooperation with the Purdue University Agricultural Experiment Station at La Fayette, Ind., resigned his position on January 31 to accept a position with the N. V. Potash Export My of Amsterdam, The Netherlands.

Dr. J. R. Holbert, agronomist in charge of the cereal-disease investigations conducted in cooperation with Funk Bros. Seed Co., Bloomington, Ill., and the Illinois Agricultural Experiment Station, was granted authority to give two 10-minute radio talks over the Prairie Farmer Radio Station, Chicago, on January 31 at 1:20 p.m., and 1:40 p.m., respectively. Dr. Holbert's subject was corn, giving him opportunity to present the very important research on control of root rot diseases of corn and on the development of cold-resistant strains of corn to an audience covering the entire Corn Belt. It is expected that these radio talks will be very beneficial to the reputation of the Federal Department of Agriculture as a research agency.

Dr. Holbert gave a talk on January 16 to the students of the Illinois State Normal University who are interested in agriculture, botany, and community development.

On February 18 Dr. Holbert will address the Kiwanis-Farmers' banquet at Bloomington, Ill. His subject will cover the results of the recent studies on cold-resistance and cold-susceptibility in corn. Lantern slides will be used.

J. Foster Martin, agent in the cooperative nursery and breeding experiments conducted at the Sherman County Branch Station, Moro, Oreg., came to Washington on January 22 to confer with members of the Office and to prepare a report of the experiments at Moro. Mr. Martin also was authorized to stop en route at St. Paul, Minn., Madison, Wis., and Manhattan, Kans., to confer with cereal research workers.

Miss Mary L. Martini, assistant botanist in barley investigations, left Washington on January 30 for Sacaton, Ariz., to assist Dr. H. V. Harlan in breeding and selection experiments with barley in the cooperative nurseries at the U. S. Field Station. Miss Martini also will make similar studies at the Aberdeen Substation, Aberdeen, Idaho, and at points in California, Oregon Washington, and Utah. Upon completion of the season's work she will return to Washington, D. C.

Walter F. Reddy, State Leader of barberry eradication in Michigan, came to Washington on January 26 to assist the associate pathologist in charge of barberry eradication in summarizing progress and cost data of the barberry eradication campaign for the past calendar year and determining field polici for the current year. Mr. Reddy will remain in Washington for about three weeks.

Hugo Stoneberg, assistant agronomist in the corn investigations conducted at Baton Rouge, La., in cooperation with the Louisiana Agricultural Experiment Station, has been granted authority to attend the meetings of the Southern Agricultural Workers to be held at Houston from February 5 to 8, inclusive.

Correction

Since April 1, 1928, Dr. J. D. Sayre, who was referred to in the Cereal Courier, Vol. 21, No. 1, Jan. 15, 1929, as of the department of botany of the Ohio State University, has been an agent of this Office in charge of the physiological phases of the special agronomic corn-borer research cooperative with the Ohio Agricultural Experiment Station and the Ohio State University.

VISITORS

Dr. C. W. Hungerford, assistant director of the Idaho Agricultural Experiment Station, was in the Office on January 22 to discuss cooperative projects.

Hickman Price, 420 Madison Avenue, New York, N. Y., an extensive wheat grower in Swisher County, Texas, was an Office visitor on January 26. In 1928, Mr. Price grew 14,000 acres of wheat and in 1929 he expects to grow 20,000 acres.

Dr. E. R. Schulz, formerly agent in connection with barberry eradication at Madison, Wis., was an Office visitor on January 31. While connected with this Office Dr. Schulz was engaged in the investigation of the effectiveness of chemicals in the eradication of the common barberry.

Dr. W. H. Tisdale, of the E. I. Du Pont de Nemours and Co., Inc., Wilmington, Del., was an Office visitor on January 18 and 19.

MANUSCRIPTS AND PUBLICATIONS

5 Manuscript of Misc. Pub. No. 21 (Revised), by V. F. Tapke, was submitted on January 10 for an edition of 100,000 copies. Galley proof was read on January 31.

6 A manuscript entitled "Breeding Hard Red Winter Wheat for Winter Hardiness and High Yield," by Karl S. Quisenberry and J. Allen Clark, was submitted on January 19 for publication in the Technical Bulletin series.

7 A manuscript entitled "The Occurrence of Strains Resistant to Leaf Rust in Certain Varieties of Wheat," by C. O. Johnston, was approved on January 24 for publication in the Journal of the American Society of Agronomy.

8 A manuscript entitled "The Relation of Stomatal Behavior to Stem Rust Resistance in Wheat," by Helen Hart, was submitted on January 28 for publication in the Journal of Agricultural Research.

Circular 43 entitled "Distribution of the Classes and Varieties of Wheat in the United States," by J. Allen Clark, et al., has been placed in the Department Bulletin series and will appear as Department Bulletin 1498.

Galley proof of Tech. Bul. 96 entitled "Yields of Barley in the United States and Canada, 1922-1926," by H. V. Harlan, L. H. Newman, and Mary L. Martini, was read on January 23.

Galley proof of article entitled "Greenhouse Studies on the Relation of Age of Wheat Plants to Infection by Puccinia triticina," by C. O. Johnston and L. E. Melchers, was read on January 23.

Galley proof of article entitled "Interpreting Correlation Coefficients," by Frederick D. Richey, for publication in the Journal of American Society of Agronomy, was read on January 30.

The article entitled "Some Chemical and Morphological Phenomena Attending Infection of the Wheat Plant by Ophiobolus graminis," by Hurley Fellows, appear in the Journal of Agricultural Research 37 (11): 647-661, pls. 1-2, figs. 1-5. December 1, 1928. (Cooperation between Office of Cereal Crops and Diseases and the Kansas Agricultural Experiment Station.)

The article entitled "Technic of Rice Hybridization in California," by Jenkin W. Jones, appears in the Journal of the American Society of Agronomy 21 (1): 35-40. January, 1929.

The paper entitled "Effects of Dehulling Seed and of Date of Seeding on Germination and Smut Infection in Oats," by B. B. Bayles and F. A. Coffman, appears in the Journal of the American Society of Agronomy 21 (1): 41-51, fig. 1. January, 1929.

ANNUAL REPORT OF PUBLICATIONS AND MANUSCRIPTS

OFFICE OF CEREAL CROPS AND DISEASES

January . to December, 1928

In the calendar year 1928, 82 articles, papers, and abstracts were published in the various series of Department publications, in publications of
cooperating State agricultural organizations, and in private journals. These
represent 38 manuscripts submitted in 1928, 42 submitted in 1927, one in 1926,
and one in 1925.

In the calendar year 1928, 92 manuscripts were submitted for publication
in the above mentioned channels. Of these, 38 were published, leaving 54 manuscripts in press on December 31, 1928. Nine of the manuscripts submitted in
1927, two submitted in 1926, and three submitted in 1925 also are still in
press. Total, 68.

GENERAL OR MISCELLANEOUS

Ball, Carleton R. The Merchant and Agriculture. Off. Yearbook N. Dak.
Retail Merchants Assoc.; 39-55. 1928.

_____ English or Latin Plurals for Anglicized Latin Nouns?
Amer. Speech 3 (4): 291-325. April, 1928.

_____ Cooperation in Corn Borer Research. Jour. Amer. Soc.
Agron. 20 (10): 1033-1047. October, 1928.

_____, Homer L. Shantz, and Charles F. Shaw. Median Terms in
Adjectives of Comparison. Jour. Amer. Soc. Agron. 20 (2): 182-191, fig. 1.
February, 1928.

Reynoldson, L. A., R. S. Kifer, J. H. Martin, and W. R. Humphries. The
Combined Harvester-Thresher in the Great Plains. U. S. Dept. Agr. Tech. Bul.
70: 1-60, figs. 1-18. February, 1928. (Cooperation among the Bureau of Agricultural Economics, Bureau of Plant Industry, and Bureau of Public Roads, and
the agricultural experiment stations of Texas, Oklahoma, Kansas, Nebraska, and
Montana.)

_____, J. H. Martin, and W. R. Humphries. Shall I Buy a
Combine? U. S. Dept. Agr.Farmers' Bul. 1565: 1-18, figs. 1-6. April, 1928.
(Cooperation among Bureau of Agricultural Economics, Bureau of Plant Industry,
and Bureau of Public Roads.)

AGRONOMIC SUBJECTS

Barley

Harlan, H. V., R. G. Wiggans, and L. H. Newman. Barley Varieties Registered, II. Jour. Amer. Soc. Agron. 20 (12): 1326-1328. December, 1928.

Henry, A. W. and Chi Tu. Natural Crossing in Barley. Jour. Amer. Soc. Agron. 20 (11): 1183-1192. November, 1928. (Cooperative investigations between the Minnesota Agricultural Experiment Station and the Office of Cereal Crops and Diseases and the Office of Fiber Plants.)

Corn

Hauge, Sigfred M. and John F. Trost. An Inheritance Study of the Distribution of Vitamin A in Maize. Jour. Biol. Chem. 80 (1): 107-114, chart 1. November, 1928. (Cooperation between the Office of Cereal Crops and Diseases and the Purdue University Agricultural Experiment Station.)

Mayer, L. S. Corn Improvement Work. Tenn. Agr. Expt. Sta. Ann. Rpt. 40 (1927): 30-31. [1928] (Cooperation between the Office of Cereal Crops and Diseases and the Tennessee Agricultural Experiment Station.)

Randolph, L. F Chromosome Numbers in Zea mays L. New York Cornell Agr. Expt. Sta. Mem. 117: 3-44, pls. I-III. June, 1928. (Cooperation between the Office of Cereal Crops and Diseases and the New York State College of Agriculture, Ithaca, N. Y.)

Richey, Frederick D. The Intensive Production of Single Crosses between Selfed Lines of Corn for Double Crossing. Jour Amer. Soc. Agron. 20 (9): 942-946, figs. 1-2. September, 1928.

_____ and H. S. Garrison. Equality of Kernal Row Numbers in Reciprocal Corn Crosses. Jour. Amer. Soc. Agron. 20 (10): 1069-1072. October, 1928.

Robinson, Joe L. and A. A. Bryan. Iowa Corn Yield Test. Results of 1927 Tests. Iowa Corn and Small Grain Growers' Assoc. [1927]: 3-24, figs. 1-5. [1928] (Cooperation between the Office of Cereal Crops and Diseases and the Iowa Agricultural Experiment Station and the Iowa Corn and Small Grain Growers Association.)

Flax

Dillman A. C. Daily Growth and Oil Content of Flaxseeds. Jour. Agr. Research 37 (6): 357-377, figs. 1-12. Sept. 15, 1928.

Stakman, E. C. Flax Resistant to Wilt and Sown Early Helps to Cut Losses. U. S. Dept. Agr. Yearbook 1927: 305-307. 1928.

Grain Sorghums

Martin, J. H. Sorghum Grain Can Be Harvested with an Adjusted Combine. U. S. Dept. Agr. Yearbook 1927: 597-599, fig. 224. 1928.

_____ Plant Characters and Yield in Grain Sorghums. Jour. Amer. Soc. Agron. 20 (11): 1177-1182, fig. 1. November, 1928.

_____, L. A. Reynoldson, B. E. Rothgeb, and W. M. Hurst. Harvesting Grain Sorghums. U. S. Dept. Agr. Farmers' Bul. 1577: 1-16, figs. 1-13. September, 1928. (Bureaus of Agricultural Economics, Public Roads, and Plant Industry, U. S. Department of Agriculture, the Kansas Engineering Experiment Station, and the Kansas and Oklahoma agricultural experiment stations, cooperating.)

Sieglinger, John B. Broomcorn Experiments at the United States Dry-Land Field Station, Woodward, Okla. U. S. Dept. Agr. Tech. Bul. 51: 1-32, figs. 1-8. February, 1928.

Swanson, Arthur F. Seed-Coat Structure and Inheritance of Seed Color in Sorghums. Jour. Agr. Research 37 (10): 577-588, fig. 1. Nov. 15, 1928.

Oats

Burnett. L. C. Iogold Oats. Iowa Agr. Expt. Sta. Bul. 247: 187-198, figs. 1-5. February, 1928. (Cooperation between the Office of Cereal Crops and Diseases and the Iowa Agricultural Experiment Station.)

Stanton, T. R. Oats of New and Improved Sorts May Now Be Registered. U. S. Dept. Agr. Yearbook 1927: 486-489. 1928.

_____ How to Grow Better Oats. Natl. Crop Impr. Com. [Circ.], 4 p. [February, 1928.]

_____ and V. H. Florell. The Fulghum Oat in California. Calif. Cult. 71 (16): 381, 403. illus. Oct. 20, 1928.

_____, H. H. Love, and E. F. Gaines. Registration of Varieties and Strains of Oats, III. Jour. Amer. Soc. Agron. 20 (12): 1323-1325. December, 1928. (Published under a cooperative agreement between the American Society of Agronomy and the Bureau of Plant Industry.)

Stanton, T. R., D. E. Stephens, and B. B. Bayles. Relative Resistance of Oat Varieties to Shattering at Moro, Oregon. (Note) Jour. Amer. Soc. Agron. 20 (3): 304-305. March, 1928. (Cooperation between the Office of Cereal Crops and Diseases and the Oregon Agricultural Experiment Station.)

Rice

Dunshee, Carroll F. Rice Experiments in Sacramento Valley 1922-1927. Calif. Agr. Expt. Sta. Bul. 454: 3-14, figs. 1-3. May, 1928. (The data in this bulletin were gathered in part in cooperation with the Office of Cereal Crops and Diseases, Bureau of Plant Industry; and in part in cooperation with the Division of Agricultural Engineering, U. S. Department of Agriculture, and the Division of Water Rights, California Department of Public Works.)

Jones, Jenkin W. Rice Yield Increased in California by Ammonium Sulphate U. S. Dept. Agr. Yearbook 1927: 558-559. 1928.

_____ Inheritance of Earliness and Other Agronomic Characters in Rice. Jour. Agr. Research 36 (7): 581-601, figs. 1-5 April 1, 1928. (Cooperation between the Office of Cereal Crops and Diseases and the California Agricultural Experiment Station.)

_____ Polyembryony in Rice. (Note) (Jour. Amer. Soc. Agron. 20 (7): 774. July, 1928.

Wheat

Ball, Carleton R. Seeing All Sides of a Complex Problem. Rpt. First Ann. Hard Spring Wheat Conf. (held at the N. Dak. Agr. Col., Fargo, N. Dak., March 27, 1928). Mimeographed, pp. 3-8. 1928.

Clark, J. Allen. Wheat Breeding for Yield, Quality, and Disease Resistance. Rpt. First Ann. Hard Spring Wheat Conf. (held at the N. Dak. Agr. Col. Fargo, N. Dak., March 27, 1928). Mimeographed, pp. 9-27. 1928.

_____ and E. R. Ausemus. Inheritance of Immunity from Black Stem Rust, Yield, and Protein Content in Hope Wheat Crosses with Susceptible and Resistant Varieties. [Mimeographed] [Washington, 1928]

_____ Immunity of Hope Wheat from Black Stem Rust Inherited as a Dominant Character. Jour. Amer. Soc. Agron. 20 (2): 152-159, fig. 1. February, 1928.

_____, Victor H. Florell, and John R. Hooker. Inheritance of Awnedness, Yield, and Quality in Crosses between Bobs, Hard Federation, and Propo Wheats at Davis, California. U. S. Dept. Agr. Tech. Bul. 39: 1-40, figs. 1-6. February, 1928. (Cooperation between the Office of Cereal Crops and Diseases and the California Agricultural Experiment Station.)

Clark, J. Allen, J. H. Parker, and L. R. Waldron. Registration of
Improved Wheat Varieties, III. Jour. Amer. Soc. Agron. 20 (12): 1318-1322.
December, 1928. (Published under a cooperative agreement between the American
Society of Agronomy and the Bureau of Plant Industry.)

_____ and Ralph W. Smith. Inheritance in Nodak and Kahla Durum
Wheat Crosses for Rust Resistance, Yield, and Quality at Dickinson, North
Dakota. Jour. Amer. Soc. Agron. 20 (12): 1297-1304. December, 1928. (Cooper-
ation between the Office of Cereal Crops and Diseases and the North Dakota
Agricultural Experiment Station.)

Kezer, Alvin, F. A. Coffman, D. W. Robertson, Dwight Koonce, and G. W.
Deming. Colorado Wheat Varieties. Colo. Agr. Expt. Sta. Bul. 329: 3-55, figs.
1-9. January, 1928. (This bulletin is the result of experiments carried on
by the Agronomy section, Colorado Experiment Station at Fort Collins and Fort
Lewis and by the Office of Cereal Crops and Diseases, at Akron, cooperating
with the Office of Dry Land Agriculture, and the Colorado Experiment Station.)

Leighty, C. E. and W. J. Sando. Natural and Artificial Hybrids of a
Chinese Wheat and Rye. Jour. Heredity 19 (1): 23-27, fig. 11. January, 1928.

Quisenberry, Karl S. Some Plant Characters Determining Yields in Fields
of Winter and Spring Wheat in 1926. Jour. Amer. Soc. Agron. 20 (5): 492-499.
May, 1928.

_____, J. Allen Clark, and B. B. Bayles. The Prevalence
of Mixtures in Marquis Wheat Grown in Central Montana in 1923. Jour. Amer.
Soc. Agron. 20 (10): 1055-1063. October, 1928.

Stephens, D. E. Oregon Gains by the Breeding of Better Wheats. Oregon
2 (1): 8-11, illus. December, 1927-January, 1928. (Cooperation between the
Office of Cereal Crops and Diseases and the Oregon Agricultural Experiment
Station.)

Taylor, J. W. Effect of the Continuous Selection of Large and Small
Wheat Seed on Yield, Bushel Weight, Varietal Purity, and Loose Smut Infection. Jour. Amer. Soc. Agron. 20 (8): 856-867. August, 1928.

PATHOLOGIC SUBJECTS

Imperfect and Sac Fungi

Dickson, James G. Wheat-Scab Control Effected by Cleaning up Refuse of Crops. U. S. Dept. Agr. Yearbook 1927: 702-706, figs. 280-283. 1928.

_____ and James R. Holbert. The Relation of Temperature to the Development of Disease in Plants. Amer. Nat. 62 (681): 311-333, illus. July-Aug., 1928. (Cooperation between the Office of Cereal Crops and Diseases, the Wisconsin Agricultural Experiment Station, and the Funk Brothers Seed Company of Bloomington, Ill.)

Drechsler, Charles. Pythium arrhenomanes n. sp., a Parasite Causing Maize Root Rot. Phytopath. 18 (10): 873-875. October, 1928.

_____ Zonate Eyespot of Grasses Caused by Helminthosporium giganteum. Jour. Agr. Research 37 (8): 473-492, pls. 1-8, figs. 1-3. Oct. 15, 1928. (Informal cooperation between the Office of Cereal Crops and Diseases and the Office of Vegetable and Forage Diseases.)

Fellows, Hurley. The Influence of Oxygen and Carbon Dioxide on the Growth of Ophiobolus graminis in Pure Culture. Jour. Agr. Research 37(6): 349-355, figs. 1-5. Sept. 15, 1928. (Cooperation between the Office of Cereal Crops and Diseases and the Kansas Agricultural Experiment Station.)

_____ Some Chemical and Morphological Phenomena Attending Infection of the Wheat Plant by Ophiobolus graminis. Jour. Agr. Research 37 (11): 647-661, pls. 1-2, figs. 1-5. December 1, 1928. (Cooperation between the Office of Cereal Crops and Diseases and the Kansas Agricultural Experiment Station)

Holbert, J. R. Corn Seed Treatment of Dent Varieties in Commercial Practice. U. S. Dept. Agr. Yearbook 1927: 210-212, fig. 52. 1928.

_____, C. S. Reddy, and Benjamin Koehler. Chemical-Dust Seed Treatments for Dent Corn. U. S. Dept. Agr. Circ. 34: 1-5. February, 1928. (Cooperation between the Office of Cereal Crops and Diseases and the Illinois Agricultural Experiment Station.)

Johann, Helen. Penicillium Injury to Corn Seedlings. Phytopath. 18 (2): 239-242. February, 1928. (Cooperation between the Office of Cereal Crops and Diseases and the Wisconsin Agricultural Experiment Station.)

_____ Grated Carrot Agar Favorable for Studies of Pythium. (Phytopath. Notes) Phytopath. 18 (8): 710. August, 1928. (Cooperation between the Office of Cereal Crops and Diseases and the Wisconsin Agricultural Experiment Station.)

Johann, Helen, James R. Holbert, and James G. Dickson. A Pythium Seedling Blight and Root Rot of Dent Corn. Jour. Agr. Research 37 (8): 443-477, pl. 1, figs. 1-9. Oct. 15, 1928. (Cooperation between the Office of Cereal Crops and Diseases, the Wisconsin Agricultural Experiment Station and the Funk Bros. Seed Co., of Bloomington, Ill.)

Reddy, C. S. and J. R. Holbert. Further Experiments with Seed Treatments for Sweet-Corn Diseases. Jour. Agr. Research 36 (3): 237-247, figs. 1-5. February 1, 1928. (Cooperative investigations between the Office of Cereal Crops and Diseases and the Funk Bros. Seed Co., of Bloomington, Ill.)

Virus Diseases

McKinney, H. H. Virus Diseases Observed by the Allison V. Armour Expedition. (Abs.) Phytopath. 18 (1): 155. January, 1928.

_____ Centrifuging Filtrable Viruses. Science 67 (1732): 271. March 9, 1928.

_____ Further Studies in Quantitative Virological Methods. Science 68 (1764): 380-382. Oct. 19, 1928.

Webb, Robert W. Further Studies on the Soil Relationships of the Mosaic Disease of Winter Wheat. Jour. Agr. Research 36 (1): 53-75, figs. 1-4. Jan. 1, 1928. (Cooperation between the Office of Cereal Crops and Diseases and the Wisconsin Agricultural Experiment Station.)

Rusts

Allen, Ruth F. A Cytological Study of Puccinia glumarum on Bromus marginatus and Triticum vulgare. Jour. Agr. Research 36 (6): 487-513, pls. 1-12. March 15, 1928. (Cooperation between the Office of Cereal Crops and Diseases and the California Agricultural Experiment Station.)

Dietz, S. M. Inheritance of Resistance in Oats to Puccinia graminis avenae. Jour. Agr. Research 37 (1): 1-23, figs. 1-5. July 1, 1928. (Cooperation between the Office of Cereal Crops and Diseases and the Iowa Agricultural Experiment Station.)

_____ and L. D. Leach. The Effective Methods of Eradicating Rhamnus Species Susceptible to Puccinia coronata Corda. (Abs.) Phytopath. 18 (1): 138. January, 1928. (Cooperation between the Office of Cereal Crops and Diseases and the Iowa Agricultural Experiment Station.)

Levine, Moses N. Biometrical Studies on the Variation of Physiologic Forms of Puccinia graminis tritici and the Effects of Ecological Factors on the Susceptibility of Wheat Varieties. Phytopath. 18 (1): 7-123, pl. 1, figs. 1-37. January, 1928. (Cooperation between the Office of Cereal Crops and Diseases and the Minnesota Agricultural Experiment Station.)

Mains, E. B. Inheritance of Resistance to Puccinia sorghi in Maize.
(Abs.) Phytopath. 18 (1): 138. January, 1928. (Cooperation between the
Office of Cereal Crops and Diseases and the Purdue University Agricultural
Experiment Station.)

Stakman, E. C. and E. B. Lambert. The Relation of Temperature during
the Growing Season in the Spring Wheat Area of the United States to the Occurrence of Stem Rust Epidemics. Phytopath. 18 (4): 369-374, figs. 1-3. April,
1928. (Cooperation between the Office of Cereal Crops and Diseases and the
Minnesota Agricultural Experiment Station.)

Barberry Eradication

Hutton, Lynn D. Barberry Eradication Reducing Stem Rust Losses in Wide
Area. U. S. Dept. Agr. Yearbook 1927: 114-118, fig. 16. 1928.

_____ Barberry Species that Spread Stem Rust. Natl. Hort. Mag.
1928: 5-8, 2 figs. January, 1928.

_____ and John W. Baringer. Annual Report of the Barberry
Eradication Campaign, 1927, with Summarized Results for 1918-1927, Inclusive.
Mimeographed pamphlet, 31 p., 2 maps. February, 1928.

Patch, Edith M. Bread or Barberries. U. S. Dept. Agr. Misc. Pub. 7:
1-14, figs. 1-8. January, 1928.

Downy Mildews

Weston, William H., Jr., and George F. Weber. Downy mildew (Sclerospora
graminicola) on Everglade Millet in Florida. Jour. Agr. Research 36 (11): 935-
975, figs. 1-4. June 1, 1928.

Smuts

Gaines, E. F. New Physiologic Forms of Tilletia tritici in Wheat. (Abs.)
Phytopath. 18 (1): 139. January, 1928. (Cooperation between the Office of
Cereal Crops and Diseases and the Washington Agricultural Experiment Station.)

_____ New Physiologic Forms of Tilletia levis and T. tritici.
Phytopath. 18 (7): 579-588. July, 1928. (Cooperation between the Office of
Cereal Crops and Diseases and the Washington Agricultural Experiment Station.)

Griffiths, Marion A. Smut Susceptibility of Naturally Resistant Corn Whe
Artificially Inoculated. Jour. Agr. Research 36 (1): 77-89, figs. 1-4.
Jan. 1, 1928.

Johnston, C. O. and L. E. Melchers. The Control of Sorghum Kernel Smut and the Effect of Seed Treatments on Vitality of Sorghum Seed. Kans. Agr. Expt. Sta. Tech. Bul. 22: 3-37. February, 1928. (Cooperation between the Office of Cereal Crops and Diseases and the Kansas Agricultural Experiment Station.)

Tapke, V. F. Wheat Stinking-Smut Control by Copper Carbonate Method. U. S. Dept. Agr. Yearbook 1927: 707-708, fig. 284. 1928.

_____ Formaldehyde Seed Treatment for Oat Smuts. U. S. Dept. Agr. Misc. Pub. 21: 1-4, illus. [March], 1928.

_____ and F. C. Meier. Copper-Carbonate Seed Treatment for Stinking Smut of Wheat. U. S. Dept. Agr. Misc. Circ. 108 (Revised): 1-4, illus. February, 1928. (Cooperation between the Office of Cereal Crops and Diseases and the Office of Cooperative Extension Work.)

Bacteriologic Diseases

Reddy, C. S. and J. R. Holbert. Differences in Resistance to Bacterial Wilt in Inbred Strains and Crosses of Dent Corn. Jour. Agr. Research 36 (10): 905-910, figs. 1-2. May 15, 1928. (Cooperation between the Office of Cereal Crops and Diseases and the Funk Bros. Seed Co., Bloomington, Ill.)

General Cereal Diseases

Mackie, W. W. A Field Method of Insuring Positive Attack with Some Cereal Diseases. Phytopath. 18 (7): 617-621. July, 1928. (Cooperation between the Office of Cereal Crops and Diseases and the California Agricultural Experiment Station.)

PHYSIOLOGICAL AND CHEMICAL SUBJECTS

Hoffer, George N. Cornstalk Testing by Chemicals Indicates Food Needs of Plant. U. S. Dept. Agr. Yearbook 1927: 212-215, figs. 53-55. 1928.

Hurd-Karrer, Annie M. Changes in the Buffer System of the Wheat Plant During Its Development. Plant Physiol. 3 (2): 131-153, figs. 1-12. 1928.

The following publications were omitted from the Annual Report of Publications and Manuscripts for the calendar year 1927.

AGRONOMIC SUBJECTS

Leighty, C. E. and J. W. Taylor. Rate and Date of Seeding and Seed-Bed Preparation for Winter Wheat at Arlington Experiment Farm. U. S. Dept. Agr. Tech. Bul. 38: 1-19, figs. 1-7. November, 1927.

_____ Studies in Natural Hybridization of Wheat. Jour. Agr. Research 35 (10): 865-887, fig. 1. Nov. 15, 1927.

May, R. W. Wheats in Central Montana. Mont. Agr. Expt. Sta. Bul. 203: 2-28, figs. 1-8. May, 1927. (Cooperation between the Office of Cereal Crops and Diseases and the Montana Agricultural Experiment Station at the Judith Basin Branch Station.)

_____ Oats and Barley in Central Montana. Mont. Agr. Expt. Sta. B 209: 2-24, figs. 1-8. October, 1927. (Cooperation between the Office of Cer Crops and Diseases and the Montana Agricultural Experiment Station at the Jud Basin Branch Station.)

Richey, Frederick D. Corn Breeding. U. S. Dept. Agr. Bul. 1489: 1-63, pls. 1-12, figs. 1-8. November, 1927.

PATHOLOGIC SUBJECTS

Briggs, Fred N. Dehulling Barley Seed with Sulphuric Acid to Induce In tion with Covered Smut. Jour. Agr. Research 35 (10): 907-914. Nov. 15, 192 (Cooperation between the Office of Cereal Crops and Diseases and the Califor Agricultural Experiment Station.)

Tisdale, W. H. and V. F. Tapke. Smuts of Wheat and Rye and Their Contr U. S. Dept. Agr. Farmers' Bul. 1540: 1-16, figs. 1-8. December, 1927.

PHYSIOLOGICAL AND CHEMICAL SUBJECTS

Rose, Dean H. and Annie M. Hurd-Karrer. Differential Staining of Specialized Cells in Begonia with Indicators. Plant Physiol. 2 (4): 441-45 figs. 1-3. October, 1927.

CEREAL COURIER

Official Messenger of the Office of Cereal Crops and Diseases
Bureau of Plant Industry, U. S. Department of Agriculture
(NOT FOR PUBLICATION)

Vol. 21   No. 3
February 15, 1929
Personnel (Feb. 1-15) and Field Station (Jan. 16-31) Issue

PERSONNEL ITEMS

Dr. O. S. Aamodt, formerly associate pathologist in charge of the
cooperative wheat-breeding experiments at University Farm, St. Paul,
Minn., and now associate professor of genetics and plant breeding in the
College of Agriculture of the University of Alberta, Edmonton, Alta.,
Canada, recently wrote to Dr. C. R. Ball as follows:

"I received your letters some time ago and also the article from
the Northwestern Miller entitled "Wheat Belt Keeps Moving North." I
wish to thank you for remembering me in this way. I was glad to learn
that you are still thinking of me in my new position.

"I expect to spend a large portion of my time during the coming
summer in making the acquaintance of the Province and the various conditions with which I shall have to deal in my work in the future. Whether
it is this year or some future time that you are able to make a trip to
the Peace River, I hope you will let me know in advance regarding your
plans, as nothing would be a greater pleasure, and I am sure more instructive, than such a field trip in your company.

"My work here is going along very nicely. I am teaching one class
in advanced Genetics and Cytology; otherwise I am kept busy on general
administrative work, Dr. Newton being on a six months leave of absence,
and in the organization of my research program in cereal breeding. We
are very fortunate in having just had made available for our work a new

laboratory and greenhouses. Both units are very well equipped; the greenhouses are all automatically controlled for both heating and air circula-
tion; they are also well equipped with electric lights. Some varieties of
wheat and F_1 hybrids, the crosses of which were made for me last summer,
were planted in November and are already coming into head. I thought it
might interest you to know too that I have just received a set of Percival
wheat collection containing 1,300 specimens. I believe this is the only
set of Percival's material in America, so probably when you come this way
I can show you something that you haven't got in the United States as far
as I know. "

R. O. Bulger, State Leader of barberry eradication in South Dakota,
who spent two weeks in Washington assisting the associate pathologist in
charge of barberry eradication, left on February 11 to return to his headquarters at Brookings, S. Dak.

Allan D. Dickson, agent in the cooperative cereal-disease experiments
conducted at Madison, Wis., has been given a temporary detail to Washington
effective February 1, to assist in the physiological studies of wheat under
the direction of Dr. A. M. Hurd-Karrer.

Dr. J. R. Holbert, agronomist in charge of the cereal-disease investigation conducted in cooperation with Funk Bros. Seed Co., Bloomington,
Ill., and the Illinois Agricultural Experiment Station, spoke before the
Plant Seminar of the College of Agriculture at Urbana on February 25 on
the subject of cold resistance and cold-susceptibility in corn.

Vincent C. Hubbard was appointed agent, effective February 1, to
assist in the cereal experiments that are being conducted at Manhattan,
Kans., in cooperation with the Kansas Agricultural Experiment Station
under the direction of Dr. John H. Parker. Mr. Hubbard takes the place
of Loren L. Davis, whose transfer to Aberdeen, Idaho, became effective
on January 16.

W. F. Reddy, State Leader of barberry eradication in Michigan, who
spent two weeks in Washington assisting the associate pathologist in charge
of barberry eradication, left Washington on February 12 for his headquarters at East Lansing, Mich.

G. F. Sprague, assistant agronomist in charge of cooperative cereal
experiments at the North Platte Substation, North Platte, Nebr., was
authorized on February 4 to go from North Platte to Lincoln, Nebr., to
remain for several weeks at the Nebraska Agricultural Experiment Station.
Mr. Sprague will prepare his annual report of the experiments at North
Platte and other manuscripts and consult with Station officials.

D. E. Stephens, superintendent of the Sherman County Branch Station, Moro, Oreg., who came to Washington on January 20 for conferences with members of the Office of Dry Land Agriculture left on February 8 to return to his headquarters at Moro.

A. F. Swanson, associate agronomist in charge of the cooperative cereal investigations at the Fort Hays Branch Experiment Station, Hays, Kans., came to Washington on February 4 for conferences with members of the Office staff and to prepare reports and manuscripts on the experiments conducted at Hays. Mr. Swanson will be in Washington about a month.

MANUSCRIPTS AND PUBLICATIONS

9 A manuscript entitled "Bulked-Population Method of Handling Cereal Hybrids," by Victor H. Florell, was approved on February 7 for publication in the Journal of the American Society of Agronomy.

10 A manuscript entitled "Tenuous Kafir Plants," by John B. Sieglinger, was approved on February 8 for publication in the Journal of Heredity.

Galley proof of article entitled "Inheritance of Yield and Protein Content in Crosses of Marquis and Kota Spring Wheats Grown in Montana," by J. Allen Clark and Karl S. Quisenberry, for publication in the Journal of Agricultural Research, was read on February 8.

Galley proof was read on February 15 of nine of the ten articles submitted by this Office for publication in the Department of Agriculture Yearbook for 1928.

The paper entitled "The Relation of Weather to the Development of Stem Rust in the Mississippi Valley," by Edmund B. Lambert, appears in Phytopathology 19(1): 1-71, figs. 1-11. January, 1929. (Cooperation between the Office of Cereal Crops and Diseases and the Department of Agriculture of the University of Minnesota.)

An article entitled "Weather and Plant Diseases," by R. O. Bulger, appears in the Dakota Farmer 49(4): 188-189. February 15, 1929.

The following abstracts relating to the work of the Office of Cereal Crops and Diseases were presented at the Twentieth Annual Meeting of the American Phytopathological Society, New York, N. Y., December 28, 1928, to January 1, 1929, and appear in Phytopathology vol. 19, no. 1. January 1929.

Dickson, James G., P. E. Hoppe. J. R. Holbert, and George Janssen. The Influence of Environment during Maturation upon Predisposition to Seedling Blight in Wheat and Corn Strains. (Abs.) Phytopath. 19(1): 79 January, 1929. (Cooperation between the Office of Cereal Crops and Diseases and the Wisconsin Agricultural Experiment Station and Funk Bros. Seed Co.)

Dickson, James G., E. B. Mains, and Helen Johann. Progress Report on Cereal Scab Development during the Season of 1928. (Abs.) Phytopath. 19(1): 108. January 1929. (Cooperation between the Office of Cereal Crops and Diseases and the Wisconsin and Purdue University agricultural experiment stations.)

Elliott, Charlotte Another Bacterial Leaf Spot of Sorghum. (Abs.)
Phytopath. 19(1): 82. January, 1929.

Fellows, Hurley. Studies of Certain Soil Phases of the Wheat
Take-All Problem. (Abs.) Phytopath. 19(1): 103. January, 1929.
(Cooperation between the Office of Cereal Crops and Diseases and the
Kansas Agricultural Experiment Station.)

Fellows, Hurley. Some Chemical and Morphological Phenomena Attending Infection of the Wheat Plant by Ophiobolus graminis Sacc. (Abs.)
Phytopath. 19(1): 103-104. January, 1929. (Cooperation between the
Office of Cereal Crops and Diseases and the Kansas Agricultural Experiment Station.)

Holbert, J. R. and W. L. Burlison. Studies of Cold Resistance and
Susceptibility in Corn. (Abs.) Phytopath. 19(1): 105-106. January,
1929. (Cooperation between the Office of Cereal Crops and Diseases and
the Illinois Agricultural Experiment Station and Funk Bros. Seed Co.)

Hoppe, P. E. Inheritance of Resistance to Seedling Blight of Corn
Caused by Gibberella saubinetii. (Abs.) Phytopath. 19(1): 79-80. January, 1929. (Cooperation between the Office of Cereal Crops and Diseases
and the Wisconsin Agricultural Experiment Station.)

Johann, Helen. Further studies on Penicillium Injury to Corn. (Abs.)
Phytopath. 19(1): 105. January, 1929. (Cooperation between the Office
of Cereal Crops and Diseases and the Wisconsin Agricultural Experiment
Station and Funk Bros. Seed Co.)

Johnson, A. G., Lillian Cash, and W. A. Gardner. Preliminary Report
on a Bacterial Disease of Corn. (Abs.) Phytopath. 19(1): 81-82. January, 1929. (Cooperation between Office of Cereal Crops and Diseases and
the Alabama Agricultural Experiment Station.)

Leukel, R. W. Experiments with Liquid and Dust Seed Disinfectants
for Controlling Covered Smut of Barley and Stinking Smut of Wheat, 1926-
1928. (Abs.) Phytopath. 19(1): 81. January, 1929.

Leukel, R. W., J. G. Dickson, and A. G. Johnson. Experiments on
Stripe Disease of Barley and Its Control. (Abs.) Phytopath. 19(1): 81.
January, 1929. (Cooperation between Office of Cereal Crops and Dis-
eases and the Wisconsin Agricultural Experiment Station.)

Mains, E. B. Relative Susceptibility of Various Varieties of
Sorghum to Rust, Puccinia purpurea. (Abs.) Phytopath. 19(1): 104.
January, 1929. (Cooperation between the Office of Cereal Crops and
Diseases and the Purdue University Agricultural Experiment Station.)

Tapke, V. F. The Rôle of Humidity in the Life Cycle, Distribution, and Control of the Loose-Smut Fungus of Wheat. (Abs.) Phytopath
19(1): 103. January, 1929.

FIELD STATION CONDITION AND PROGRESS

HUMID ATLANTIC COAST AREA (South to North)

GEORGIA

State College of Agriculture, Athens (Cereal Agronomy, R. R. Childs)

VIRGINIA

Arlington Experiment Farm, Rosslyn (Small Grain Agronomy, J. W. Taylor)

Arlington Experiment Farm, Rosslyn (Corn Breeding, F. D. Richey)

Arlington Experiment Farm, Rosslyn (Cereal Smuts, V. F. Tapke, Acting in Charge)

Arlington Experiment Farm, Rosslyn (Virus Diseases, H. H. McKinney)

NEW YORK

Cornell University Agricultural Experiment Station, Ithaca (Cereal Breeding, H. H. Love)

HUMID MISSISSIPPI VALLEY AREA (South to North)

LOUISIANA

Rice Experiment Station, Crowley (Rice Agronomy, J. M. Jenkins)

Agricultural Experiment Station, Baton Rouge (Corn Breeding, H. F. Stoneberg)

MISSOURI

Agricultural Experiment Station, Columbia (Cereal Agronomy, L. J. Stadler)

TENNESSEE

Agricultural Experiment Station, Knoxville (Corn Breeding, L. S. Mayer)

IOWA

Agricultural Experiment Station, Ames (Oat Breeding, L. C. Burnett)

Agricultural Experiment Station, Ames (Corn Breeding, M. T. Jenkins)

Agricultural Experiment Station, Ames (Crown Rust of Oats, S. M. Dietz)
(H. C. Murphy) (February 6)

In the year 1928, 26 F_9 selections from the cross Richland (C.I. No. 787) (Iowa No. 105) X Green Russian were tested for yielding capacity in comparison with Iogold C.I. No. 2329, (Iowa No. 109). Iogold is one of the highest yielding varieties at the Iowa station and is highly resistant to the local forms of stem rust but possesses no known resistance to crown rust. The hybrid selections tested are all highly resistant to the local forms of stem rust and are very resistant to certain physiologic forms of crown rust. Seventeen of these hybrid selections were tested in 20th-acre plots with two replications. The remaining nine selections represent a series that were selected with reference to desirable glume color. They were grown in rod rows with thirty replications. In each test Iogold was sown every tenth row and used as a check. The following tables give the results of the two tests.

Average corrected yield of 19 F_9 selections of Richland (Iowa No. 105) X Green Russian, replicated two times in 20th-acre plots, in comparison with Iogold in 1928.

Selection number	Yield (Bu. per acre)	Difference from check	Rank
2	95.4	4.1	7
3	96.0	4.6	6
4	90.7	-0.7	11
5	96.5	5.1	5
8	98.9	7.5	2
14	89.7	-1.7	13
21	88.3	-3.1	14
24	89.9	-1.5	12
25	85.4	-6.0	16
26	81.6	-9.8	17
32	85.5	-5.9	15
67	101.0	9.6	1
69	92.8	1.4	9
71	78.8	-12.6	18
77	98.0	6.6	3
86	93.2	1.8	8
102a/	97.3	5.9	4
Iogold	91.4	---	10

a/ No. 102 replicated four times

Average corrected yields of 9 F_9 selections of Richland (Iowa No. 105) X Green Russian, replicated thirty times in rod rows, in comparison with Iogold in 1928.

Selection number	Yield (Bu. per acre)	Difference from check	Rank
16	76.8	16.1	5
18	69.0	8.3	8
19	82.0	21.3	2
34	75.6	14.9	6
52	74.5	13.8	7
62	67.0	6.3	9
99	84.5	23.8	1
104	77.8	17.1	4
112	79.7	19.0	3
Iogold	60.7	----	10

It should be mentioned that stem-rust infection was negligible in both tests. The crown-rust infection in the 20th-acre plots was merely a trace, while in the rod-row tests it was extremely abundant due to an artificial epidemic. The crown-rust infection probably accounts somewhat for the great difference in yield in the two tests.

ILLINOIS

Funk Bros. Seed Co., Bloomington (Corn Root, Stalk and Ear Rots, J. R. Holbert)

INDIANA

Purdue University Agricultural Experiment Station, La Fayette (Corn Rots and Metallic Poisoning, -----------)

Purdue University Agricultural Experiment Station, La Fayette (Leaf Rusts, E. B. Mains)

WISCONSIN

Agricultural Experiment Station, Madison (Wheat Scab, J. G. Dickson)

MINNESOTA

Agricultural Experiment Station, University Farm, St. Paul (Wheat Breeding, K. S. Quisenberry, Acting in Charge)

Agricultural Experiment Station, University Farm, St. Paul (Stem Rust, E. C. Stakman)

Agricultural Experiment Station, University Farm, St. Paul (Flax Rust, H. A. Rodenhiser)

GREAT PLAINS AREA (South to North)

OKLAHOMA

Woodward Field Station, Woodward (Grain Sorghum and Broomcorn, J. B. Sieglinger)

KANSAS

Agricultural Experiment Station, Manhattan (Cereal Breeding, J. H. Parker)

Agricultural Experiment Station, Manhattan (Corn Breeding, A. M. Brunson) (February 2)

The month of January has been characterized by consistently low temperatures and more than the average covering of snow. The mean temperature for the month was 21.3°, or 5.2° below normal and was the coldest January since 1918. No extremely cold periods occurred, the minimum temperature being one° below, but neither were there any warm periods such as usually occur. The total precipitation was 1.95 inches as compared to a normal of 0.72. The snowfall measured 8.5 inches.

Wheat apparently is in very good condition, except in localities where ice sheets may have done some slight injury. The ground contains much more than a normal reserve of moisture for this time of year.

We have been busy during the last month calculating corn yields and making popping tests with pop corn. Individual tests of over a thousand ears showed a range of 16 to 33 volumes expansion.

Agricultural Experiment Station, Manhattan (Wheat Foot Rots, Hurley Fellows)

Agricultural Experiment Station, Manhattan (Wheat Leaf Rust, C. O. Johnston

Hays Branch Experiment Station, Hays (Cereal Agronomy, A. F. Swanso

NEBRASKA

North Platte Substation, North Platte (Cereal Agronomy, G. F. Sprag (January 31)

The yields in bushels per acre of spring wheat varieties and hybrid selections grown in plots and nursery at North Platte, Nebr., are presented in the following tables:

Yield in bushels per acre of spring-wheat varieties grown in four systematically replicated plot experiments at the North Platte Substatio North Platte, Nebr., in 1928.

Class and Variety	C.I. No.	Yield (Bu. per acre)
Hard Red Spring		
Ceres	6900	31.8
Marquillo	6887	29.3
Reliance	7370	28.3
Marquis	3641	27.3
Progress	6902	27.2
Kota	5878	26.9
Garnet	8181	26.7
Reward	8182	24.2
Java (Kearney Co.)	----	24.0
Ruby	6047	22.0
Durum		
Nodak	6519	28.4
Mindum	5296	26.3
Akrona	6881	25.9
Kubanka	1440	23.8
White		
Quality	6607	26.1
Hard Federation	4733	24.4

Yield of spring wheat selections grown in the nursery at the North
Platte Substation, North Platte, Nebr., in 1928.

Variety or Hybrid	C. I. No.	Nursery No.	Yield (Bu. per acre)
Kanred x Marquis, II-17-40	8018	---	48.7
Kota x Hd. Fed. 8A-1-16-8-4	----	295	48.4
Kota x Marquis	8004	---	47.1
Marquis x Hd. Fed. A-2-34-3-1	----	710	46.6
Reliance B-8-11-22	----	17	44.8
Kanred x Marq. B-9-11-50	----	33	44.8
Do B-2-14-20	----	11	43.3
Do B-9-11-40	----	---	43.0
Kota x Marquis	6898	---	42.3
Marquis x Hd. Fed. B3-53-3-6	----	674	42.3
Kota x Webster, H-151-25	----	---	42.0
Kota x Hd. Fed. x Kanred x Marquis, B-2-1-2	----	702	42.0
Kanred x Marquis B9-11-21	----	---	41.9
Kota x Webster, H-209-25	----	---	41.9
Reliance B-8-11-16	----	14	41.8
Kota x Webster H 81-25	----	---	41.3
Kanred x Marquis B-2-14-2	----	---	40.6
Reliance B-8-11-64	----	22	40.2
Marquis x Hd. Fed. 2B-1-24-29	----	394	40.0
Reliance	7370	---	39.7
Kota x Kanred B1-12-1	----	---	39.7
Marquis x Hd. Fed. B1-24-44	----	395	39.5
Garnet	8181	---	39.3
Kanred x Marquis B-9-11-27	----	28	39.2
Ceres	6900	---	39.2
Kota x Galgalos A5-11-1	----	364	39.1
Kanred x Marquis B2-14-4	----	---	39.1
Kota x Marquis	8005	---	38.9
Kota x Hd. Fed. x Kanred x Marquis	----	701	38.9
Marq. x Hd. Fed. 2A-1-34-35-1	----	709	38.5
Marq. x Hd. Fed. B1-93-52	----	421	38.3
Kanred x Marquis B-9-11-42	----	41	38.3
Hd. Fed. x Marq. 3A-1-95-30-3	----	677	38.2
Marq. x Hd. Fed. 2B-3-39-28	----	434	38.1
Kota x Marquis	8185	---	38.0
Kanred x Marquis B9-11-48	----	---	37.9
Reward	8182	---	37.6
Hd. Fed. x Marquis 3A2-77-30	----	457	37.5
Marquis x Hd. Fed. 2 A-1-34-31-1	----	708	37.2
Do B-1-24-60	----	398	37.1
Kota x Hd. Fed. 8E-9-2-1	----	318	37.0
Kanred x Marquis B9-14-24	----	37	36.8
Marquis x Hd. Fed. 2 A-1-34-28-1	----	707	36.4
Marquis x Hd. Fed. B-1-78-26-12	----	666	36.3

(Continued)

Variety or Hybrid	C. I. No.	Nursery No.	Yield (Bu. per ac
Hard Federation	4733	---	36.2
Marquis x Erivan B3-19-3	----	473	36.0
Marquis x Hd. Fed. 2 A1-34-35	----	378	35.9
Marquis x Hd. Fed. B3-49-30-2	----	676	35.8
H-44	8177	---	35.4
Marquis x Hd. Fed. 2 B1-24-25	----	393	35.0
Hard Federation x Kota 9 D-3.3-1	----	340	34.9
Kanred x Marquis B-15-14-3	----	---	34.8
Hd. Fed. x Marq. 3A-2-77-47-9	----	679	34.7
Marquillo	6887	---	34.6
H. Fed. x Marquis 3A2-46-5-2	----	678	34.5
Marquis x Hd. Fed. 2 A1-34-31	----	377	34.3
Marquis	----	---	33.9
Marquis x Hd. Fed. B1-24-67	----	400	33.4
Hd. Fed. x Marquis	----	680	33.3
Kota x Hd. Fed. x Kanred			
x Marquis A3-6-4	----	700	32.8
Kota x Webster H178-25	----	---	32.3
Hd. Fed. x Marquis 3 A-1-24-9-5	----	675	32.2
Progress	6902	---	32.2
Hd. Fed. x Kota 9 C-6-4-1	----	338	32.1
Marquis x Hd. Fed. 2A-1-34-1-1	----	705	31.8
Axminster	8196	---	31.5
Marquis x Hd. Fed. 2B2-100-22-1	----	672	31.5
Hd. Fed. x Marq. 3A2-77-47-17	----	680	31.4
Hd. Fed. x Marq. 3A2-46-5-2	----	678	31.0
Kota x Hd. Fed. 8A1-16-4-3	8197	285	30.7
Hope	8178	---	30.7
Marquis x Prelude 5A2-15-5	----	---	30.5
Marquis x Erivan A3-12-6	----	---	30.4
Marquis x Hd. Fed. B-1-78-17-9	----	663	30.1
Marquis x Erivan A4-6-1	----	---	29.7
Supreme	8026	---	29.3
Kota x Hd. Fed. D4-34-2	----	317	29.1
Kanred x Marquis B9-14-22	----	36	28.6
Marquis x Sunset 7A-1-16-6	----	346	28.3
Kota	5878	---	28.0
Kanred x Marquis B-9-14	----	---	27.4
Hd. Fed. x Prelude 5A-29-13-1	----	257	27.4
Marquis x Hd. Fed. A2-6-1	----	381	27.0
Hd. Fed. x Prelude 5A-2-11-9-1	----	---	26.7
Marquis x Hd. Fed. A7-26-47-12	----	687	26.1
Erivan	2397	---	23.5
Sunset	4728	---	20.0
Prelude	4323	---	18.7

NORTH DAKOTA

Agricultural Experiment Station, State College Station, Fargo (Flax Diseases, L. W. Boyle)

Dickinson Substation, Dickinson (Cereal Agronomy, R. W. Smith) (January 16)

The mild aspect of our winter has changed somewhat since the last report. Mild weather continued up until New Year's Day and the ground was bare. During much of the time since then the temperature has been colder than usual. Snow has fallen on a majority of the days this month. It is now about eight inches deep. Snow is still falling. The minimum temperature has been around 20 degrees below zero several times, 23 below being reached on January 13 and 14.

The winter grain has been protected by snow during the coldest weather and the prospect is good for ample snow protection during the rest of the winter.

Supt. Leroy Moomaw is in Fargo for a few days, attending the annual meeting of Substation Superintendents and other meetings in connection with Farmer's Week programs being held at the Agricultural College.

(February 1)

The year 1929 already has begun to set new weather records. During December the temperatures had been considerably above normal and the ground was practically bare throughout the month. It began to snow on New Year's Day and a measurable amount of snow fell on 19 days in January and a trace was recorded on three other days. About 18 inches of snow fell during the month and the snow is now about 12 inches deep. This seems to be the high record for January snow at Dickinson for the 37 years covered by weather records. The average January snowfall for this Substation is only about 4 inches.

Winter wheat has thus been well protected by snow during the past month. This protection was needed, as the month was one of the coldest ever recorded here. The minimum temperature was below zero on 26 days and the maximum below zero every day for the past 10 days, getting up to zero this afternoon for the first time since January 21. The mean temperature here during the past 10 days was 19.8 degrees below zero. This probably was the coldest 10-day period in the history of the Substation. The mean temperature for the month was 4.5 degrees below zero as compared with a normal January temperature of 10.3 degrees above zero. The lowest temperature for the month and the lowest here for 12 years was 39 below on the 25th.

Fortunately the wind velocity was low, averaging 5.2 miles per hour for the month. A few winds the past week have caused the roads to become almost impassable. Rural mail carriers are able to travel by using runners under the front end of the car and a caterpillar tread under the rest of the car.

Due to the condition of the roads but little wheat has been marketed here during the past two weeks. One commodity that has kept moving is lignite coal which is obtained on many farms in this vicinity, in some cases being in beds but a few feet below the wheat fields growing on the surface. At Lehigh, four miles east of Dickinson, there has been in process of erection for the past year a large industrial plant for the manufacture of lignite briquets. This plant began turning out briquets on January 26. It is said to be the first completed plant of its kind in the United States, making briquets of lignite coal by a low temperature carbonizing process, using pitch extracted from the coal to bind the crushed dried coal together into briquets about the size and shape of an egg. Several by-products will be obtained in the process.

Northern Great Plains Field Station, Mandan (Flax Breeding, J. C. Brinsmade, Jr.) (February 2)

The month of January, 1929, has been the coldest month since January, 1916. Average daily temperatures for the entire month were as follows: Average maximum 5°, average minimum -15°, and average mean -5°, the latter 1 degree higher than the average mean for January, 1916. The minimum temperature was -33° on January 29, compared with -43° for January, 1916. The maximum temperature for the month was 39° on January 10. During the last ten days of January the highest maximum temperature was -3° and the highest minimum -15°. For the same ten days the average maximum was -8° and the average minimum -25°.

The snowfall in January amounted to 0.80 of an inch of precipitation, more than half an inch over the average January precipitation for the past 14 years.

The flax still standing in the field is partly buried in snow. The snow has drifted over the seeding so that the depth varies from about eight inches to three feet. Plants still protruding from the snow are apparently standing up straight, and show little apparent loss of bolls and seed except in a few places where the depth of snow has given mice easy access to the heads. The scarcity of rabbit tracks has indicated very little damage from this source.

Inquiries and reports from farmers have indicated more than usual interest in Argentine flax in this locality. The past season was unusually favorable to late maturing crops so that Argentine flax generally outyielded varieties of other types.

Northern Great Plains Field Station, Mandan (Cereal Agronomy, E. R. Ausemus)

MONTANA

Judith Basin Substation, Moccasin (Cereal Agronomy, B. B. Bayles) (Joe L. Sutherland)

Montana (Western Wheat Investigations, J. Allen Clark, Senior Agronomist in Charge) (January 31)

The results from recent varietal experiments with spring wheat in Montana indicate that Reliance, Supreme, and Ceres are the most promising new varieties. There is keen interest regarding the comparative value of these new varieties in comparison with the standard Marquis. The results from the plot and nursery experiments at the Bozeman, Moccasin, and Havre stations for 1928 are shown in Table 1. These results show that, at Bozeman, Reliance was the highest yielding variety. At Moccasin, Ceres produced the highest yield, and at Havre, Supreme ranked first. The average for all experiments at the three stations in 1928 shows the varietal rank as follows: Reliance first, Supreme second, Marquis third, and Ceres fourth.

The results from four years' of plot experiments with the same varieties are given in Table 2. These show Reliance to rank first, Supreme second, and Ceres third. The yield of Reliance has been 9.2 per cent greater than that of Marquis.

Nursery experiments with 22 miscellaneous varieties and hybrid selections have been conducted in a uniform manner at the three stations, and the results are shown in Table 3. In these experiments Reliance selections 16 and 22 slightly outyielded the Reliance variety. Other selections of the Kanred x Marquis cross were among the higher yielding strains. Supreme outyielded the average of the Marquis checks, which in turn outyielded Ceres.

More promising selections from the Marquis x Hard Federation cross are included in the Montana nurseries. The results of the nursery experiments with 40 selections of this cross at Bozeman, Moccasin, and Havre, in comparison with the parents, are shown in Table 4. There were 29 selections of the cross which outyielded the higher yielding Marquis parent and all of the selections grown outyielded the Hard Federation parent. This is a striking example of transgressive segregation for yield. This increased yield over both parents has been apparent for a 5-year period and apparently is due to combining the advantages of both parents, viz, the height of Marquis and the long fruiting period of Hard Federation.

Table 1. Yield, in bushels per acre, of Reliance, Supreme, Marquis, and Ceres wheats grown in plot and nursery experiments at Bozeman, Moccasi and Havre, Mont., in 1928.

Variety	Bozeman			Moccasin			Havre			Av. all expe imen
	Plots	Nur.	Av.	Plots	Nur.	Av.	Plots	Nur.	Av.	
Reliance	77.1	50.7	63.9	40.0	23.9	32.0	46.7	37.8	42.3	46.
Supreme	70.1	41.2	55.7	41.7	23.9	32.8	49.2	44.9	47.1	45.
Marquis	65.1	40.6	52.9	38.8	22.7	30.8	42.8	40.0	41.4	41.
Ceres	62.5	34.0	48.3	42.3	28.2	35.3	42.5	37.8	40.2	41.

Table 2. Yield in bushels per acre, of Reliance, Supreme, Ceres, and Marquis wheats grown in plot experiments at Bozeman, Moccasin, and Havre, Mont., from 1925 to 1928.

Bozeman

Average

Moccasin	1 25	24.3	24.7	25.6	22.4
	1 26	32.6	29.7	30.7	30.0
	1 27	22.2	21.4	22.2	18.2
	1 28	40.0	41.7	42.3	38.8

Average

Havre	1	17.2	.9	18.1	16.4
	1	3.9	.2	3.6	2.8
	1	40.6	.3	37.1	36.8
	1	46.7	.2	42.5	42.8

Average

Station years	12	12	9	12
Variety	39.2	38.9	31.6	35.9
Marquis same years	35.9	35.9	30.4	35.9
Percentage of Marquis	109.2	108.4	103.9	100.0

Table 3. Yield, in bushels per acre, of 22 miscellaneous varieties and hybrid selections grown in nursery experiments at Bozeman, Moccasin, and Havre, Mont., in 1928.

ariety or cross		C. I. No.	Nursery No.	Station and yield			
				Bozeman	Moccasin	Havre	Av.
cliance Sel. 16		----	14	50.2	25.0	39.8	38.3
cliance Sel. 22		----	17	42.7	30.3	40.0	37.7
cliance		7370	--	50.7	23.9	37.8	37.5
cliance Sel. 64		----	22	47.6	24.7	39.9	37.4
anred x Marquis 2-14-20		----	11	46.3	23.6	42.1	37.3
upreme		8026	--	41.2	23.9	44.9	36.7
anred x Marquis		8018	II-17-40	46.3	24.5	39.1	36.6
Do	9-11-50	----	33	41.2	23.5	37.3	35.7
Do	9-14-42	----	41	35.8	24.8	44.4	35.0
Do	9-14-24	----	37	39.9	23.7	40.2	34.6
ondak		7287	--	49.9	20.4	33.1	34.5
arquis (checks)		3641	--	40.6	22.7	40.0	34.4
anred x Marquis 5-14-3			13	44.4	21.5	36.1	34.0
ota		5878	14	44.9	23.6	32.6	33.7
ores		6900	--	34.0	28.2	37.8	33.3
ota x Marquis			1656.84	33.5	27.0	38.6	33.0
ard Federation		4733	--	42.7	21.5	34.6	32.9
anred x Marquis 9-11-27			28	37.4	22.4	34.5	31.4
ota x Marquis			1656.81	33.2	22.5	33.7	29.8
ope		S178	--	37.9	18.5	31.1	29.2
ota x Marquis			1656.125	29.9	21.7	32.4	28.0
ota x Hard Federation		5197	285	33.2	16.1	29.6	26.3

Table 4. Yield, in bushels per acre, of 40 selections from the Marquis x Hard Federation and reciprocal crosses, and of both parents grown in nursery experiments at Bozeman, Moccasin, and Havre, Mont., in 1928.

Parent or cross	C. I. No.	Nursery No.	Bozeman	Moccasin	Havre	Av.
Marquis x Hard Federation	----	666	56.1	29.5	41.1	43.9
Do	----	673	59.5	27.1	45.1	43.9
Do	----	657	54.5	29.3	46.8	43.5
Do	----	674	46.3	28.3	50.7	41.8
Do	----	736	52.4	25.1	48.2	41.9
Do	----	402	56.0	23.7	43.8	41.2
Do	----	675	56.1	24.6	42.7	41.1
Do	----	456	49.0	29.7	43.8	40.8
Do	----	687	50.1	26.7	44.0	40.3
Do	----	671	52.0	23.3	45.2	40.2
Do	----	393	47.9	23.1	49.2	40.1
Do	----	421	47.8	23.7	47.8	39.8
Do	----	651	48.2	25.6	44.2	39.3
Do	----	409	50.3	24.9	42.5	39.2
Do	----	659	52.0	27.6	37.6	39.1
Do	----	670	43.8	24.7	48.6	39.
Do	----	705	50.8	22.1	43.9	38.
Do	----	668	46.7	23.9	45.6	38.
Do	----	398	45.6	25.5	44.7	38.
Do	----	418	51.5	22.5	41.7	38.
Do	----	656	49.2	25.2	41.3	38.
Do	----	653	52.2	21.2	41.9	38.
Do	----	734	46.5	23.9	43.8	38.
Do	----	649	42.4	22.6	47.8	37.
Do	----	676	41.0	24.3	47.3	37.
Do	----	716	49.8	22.2	40.4	37.
Do	----	727	43.6	26.3	42.5	37.
Do	----	395	39.8	24.4	47.6	37.
Do	----	710	43.5	24.4	43.9	37
Marquis	3641	---	47.7	22.7	40.0	36
Marquis x Hard Federation	----	678	35.9	28.1	46.1	36
Do	----	663	37.1	27.3	45.0	36
Do	----	377	41.1	21.2	46.1	36
Do	----	677	43.4	23.7	41.2	36
Do	----	381	41.3	22.5	44.0	35
Do	----	661	42.8	23.7	41.1	35
Do	----	672	39.9	25.3	40.1	35
Do	----	709	45.7	18.1	41.5	35
Do	----	378	35.7	26.0	42.8	34
Do	----	400	36.7	24.5	43.3	3
Do	----	399	30.2	23.9	46.7	3
Hard Federation	4733	---	42.7	21.5	34.6	3

WESTERN BASIN AND COAST AREAS (North to West and South)

IDAHO

Aberdeen Substation, Aberdeen (Cereal Agronomy, G. A. Wiebe)

Agricultural Experiment Station, Moscow (Stripe Rust, C. W. Hungerford)

WASHINGTON

Agricultural Experiment Station, Pullman (Cereal Breeding, E. F. Gaines)
[February 15]

The following table gives the amount of smut produced on 10 different spring wheats when inoculated with smut collections from four different sources. If these results are compared with those obtained on the 10 winter wheats mentioned in the Cereal Courier 20 (19):236-237, August 10, 1928, a better idea of variation in the pathogenicity of the collections may be obtained. The Tilletia levis collection from Waterville and the T. levis collection from Pullman on Albit were examined in the heads, and those showing T. tritici were discarded before inoculating the spring wheats, so that the experiments on spring and fall-sown wheat are not entirely comparable.

Blueston, Baart, Jenkin, and Federation are susceptible to all four collections. Marquis and Kubanka are resistant to all forms. Alaska and Hope appear practically immune, while Khapli produced respectively 15 and 17 per cent of bunted heads from the two Pullman collections. Marquis X Turkey, on the other hand, appeared most susceptible to the smuts from Lind and Waterville.

The seed inoculated with a composite inoculum consisting of proportionate parts of the four collections of smut produced, on the average, slightly less bunt than the seed inoculated with the most virulent inoculum for that particular host. Fifteen plants were found as a result of this mixed inoculum, each of which had both levis and tritici on different heads of the same plant. In fact, two heads were found that had levis and tritici in different smut balls on the same head. Seven smut balls contained a mixture of both rough and smooth spores, showing that the two species of bunt had infected the same ovary seven times in the 450 balls examined.

Porcentage of smut on 10 varieties of spring wheat inoculated with four collections of smut from different sources. Sown on two different dates.

Variety	Source, species and percentage of smut									
	Pullman T. tritici		Lind T. levis		Waterville T. levis		Pullman T. levis[a]		Composite, all collect (3 T. levis, 1 T. tri	
	4-11	4-14	4-11	4-14	4-11	4-14	4-11	4-14	4-11	4-14
Bluesten	28	80	34	60	47	74	27	43	17	66
Baart	17	51	16	50	10	51	13	55	25	57
Marquis	0	0	0	6	1	7	0	2	1	3
Kubanka	0	0	2	1	1	0.2	0	0	0	8
Jenkin	28	70	34	63	40	65	25	62	39	45
Alaska	0	0	0	0	0	0	0	0.3	0	0
Khapli	6	17	3	9	0	0	6	15	6	14
Federation	22	63	16	58	11	48	9	41	14	52
Marquis X Turkey	0	0	1	13	4	13	0.3	3	0.2	14
Hope	0	0	0	0	0	0	0	0	0	1

a/ From smutted heads of Albit.

OREGON

Sherman County Branch Station, Moro (Cereal Agronomy, D. E. Steph (February 15)

The following table gives the results obtained from an experiment conducted in cooperation with the Oregon Agricultural Experiment Station in 1927-28 at Moro, Oreg., to determine the existence and distribution of physiologic forms of stinking smut. Collections of smut from 45 localities, four of which were originally from foreign countries, were obtained by Prof. E. N. Bressman, of the Oregon Station, who determined whether the smuts were T. laevis or T. tritici, and inoculated the seed. Subsequent examination, by the Office of Cereal Crops and Diseases, of smutted heads of Ridit produced from some of the smut collections showed that both species were present in the heads from single collections. Sowings were made at Corvallis and at Moro, each collection being used on 10 varieties of winter wheat.

The results obtained at Moro are given in the following table, the smuts from the various localities being grouped according to their behavior on the 10 varieties. Prof. Bressman's results at Corvallis agree very closely with those obtained at Moro, except in three instances where there were wide discrepancies. These were with smuts No. 1d, 3, and 8b.

Of the 27 smuts in group 1, 15 were determined as T. laevis and 12 as T. tritici. In this group 15 States are represented. The smuts in this group appear to be the most widely disseminated. The nine varieties which until 1927 proved resistant for many years at Moro are all resistant to the collections in this group. Smuts No. 4, No. 8c and No. 1b listed in this group may not belong here because of the rather high percentage of smut obtained in Albit with smuts No. 8c and No. 4, and in Banner Berkeley with smut No. 1b.

Five of the varieties resistant to the smuts in group 1 proved susceptible to those listed in group 2.

The results with Hussar separate the smuts in group 3 from those in group 2. The smut known as Palouse smut is grouped here because of the similarity of reaction on several varieties although it was not tested on Hussar. The two smuts in group 4 differ from those in group 2 in their behavior on the variety Martin.

White Odessa was the only one of the resistant varieties which was susceptible to the two smuts in group 5.

The one smut in group 6 is distinctly different from all the others in its result on Oro. Of 45 collections, this is the only smut to which Oro quite completely succumbed.

Ridit was the most resistant variety, averaging one per cent of smut. The highest percentage of smut in Ridit was 9.1 from a strain of smut grown at Moro in 1927, which was originally obtained from a sample of wheat grown in the Palouse section of Washington.

The second most resistant variety was Turkey X Bd. Minn. 48, which proved resistant to all forms.

The most virulent smut was one obtained near Heppner, Oreg. When inoculated with this smut, Regal produced 79.0 per cent of smutted heads, Albit 70.0 per cent and White Odessa 70.2 per cent.

Percentage of bunt in 10 winter-wheat varieties grown at Moro, Oreg., in 1928 with seed inoculated with Tilletia from 45 localities. Both species are grouped together on the basis of pathogenicity on 10 varieties.

No.	Source of Inoculum	Oro	Turkey x Bd. Minn. 48	Regal	Ridit	Hybrid 128	Albit	Hussar	Martin	Bammor Berkeley	White Odessa	Av. (excluding
	GROUP 1											
	T. tritici [a]											
5	Lakeview, Oreg.	0.5	0.7	0.9	0.0	64.0	0.0	0.2	0.0	0.3	0.7	.
6a	Morrow Co.,Oreg.	0.5	0.8	0.0	0.4	39.8	0.6	0.0	3.0	0.0	0.3	.
6b	Do Do	0.3	0.0	0.1	0.7	14.1	0.0	0.0	0.0	0.0	0.0	.
7b	Pendleton, Oreg.	0.8	0.0	1.6	0.4	68.2	0.0	0.0	1.0	0.8	0.3	.
20	Hillsboro, Oreg.	0.7	1.5	2.3	0.4	80.9	1.1	0.2	0.4	3.0	0.6	1.
	Sherman Co.,Oreg.	1.7	---	2.0	1.1	---	---	---	0.0	---	1.1	1.
4	Redmond, Oreg.	4.8	5.7	2.2	2.7	91.7	12.5	1.5	4.9	6.1	4.1	4.
8c	Pullman, Wash.	0.8	0.4	3.5	0.0	87.3	14.5	1.6	0.2	3.4	1.7	2.
10	Davis, Calif	1.3	2.0	3.0	0.0	74.7	1.5	0.4	0.6	0.0	0.4	1.
12a	Tucson, Ariz.	0.2	1.1	3.3	0.0	62.8	0.4	0.0	0.2	0.0	0.0	.
12b	Tucson, Ariz.	0.0	0.0	0.0	0.3	66.1	0.0	0.0	1.1	0.0	0.0	.
19b	St. Paul, Minn. (Sweden)	3.5	7.8	2.0	1.0	93.4	1.0	1.7	0.7	0.0	0.0	2.
	T. laevis [a]											
1a	Corvallis, Oreg.	1.2	1.2	1.5	1.0	92.5	0.2	0.0	2.2	0.0	0.0	.
2	Camas Valley,Oreg.	0.7	2.7	1.5	0.6	94.4	0.5	0.0	0.3	0.0	0	.
1b	Corvallis, Oreg.	0.9	0.8	1.3	0.2	94.1	2.5	0.8	0.2	18.8	8	3.
13	Bozeman, Mont.	3.0	3.2	4.6	2.3	95.2	4.3	1.6	0.7	1	7.7	3.
11	Pierre, S. Dak.	1.8	5.4	2.5	0.0	92.6	0.2	0.3	1.2	0	4.4	1.
14	Ames, Iowa	0.9	4.4	0.9	0.3	86.7	0.8	1.7	2.3	0.0	.	1.
16a	Lincoln, Nebr.	6.3	1.2	2.3	0.6	89.0	0.2	0.0	0.0	0.0	0.0	1.
16b	Lincoln, Nebr.	1.5	1.4	3.4	2.1	91.6	0.2	0.0	1.0	0.0	0.0	1.1

ntinued

:Source of Inoculum	Oro	Turkey x Bd. Minn. 48	Regal	Radit	Hybrid 128	Albit	Hussar	Martin	Banner Berkeley	White Odessa	Av. (excluding Hybrid 128)
GROUP 1 Cont'd T. laevis a/											
Hutchinson, Kans.	2.3	1.4	3.9	0.6	82.1	2.3	0.0	2.5	3.4	4.5	2.3
Denton, Tex.	1.0	0.4	0.5	0.0	68.2	2.2	0.0	1.8	0.0	0.0	.7
c:St. Paul, Minn.											
: (New Zealand)	0.7	0.0	0.3	0.0	73.1	4.8	1.2	1.1	0.0	0.0	.9
:Portage, Wis.	3.0	0.3	0.8	0.0	49.1	0.5	0.0	1.4	0.0	0.0	.7
:Hoopstown, Ill.	0.7	0.6	3.0	0.2	47.8	1.1	1.0	0.3	0.0	0.7	.8
:Ithaca, N. Y.	1.3	1.0	2.0	2.2	74.1	0.4	0.0	1.1	8.0	4.0	2.2
:State College, Pa.	4.5	2.3	1.4	0.0	85.7	3.9	1.1	1.9	1.4	2.7	2.1
GROUP 2 T. tritici a/											
d:Corvallis, Oreg.	3.0	4.1	59.5	0.5	93.4	69.9	3.2	61.8	82.5	27.0	34.6
c:Corvallis, Oreg.	5.9	2.2	42.5	0.0	52.1	50.4	1.2	24.6	55.3	75.1	28.6
d:St. Paul, Minn.											
: (Norway)	0.9	2.7	33.1	0.0	77.9	75.1	2.3	54.5	58.9	67.8	32.8
T. laevis a/											
:Fort Collins, Colo.	4.5	0.8	7.4	0.0	91.0	32.6	0.2	12.1	26.1	36.1	13.3
a:St. Paul, Minn.	3.0	2.0	24.7	0.0	89.7	47.0	3.1	32.9	27.4	37.9	19.8
c:St. Paul, Minn.											
: (Italy)	0.6	3.9	41.3	0.9	63.1	47.1	8.1	25.5	20.4	90.2	26.4
:Lancaster, Wis.	1.1	1.2	22.0	0.0	57.6	39.8	2.2	16.3	32.7	91.6	23.0
:Tippecanoe Co., Ind.	0.4	1.7	37.3	0.0	86.0	45.0	4.5	35.8	43.9	54.8	24.8
GROUP 3 T. tritici a/											
:Redmond, Oreg.	4.0	1.7	32.4	2.2	76.5	26.3	23.6	24.2	40.4	61.8	24.1
:Heppner, Oreg.	1.6	2.8	79.0	0.0	81.6	70.0	36.9	59.5	65.9	70.2	42.9
:Palouse Smut (Moro)	5.6	---	36.8	9.1	----	----	----	46.1	----	59.5	31.4

Continued

No. Source of Inoculum	: Oro	Turkey x Bd. Minn. 48	Regal	Ridit	Hybrid 128	Albit	Hussar	Martin	Banner Berkeley	White Odessa
GROUP 3 Cont'd										
T. laevis a/										
1c: Corvallis, Oreg.	5.5	1.0	59.9	2.2	71.9	25.1	17.5	23.9	57.6	41.4
8b: Pullman, Wash.	4.6	2.1	61.5	1.2	61.1	51.7	20.7	34.3	66.3	61.2
GROUP 4										
T. tritici a/										
7a: Pendleton, Oreg.	1.7	2.1	29.3	0.0	83.3	35.9	6.4	1.3	8.0	24.5
T. laevis a/										
27 : Waterville, Wash.	8.4	0.7	8.0	1.8	85.2	32.6	4.7	1.2	13.7	14.0
GROUP 5										
T. tritici a/										
7c: Pendleton, Oreg.	0.0	0.0	0.6	0.0	25.7	0.2	0.0	1.2	0.0	32.4
8a: Pullman, Wash.	1.0	2.2	6.6	2.1	70.3	0.6	4.9	2.0	1.6	25.2
GROUP 6										
T. laevis a/										
28 : Moccasin, Mont.	72.8	6.7	20.5	5.2	18.2	9.5	1.4	22.7	3.8	17.8
AVERAGE	3.8	2.0	14.5	0.9	73.1	16.6	3.6	11.3	15.1	20.6

a/ The identity of these smut collections used in this experiment was dete mined by Prof. E. N. Brossman. However, an examination of smutted heads o Ridit from some collections showed that both T. tritici and T. laevis were present in the smutted heads produced from a single collection.

CALIFORNIA

Biggs Rice Field Station, Biggs (Rice Agronomy, J. W. Jones)

University Farm, Davis (Cereal Agronomy, V. H. Florell)

Agricultural Experiment Station, Berkeley (Cereal Smuts, F. N. Briggs)

BARBERRY ERADICATION PROGRESS

OHIO

Ohio State University, College of Agriculture, Columbus, J. W. Baringer (January 31)

Tabulation of barberry records, compilation of reports, the preparation of educational material for use in Ohio grade schools, and the making of plans for a barberry-eradication lesson plan contest for teachers occupied the time in January.

Eight copies of the annual report on barberry eradication in Ohio for the calendar year 1928 were mailed to cooperators the latter part of the month.

Approximately 200 instructors in Ohio normal schools, colleges, and universities besides 200 Smith-Hughes teachers of agriculture have been invited to participate in a barberry-eradication lesson plan contest. Packets of relevant material were mailed to them early in January.

It is with gratification that we are able at this time to report the passage, in January, of an appropriation by the Ohio Legislature of $2,250.00 for barberry eradication for the period from Jan. 1 to June 30, 1929.

Plans for the preparation of a barberry-eradication demonstration to be held in connection with the Annual Farmers' Week at the Ohio State University are now in progress. Farmers' Week will be held this year from Feb. 4 to 8, inclusive.

INDIANA

Purdue University College of Agriculture, La Fayette, W. E. Leer (January 25)

The active field season in Indiana closed late in November. The unusually favorable fall weather permitted continuous work in areas of escaped bushes.

During the last week of November and the first week of December, a barberry demonstration was placed at the International Grain and Hay Show at Chicago. As in the past, the demonstration attracted many

interested people. It is pleasing to one conected with the campaign to
be able to note with certainty the annual increase in the "barberry
intelligence" of people in the past five years. Our various activities
are beginning to impress themselves on the minds of the public. Dealing with an individual antagonistic toward the campaign is no longer
the problem of the demonstration explainer. The problem is to give out
more detailed information about stem-rust losses, identification of the
barberry, and how to kill the barberry.

Since the International Show, most of the time has been devoted to
the preparation of the annual report of the progress of barberry eradication in Indiana for 1928.

MICHIGAN

Agricultural College, East Lansing, W. F. Reddy

WISCONSIN

Department of Agriculture, State Capitol Annex, Madison, R. M.
Caldwell (February 11)

Activities in barberry eradication in Wisconsin have been limited
to educational work since the close of the fall survey.

Recently a small pamphlet has been prepared, summarizing the results
of the campaign since its initiation. This pamphlet gives special emphasis to problems and results of 1928. It has been distributed to the
leading farmers, educators, and others interested in the agricultural
progress of the State. Copies also have been supplied to all Wisconsin
public libraries.

Material which makes possible a very intensive study of the stem-
rust fungus in relation to both the uredinial and aecial hosts is now
being supplied to all the high schools of the State. Such a study is
of special value as a part of agricultural courses where a type study
of one such fungous disease of plants is very useful for reference when
a less intensive consideration is being given to other fungous diseases.

Plans also are being made for supplying study materials to about
one-third of the rural and urban graded schools of the State. The
studies made in these schools will stress the recognition of the disease
and the comprehension of its great economic importance as well as the
identification of the common barberry.

ILLINOIS

Box 72, Post Office Building, Urbana, R. W. Bills (January 25)

Educational and publicity activities have followed the completion of field survey and this phase of the campaign is now the principal activity. A plan is being developed to make a study of the common barberry a part of the nature-study class work in the rural schools. Twenty-two counties in Southern Illinois that have had little publicity in the past, are being made the field of operations.

Mr. L. H. Corbin is at present giving illustrated lectures in the high schools of these counties to classes in vocational agriculture and science and before the high school assemblies. A fine spirit of cooperation is being shown in the schools.

At Mt. Vernon High School the agricultural students had a planting of common barberry all ready to report when Mr. Corbin arrived. The instructor, Mr. Anderson, will have a class exercise in eradication in the spring, at which time the bushes will be destroyed.

IOWA

Iowa State College, Ames, P. W. Rohrbaugh (January 25)

A thick coating of ice has covered the State of Iowa for several days and has been followed by a heavy coating of snow. It is quite possible that this may cause serious damage to winter wheat. January has been extremely cold and has had a record-breaking snowfall for Iowa.

Mr. Jount, who served as assistant State Leader of barberry last summer, is now taking graduate work at the University of Minnesota.

The barberry office force has been spending its time for the past several weeks on the annual report of the progress of barberry eradication in Iowa, and on a paper dealing with the importation of the barberry into Iowa and its effect on the rust situation.

MINNESOTA

Agricultural Experiment Station, University Farm, St. Paul, L. W. Melander (January 26)

The 1928 field season was terminated on November 30. This is the latest date for work in the field in the history of the barberry campaign in Minnesota. Ideal weather conditions in November permitted survey so late in the season. The most outstanding thing about fall survey is the fact that practically all the trees and shrubs, except common barberry, lose their leaves after the first frost. With the absence of leaves on other shrubs, it is very easy to see the barberry. Accordingly, the highest efficiency in finding barberries, especially in heavy underbrush, and speed of survey are obtained in the late fall.

From October 15 to November 30 an intense survey was made of the Minnesota River Valley starting at Ortonville. The survey almost reached Redwood Falls by November 30. Two new locations of barberry were found in a small area of escaped bushes near Montevideo. In most instances we surveyed about a mile of the tributary rivers and creeks. One of these plantings was found a short distance up the Chippewa River near Montevideo.

This year a planting of barberry in Clay County was reported at a fair in North Dakota. On investigating this location, the remains of a hedge over 40 years old which had been cut off was found in Moland Township, Clay County. In addition, 21 escaped barberry bushes were found growing along the Buffalo River. In 1925, Dr. H. L. Bolley, of the North Dakota Experiment Station, took a group of cereal pathologists, who were attending the summer meeting of the American Phytopathological Society, to this farm and showed them a very heavy infection of stemrust. At that time he stated that he came to this farm every year to find the first stem rust and that he was convinced that there were barberries in the vicinity. The bushes which spread this rust now have been found and eradicated. Recently, three farmers each signed an affidavit to the effect that stem rust always has been worse on his farm than on farms five to ten miles distant.

(February 2)

You may be interested to know that the average temperature for January in Minnesota was 10 degrees below normal and there was lots of snow. It is the coldest January reported since 1912.

NEBRASKA

College of Agriculture, University Farm, Lincoln, A. F. Thiel
(January 25)

The oldest known barberry bushes so far found in the State were located on the Bruner Estate near West Point. Mr. Edgar Bruner planted about six barberry bushes in 1870. The age of the escaped bushes near the planted bushes indicate that birds had scattered seeds in the orchards, planted groves, and native woods of the vicinity within a few years after the original planting had been made.

This area was surveyed last summer and 343 escaped barberry bushes and 576 seedlings were found on nine properties. The area covers parts of three different sections in the immediate vicinity of West Point. With the exception of the area in northern Cedar County where escaped bushes were found along the Missouri River, this is the largest area of escaped bushes found in Nebraska to date. It is a common thing to find escaped barberry bushes on properties having old planted bushes.

SOUTH DAKOTA

College of Agriculture, Brookings, R. O. Bulger

NORTH DAKOTA

Agricultural Experiment Station, State College Station, Fargo, G. C. Mayoue (January 29)

In January, demonstrations and talks supplemented with lantern slides were made in two rural schools and four town schools as well as before the annual State conventions of the county superintendents of schools at Bismarck and the County Commissioners at Valley City. Valuable contacts were made at both of these gatherings.

An effort is being made to obtain a new lesson plan especially adapted to the seventh and eighth grades. Two years ago a lesson plan was prepared for use in the grade schools of North Dakota. It has served its purpose well. However, there is need for a new up-to-date plan. The Conference for the Prevention of Grain Rust, of Minneapolis, is sponsoring this lesson-plan contest, offering in cash $100 for the most satisfactory plan submitted by an instructor of teacher training courses of science within the 13 States of the barberry-eradication area. The Greater North Dakota Association, of Fargo, is offering in addition 1st, 2nd, 3rd, and 4th prizes aggregating $100.

Educational materials are being mailed to all of the rural and urban grade schools of approximately one-third of the counties and to all of the high schools of the State. The material consists of bulletins, circulars, colored plates, lesson plans, specimens of barberry, rusted grain, and shriveled wheat. Circular letters from the State Leader and the State Superintendent of Public Instruction accompany this material. All of these schools will be circularized by the middle of March.

Among the recent visitors in the office were Governor Walter
.Maddock, Mr. Joseph A. Kitchen, Commissioner of Agriculture and Labor,
and Mr. M. S. Hagen, manager of the State Hail Insurance Department.

MONTANA

State College of Agriculture, Bozeman, W. L. Popham [February 5]

A summary of the rust observations made in Montana in 1928 shows
that leaf rust was reported in 32 counties, stem rust in 30 counties,
and stripe rust in five of the 56 counties of the State. Leaf rust
was collected early in April before the weather had been sufficiently
warm for the winter wheat to start growing. Entire wheat plants were
taken up and transplanted in the greenhouse where they were grown to
maturity, and the rust infection observed from time to time. No stem
rust developed on any of these plants.

No stem rust was reported in Montana until the week of July 22.
During the latter part of July and the first part of August a general
infection occurred throughout the eastern half of Montana. However,
this late infection did very little damage, as the major portion of
the spring-wheat crop was matured by August 15. The only noticeable
losses from stem rust were in fields of late seeded spring wheat.
Supreme wheat appeared more susceptible to stem rust than Marquis.

An epidemic of stripe rust developed on Jones Fife wheat in the
Flathead Valley late in June. Turkey and Marquis wheat growing in
the infected area were fairly resistant. Observation and inquiries
made at threshing time indicated that although some damage occurred
throughout the Valley in Jones Fife fields the losses were not great.
It is estimated that about two-thirds of the winter wheat grown in
the Flathead Valley in 1928 was Jones Fife.

WYOMING

College of Agriculture, University of Wyoming, Laramie, W. L.
Popham

COLORADO

Agricultural College, Ft. Collins, E. A. Lungren (January 26)

During the winter season we have been carrying on a very interesting activity in connection with barberry eradication. Through the

cooperation of the Smith-Hughes teachers and county agents, especially those in Larimer and Weld counties, a series of night classes for farmers have been conducted. Thus far we have reached four communities and have had five meetings in each. The average attendance has been 22 in each community.

Special provisions have been made to equip each farmer at these schools with microscopes and other working materials. The course is taught in the nature of a laboratory class. The first 15 or 20 minutes are devoted to explanation, following which materials are passed out, and the farmer makes his own observations of the disease. The first lessons are the study of the plant and how it is constructed; following this a study is made of the important plant diseases. With the knowledge the farmer has of the plant, he is in a much better position to understand how diseases like black stem rust infect and damage the plant.

At one of the meetings west of Loveland, a farmer reported finding a common barberry growing along a ditch in a very out-of-the-way place. He carefully dug it up and brought it to the next class, explained how he found it and described its characteristics to the class. There has been much enthusiasm in these classes, and the demand for them has become greater.

C E R E A L   C O U R I E R

Official Messenger of the Office of Cereal Crops and Diseases
Bureau of Plant Industry, U. S. Department of Agriculture
(NOT FOR PUBLICATION)

Vol. 21   No. 4

February 28, 1929
Personnel (Feb. 16-28) and Project Issue

PERSONNEL ITEMS

C. E. Chambliss, associate agronomist in charge of rice investigations, was in Camden, N. J., on February 20 to conduct cooking and processing tests with Fortuna rice in comparison with imported Patna rice from India in co-operation with the laboratory and factory of the Campbell Soup Company.

Clarence C. Colcord was transferred to this Office on February 16 from the Bureau of Agricultural Economics. Mr. Colcord was appointed as scientific aid to fill the vacancy in western wheat investigations caused by the resignation of John R. Hooker in May, 1928.

A. C. Dillman, associate agronomist in charge of flax investigations, has been authorized to attend the meeting of The Flax Development Committee at St. Paul, Minn., on March 8, on invitation of the Committee. While at St. Paul Mr. Dillman will confer with agronomists and linseed crushers of the flax-producing States, Minnesota, North and South Dakota, and Montana.

Dr. H. V. Harlan, principal agronomist in charge of barley investigations, wrote to Dr. Ball from Sacaton, Ariz., on February 19 that the barleys in the nurseries are growing rapidly and that some interesting observations already have been made.

The automobile trip from Washington, D. C., to Sacaton was made on schedule, a daily average of 303 miles being maintained. From Washington the party went south to Jacksonville, Fla. It was expected that the schedule for the entire trip would be shorter by one day than that of last year. Severe weather in west Texas delayed progress, however. Dr. Harlan writes:

"A 'norther' slipped down on us when we got out where there were no towns and we woke up one morning surrounded by and engulfed in clouds with the temperature 10 above zero. Our run for the day was 3 miles---1-1/2 miles out and 1-1/2 miles back. In those three miles I scraped the windshield three times with a pocket knife to find where the road was and it was not where I thought it should be. Even the buses gave up--some of them giving up in the ditch............The roads were vastly better than they were last year. We did not change a tire all the way out."

Dr. Harry V. Harlan, principal agronomist in charge of barley investigations, and Dr. James R. Holbert, agronomist in charge of the cereal-disease investigations conducted in cooperation with Funk Bros. Seed Co., Bloomington, Ill., and the Illinois Agricultural Experiment Station, were elected Fellows of the American Association for the Advancement of Science at the meetings in New York City, December 27, 1928, to January 2, 1929.

J. Mitchell Jenkins, associate agronomist in charge of the cooperative rice experiments conducted at the Rice Experiment Station, Crowley, La., has been authorized to go to Nome, Texas, to attend a meeting of rice farmers on March 6.

Dr. Merle T. Jenkins, associate agronomist in the cooperative corn investigations at Ames, Iowa, was authorized on February 26 to go to Madison, Wis., to take notes on the condition of seedlings of his breeding stocks grown under controlled-temperature conditions through the courtesy of Dr. J. G. Dickson in the latter's laboratory. Dr. Jenkins expects to return to Ames about March 5.

C. H. Kyle, senior agronomist in corn investigations, and M. A. McCall, principal agronomist in charge of cereal agronomy, left Washington on February 24 to visit agricultural experiment stations in Alabama, Louisiana, Georgia, South Carolina, and North Carolina to consult station officials and others about cooperative corn experiments. They will return to Washington about March 7.

J. Foster Martin, junior agronomist in the cooperative nursery and breeding experiments conducted at the Sherman County Branch Station, Moro, Oreg., who came to Washington the latter part of January for conferences and to prepare a report on the experiments at Moro, left on February 23 to return to his headquarters.

Dr. John H. Parker, agronomist in the breeding experiments with small grains and sorghums conducted in cooperation with the Kansas Agricultural Experiment Station, wrote to Dr. Ball on February 26 that it was snowing and sleeting at Manhattan that day and that on the preceding day there had been a heavy rainfall. Mr. Parker added: "These conditions are not very favorable for winter wheat, but so far we know of no serious losses to the crop."

VISITORS

Dean Samuel W. Beyer, of the Industrial Science Division of Iowa State College, was an Office caller on February 23 to discuss cooperative research projects and their organization.

Charles H. Clark, formerly assistant agronomist in charge of flax investigations, now vice-president of the John L. Kellogg Seed Co., of Chicago, Ill., was an Office visitor on February 25.

Dr. and Mrs. E. M. Freeman, of St. Paul, Minn., were Office callers on February 26 on their way home from a vacation in the East and South.

Messrs. P. L. Gowen, of the National Canners' Association, Philip F. Nieukirk, General Purchasing Agent of the Campbell Soup Co., and F. B. Wise, Secretary-Treasurer of the Rice Millers' Association, of New Orleans, were Office visitors at different times in February to inspect the results of cooking experiments with Fortuna and imported Patna rice as used in soups.

Dr. F. E. Kempton, formerly pathologist in charge of barberry eradication, and now instructor of biology and zoology at Mt. Union College, Alliance, Ohio, was an Office caller on February 23.

MANUSCRIPTS AND PUBLICATIONS

11 A manuscript entitled "Date of Seeding Cereals As It Affects the Results of Cereal Varietal Experiments," by V. H. Florell, was approved on February 19 for publication in the Journal of the American Society of Agronomy.

12 A manuscript entitled "Sulphur Dusting for the Prevention of Stem Rust of Wheat," by E. B. Lambert and E. C. Stakman, was approved on February 25 for publication in Phytopathology.

13 A manuscript entitled "The Influence of the Combine on Agronomic Practices and Research," by John H. Martin, was approved on February 25 for publication in the Journal of the American Society of Agronomy.

The article entitled "Interpreting Correlation Coefficients," by Frederick D. Richey, appears in the Journal of the American Society of Agronomy 21 (2): 232-234. February, 1929.

The article entitled "A Bacterial Stripe Disease of Sorghum," by Charlotte Elliott and Erwin F. Smith, appears in the Journal of Agricultural Research 38 (1): 1-22, pls. 1-9. January 1, 1929. (Received February 27)

The article entitled "Yellow-Kerneled Fatuoid Oats," by T. R. Stanton and F. A. Coffman, appears in the Journal of Heredity 20 (2): [66]-70, figs. 3-4. February, 1929.

NOTICE ABOUT SEPARATES OF J. A. R. ARTICLES

After January 1, 1929, only 35 separates of articles published in the Journal of Agricultural Research will be allotted to the author (or authors) and 35 copies to the Office from which the article is a contribution.

RECENT DECISIONS OF THE COMPTROLLER GENERAL

(A-25121)
8 Comp. Gen. p. 261

COMPENSATION - DOUBLE

In determining whether the combined amount of more than one salary received in more than one position under the Government exceeds the sum of $2,000 per annum, the maximum authorized by the act of May 10, 1916, 39 Stat. 120, as amended by the act of August 29, 1916, 39 Stat. 582, the basis is the rate per annum of the combined salaries and not the aggregate amount actually received during a portion of the year, whether the measure of time for payment of salary under one or more positions is per annum, per diem, or per hour, it being necessary to determine in each instance the per annum rate equivalent to the rate based on a measure of time less than a year.

(A-25192)
8 Comp. Gen. 275

CLASSIFICATION OF CIVILIAN EMPLOYEES - REALLOCATION OF POSITION TO A LOWER GRADE

Upon reallocation of a position by the Personnel Classification Board from a higher to a lower grade, the initial salary rate properly payable is the minimum salary rate of the lower grade in which the position is reallocated, and any administrative promotion thereafter to a higher salary rate in the lower grade depends on the availability of appropriation, the comparative efficiency of the employee, and compliance with the average provision. 6 Comp. Gen. 413, distinguished.

C E R E A L   C O U R I E R

Official Messenger of the Office of Cereal Crops and Diseases,
Bureau of Plant Industry, U. S. Department of Agriculture
(NOT FOR PUBLICATION)

Vol. 21   No. 5

March 15, 1929
Personnel (March 1-15) and Field Station (Feb. 16-28) Issue

NOTICE

Beginning with the issue of April 10, 1929, the Cereal Courier will
appear three times a month, namely, on the 10th, 20th, and last days of
the month. The courtesy will be greatly appreciated if all contributors
at agronomic, pathologic, and barberry-eradication headquarters will mail
field reports promptly on the 15th and last days of the month. Field reports are issued on the 10th and 20th days of the month.

PERSONNEL ITEMS

A. C. Dillman, associate agronomist in charge of flax investigations,
returned to Washington on March 13 from St. Paul, Minn., where he attended
the annual meeting of the Flax Development Committee on March 8. Papers
were read by agronomists of the several flax producing States, and a summary of the outlook for the consumption of linseed oil for the coming year
was presented by the linseed crushers. Mr. Dillman gave a brief report of
experiments which he has conducted on the rate of absorption of hydroscopic
moisture in flax seeds and wheat exposed to atmospheres of different relative humidity.

Experiments at the several agricultural experiment stations have shown
the great advantage of early seeding of flax both in regard to control of
weeds and higher acre yields. Buda and Bison are two new varieties of flax
that have been developed by Prof. H. L. Bolley of the North Dakota station.
These varieties produce somewhat better yields than Linota, the former
standard variety in North Dakota.

Dr. J. R. Holbert, senior agronomist in charge of the cereal-disease investigations conducted in cooperation with Funk Bros. Seed Co., of Bloomington, Ill., and the Illinois Agricultural Experiment Station, wro on March 2 concerning the experiences of Mr. Baldwin, manager of the Dud Farms, Decatur, Ill., with tested and untested seed corn. In 1928 appro: mately 500 acres were planted with untested seed and 300 acres with seed tested by the Illinois Seed Testing Laboratory at Bloomington. The corn has been shelled and delivered to the elevators. That from the fields planted with tested seed yielded eight bushels more to the acre. The co from the tested seed had a test-weight per bushel of 56 pounds, while th from the untested seed had a test-weight per bushel of 52 pounds. The c from the tested seed had 16 per cent moisture and that from the untested seed had 19 per cent moisture. One graded No. 3 and the other graded No. Mr. Baldwin reported that the corn from the hybrid seed produced very sa factory results.

Robert B. Hoskinson was appointed agent, effective March 1, to have immediate charge of field work in connection with the cooperative dry-la cereal investigations at the Sherman County Branch Station, Moro, Oreg., under the direction of Superintendent D. E. Stephens.

Jenkin W. Jones, superintendent of the Biggs Rice Field Station, Bi Calif., who came to Washington late last December left on March 9 to ret to his headquarters.

M. A. McCall, principal agronomist in charge of cereal agronomy, an C. H. Kyle, senior agronomist in corn investigations, returned to Washin ton on March 8 from a trip in the southern and southeastern States in th interests of cooperative investigations of corn. Stops were made in Louisiana, Alabama, Georgia, and South and North Carolina. Arrangements were made for growing Mr. Kyle's corn breeding material at Tifton, Ga., and for general tests throughout the area of crosses developed in his b ing program. Plans for developing a well-coordinated corn improvement breeding program for the entire South were discussed with Station direc and agronomists and were received with hearty approval and the promise future support in so far as funds and facilities may be available.

Edgar C. Tullis, agent in the cooperative rice-disease investigati conducted at Fayetteville, Ark., was authorized on March 9 to go to Man tan, Kans., to confer with Dr. Hurley Fellows on the subject of Ophiobo He also will go to Lincoln, Nebr., to discuss with Dr. G. L. Peltier pr lems of technique and the subject of humidity and temperature control i greenhouses. Before returning to his headquarters Mr. Tullis will come Washington to confer with Department officials about the rice-disease i tigations at Fayetteville.

G. A. Wiebe, formerly assistant agronomist in charge of the cooperative cereal experiments at the Aberdeen Substation, Aberdeen, Idaho, was transferred on March 1 to his new headquarters at Davis, Calif., where he will assist in the investigations and experiments in the production and improvement of cereals in cooperation with the California Agricultural Experiment Station.

VISITORS

H. T. Corson, of the National Food Bureau, 844 Rush Street, Chicago, Ill., was an Office caller on March 5 to discuss with Dr. Ball the factors influencing the per capita consumption of wheat.

Ross R. Childs, agent in charge of cereal agronomy investigations in cooperation with the Georgia State College of Agriculture, Athens, Ga., was an Office visitor on March 15 and 16.

E. A. Žemčužnikov, professor of plant physiology, Don College of Agriculture and Amelioration, Novocherkassk, Northern Caucasus, U. S. S. R. (Russia), was an Office visitor on several occasions the week of March 11. Prof. Žemčužnikov was interested in the rice and wheat projects of the Office and in projects involving problems and methods in fundamental plant physiology both in the Office and at Arlington Experiment Farm.

MANUSCRIPTS AND PUBLICATIONS

14 A manuscript entitled "Scab of Barley and Wheat and Its Control by James G. Dickson and E. B. Mains, was submitted on March 1 for public tion in the Farmers' Bulletin series.

15 A manuscript entitled "Dehiscence of the Flax Boll," by A. C. Dillman, was approved on March 5 for publication in the Journal of the American Society of Agronomy.

16 A manuscript entitled "Moisture Content of Flaxseed and Its Rel tion to Harvesting," by A. C. Dillman and R. H. Black, was approved on M 5 for publication in the Journal of the American Society of Agronomy.

17 A manuscript entitled "Observations on the Distribution of Anth cyan Pigments in Rice Varieties," by Jenkin W. Jones, was approved on Ma 9 for publication in the Journal of the American Society of Agronomy.

18 A manuscript entitled "The Inheritance of Anthocyan Pigmentatio Rice," by Jenkin W. Jones, was submitted on March 9 for publication in t Journal of Agricultural Research.

19 A manuscript entitled "Correlations between Seed Ear and Kernel Characters and Yield of Corn," by Arthur M. Brunson and J. G. Willier, approved on March 12 for publication in the Journal of the American Soc of Agronomy.

20 A manuscript entitled "Review of the Literature on Pollination Hour of Blooming, and Natural Crossing in Rice," by Jenkin W. Jones, wa approved on March 12 for publication in the Journal of the American Soc of Agronomy.

21 A manuscript entitled "The Effects of Leaf Rust, Puccinia trit Eriks., on the Yield of Wheat," by E. B. Mains, was submitted on March for publication in the Journal of Agricultural Research.

U. S. Dept. Agr. Misc. Pub. 21 (Revised) entitled "Formaldehyde S Treatment for Oat Smuts," by V. F. Tapke, was received from the Governm Printing Office on March 3, bearing date of February, 1929.

Dr. C. E. Leighty, principal agronomist in charge of eastern whea investigations, is fourth author of U. S. Dept. Agr. Leaflet 33, Febr 1929, entitled "The Combination Cleaning and Treating of Seed Wheat," F. C. Meier, Extension Plant Pathologist, Extension Service; E. G. Bo Senior Marketing Specialist; G. P. Bodnar, Assistant Marketing Special Grain Division, Bureau of Agricultural Economics; C. E. Leighty, Princ Agronomist, Office of Cereal Crops and Diseases, Bureau of Plant Indus United States Department of Agriculture, and J. Earl Coke, Extension Specialist in Agronomy, California State Extension Service.

The article entitled "Greenhouse Studies on the Relation of Age of Wheat Plants to Infection by Puccinia triticina," by C. O. Johnston and L. E. Melchers, appears in the Journal of Agricultural Research 38 (3): 147-157, pls. 1-3. Feb. 1, 1929. (Cooperation between the Office of Cereal Crops and Diseases and the department of botany of the Kansas State Agricultural College.)

The article entitled "Inheritance of Yield and Protein Content in Crosses of Marquis and Kota Spring Wheats Grown in Montana," by J. Allen Clark and Karl S. Quisenberry, appears in the Journal of Agricultural Research 38 (4): 205-217. Feb. 15, 1929. (Cooperation between the Office of Cereal Crops and Diseases and the Montana Agricultural Experiment Station.)

The article entitled "What Sorghum Variety is Best?" by John B. Sieglinger, appears in the Oklahoma Farmer-Stockman 42 (5): 16 (200). March 1, 1929.

The 30-page pamphlet entitled "Iowa Corn Yield Test. Results for 1928," by Joe L. Robinson and A. A. Bryan, published by the Iowa Corn and Small Grain Growers' Association, was received on March 12. (The Iowa State Corn Yield Test is conducted by the Iowa Corn and Small Grain Growers' Association in cooperation with the Farm Crops Section, Iowa Agricultural Experiment Station and the Office of Cereal Crops and Diseases, Bureau of Plant Industry, United States Department of Agriculture.)

ANNOUNCEMENT

The Eleventh Annual Conference of the State Leaders of Barberry Eradication will be held at Bozeman, Montana, from March 25 to 30, inclusive.

FIELD STATION CONDITION AND PROGRESS

HUMID ATLANTIC COAST AREA (South to North)

GEORGIA

State College of Agriculture, Athens (Cereal Agronomy, R. R. Childs

VIRGINIA

Arlington Experiment Farm, Rosslyn (Small Grain Agronomy, J. W. Tay.

Arlington Experiment Farm, Rosslyn (Corn Breeding, F. D. Richey)

Arlington Experiment Farm, Rosslyn (Cereal Smuts, V. F. Tapke, Actin in Charge)

Arlington Experiment Farm, Rosslyn (Virus Diseases, H. H. McKinney)

NEW YORK

Cornell University Agricultural Experiment Station, Ithaca (Cereal Breeding, H. H. Love)

HUMID MISSISSIPPI VALLEY AREA (South to North)

LOUISIANA

Rice Experiment Station, Crowley (Rice Agronomy, J. M. Jenkins)

Agricultural Experiment Station, Baton Rouge (Corn Breeding, H. F. Stoneberg)

MISSOURI

Agricultural Experiment Station, Columbia (Cereal Agronomy, L.J.St

TENNESSEE

Agricultural Experiment Station, Knoxville (Corn Breeding, L. S. M

IOWA

Agricultural Experiment Station, Ames (Oat Breeding, L. C. Burnett)

Agricultural Experiment Station, Ames (Corn Breeding, M. T. Jenkins)

Agricultural Experiment Station, Ames (Crown Rust of Oats, S.M.Dietz)

ILLINOIS

Funk Bros. Seed Co., Bloomington (Corn Root, Stalk and Ear Rots, J. R. Holbert)

INDIANA

Purdue University Agricultural Experiment Station, La Fayette (Corn Rots and Metallic Poisoning, ------------)

Purdue University Agricultural Experiment Station, La Fayette (Leaf Rusts, E. B. Mains)

WISCONSIN

Agricultural Experiment Station, Madison (Wheat Scab, J. G. Dickson)

MINNESOTA

Agricultural Experiment Station, University Farm, St. Paul (Wheat Breeding, K. S. Quisenberry, Acting in Charge)

Agricultural Experiment Station, University Farm, St. Paul (Stem Rust, E. C. Stakman)

Agricultural Experiment Station, University Farm, St. Paul (Flax Rust, H. A. Rodenhiser)

GREAT PLAINS AREA (South to North)

OKLAHOMA

Woodward Field Station, Woodward (Grain Sorghum and Broomcorn, J. B. Sieglinger)

KANSAS

Agricultural Experiment Station, Manhattan (Cereal Breeding, J. H. Parker)

Agricultural Experiment Station, Manhattan (Corn Breeding, A.M.Bruns (March 2)

February has continued the cold-weather record generally prevalent this winter. The mean temperature of 23.9 degress was 6.6 degrees below normal and was the lowest February mean since 1905. The minimum temperature for the month was 14 degrees below zero on February 9 and the maximum 55 degrees on February 23. A snowfall of 6.25 inches was recorded for the month. The total precipitation was 0.82 of an inch as compared to a norm of 1.25 inches.

Farm and Home Week at the Kansas State Agricultural College held from February 5 to 8, inclusive, attracted a good crowd in spite of cold, stormy weather. The winner of the 5-acre corn contest for 1928 was announced as Mr. Brox, of Atchison County. He had obtained an acre yield of 110 bushels of excellent quality corn. The highest yield of the contest was 117.2 bushels, and 21 contestants made yields of over 100 bushels per acre. Fourteen counties finished the contest.

Substation workers met at the College on February 19 and 20 for their annual conference. Soil erosion and terracing were the special topics of discussion. Dr. A. G. McCall, of the Bureau of Soils and Chemistry, U. S. Dept. Agr., and Mr. R. E. Dickson of the Spur (Texas) Substation were out-of-State speakers. The resignation of Mr. B. F. Barnes as superintendent of the Colby Substation was announced. He will be succeeded by Mr. E. H. Coles, at present associate agronomist in the Office of Dry-Land Agriculture at Garden City, Kans.

Thus far there have been few reports of serious injury to wheat. An existing injury will become apparent this month and may be augmented by freezing and thawing because of the considerable amount of frost in the ground. Early farm work promises to be somewhat delayed by an unseasonal late spring. Country roads are nearly impassable at the present time.

Agricultural Experiment Station, Manhattan (Wheat Foot Rots, Hurley Fellows)

Agricultural Experiment Station, Manhattan (Wheat Leaf Rust, C. O. Johnston)

Hays Branch Experiment Station, Hays (Cereal Agronomy, A. F. Swanson)

NEBRASKA

North Platte Substation, North Platte (Cereal Agronomy, G. F. Sprague)

SOUTH DAKOTA

Ardmore Field Station, Office of Dry-Land Agriculture (Oscar R. Mathews) (March 8)

Yields in bushels per acre of 10 spring-wheat varieties grown in plot experiments at the Ardmore Field Station, Ardmore, S. Dak., in 1928

Class and Variety	C. I. No.	Yield (Bu. per acre)
Hard Red Spring		
Reliance	7370	22.5
Ceres	6900	20.0
Marquis	3641	20.0
Kota	5878	18.9
Supreme	8026	18.0
Durum		
Kubanka	1440	21.1
Acme	5284	19.5
Nodak	6519	18.1
Peliss	1584	16.9
Mindum	5296	14.4

NORTH DAKOTA

Agricultural Experiment Station, State College Station, Fargo (Flax Diseases, L. W. Boyle)

Dickinson Substation, Dickinson (Cereal Agronomy, R. W. Smith) (February 16)

The extremely cold weather of January has continued during the first half of February with slight abatement the past two days. The minimum temperature was down to zero or below every morning during the first two weeks of this month.

Country cross roads are still impassable except for bobsleds. The condition of the roads since the first of January has interfered with the usual marketing of wheat in winter. A small quantity is still being marketed, however, with the use of bobsleds.

A series of pure-seed meetings is being held throughout the State this winter under the auspices of the Greater North Dakota Association in cooperation with State and Federal workers. Three meetings were held in Stark County conducted by Mr. F. R. Cook for the Greater North Dakota Association, Mr. M. J. Johnson, of the Federal grain grading department in Minneapolis, and Mr. C. B. Aamodt and Mr. C. C. Eastgate of the State and local extension forces. The importance of growing pure seed of approved varieties, free from disease, was emphasized. Farmers were direc to sources of pure seed of approved varieties. The varieties recommende for different parts of the State were Marquis, Ceres, Kubanka, and Mindu wheat; Victory and Gopher oats; Hannchen, Manchuria, and Trebi barley; Bison, Linota, and N. D. R. 119 flax. These meetings will be continued until seeding time. The attendance of farmers at these meetings in the county was small because of severe weather and blocked roads.

A permanent organization to encourage the production of pure seeds of cereal crops in the State was formed in January when the North Dakota Crop Improvement Association was organized in Fargo. The object of this association, as given in the bylaws, is "To organize an independent grou of farmers for the purpose of cooperating with the state experiment stat. the pure seed laboratory, and the extension service, in developing and growing supplies of seeds of the varieties best adapted to the state, an to make these supplies of seed easily available to the farmers of the state."

(March 2)

The severe weather that prevailed in January and most of February, moderated somewhat during the last week of February. March has begun wi a mixture of rain and snow and temperatures about freezing. The lowest temperature for the winter at this Substation was 40 degrees below zero on February 19. The temperature had risen to 27 degrees above zero the next morning making a rise of 67 degrees in a little more than 24 hours. The mean temperature for February was 2.8 degrees as compared with a nor mal mean of about 12.5 degrees. The precipitation for February was 0.39 of an inch. The snow was still about 10 inches deep on the last of the month but has melted somewhat since.

Northern Great Plains Field Station, Mandan (Flax Breeding, J. C. Brinsmade, Jr.) (March 1)

February, 1929, was one of the coldest on record. The maximum tem ature during the month was 33 degrees on February 3, and the minimum, -1 degrees on February 18. The latter was the coldest temperature recorded here since January, 1916, and the coldest ever recorded here in Februar

January and February together made a record for average low temperatures during the first two months of the year, or for any two consecutive months. Average daily temperatures for the two months of January and February, 1929, were as follows: Average maximum, 10 degrees; average minimum, -12 degrees; and average mean, -1 degree.

Frequent light snowfalls in February amounted to 0.31 of an inch precipitation, which is about normal for February. The ground is still covered with snow to a depth of several inches. The bare ground shows only in spots, chiefly on south slopes. Snow, drifted to a depth of over two feet, still remains over the flax left standing in the field.

There might be danger of a severe river flood if the weather should turn suddenly warm. Continuance of the moderate weather that has prevailed for several days would tend to melt the snow gradually and thus avert a serious flood when the ice goes out.

Northern Great Plains Field Station, Mandan (Cereal Agronomy, E. R. Ausemus)

MONTANA

Judith Basin Substation, Moccasin (Cereal Agronomy, B. B. Bayles)

WESTERN BASIN AND COAST AREAS (North to West and South)

IDAHO

Aberdeen Substation, Aberdeen (Cereal Agronomy, G. A. Wiebe)

Agricultural Experiment Station, Moscow (Stripe Rust, C.W.Hungerford)

WASHINGTON

Agricultural Experiment Station, Pullman (Cereal Breeding, E. F. Gaines)

OREGON

Sherman County Branch Station, Moro (Cereal Agronomy, D. E. Stephens)

CALIFORNIA

Biggs Rice Field Station, Biggs (Rice Agronomy, J. W. Jones)

University Farm, Davis (Cereal Agronomy, V. H. Florell)

Agricultural Experiment Station, Berkeley (Cereal Smuts, F. N. Brig
(February 22)

I have just returned from Davis where I had an opportunity to inspe
the cereal nurseries. Although the rainfall is below normal and the wea
has been uniformly cold, the grain looks very healthy. However, it has
grown much because of the cold weather.

Albino plants were found both in wheats and barleys. Counts on 55
of the 115 varieties and strains of barley in the smut nursery showed an
average of 12.3 per cent of albino plants. Only one variety, a hull-les
barley, had no albino plants, while 34.3 per cent of the plants in one
variety were white. Dr. J. L. Collins, of the Division of Genetics, has
studied this character and found that it is expressed only in cold weath
Also, the plants may recover with warm weather.

Albino plants were not so numerous in the wheat varieties. Counts
were not made, but it was estimated that the number was less than one pe
cent. However, some white plants were found in every variety being grow
in the 1/50-acre plots.

BARBERRY ERADICATION PROGRESS

OHIO

Ohio State University, College of Agriculture, Columbus, J.W.Baringer
(February 28)

A barberry-eradication demonstration was held during the period from February 4 to February 8, inclusive, in connection with the Farmers' Week Hay and Grain Show, at Ohio State University. The death-cell arrangement was used in connection with a specially prepared prison-wall background. Potted barberries, bundles of rusted grain, samples of rust-shriveled and healthy grain, appropriate signs and pertinent literature completed the demonstration. The appearance of the death-cell door challenged to such a degree the curiosity of most people who chanced to glance at it that they were compelled to go nearer in order that they might discover what might be behind those bars. Interest in the demonstration was fair, as compared to other years, in spite of a smaller attendance due to icy roads during the week.

Much time has been given in February to the preparation of packets of study materials for schools. Some of the packets have been placed in the mails but many more are yet to be sent. It is hoped to reach all sixth grades in Ohio in addition to all high schools during this winter.

Replies to questionnaires from State Leaders who are preparing talks for the annual State Leaders' Conference, to be held next month at Bozeman, Mont., have demanded much attention during the last two weeks.

INDIANA

Purdue University College of Agriculture, La Fayette, W. E. Leer
(February 14)

Educational activities are receiving the greatest attention at this period. Study materials have been sent to the grade schools in the 26 southern counties in the State. Similar materials were sent into the schools in the 38 northern counties in 1926, and into the schools in the 28 central counties in 1927.

One of the field agents with special educational training has been retained during the winter months to visit all of the high schools in Henry, Rush, and Wayne counties, which are to be surveyed in 1929. Lantern-slide lectures are given before the school assemblies and a special lecture before the agricultural and science classes.

A barberry demonstration was placed at Purdue at the time of the annual Agricultural Conference, held January 14 to 18, 1929.

(February 28

Educational materials are being sent into the high schools, normal schools, colleges, and universities of the State at this time. This is an annual practice.

The State Leader visited the eight district meetings of county agricu tural agents and led a short discussion on the present status of barberry-eradication in the whole area and in Indiana.

The field scout who has been doing educational work during the winter is now engaged in working with the Smith-Hughes agricultural teachers. It is planned that each vocational department be visited this spring.

Considerable attention is being given at this time to the organizatio of the field force for the summer. Fortunately, the field force will be composed almost entirely of experienced men.

MICHIGAN

Agricultural College, East Lansing, W. F. Reddy

WISCONSIN

Department of Agriculture, State Capitol Annex, Madison, R.M. Caldwell

ILLINOIS

Box 72, Post Office Building, Urbana, R. W. Bills (March 1)

The educational and publicity activities that were started in 22 cou ties of southern Illinois in January have been completed. During the lan-tern-slide lecture tour of the high schools in this area 51 schools were visited. The barberry and rust story reached 5,230 high school students, 488 grade students, 287 teachers, and 30 visitors, composed of farmers, farm advisers, and county school superintendents. A grand total of 6,035 people heard the story.

Mr. Corbin interviewed the farm bureau agents in the various countie told them of the progress of the campaign, the results obtained and invit them to attend the lecture to be given at the high schools. Those who could attended and all promised aid in ways possible for their organizati to render.

A short interview was held with the superintendent of schools of eac county in regard to study material that was being sent to the grade schoo both rural and village. One hundred per cent cooperation was received fr the superintendents.

The teachers of agriculture in several schools arranged for the lecture to be given to the entire assembly. One outstanding example was at Marion, where Mr. O. H. Guenther planned the meeting for the student body of 740.

The lantern-slide lecture was given by request at a Teachers' Institute in Vienna, Johnson County, on a day set aside for agricultural subjects. Hearty cooperation was received.

At the Metropolis High School in Massac County 21 boys studying agriculture volunteered, after the illustrated lecture, to make a survey for barberry of the entire county under the supervision of the agriculture teacher, Mr. George Sullivan. Mr. Sullivan, a former barberry scout, promised to have a report of this work in the Urbana office by July or August of this year.

Mr. L. W. Brown, County Superintendent of Schools in Union County, and Mr. L. H. Zimmer, County Superintendent of Schools in Monroe County, requested the lecture at their Teachers' Institute, but previous arrangements prevented Mr. Corbin from meeting with these groups.

The Southern Illinois Teachers' College at Carbondale was included in the list of schools to be visited. Prof. Muckleroy, head of the agricultural department, and Prof. Bailey, head of the biology department, combined their regular Wednesday evening club meetings, and the lantern-slide lecture was given to the joint group.

The above illustrations show the spirit in which the work was received and proves without doubt the great value of the educational system that was used.

IOWA

Iowa State College, Ames, P. W. Rohrbaugh (March 1)

In spite of the heavy blanket of snow which has covered the State for the past two months, several locations of barberry bushes have been reported.

Mr. Yount is expecting to return to Iowa and take up the educational work in the schools of the State about April 1.

(March 15)

Most of the snow has disappeared in the last few days, leaving plenty of mud and water, and reminding us that it will not be long until barberries will be rusting again.

The process of selecting and training field men for barberry eradication for the coming summer is in progress. Some very fine men have been lined up for this year. At least two men will start out, as soon as the barberries leaf out, to pick up the scattered bushes which have been reported.

NEBRASKA

College of Agriculture, University Farm, Lincoln, A. F. Thiel
(March 6)

Barberry educational material is being prepared in the office at the present time. This material will be sent to county superintendents of 30 counties in August, 1929. The material consists of bulletins, lesson plans, colored plates, specimens of the common barberry, and rusted grain straw.

During the past week two leads were obtained from school children which may prove fruitful. The leads will be investigated in April. In one case, escaped barberries were found on the property previously surveyed by Federal scouts, and it is possible that new barberry bushes have appeared from seeds of the original planting.

A digest of the annual report of the barberry-eradication campaign in Nebraska for 1928 is being sent to 3,000 individuals who are especially interested in agriculture.

SOUTH DAKOTA

College of Agriculture, Brookings, R. O. Bulger (February 16)

Educational work constituted the major activity of the barberry-eradication campaign in South Dakota this winter. Materials for the study of black stem rust and the common barberry were sent to all grade schools in 19 different counties. These are the counties that did not join the essay-writing and speaking contest on "Black Stem Rust and the Common Barberry" which was conducted last year in cooperation with the Young Citizens League. Consequently in the last two years the grade schools in every county of the State have received study material from this office.

The material sent out this year included the National Rust Buster's Button, which is being given to the boy or girl in each school who has the best lesson or does the best work on stem rust and the barberry. These buttons are furnished by The Conference for the Prevention of Grain Rust, Minneapolis, Minn. It is believed that these buttons will help to stimulate interest in the subject.

Through the cooperation of the Extension Service of the South Dakota State College the State Leader was scheduled to give talks at 30 different agricultural short courses in the State this winter. Due to conflicting engagements it was necessary to hire someone to substitute for the State Leader on part of these short courses. The short courses are sponsored by the Extension Service in cooperation with the different communities who desire this service. Talks on agricultural subjects are given by extension specialists, farm men and women, and by local cooperators.

Reports to date indicate that these agricultural short courses are being
well received by the people of the State. In addition to a talk in the
afternoon and evening, the State Leader also arranged a demonstration on
stem rust and the barberry in connection with the local exhibits of corn,
grains, foods, and sewing.

NORTH DAKOTA

Agricultural Extension Division, State College Station, Fargo,
G. C. Mayoue (March 5)

The principal activity in February was the mailing of educational materials to rural and urban schools. Display cards are being placed in the
Smith-Hughes schools. The superintendents and agricultural instructors of
these schools are manifesting considerable interest in these displays. The
people of the various communities also are showing much interest in this
educational feature.

Sets of microscope slides showing the life cycle of black stem rust
have been supplied to all of the institutions of higher learning, as well
as to all high schools of the towns with a population of more than 1,000.
There probably is a sufficient number of these slides still on hand to
supply also the schools of towns with a population of between 500 and 1,000.
Teachers have made very favorable comments regarding the use of these slides
in connection with their class work. In addition to the slides the schools
were supplied with a Laboratory Outline explaining the use of them.

A very interesting feature of the past month was a window display
placed in the show window of the Merchants National Bank at Fargo, at the
time of the State Annual Convention of Grain Dealers, February 4 to 9. In
addition to the regular window display, maps, charts, and specimens of barberry, as well as samples of plump and shriveled wheat, were shown in connection with a miniature model farm which formed the center of attraction.
This demonstration created a great deal of interest not only on the part
of the people of Fargo, but with visitors as well. It is estimated that
1,600 grain dealers were in the city during that week. This display was
announced at the regular meetings of the convention.

Besides the mailing of educational materials this office has been
busy with the lesson-plan contest and the preparation of various reports,
including those intended for papers to be presented at the annual State
Leaders' Conference in Bozeman during the last week of March.

MONTANA

State College of Agriculture, Bozeman, W. L. Popham

WYOMING

College of Agriculture, University of Wyoming, Laramie, W. L. Poph

COLORADO

Agricultural College, Ft. Collins, E. A. Lungren

C E R E A L   C O U R I E R

Official Messenger of the Office of Cereal Crops and Diseases
Bureau of Plant Industry, U. S. Department of Agriculture
(NOT FOR PUBLICATION)

----

ol. 21   No. 6

March 31, 1929
Personnel (March 16-31) and Project Issue

PERSONNEL ITEMS

E. R. Ausemus left Washington on March 29 for his headquarters at Mandan,
N. Dak. He was authorized to make stops at Madison, Wis., and St. Paul, Minn.,
to confer with officials of the State agricultural experiment stations at
those points. Mr. Ausemus, who is the assistant agronomist in charge of the
cooperative small-grain investigations at the Northern Great Plains Field Station, had been in Washington since last October assisting the senior agronomist in charge of western wheat investigations in the temporary absence of Mr.
K. S. Quisenberry.

J. M. Hammerly, senior scientific aid, and C. H. Kyle, senior agronomist
in corn investigations, will leave Washington about April 6 for Tifton, Ga.,
and Florence, S. C., to plant experimental corn plots. They will be gone
about two weeks.

Dr. H. B. Humphrey, principal pathologist in charge of cereal-rust investigations, will leave Washington about April 4 to confer with members of the
office staff and with officials of the agricultural experiment stations at
La Fayette, Ind., Ames, Iowa, Manhattan, Kans., St. Paul, Minn., and Madison,
Wis., regarding rust studies and plans for the study of rust epidemiology this
summer and to inspect results of greenhouse experiments conducted during the
past winter. Dr. Humphrey will be gone about three weeks.

L. D. Hutton, pathologist in charge of barberry eradication, left Washington on March 21 for Bozeman, Mont., where the Eleventh Annual Conference
of the State Leaders of Barberry Eradication was scheduled for March 25 to
30, inclusive. Thereafter Mr. Hutton will visit cooperative operations of
the barberry eradication campaign in North Dakota, South Dakota, Minnesota,
and Michigan.

Dr. A. G. Johnson, principal pathologist in charge of cereal-disease investigations, was authorized to go to Cincinnati, Ohio, on March 30, to meet Dr. Hurley Fellows, of Manhattan, Kans., and discuss with Mr. Roderick Sprague, of the University of Cincinnati, the investigation of wheat foot-rot. Dr. Johnson is expected back in Washington on April 2.

Dr. C. E. Leighty, principal agronomist in charge of eastern wheat investigations, has been authorized to attend the Tri-State Wheat Conference to be held at Toledo, Ohio, on April 3. At this Conference representatives of departments of agronomy and milling firms in Michigan, Indiana, and Ohio will be present. Dr. Leighty will present a paper on The Relation of Environment to Quality in Wheat.

Dr F. B. Mains, agent in the cereal-disease investigations in cooperation with the Purdue University Agricultural Experiment Station at La Fayette, Ind., has been authorized to start early in April for Tennessee, Georgia, and North Carolina to inspect seedings of cereals in plot experiments for the occurrence of leaf rust. Dr. Mains also will come to Washington for about 10 days to confer with members of the Office staff and to take notes on the occurrence of leaf rust in cereals in the experiments at Arlington Experiment Farm.

J. Foster Martin writes from Moro, Oreg., on March 23 that the seeding of the cereal nursery was finished the day before. Mr. Martin is junior agronomist in charge of the cooperative nursery and breeding experiments at the Sherman County Branch Station, Moro, Oreg.

M. A. McCall, principal agronomist in charge of cereal agronomy, left Washington on March 31 for points in Ohio, Indiana, South Dakota, North Dakota, Montana, Minnesota, and Wisconsin to confer with members of the Office staff and with officials of agricultural experiment stations. Mr. McCall will return to Washington about April 22.

Edgar S. McFadden, of Webster, S. Dak., was appointed associate agronomist effective March 22, to conduct experiments on the improvement and genetics of cereals, particularly wheat, at the Redfield Field Station, Redfield, S. Dak.

F. D. Richey, senior agronomist in charge of corn investigations, left Washington on March 30 for points in Ohio, Indiana, Iowa, Nebraska, Missouri, and Kansas to confer with members of the office staff and with officials of the agricultural experiment stations in these States regarding the progress of cooperative corn experiments. Mr. Richey will be gone about three weeks.

of Hays, Kans., left Washington on March 16 for his head-
Hays Branch Experiment Station, stopping at Manhattan,
Mr. Swanson had been in Washington since the early part
ferences with members of the Off.ce staff and the prepara-
manuscripts on the work conducted at the Ft. Hays station.

agent in the cooperative studies of rice diseases in Arkan-
. at Fayetteville, was in Washington from March 18 to 27
.. rs of the Office staff regarding the plan and scope of his

MANUSCRIPTS AND PUBLICATIONS

22 A manuscript entitled "The Inheritance of the Second Factor for Resistance to Bunt, Tilletia tritici, in Hussar Wheat," by F. N. Briggs, was submitted on March 20, for publication in the Journal of Agricultural Research

23 A manuscript entitled "The Synthetic Formation of Avena sterilis," by V. H. Florell, was approved on March 23 for publication in the Journal of Heredity.

24 A manuscript entitled "Wheat Production in America," by Carleton R. Ball, was approved on March 23 for publication in the Encyclopedia Britannica

25 A manuscript entitled "Field Studies of the Rust Resistance of Oat Varieties," by M. N. Levine, E. C. Stakman, and T. R. Stanton, was submitted on March 28 for publication as a Technical Bulletin.

Galley proof of article entitled "The Occurrence of Sclerospora graminic on Maize in Wisconsin," by Wm. H. Weston, Jr., for publication in Phytopathol was read on March 20.

Galley proof was read March 22 of two articles to be published in the Journal of the American Society of Agronomy, namely, "A Composite Hybrid Mixture," by Harry V. Harlan and Mary L. Martini, and "Barley Variety Tests at a High-Altitude Ranch near Obsidian, Idaho," by Harry V. Harlan and F. W. Shaw.

Page proof of Department Bulletin 1498 entitled "Distribution of the Classes and Varieties of Wheat in the United States," by J. Allen Clark, John H. Martin, Karl S. Quisenberry, John R. Hooker, C. E. Leighty, and Chester N. Dubois, was read on March 18.

Farmers' Bulletin 1358 (Revised) entitled "Growing Rye in the Western Half of the United States," by John H. Martin and Ralph W. Smith, was recentl received from the Government Printing Office bearing date of November, 1928. Farmers' Bulletin 1358 was originally issued in September, 1923.

NOTICE TO FIELD MEN

The field employees of this Office who recently have received a supply of return envelopes addressed only to the Bureau of Plant Industry, that is, without the name of the Office of Cereal Crops and Diseases, will kindly write the latter part of the address on the envelopes when mailing vouchers, transportation request coupons, or any other matter intended for this Office. This precaution is necessary in order that vouchers, transportation requests, etc., may come direct to this Office where they must be entered and recorded in the fiscal division.

MEMORANDUM FROM DIRECTOR OF PERSONNEL AND BUSINESS ADMINISTRATION

March 25, 1929

CHIEFS OF BUREAUS AND OFFICES:

The General Accounting Office has drawn the attention of the Department to the growing frequency with which there are appearing in the personal expense accounts of our employees items for cash payment of transportation in excess of $1.00 without explanation of any kind of the failure to use transportation request.

Par. 20 of the Standardized Government Travel Regulations requires use of the requests "when practicable, to obtain all official transportation whe the amount involved is $1.00 or more." The phrase, "when practicable," is construed as calling for an explanation on the voucher of the circumstances which precluded use of the request. Requests are to be used not for rail an steamer travel alone, but for motor-bus transportation also where the line i operated as a public transportation facility "commonly recognized as such."

The Standardized Travel Regulations are established by direction of the President as the rule of practice in Government travel and vouchering, and their provisions should be observed. Bureaus are requested to take the nece sary steps for correcting tendencies on the part of employees unnecessarily to substitute cash payment for transportation requests and to omit explanation where cash payment can not be avoided.

W. W. STOCKBERGER

Director

RECENT DECISIONS OF THE COMPTROLLER GENERAL

(A-25283)
8 Comp. Gen. page 299

ADVERTISING-BIDS-ACCEPTANCE ON BASIS OF ELEMENT NOT MENTIONED IN ADVERTISEMENT

A bid should not be accepted because the bidder proposes to do the work in less time than the lowest bidder when the advertisement for proposals has not notified all concorned that the time element would be considered in the acceptance of bids.

(A-24969)
8 Comp. Gen. 354

CONTRACTS--PURCHASES OF INDEFINITE QUANTITIES

While it may be proper in inviting bids and making contracts for the furnishing of supplies to provide for a reasonable variance from the quantities stated, this should be done by specifying not exceeding a maximum percentage for such variance--such as 10 per cent or 20 per cent, depending upon the articles or supplies to be purchased--so that a bidder may know the maximum quantity he may be called upon to furnish, and the maximum amount of the obligation against the appropriation may be determined at the time the contract is made. Where it is found that a quantity in excess of the maximum percentage variance is required such excess should be purchased independently of the original contract and after proper advertising.

(A-25243)
8 Comp. Gen. 357

SUBSISTENCE EXPENSES--EMPLOYEE USING OWN AUTOMOBILE

Under regulations of the internal revenue, limiting reimbursement of subsistence expenses or per diem when travel is by own automobile to not exceeding what the employee would have been entitled to had he traveled by train, there is for consideration so far as subsistence is concerned only the time which would have been required for the journey by train. If such time is less than 24 hours only actual expenses for the number of meals involved are payable.

(A-25599)
8 Comp. Gen. 391
TRAVELING EXPENSES - PULLMAN RECEIPTS

Paragraph 95 (r) of the Standardized Government Travel Regulations requires that receipts be furnished in support of travel voucher claiming reimbursement for sleeping-car, parlor-car, and stateroom fares when paid in cash, and an affidavit that such receipts have been lost can not be accepted as authorizing reimbursement of such expenses. 3 Comp. Gen. 775 no longer applicable. 6 Comp. Gen. 116 distinguished.

HAYS GOLDEN DENT, AN EARLY YELLOW CORN IN KANSAS

(A. F. Swanson, Fort Hays Branch Experiment Station)

Hays Golden Dent, an early variety of yellow corn, has been recommended for distribution by the Kansas Agricultural Experiment Station. The variety has been approved for certification by the Kansas Crop Improvement Associatic

Hays Golden Dent was grown for a number of years in a small isolated are in central Kansas. While on a field trip in 1923, A. F. Swanson, associate agronomist of the Office of Cereal Crops and Diseases, was impressed with its hardiness and ability to produce good yields under adverse conditions. He ob tained a supply of seed and took it back to the Ft. Hays Experiment Station, Hays, Kans. For five years he carefully selected and tested it in comparison with standard varieties. During the last three years the variety was include in State-wide tests, and in limited tests in Colorado and New Mexico.

It proved to be well adapted to the uplands of eastern Kansas, and was about equal in yield to the best recommended white dent varieties in the west ern part of the State. Adapted white dent varieties are generally grown in western Kansas because of the greater yields obtained as compared to yellow varieties. For a number of years, however, there has been an urgent demand for a yellow corn for feeding. Since Hays Golden Dent compares favorably in yield with the best adapted white dent varieties, and as it is yellow, it promises to meet a definite need in the western part of the State.

Apparently Hays Golden Dent is adapted over a wide area, judging from the relatively high yields obtained from it in eastern Colorado and north-eastern New Mexico, as well as on the uplands of eastern Kansas, in unfavor-able years. It has a sturdy uniform stalk of medium height, is very resist-ant to lodging, and has the ears well attached. The ears are solid but show considerable variation in type.

C E R E A L   C O U R I E R

Official Messenger of the Office of Cereal Crops and Diseases
Bureau of Plant Industry, U. S. Department of Agriculture
(NOT FOR PUBLICATION)

Vol. 21   No. 7

April 10, 1929
Personnel (April 1-10) and Field Station (March 1-31) Issue

PERSONNEL ITEMS

Bert Ball, Director of Plans, National Crop Improvement Committee, 105 La Salle Street, Chicago, Ill., who was a frequent Office visitor for many years, recently passed away suddenly while on a business trip in St. Louis, Mo.

The appointment of **Dr. Joseph F. Haskins**, agent in the agronomic corn-borer research at Wooster, Ohio, in cooperation with the Ohio Agricultural Experiment Station, was terminated on September 14, 1928.

L. D. Hutton, pathologist in charge of barberry eradication, and **H. E. Clark** returned to Washington on April 10 after attending the Eleventh Annual Conference of the State Leaders of Barberry Eradication at Bozeman, Mont., March 25 to 30, and stopping in North and South Dakota, Minnesota, and Wisconsin to look over cooperative barberry-eradication operations.

Prof. H. S. Jackson, agent of this Office in the identification and description of new or little-known rusts and smuts in cooperation with the Purdue University Agricultural Experiment Station, accepted the position of mycologist in the department of plant pathology of Toronto University, Toronto, Canada, on January 1, 1929. Prof. Jackson's appointment as agent was terminated on December 31, 1928.

Roebush G. Shands was appointed agent, effective April 1, in investigations of barley diseases conducted in cooperation with the Wisconsin Agricultural Experiment Station at Madison, Wis.

VISITORS

Dr. F. P. Bussell, professor of plant breeding in the New York State College of Agriculture of Cornell University, was an Office visitor on April 1.

Homer L. Brinkley, General Manager of the American Rice Growers' Asso ciation, of Lake Charles, La., was an Office caller on April 1.

Messrs. J. B. Cotner and G. M. Garren, of the department of agronomy, North Carolina State College of Agriculture and Agricultural Experiment Sta tion, called on members of the Office staff on April 3. They were especia‍ interested in seeing the various nursery threshers and the winter oat expe. ments at the Arlington Experiment Farm.

MANUSCRIPTS AND PUBLICATIONS

26 A manuscript entitled "Experiments with Seed Treatments for the Prevention of Flax Wilt," by W. E. Brentzel, was submitted on April 3 for publication in the Journal of Agricultural Research.

28 A manuscript entitled "Argentine Flax," by J. C. Brinsmade, Jr., was approved on April 3 for publication in The Dakota Farmer, Aberdeen, S. Dak.

29 A manuscript entitled "The Nematode Disease of Wheat and Rye," by R. W. Leukel, was submitted on April 4 for publication in the Farmers' Bulletin series.

30 A manuscript entitled "Concerning Heterothollism in Puccinia graminis," by Ruth F. Allen, was approved on April 10 for publication in Science.

FIELD STATION CONDITION AND PROGRESS

HUMID ATLANTIC COAST AREA (South to North)

GEORGIA

State College of Agriculture, Athens (Cereal Agronomy, R. R. Childs)

VIRGINIA

Arlington Experiment Farm, Rosslyn (Small Grain Agronomy, J. W. Tayl (April 9)

The winter of 1928-29 was rather mild in the vicinity of the Arlingt Experiment Farm. There were no sudden changes from high to extremely low temperatures. However, there was some injury to small grains on the Farm as the result of heaving and also from the depredations of the green bug the fall and early winter. Spaced plants in the nursery intended for use genetic studies are almost a total loss. There are average stands in the drilled plots and in rows of all small grains, and the vegetative growth advanced from 10 days to two weeks. Rye is now starting to head.

Spring weeds, mostly German knotgrass (knawel), fennel, and red dead nettle, are unusually abundant and harmful. The first named weed has not been observed before on the sections used for small grains at Arlington F It probably was introduced in the Sudan grass and cowpea mixture that was grown on the land last year.

The minimum and maximum temperatures and the precipitation for the n of November, 1928, to March, 1929, inclusive, and from April 1 to 8, incl are as follows:

Month	Temperature (Degrees)		Precipitation (Inches)
	Minimum	Maximum	
November	24	79	1.98
December	15	61	1.30
January	9	68	2.45
February	13	62	3.13
March	14	85	2.68
April 1-8	35	95	----

Arlington Experiment Farm, Rosslyn (Corn Breeding, F. D. Richey)

Arlington Experiment Farm, Rosslyn (Cereal Smuts, V. F. Tapke, Acti in Charge)

Arlington Experiment Farm, Rosslyn (Virus Diseases, H. H. McKinney)

NEW YORK

Cornell University Agricultural Experiment Station, Ithaca (Cereal Breeding, H. H. Love)

HUMID MISSISSIPPI VALLEY AREA (South to North)

LOUISIANA

Rice Experiment Station, Crowley (Rice Agronomy, J. M. Jenkins)

Agricultural Experiment Station, Baton Rouge (Corn Breeding, H. F. Stoneberg)

MISSOURI

Agricultural Experiment Station, Columbia (Cereal Agronomy, L. J. Stadler)

TENNESSEE

Agricultural Experiment Station, Knoxville (Corn Breeding, L. S. Mayer)

IOWA

Agricultural Experiment Station, Ames (Oat Breeding, L. C. Burnett)

Agricultural Experiment Station, Ames (Corn Breeding, M. T. Jenkins)

Agricultural Experiment Station, Ames (Crown Rust of Oats, S. M. Dietz)

ILLINOIS

Funk Bros. Seed Co., Bloomington (Corn Root, Stalk and Ear Rots, J. R. Holbert) (March 18)

We are supplying the Bureau of Entomology with a sufficient quantity of F_1 seed of Hybrid 365 to plant four small fields of five acres each. We also are supplying them with a similar quantity of Hybrid 517. I think many people are going to be interested in the outcome of the use of larger plots for a study of the reaction of various strains of corn to the corn borer.

INDIANA

Purdue University Agricultural Experiment Station, La Fayette (Corn Rots and Metallic Poisoning, ----------)

Purdue University Agricultural Experiment Station, La Fayette (Leaf R̶ E. B. Mains)

WISCONSIN

Agricultural Experiment Station, Madison (Wheat Scab, J. G. Dickson)

MINNESOTA

Agricultural Experiment Station, University Farm, St. Paul (Wheat Bree ing, K. S. Quisenberry, Acting in Charge)

Agricultural Experiment Station, University Farm, St. Paul (Stem Rust, E. C. Stakman)

Agricultural Experiment Station, University Farm, St. Paul (Flax Rust, H. A. Rodenhiser)

GREAT PLAINS AREA (South to North)

OKLAHOMA

Woodward Field Station, Woodward (Grain Sorghum and Broomcorn, J. B. Sieglinger)

KANSAS

Agricultural Experiment Station, Manhattan (Cereal Breeding, J.H.Park (April 2)

An Outline of Nursery Plantings of Spring Oats and Barley, Manhattan, Kansas, 1929

Ground for the spring nursery was plowed on March 15 and prepared fo planting on March 16. Nursery plots were staked and rows marked on March Seeding was begun the same day and completed on March 23. The ground was somewhat cloddy, and for this reason germination was neither very prompt very uniform. A rain of 0.68 of an inch on March 30 provided ample moist

The oats seedings included 2,075 rod rows, 515 rows 7-1/2 feet long, and 880 headrows. The barley seedings included 1,130 rod rows and 100 head rows. In addition, 27 strains of spring wheat (U.S.D.A. uniform rust nursery) were sown in 8-foot rows.

The advanced test of promising strains of oats includes 18 strains (12 pedigree selections of Kanota, 5 of Fulghum, 1 of Red Texas) in 3-row plots replicated nine times (10 series). Kanota is used as a check every fourth plot in each series.

The replicated rod rows include 60 strains in 3-row plots, replicated three times (4 series). Kanota is used as a check every sixth plot in each series. These 60 strains include 14 pedigree selections of Burt, 4 of Burt x Sixty-Day, 2 of Kanota, 29 of Fulghum, 2 of Fulghum x Swedish Select, 3 of the unnamed oat, C. I. 357. The four foreign varieties, Desi, Ruakura, Glen Innis, and Hajira, complete the list.

The triplicated rod rows include 113 strains sown in three distributed single-rod rows, with checks of Kanota every tenth row. These seedings include six pedigree selections of Burt, 77 of Fulghum, 4 strains of Red Rustproof, 9 selections from the cross Sixty-Day x Markton, 7 of the unnamed oat, C. I. 357, and the following foreign introductions, Bathurst, Cowra, Lachlan, and Sunrise.

The single rod rows include three varieties from the Alaska station (Hybrid 102, Alaska Black, and Canadian) and four varieties, White Tartar, Red Rustproof, Joanette, and Green Mountain, received from the Oregon station and which showed some resistance to crown rust in Oregon. The uniform U.S. D.A. oats rust nursery of 27 strains also is seeded in single-rod rows.

The F_4 hybrid selections were sown in 7-1/2 foot rows and include 99 individual plant selections of Fulghum x Green Russian, 106 of Richland x Markton, and 265 of Fulghum x Markton. The last cross is the one in which we are most interested, because of the need of developing a new oat for Kansas having the earliness, high yield, and high test weight of Kanota, combined with the smut resistance (new physiologic forms) of Markton. Seed for all of these rows was smutted before sowing.

Loren L. Davis, now at Aberdeen, Idaho, made the following oat crosses in 1927: Markton x Kanota (and reciprocal), Navarro (Ferguson Navarro) x Kanota, and Hull-less x Kanota. F_1 plants were grown in 1928. Twelve F_2 populations of these three crosses are space-planted in the 1929 nursery. This seed was all smutted before sowing.

A new cooperative project on rust resistance in oats was outlined during the winter by leaders of the oats and rust projects, of the Office of Cereal Crops and Diseases, and cooperators of the departments of botany and agronomy of the Kansas station. H. C. Murphy, of the Iowa station, also will cooperate with us, with the idea of extending the cooperative rust studies conducted at the Iowa station, mostly with varieties of _Avena sativa_ adapted to the central and northern States, to include the spring-sown varieties of _Avena byzantina_ grown in Kansas and other States.

The seedings made at Manhattan for these rust studies include the following:

1. Twenty-nine strains received from Ames, Iowa, grown in single-rows.

2. Bulked seed from Washington, D. C., of F_2 plants of the crosse Edkin x Markton, Richland x Markton, Silvermine x Edkin, Markton x Iogo Fulghum x Markton. Ten 7-1/2 foot rows of each of these crosses were s

3. More than 500 strains of oats received from Washington, D. C., in head rows.

4. More than 200 strains of oats received from the Iowa station, grown in head rows.

All seed sown in the crown-rust nursery was smutted.

In the barley nursery at Manhattan the seedings are more extensive year than usual. The indications are that chinch bugs will not be nume and for this reason it seems likely that we may be able to obtain more pendable data than usual.

The advanced test includes 14 strains in 3-row plots, replicated 9 (10 plots). There are no checks. The strains are: Club Mariout, Flyn Flynn Selection (from Moro, Oreg.), Stavropol Selection (Hays No. 249), Local Six Row, Huntington, Vaughn, Vaughn Selections (C. I. 1367-1 and from Davis, Calif.), Comfort, Glabron, and Velvet. Two different lots of Comfort and Glabron were used, one previously grown in Kansas, and (the Nebraska station.

The triplicated rod rows include 155 strains, three distributed s rod rows of each, "trio" checks of Flynn, Stavropol Selection (Hays No and Vaughn after every tenth variety. These seedings are largely a du tion of the same strains that are being grown at Hays. Among the 133 row barleys in this series are five pedigree selections of Vaughn, six Flynn, and 55 of Colby Local. Twenty-two strains of two-row barleys a being tested.

The single rod rows include about 60 pedigree selections of Vaugh ley received from Davis, Calif. Six varieties from the Alaska statior are sown in single-rod rows.

Because of the favorable showing made by Vaughn barley in the Kal nursery tests, and in California, about 100 head selections of this va were made in the Manhattan nursery in 1928. These are being grown in rows in 1929.

Agricultural Experiment Station, Manhattan (Corn Breeding, A. M. Brunson)

Agricultural Experiment Station, Manhattan (Wheat Foot Rots, Hurley Fellows)

Agricultural Experiment Station, Manhattan (Wheat Leaf Rust, C. O. Johnston) (April 4)

The past winter in the southern Great Plains was characterized by unusually long periods of low temperature. Spring is late and rather backward. In much of this area winter wheat was late in germinating last fall and consequently went into the winter with a very short top growth. Fortunately, however, there was an unusually good snow cover during the severe weather of January and February, and wheat came through in excellent condition. At present wheat is growing rapidly and looks very well. There seems to be an abundance of soil moisture and so far not much wheat has been blown out by high winds.

Leaf rust apparently overwintered in most localities in Texas, Oklahoma, and Kansas where it was prevalent last fall. Some leaf rust was present at College Station, Tex., early in December and has increased slowly since that time. There was very little leaf rust in northern Texas and Oklahoma last fall, and infection was difficult to find at Denton, Tex., and Stillwater, Okla., until recently. At Manhattan, Kans., on March 18 a small quantity of leaf rust was found on the lower leaves of wheat plants in the leaf-rust nursery. These were plants on which flecks developed late last fall, but no uredinia appeared. There is excellent evidence that the rust survived as mycelium in the leaf tissues.

Spring wheats were sown in the leaf-rust nursery at Manhattan on March 19, and have emerged in good condition. A light rain on March 31, and rising temperatures, since that time have made conditions very favorable for the growth of wheat. Conditions still are not very favorable for the rapid spread of rust, however, the night temperatures apparently being too low. As a consequence the infection present in the nursery is not spreading to any appreciable extent.

Greenhouse experiments are now being brought to a close as rapidly as possible, the high temperatures under glass being unfavorable for normal leaf-rust development. High winds and the necessity of keeping the ventilators open makes it practically impossible to keep rust cultures pure. More than 60 collections of leaf rust have been tested for physiologic forms so far this year. The data have not been summarized but physiologic form 9 seems to have been the prevalent form again in 1928. Physiologic forms 3 and 5 and several new forms also were present in considerable number in 1928.

Hays Branch Experiment Station, Hays (Cereal Agronomy, A. F. Swanson)
(March 30)

Seeding of the varietal and nursery plots of spring wheat, oats, barl
and flax was completed on March 27. Conditions were ideal for seeding.
There is an abundance of stored moisture in the soil. At the present time
the plots are being trimmed.

Winter wheat is making rapid growth. Most of the fields are green an
sufficiently covered to prevent much soil blowing. There were two days of
severe soil blowing early in March and in some fields slight injury result
Although January and February were unusually cold months there was no wint
killing of wheat. As noted by the writer, the prospects for wheat are exc
lent in the district from Kansas City west to Hays.

Winter wheat is being pastured again.

NEBRASKA

North Platte Substation, North Platte (Cereal Agronomy, G. F. Sprague

NORTH DAKOTA

Agricultural Experiment Station, State College Station, Fargo (Flax
Diseases, L. W. Boyle)

Dickinson Substation, Dickinson (Cereal Agronomy, R. W. Smith) (Marc

The month of March is keeping up the high record set by the precedin
two months for heavy snowfall, about 9 inches of snow and 1.11 inches of
cipitation having fallen so far this month. About 33 inches of snow have
fallen since the beginning of the year. This is much above the normal sn
fall, as is shown by the fact that only about 20 inches of snow fell at t
Substation during the entire year, 1928.

Country roads still are impassable for autos and trucks. A consider
quantity of wheat is on the farms still unsold, due partly to the diffic
of transportation during the winter.

A considerable quantity of seed has been distributed from the Substa
this season at the request of the Office of Cereal Crops and Diseases and
various experiment stations. Most of this seed has been sent to stations
this and adjoining States. A few samples have been sent to distant stati
oats being sent to Oregon, corn to New Jersey, barley to Saskatchewan, an
three varieties of wheat to Mexico.

Comparatively uniform temperatures have prevailed this month, the m
being 49 degrees on the 11th, and the minimum 5 degrees above zero on Ma
and 15, respectively.

WESTERN BASIN AND COAST AREAS (North to West and South)

IDAHO

Aberdeen Substation, Aberdeen (Cereal Agronomy, **L. L. Davis**)

Agricultural Experiment Station, Moscow (Stripe Rust, C. W. Hungerford)

WASHINGTON

Agricultural Experiment Station, Pullman (Cereal Breeding, E. F. Gaines)

OREGON

Sherman County Branch Station, Moro (Cereal Agronomy, D. E. Stephens)
[March 16]

The winter of 1928-29 in the Pacific Northwest was the coldest in many years. The severely cold weather and the heavy snowfall, which remained on the ground for a long period, caused considerable trouble to livestock owners. In some sections there is a serious shortage of hay.

At Moro there were five days in January with below zero temperatures, the lowest being -6 degrees on the 29th. In February there were seven successive days, the 6th to the 13th inclusive, with below zero temperatures, -14 degrees being the lowest.

Because of a heavy snow covering during most of the cold weather, there has been little winterkilling of the fall-sown grains. In some instances winter grain still has failed to emerge because of the unusually dry autumn weather followed by continued cold weather in December, January, and February. Some reseeding will be necessary in the Columbia River Basin. Many farmers are not yet certain as to whether reseeding will be necessary, and many fields no doubt will be left with thin stands.

On the Station most of the winter wheat has emerged with fair stands. The latest sowings in the date-of-seeding experiments have not emerged, and probably will not because the surface of the ground is now crusted and the plants probably will not be able to push through. A small increase field of winter barley will have to be reseeded. The shallow sown grain seems to be in worse condition than that sown comparatively deep.

In the nursery there probably will be fair stands of everything except the grain sown in the experiments to determine the existence of different strains or forms of stinking smut.

Mild weather has prevailed during the past three weeks. Field opera
tions were started early in the month. It is hoped to have all the sprin
grains seeded early next week.

The total precipitation at Moro for January and February and so far
March has been only 2.76 inches. All the precipitation in January and Fe
ruary was in the form of snow, most of which fell on frozen ground and wa
lost as run-off. In stubble ground the moisture has penetrated less than
two feet.

J. Foster Martin returned to Moro from Washington, D. C., on March 1

CALIFORNIA

Biggs Rice Field Station, Biggs (Rice Agronomy, J. W. Jones) (March

The precipitation at the Station for the period from October, 1928,
February, 1929, inclusive, was only 10.28 inches as compared with a norma
for the same period of 16.24 inches. Many rice farmers now are plowing o
the well-drained lands, and if the favorable weather continues field oper
tions will be started in a day or two.

Wheat and barley on commercial fields is shorter than usual due to t
cold winter weather.

The rice market is quiet and present indications are that the acreag
sown to rice in California will be much less than that of last year. How
ever, if the market should improve before seeding time some of the grower
who expect to grow other crops may sow rice.

University Farm, Davis (Cereal Agronomy, G. A. Wiebe)

Agricultural Experiment Station, Berkeley (Cereal Smuts, F. N. Brigg

BARBERRY·ERADICATION PROGRESS

OHIO

Ohio State University, College of Agriculture, Columbus, J. W. Baringer
(March 31)

The major activity in the Ohio barberry-eradication office in March
consisted of the preparation of packets of study materials for schools.
All rural sixth grades in the county-school systems of 50 counties were provided with supplies. Packets now are being prepared for all sixth grades
in the exempted and independent city and village schools in the State in
addition to all high schools in Ohio. These packets contain 12 enclosures,
namely, bulletins, circulars, circular letters, barberry twig specimens,
rusted straw, shriveled wheat, plump wheat, charts, posters, lesson plans,
novelties, etc.

Considerable time also was devoted to the compilation of data, pertinent
to the progress of the barberry-eradication campaign in Ohio, for presentation at the annual State Leaders' Conference held at Bozeman, Mont., March
25 to 30, inclusive. The writer had the pleasure of attending this Conference.

Leaves on common barberries at Columbus were unfolding from the buds
rapidly in the last week in March.

INDIANA

Purdue University College of Agriculture, La Fayette, W. E. Leer
(March 20)

The State Leader has been in personal contact with all the departments
of botany in the universities, colleges, and normal schools in Indiana for
the past few weeks. An effort was made to find out what materials are
needed for class work. During the summer, the different departments will
be supplied with the materials desired. It is becoming rather difficult
for those not directly connected with the barberry-eradication campaign to
find suitable material for the study of black-stem rust and the common barberry.

The special educational agent is continuing his work with the vocational
agricultural teachers, and at the same time is investigating leads sent in
by school teachers and others interested in the campaign. Only a short time
ago he found a new area of escaped bushes in Owen County which had been reported by a seventh-grade teacher at Freedom, Ind. It seems that the area
may be quite extensive. The results of the educational program are beginning to be evident.

MICHIGAN

Agricultural College, East Lansing, W. F. Reddy

WISCONSIN

Department of Agriculture, State Capitol Annex, Madison, R. M.

ILLINOIS

Box 72, Post Office Building, Urbana, R. W. Bills

IOWA

Iowa State College, Ames, P. W. Rohrbaugh

MINNESOTA

Agricultural Experiment Station, University Farm, St. Paul, L.

NEBRASKA

College of Agriculture, University Farm, Lincoln, A. F. Thiel

SOUTH DAKOTA

College of Agriculture, Brookings, R. O. Bulger

NORTH DAKOTA

Agricultural Extension Division, State College Station, Fargo Mayoue

MONTANA

State College of Agriculture, Bozeman, W. L. Popham

WYOMING

College of Agriculture, University of Wyoming, Laramie, W. L.

COLORADO

Agricultural College, Ft. Collins, E. A. Lungren

C E R E A L C O U R I E R

Official Messenger of the Office of Cereal Crops and Diseases
Bureau of Plant Industry, U. S. Department of Agriculture
(NOT FOR PUBLICATION)

ol. 21   No. 8

April 20, 1929
Personnel (April 11-20) and Field Station (April 1-15) Issue

PERSONNEL ITEMS

V. H. Florell, formerly in charge of cereal agronomy experiments at the
niversity Farm, Davis, Calif., was granted leave of absence without pay,
ffective April 1, to engage in graduate study at the University of California.

J. M. Hammerly, senior scientific aid, and C. H. Kyle, senior agronomist
in corn investigations, returned from Tifton, Ga., on April 17. Mr. Hammerly
will leave Washington on April 24 for Florence, S. C., where he will plant
corn in the cooperative plots at the Pee Dee Substation. He will be gone about
a week.

Paul E. Hoppe, who, for some time, has been under part-time appointment
in the cereal-disease investigations conducted at Madison, Wis., was appointed
full-time agent on April 1 to assist Dr. J. G. Dickson in special barley-
disease investigations.

Dr. H. B. Humphrey, principal pathologist in charge of cereal-rust investigations, returned to Washington on April 18 from points in Indiana, Iowa,
Kansas, Minnesota, and Wisconsin, where he consulted with members of the Office
staff and officials of agricultural experiment stations regarding cereal-rust
investigations.

M. A. McCall, principal agronomist in charge of cereal agronomy, returned
to Washington on April 15 from points in Ohio, Indiana, South Dakota, North
Dakota, Minnesota, and Wisconsin where he conferred with members of the office
and officials of State agricultural experiment stations.

H. H. McKinney will leave Washington on April 27 for Granite City, Ill.
where he will make observations on wheat mosaic on the cooperative experimen
plots. He also will go to Manhattan, Kans., to examine wheat fields at the
agricultural experiment station in which it is thought there may be mosaic
disease. Mr. McKinney is senior pathologist in charge of cereal-virus disea
investigations.

M. T. Meyers, agent in corn-breeding investigations cooperative with th
Ohio Agricultural Experiment Station and the Ohio State University, wrote on
April 10 from Wooster, Ohio, that Mr. M. A. McCall and Mr. F. D. Richey spen
April 1 and 2 at Wooster in conference with Director C. G. Williams on the c
operative breeding, fertility, and physiologic experiments with corn in Ohio
Major emphasis was given to the phases of the work pertaining to the study o
corn-borer control.

On April 3 Messrs. Meyers and Richey were in Columbus to discuss with M
L. R. Jorgenson the cooperative corn-breeding experiments of which he is in
charge.

Each year the Department of Farm Crops of the Ohio State University giv
a series of radio talks on the weekly Farmers' Night program broadcasted by
the University over Station WEAO. This year two of these talks were assigne
to the corn crop, and the first one on "Fighting the Corn Borer by Selecting
the Right Variety" was broadcasted in the evening of March 13. This talk ha
been prepared jointly by Mr. Meyers and Dr. L. L. Huber, of the Ohio Agricultural Experiment Station. The second talk on "Starting the Corn Crop," by
Mr. Meyers, was scheduled for the evening of April 10.

F. D. Richey, senior agronomist in charge of corn investigations, retun
to Washington on April 15 from a two weeks' trip in the Corn Belt in the int
ests of cooperative corn experiments.

VISITORS

Mr. Masao Otsuki, assistant professor of agricultural economics at the
Kioto Imperial University, Kioto, Japan, was a visitor in the Office on
April 12.

Dr. Yoshihiko Tochinai, professor of plant pathology in the Botanical
Institute of the Hokkaido Imperial University, Sapporo, Japan, was in Wash-
ington early in April interviewing plant pathologists in the Bureau of Plant
Industry. Dr. Tochinai has visited various agricultural institutions in the
United States. He will soon sail for Europe.

MANUSCRIPTS AND PUBLICATIONS

Galley proof of article entitled "Wheat Production in America," by
rleton R. Ball, for publication in the Encyclopaedia Britannica, was read
April 11.

Page proof of article entitled "The Occurrence of Sclerospora graminicola
Maize in Wisconsin," by W. H. Weston, Jr., for publication in Phytopathology,
s read on April 16.

The article entitled "Barley Variety Tests at a High-Altitude Ranch near
sidian, Idaho," by Harry V. Harlan and F. W. Shaw, appears in the Journal
the American Society of Agronomy 21 (4): 439-443. April, 1929.

The article entitled "A Composite Hybrid Mixture," by Harry V. Harlan and
r L. Martini, appears in the Journal of the American Society of Agronomy 21
): 487-490. April, 1929.

The small circular entitled "Barley in Oats," by T. R. Stanton, printed
y the McClain Company, Minneapolis, Minn., for use by the National Crop Im-
rovement Committee, of Chicago, Ill,, has been received. Owing to the death
f Mr. Bert Ball, Director of Plans, for the National Crop Improvement Commit-
ee, for whom the circular was written, notice of the appearance of the circu-
ar was not received until April 12.

The article entitled "Argentine Flax Not Recommended," by J. C. Brinsmade,
r., appears in The Dakota Farmer 49 (8): 460-461. April 15, 1929.

TRANSLATIONS

Marinucci, M. Il "mal del piede" dei cereali. [Foot-rot of cereals.]
Coltivatore 73: 514-516. 1927. (Translation by Theo. Holm, December, 1928.)

Petri, L. Osservazioni sul "mal del piede" del frumento. [Observation
in "foot-rot" in cereals.] Boll. R. Staz. Patol. Veg. Rome 6: 174-178. 1926
(Translation by Theo. Holm, December, 1928.)

Peyronel, B. Osservazioni sul "mal del piede" dei cereali e sulle varie
crittogame che lo producona in Italia. [Observations of "foot-rot" of cereal:
and various cryptogams which cause it in Italy.] Boll. R. Staz. Patol. Veg.
Rome 6: 213-216. 1926. (Translation by Theo. Holm, December, 1928.)

The foregoing list of translations supplements the lists published in
earlier numbers of the Cereal Courier, as follows:

Vol. 13: 12-15, 52, 69, and 225-226. 1921.

14: 38, 39, and 99-100. 1922.

15: 11-13, and 46-47. 1923.

16: 16-18, and 127. 1924.

17: 62-63, and 326-327. 1925.

18: 4-5, 335. 1926.

19: 16 and 124-125. 1927.

Copies of these translations are on file in the Library of the Bureau of
Plant Industry.

ELEVENTH ANNUAL CONFERENCE OF BARBERRY-ERADICATION AND STEM-RUST
EPIDEMIOLOGY LEADERS

During the week of March 25 to 30, inclusive, Leaders of the barberry-
adication and stem-rust epidemiology forces, together with members of cooper-
ing agencies, met at Montana State College, Bozeman, Mont., to summarize the
rogress made and to formulate plans for the future.

In attendance at this meeting were Lynn D. Hutton and H. E. Clark, of the
ashington Office, Dr. E. C. Stakman and G. D. George, University Farm, St.
aul, D. G. Fletcher and J. L. Richardson, of The Conference for the Preven-
ion of Grain Rust, Minneapolis, and the following State Leaders of Barberry
radication: E. A. Lungren, Colorado; R. W. Bills, Illinois; W. E. Leer,
ndiana; P. W. Rohrbaugh, Iowa; W. F. Reddy, Michigan; L. W. Melander, Minneota; W. L. Popham, Montana and Wyoming; A. F. Thiel, Nebraska; G. C. Mayoue,
orth Dakota; J. W. Baringer, Ohio; R. O. Bulger, South Dakota; and R. M.
aldwell, Wisconsin. Montana people interested in this and related work also
ere present.

Among the prominent speakers outside of the barberry-eradication and stem-
st epidemiology organizations were the following from Montana State College:
r. Alfred Atkinson, President of Montana State College, Dean F. B. Linfield,
irector of the Montana Agricultural Experiment Station, Prof. Clyde M. McKee,
ead of the Department of Agronomy, Prof. D. B. Swingle, Head of the Botany
nd Bacteriology Department, Prof. H. E. Morris, Associate Botanist and Bacteri-
logist, Dean J. M. Hamilton of the Department of Economics and Farm Management,
rof. M. L. Wilson, Agricultural Economist, Mr. John Dexter, Director of Pub-
icity, and Mr. M. J. Abbey, Supervisor of Smith-Hughes work in Montana.

The program of the first day included a review of the progress of the cam-
aign from its inception in 1918 to the present time, and presentation of the
mportance of small-grain production and the control of cereal diseases to agri-
ulture in Montana. On the evening of the first day a banquet was held for
he visitors and the agricultural staff of the Montana State College. At this
anquet Dean J. M. Hamilton gave a most interesting talk on the early days of
ontana.

During the remainder of the week discussions were held on each of the
rincipal activities of the campaign. Papers on the various phases of survey,
nvestigation, education, publicity, and administration were read and dis-
ussed. Each of these activities plays an important part in the progress of
he campaign. Methods were discussed of improving surveys so that the syste-
atic location and destruction of barberry bushes may be expedited. Educa-
ional and publicity activities, which play so important a part in a campaign
f this kind, were given particular attention. A study was made of the need
or the continuation of certain investigational activities and the inception
f others. Administrative problems, including budget matters, office and
ield records, and the selection, training, and supervision of field personnel,
ere considered.

The review of the progress made revealed the following facts:

A total of 17,587,276 original bushes, sprouting bushes, and seedling has been found and destroyed in the barberry-eradication area to December 1928. In 1928, alone, 1,520,832 bushes and seedlings were destroyed.

In the first survey, 892 counties of the 921 counties needing survey have been completed. Approximately 250 counties have been covered a second time. Nearly every county needing a first survey also must be covered by a second survey. In many areas, particularly where viable seeds still lie in the ground, a third or fourth survey will be required.

Stem rust is being controlled in these States by the eradication of tl common barberry. During the six-year period from 1915 to 1920, inclusive, before the barberry-eradication campaign became effective, the average annm loss of wheat from stem rust in the 13 States was 50,420,000 bushels, while the comparable loss from this source for the next 7-year period, from 1921 1927, inclusive, amounted to only 15,967,000 bushels. This annual saving demics by eliminating the common barberry.

Public sympathy and support for the campaign have been greatly increas by the publicity and educational activities. Thousands of barberry bushes have been found as a result of reports from property owners and school chil dren. A more complete understanding of the campaign has greatly facilitate survey progress.

RECENT DECISIONS OF THE COMPTROLLER GENERAL

(A-25183)
8 Comp. Gen. 397
CONTRACTS-MISTAKE IN BID

Where a bid to furnish articles or supplies to the Government was so low
that the contracting officer believed a mistake had been made but accepted the
bid, and, upon being notified of the acceptance, the bidder alleges a mistake
in submission of its bid, and thereafter satisfactorily discloses the facts of
the mistake but is directed to furnish the articles or supplies, and does so
furnish them, the payment is authorized of the actual cost to the contractor,
the said amount being less than the lowest correct bid received.

Where a contracting officer, at the time for acceptance of bid, has reason
to think and does think that the lowest bid was the result of a mistake on the
part of the bidder, he should, before awarding the contract, if the needs of
the Government will permit of the delay incident thereto, ask the bidder to
verify its bid and, if the bidder then claims error, submit the facts with reference to the error to the Comptroller General for determination whether the
erroneous bid may be withdrawn. If the Government's needs will not permit of
the delay incident to such procedure the bid should be accepted and the bidder
instructed to perform leaving the matter of price to be determined subsequently
by the Comptroller General.

(A-25751)
8 Comp. Gen. - 400
CLASSIFICATION OF CIVILIAN EMPLOYEES--TRANSFER TO A NEW POSITION FROM A HIGHER
GRADE

When a new position is created by an administrative office and finally
allocated as provided by law the administrative office may transfer to the
new position an employee from a higher grade and pay the maximum salary rate
in the lower grade if there is no salary rate in the lower grade to which transferred equal to or greater than the salary rate being received in the higher
grade at the time of such transfer.

(A-25583)
8 Comp. Gen. 441
CLASSIFICATION OF CIVILIAN EMPLOYEES--REALLOCATION OF POSITIONS

If the administrative office finally approves or acquiesces in the action
of the Personnel Classification Board in reallocating a position, the salary
rate of the employee is for determination in the grade in which the position
has been finally allocated. 7 Comp. Gen. 820, 825 distinguished.

When there is a difference of opinion as to the duties and responsibilities
of a position between the employee on the one hand, and the administrative office
together with the Personnel Classification Board on the other, the final determination by the latter must control in fixing the salary grade of the position.

(A-25361)
8 Comp. Gen. 454

COUPON BOOKS FOR THE PROCUREMENT OF GASOLINE AND OIL

The purchase on behalf of the Government of coupon books to be used in the procurement of gasoline and oil incident to the operation of an automobile under Government control is not authorized, as such purchase involves the payment for supplies in advance of delivery in contravention of section 3648, Revised Statutes.

Reimbursement may not be made of the value of a coupon book for the procurement of gasoline and oil alleged to have been used by an employee traveling under orders, in the absence of satisfactory evidence as to the time, place, quantity, or price of the gasoline and oil that were furnished in exchange for the coupons detached from the book, and that the gasoline and oil were used on the official travel.

(A-25865)
8 Comp. Gen. 455

CONTRACTS--ACTUAL DAMAGES--DELAYS IN COMPLETION

Where no specific provision is made in a contract for either liquidated or actual damages, the contractor is, upon failure to complete the contract within the time specified therein for completion, chargeable with all expense caused the Government by reason of delays in completion for which no extensic of time is provided, as actual damages to the Government on account of such delays.

FIELD STATION CONDITION AND PROGRESS

HUMID ATLANTIC COAST AREA (South to North)

GEORGIA

State College of Agriculture, Athens (Cereal Agronomy, R. R. Childs)

VIRGINIA

Arlington Experiment Farm, Rosslyn (Small Grain Agronomy, J. W. Taylor)

Arlington Experiment Farm, Rosslyn (Corn Breeding, F. D. Richey)

Arlington Experiment Farm, Rosslyn (Cereal Smuts, V. F. Tapke, Acting n Charge)

Arlington Experiment Farm, Rosslyn (Virus Diseases, H. H. McKinney)

NEW YORK

Cornell University Agricultural Experiment Station, Ithaca (Cereal Breeding, H. H. Love)

HUMID MISSISSIPPI VALLEY AREA (South to North)

LOUISIANA

Rice Experiment Station, Crowley (Rice Agronomy, J. M. Jenkins)

Agricultural Experiment Station, Baton Rouge (Corn Breeding, H. F. Stoneberg)

MISSOURI

Agricultural Experiment Station, Columbia (Cereal Agronomy, L. J. Stadler)

TENNESSEE

Agricultural Experiment Station, Knoxville (Corn Breeding, L. S. Mayer)

IOWA

Agricultural Experiment Station, Ames (Oat Breeding, L. C. Burnett)

Agricultural Experiment Station, Ames (Corn Breeding, M. T. Jenkins)

Agricultural Experiment Station, Ames (Crown Rust of Oats, S. M. Dietz)

ILLINOIS

Funk Bros. Seed Co., Bloomington (Corn Root, Stalk and Ear Rots, J. R. Holbert)

INDIANA

Purdue University Agricultural Experiment Station, La Fayette (Corn Rot and Metallic Poisoning, ----------)

Purdue University Agricultural Experiment Station, La Fayette (Leaf Rus E. B. Mains)

WISCONSIN

Agricultural Experiment Station, Madison (Wheat Scab, J. G. Dickson)

MINNESOTA

Agricultural Experiment Station, University Farm, St. Paul (Wheat Bree K. S. Quisenberry, Acting in Charge) (April 13)

A few days ago a hurried inspection was made on the winter wheat in th nursery at University Farm. It seems that winterkilling has not been sever this season. The fall and early winter months were mild, the wheat continu ing in a growing condition until late in December. Once or twice in this period the temperature dropped below zero, and as there was no snow coverin at the time it was feared that killing might result. Soon after January 1, the ground was covered with snow which remained until late in February. January was cold (the coldest since 1912), the mean temperature being 2 deg F. This cold weather continued into February, making one of the coldest tw month periods on record here. Twice in the two months the temperature dro to 24 degrees below zero. The weather moderated by the last of February, a most of the snow was gone by March 15. In spite of this cold weather only most tender wheat varieties in the rod rows are showing any amount of kill Some of the space-planted hybrids were injured much more than the thicker seeded rod rows.

The ground was nearly dry enough to begin spring seeding when snow began
o fall on April 10, and continued for about 40 hours. There was from 6 to 8
nches of wet snow on the ground. This is now melting very rapidly. This
oisture will delay spring seeding for some time.

Recent visitors at University Farm included Mr. E. R. Ausemus on April 2
nd 3, Mr. M. A. McCall on April 12, and Dr. H. B. Humphrey on April 12 and 13.

Agricultural Experiment Station, University Farm, St. Paul (Stem Rust,
. C. Stakman)

Agricultural Experiment Station, University Farm, St. Paul (Flax Rust,
:. A. Rodenhiser)

GREAT PLAINS AREA (South to North)

OKLAHOMA

Woodward Field Station, Woodward (Grain Sorghum and Broomcorn, J. B.
ieglinger) (April 15)

Judging by the condition of trees and shrubbery spring is here. Wheat
also has made rapid growth during the last two weeks and looks well. As
usual, rain will be needed soon. At this time prospects are excellent for a
fruit crop. Peaches, cherries, plums, apricots; and apples have bloomed and
are setting, some of the apricots being over ½ inch in diameter.

Sorghum seed is moving at a fair rate for this time of the year.

A summary of precipitation and extremes of temperature for this year by
nonths is as follows:

Month	Precipitation Inches	Temperature (Degrees) Maximum	Minimum
January	0.92	59	5
February	0.20	59	-5
March	2.04	89	25
April (first half)	0.07	89	33

KANSAS

Agricultural Experiment Station, Manhattan (Cereal Breeding, J. H. Parker)

Agricultural Experiment Station, Manhattan (Corn Breeding, A. M. Brunson)

Agricultural Experiment Station, Manhattan (Wheat Foot Rots, Hurley Fe

Agricultural Experiment Station, Manhattan (Wheat Leaf Rust, C. O. Joh

Fort Hays Branch Experiment Station, Hays (Cereal Agronomy, A. F. Swar
(April 15)

Mr. R. E. Getty, associate agronomist of the Office of Forage Crops, a
for 16 years identified with the Fort Hays Branch Experiment Station, resig
to take up private farming. Mr. Getty rendered outstanding service as an
investigator of Kansas agriculture and is the author or co-author of a numb
of publications and articles. He is succeeded by Mr. D. A. Savage, who was
transferred to Hays from Moccasin, Mont.

Winter wheat and spring crops are making good growth largely on subsoi
moisture, as April rainfall so far has been limited to less than one-half i
Considerable volunteer wheat is showing up in many Kansas wheat fields. In
some cases the stand may result in from two to four bushels to the acre.
Owing to the lack of rainfall in September germination of the seed was dela
so long that the seedlings could not be killed by disking before the regula
date for seeding wheat.

The Annual Western Kansas Boys and Girls Judging contest will be held
April 25, followed by an interesting program for the "Round Up" to be held
the following day. One of the outstanding features of the latter will be a
discussion of cost of grinding feeds, and the better utilization of crops f
livestock.

NEBRASKA

North Platte Substation, North Platte (Cereal Agronomy, G. F. Sprague
(April 15)

The first small-grain seeding on the cereal project was done on March
Varietal and nursery seedings followed as weather permitted. Only the fir
seeding in the date-of-seeding experiment and the spring-wheat varieties h
emerged as yet.

Winter wheat has been damaged somewhat by winterkilling and soil blow
Stands are still fairly good, however. The Blackhull wheats showed the gr
est winter injury. Blackhull 60 and Early Blackhull apparently are less w
hardy than the original Blackhull and Superhard.

This period has been characterized by fairly high winds and relativel
low temperatures. The average daily wind velocity was 182.8 miles, with a
imum of 366 miles in one day. Minimum temperatures of 32 degrees or belov
have been recorded for most of this period. The total precipitation has l
0.45 of an inch. The accumulated rainfall deficiency to date is 1.41 inch

NORTH DAKOTA

Agricultural Experiment Station, State College Station, Fargo (Flax iseases, L. W. Boyle)

Dickinson Substation, Dickinson (Cereal Agronomy, R. W. Smith) (April 15)

Field operations in the early part of April have been rather intermittent ue to the frozen condition of the ground during part of the time. Work in he field became general last week and a little seeding has been done in this ocality.

Seeding at the Substation began Saturday with the sowing of the uniform mut experiment and the first seeding in the date-of-seeding experiment with ive varieties inoculated with smut. It is planned to continue today the eeding of the seed-treatment experiment if not prevented by rain, which hreatens. The cool, moist soil conditions should insure a maximum infection of smut in smut-inoculated seed sown at this time.

The winter-wheat nursery was protected by snow until about March 25, and the winter-wheat plots in standing corn were protected until about April 1. In spite of good winter protection the stand of winter grain is rather thin owing to extremely dry soil conditions last fall. In the plots the rather thin stand has resulted from some injury by grasshoppers.

Seed has been prepared for sowing the varietal plots of spring wheat, oats, and barley, and seed for the nursery is being prepared.

Northern Great Plains Field Station, Mandan (Flax Breeding, J. C. Brinsmade, Jr.)

Northern Great Plains Field Station, Mandan (Cereal Agronomy, E. R. Ausemus) (April 18)

The weather during the first half of April has been unfavorable for the seeding of the spring cereal crops. The maximum temperature, 73 degrees, was recorded on April 3. Since then the temperatures have been much lower with a minimum of 19 degrees on two nights, April 7 and 8. The precipitation for this period was 1.06 inches.

The varietal field plots of wheat were sown on April 16 and those of oats on April 17.

The land for the spring-wheat nursery was prepared yesterday. A part of the nursery will be grown on the State Training School land again this year. This land is being prepared today.

MONTANA

Judith Basin Substation, Moccasin (Cereal Agronomy, B. B. Bayles) (Joe L. Sutherland)

WESTERN BASIN AND COAST AREAS (North to West and South)

IDAHO

Aberdeen Substation, Aberdeen (Cereal Agronomy, L. L. Davis)

Agricultural Experiment Station, Moscow (Stripe Rust, C. W. Hungerford)

WASHINGTON

Agricultural Experiment Station, Pullman (Cereal Breeding, E. F. Gaines)

OREGON

Sherman County Branch Station, Moro (Cereal Agronomy, D. E. Stephens)
(April 15)

The weather during the latter half of March and the first half of April
was unfavorable for crop growth in eastern Oregon. For the past 60 days at
Moro there has been no precipitation of consequence. Temperatures have been
unseasonably low and the wind movement has been high. The total precipitation for March was 0.44 of an inch and for April, to date, only 0.24 of an
inch. The total precipitation from Sept. 1, 1928, to April 15, 1929, was 6.8
inches, or 2.44 inches less than the normal for that period.

On April 1 the moisture content of the soil of the tillage plots that
were fallowed last season, was less than 10 per cent, averaging the six feet.
The soil of these plots usually contains on that date between 13 and 14 per
cent moisture, 13.3 per cent being the average for an 8-year period.

Winter wheat has made very little growth during the past month, and there
has been no improvement in stands. Considerable wheat failed to emerge because
of the crust which formed soon after the melting of the snow. Harrowing or
rolling did not seem to be of any benefit. There has been considerable rese
ing of winter wheat to spring grain in certain sections of the Columbia Basin
Many fields with thin stands were left. These thin stands, the backward con
dition of the wheat, and the shortage of moisture in the soil, make prospect
for a good crop anything but favorable.

Spring grain on the Station was sown during the week of March 18 to 23.
Most of the spring grains have emerged with good stands in both field plots
and nursery.

M. M. Oveson has been employed to fill the position on the Station made
vacant by the resignation of G. A. Mitchell, who is now in charge of the Pen
dleton Field Station for the Office of Dry-Land Agriculture. Mr. Oveson has
about completed his work for his Master's degree in the Department of Soils
of the Oregon State Agricultural College.

CALIFORNIA

Biggs Rice Field Station, Biggs (Rice Agronomy, J. W. Jones)

University Farm, Davis (Cereal Agronomy, G. A. Wiebe)

Agricultural Experiment Station, Berkeley (Cereal Smuts, F. N. Briggs)

BARBERRY ERADICATION PROGRESS

OHIO

Ohio State University, College of Agriculture, Columbus, J. W. Baringer

INDIANA

Purdue University College of Agriculture, LaFayette, W. E. Leer (April

The weather conditions in Indiana this spring have been very favorable for barberry infection. However, up to April 20, no infection has been foun probably because of the small number of locations examined. By April 1, at La Fayette, the leaves on the bushes were beginning to show green, and in southern Indiana the leaves were well out by that date.

The field force in Indiana for the coming summer will be composed of 18 experienced men. Of this number, eight have had one year's experience, four two years' experience, two three years' experience, three four years' experi ence, and one six years' experience. During the past winter nine of the men have been engaged in teaching, eight have been in school, and one has been engaged in educational work in connection with barberry eradication.

It is planned to start each man in an area of escaped bushes in order t restore and improve his ability to identify barberry bushes readily. After week in an area of escaped bushes, the work then will be of an intensive sur vey type in Montgomery, Tipton, and Hamilton counties.

MICHIGAN

Agricultural College, East Lansing, W. F. Reddy

WISCONSIN

Department of Agriculture, State Capitol Annex, Madison, R. M. Caldwell

ILLINOIS

Box 72, Post Office Building, Urbana, R. W. Bills

IOWA

Iowa State College, Ames, P. W. Rohrbaugh

MINNESOTA

Agricultural Experiment Station, University Farm, St. Paul, L. W. Melander

NEBRASKA

College of Agriculture, University Farm, Lincoln, A. F. Thiel (April 15)

Barberry education work pays! Pupils of the Glendale School near Louisville, Nebr., recently found 50 common barberry bushes.

Literature and specimens of rust had been given to the County Superintendent, Miss Alpha Peterson, who supplied all of her schools with this material.
At the Glendale School, Miss Elizabeth Tritsch, in connection with the course
in agriculture, taught her class about common barberry, how to identify it,
and its relation to stem rust. Her pupils became intensely interested and began to look for barberry bushes. One day they brought in specimens of some
bushes they had found on the property of John Erwin. Their teacher identified
them as common barberry and sent them to the barberry-eradication office in
Lincoln.

It had been announced earlier in the year that The Conference for the
Prevention of Grain Rust, of Minneapolis, would give a medal to every boy and
girl who reported a property on which common barberry had been found. Accordingly, the Glendale School decided to secure a medal. It has been awarded and
will be presented to the pupils of the seventh and eighth grades at the meeting of the Community Club on April 19. A lecture will be given the same evening on the "Common Barberry and Its Relation to Stem Rust."

SOUTH DAKOTA

College of Agriculture, Brookings, R. O. Bulger (April 12)

Plans for the spring and summer in barberry eradication are being given
chief consideration at the present time. Twenty-five prospective barberry
agents are attending a school of instruction which is being held one evening
a week. This school will continue until the latter part of May, when an
examination will be given to aid in making the final selection of men.

At the present time one assistant is employed on educational work. His
duties consist of talks before the general assemblies and biology classes in
high schools in counties where an intensive survey will be carried on this
summer. On May 1 two more agents will be employed who will begin operations
in Grant County. The main barberry crew will not be appointed until about
June 15.

The principal activity of the winter months consisted of educational wo
Study materials and "helps" for teachers were sent to all of the grade scho
in 19 counties. A contest to obtain the best lesson plan for teaching the s
ject of "Black Stem Rust and the Common Barberry" was conducted this winter.
It was open to instructors in colleges, universities, normal schools, and hi
schools. Some very fine plans have been received which are now in the hands
the judges. The first prize winner in this State will receive a cash price
$10.00, and the lesson plan will be submitted in the National contest to con
pete for the $100.00 prize offered by The Conference for the Prevention of
Grain Rust, of Minneapolis.

In oooperation with the Extension Service, of the South Dakota State Co
lege, the State Leader of barberry eradication was scheduled to appear on tl
programs of the Agricultural Short Courses in 30 different cities and towns.
Because of bad weather and the poor condition of the roads it was necessary
cancel some of these engagements. However, 4,453 people were reached at 15
different places, making an average of about 297 to a town. In addition to
talks and instruction, barberry demonstrations were placed at some of the Sl
Courses where local exhibits were present.

The State Leader has been invited by the State Leader of Club Work in
South Dakota to appear on the programs of the various 4-H Club camps that
will be held in South Dakota in June and July. A talk on barberry and stem
rust will be given at the general assemblies; in addition, various groups of
boys and girls will be given instruction in their regular class work.

An unusual number of inquiries have been received this winter and sprii
from various people in the State regarding barberry eradication. In many
cases these requests are from teachers desiring material to aid in teaching
the subject in their schools.

NORTH DAKOTA

Agricultural Extension Division, State College Station, Fargo, G.C.May

MONTANA

State College of Agriculture, Bozeman, W. L. Popham [April 8]

In April particular attention will be given to the preparation of educ
tional material and its dissemination throughout the State. Most of this w
will be in connection with rural, grade and high schools. Material is now
being prepared which, together with a teacher's guide, will be sent about M
to each high school science teacher in the State. It is planned to furnish
material in May to all rural schools in the counties in which survey will b
conducted during the 1929 field season.

Some publicity material has been sent to mailing lists in the State, nd more will be mailed as the opening of the field season approaches. A ircular letter, together with Farmers' Bulletin 1544, was sent to a representative list of farmers early in the winter. County agents were supplied ith the latest available publicity material, including a oopy of the Sumary of the 1929 Annual Report. This report also has been sent to State enators and Representatives, and within the next week a oopy will be suplied to each of the daily and weekly newspapers of Montana.

A mailing list for future use now is being compiled from the State Seed aboratory records of farmers who have requested protein and pure-seed tests uring the past two years. This list will contain approximately 4,000 names f farmers particularly interested in small-grain crops.

WYOMING

College of Agriculture, University of Wyoming, Laramie, W. L. Popham

COLORADO

Agricultural College, Ft. Collins, E. A. Lungren

C E R E A L   C O U R I E R

Official Messenger of the Office of Cereal Crops and Diseases
Bureau of Plant Industry, U. S. Department of Agriculture
(NOT FOR PUBLICATION)

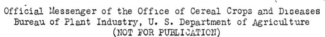

. 21   No. 9

April 30, 1929
Personnel (April 21-30) and Project Issue

PERSONNEL ITEMS

Dr. James G. Dickson, agent in the cooperative cereal disease investiga-
ons that are being conducted at Madison, Wis., came to Washington on April
for conferences with officials of the Department, especially on the research
ogram on scab of wheat and barley. Dr. Dickson will be in Washington about
n days.

J. M. Hammerly, senior scientific aid in corn investigations, returned on
ril 28 from Florence, S. C., where he had planted corn in the cooperative
ots on the Pee Dee Substation. Mr. Hammerly reports that the crops in the
cinity of Florence are looking better than they did last year at this time.

The appointment of Miss Anne E. Kimball, clerk-stenographer to the State
ader of barberry eradication in Colorado since June, 1928, was terminated on
ril 6, 1929. Miss Kimball has accepted a position in another line of work.

Dr. C. E. Leighty, principal agronomist in charge of eastern wheat inves-
gations, left Washington on April 29 for Raleigh, N. C., to confer with offi-
als of the North Carolina Agricultural Experiment Station on wheat investiga-
ons. He also will go to Athens and Experiment, Ga., to look over ooopera-
ve wheat experiment plots, and then to Sacaton, Ariz., to take notes on and
rvest wheats in the foreign introduction detention nursery on the United States
eld Station. Dr. Leighty will return to Washington about the first week in
ne.

Miss Mary L. Stonik, clerk-stenographer in eastern wheat investigations,
signed her position on April 22. Miss Stonik was married on April 16 to Dr.
orge H. Ryan, Jr., of Walpole, Mass.

VISITORS

Dr. E. D. Ball, Dean of the College of Agriculture and Director of the Agricultural Experiment Station of the University of Arizona, was an Office visitor on April 25 to discuss a wheat improvement program.

Dr. C. T. Dowell, Dean of the College of Agriculture, and Director of Stations of the Louisiana State University, called at the Office on April 2

Dr. J. Arthur Harris, of the department of botany of the University of Minnesota, Minneapolis, was an Office visitor on April 22.

Dr. L. R. Jones, Professor of Plant Pathology in the University of Wisconsin, was an Office visitor on April 30 to confer on cooperative projects

Dr. R. W. Thatcher, President of the Massachusetts Agricultural Colleg called on Dr. C. R. Ball April 22 to discuss agronomic affairs.

MANUSCRIPTS AND PUBLICATIONS

ript entitled "Oats in the Western Half of the United States,"
and F. A. Coffman, was submitted on April 30 for publication
letin.

of Technical Bulletin 120 entitled "Relation of Husk Cover-
rn Ears," by C. H. Kyle, was read on April 24.

C E R E A L   C O U R I E R

Official Messenger of the Office of Cereal Crops and Diseases
Bureau of Plant Industry, U. S. Department of Agriculture
(NOT FOR PUBLICATION)

Vol. 21   No. 10

May 10,.1929
Personnel (May 1-10) and Field Station (April 16-30) Issue

PERSONNEL ITEMS

M. A. McCall, principal agronomist in charge of cereal agronomy, left
Washington on May 5 for points in Missouri, Kansas, Louisiana, and Arkansas,
for conferences with experiment station officials relative to cooperative
cereal experiments.

Miss Margaret V. Paden, junior clerk-stenographer for Dr. A. M. Brunson
and Dr. J. H. Parker in the cooperative cereal experiments at Manhattan, Kans.,
was married on May 1 to Mr. Fred Hazel, and her name on the rolls has been
changed to Mrs. Margaret P. Hazel.

T. R. Stanton, senior agronomist in charge of oat investigations, left
Washington on May 8 for an extended trip through the South and the southwestern States in the interest of oat investigations. Mr. Stanton will visit
experiment stations and confer with agronomists in Virginia, North Carolina,
South Carolina, Georgia, Alabama, Mississippi, Tennessee, Louisiana, Texas,
Oklahoma, Kansas, and Missouri. On the trip from Experiment, Ga., to Manhattan, Kans., Mr. Stanton will be accompanied by Mr. H. C. Murphy, assistant
pathologist in crown-rust investigations, stationed at Ames, Iowa. They will
inspect the uniform crown-rust nurseries located at Experiment and Tifton,
Ga., A. & M. College, Miss., Baton Rouge, La., Denton, Tex., Stillwater,
Okla., and Manhattan, Kans. Several days will be spent at A. & M. College,
Miss., and Manhattan, Kans., in studying the varieties and strains of oats
included in the general crown-rust nurseries which are being conducted at
these stations. Mr. Stanton will return to Washington about June 20.

John F. Trost, associate pathologist in the cooperative cereal-disease
investigations conducted at Purdue University Agricultural Experiment Station,
LaFayette, Ind., came to Washington on May 2 to confer with members of the
Office staff. He left on May 4 to return to his headquarters.

MANUSCRIPTS AND PUBLICATIONS

Galley proof of article entitled "Smuts and Rusts Produced in Cereals by Hypodermic Injection of Inoculum," by Marion A. Griffiths and Harry B. Humphrey, for publication in the Journal of Agricultural Research, was read May 3.

The article entitled "The Occurrence of Sclerospora graminicola on Maize in Wisconsin," by Wm. H. Weston, Jr., appears in Phytopathology 19 (4): 391-397. April, 1929.

Galley proof of Farmers' Bulletin 1581, "Oats in the North-Central States," by T. R. Stanton and F. A. Coffman, was read on May 7.

Galley proof of Farmers' Bulletin 1583, "Spring-Sown Red Oats," by T. R. Stanton and F. A. Coffman, was read on May 7.

Page proof of Tech. Bul. 120 entitled "Relation of Husk Covering to Smut of Corn Ears," by C. H. Kyle, was read on May 7.

FIELD STATION CONDITION AND PROGRESS

HUMID ATLANTIC COAST AREA (South to North)

GEORGIA

State College of Agriculture, Athens (Cereal Agronomy, R. R. Childs)

VIRGINIA

Arlington Experiment Farm, Rosslyn (Small Grain Agronomy, J. W. Taylor)
(May 9)

The weather this spring has been unfavorable to small grains. The total
rainfall for April was 7.06 inches, which is almost twice the average for the
month. The frequent showers in the first nine days of May have totaled 1.20
inches. The excessive rains and lack of sunshine have caused rank vegetative
growth, particularly in wheat, rye, and barley. Lodging has begun and more
is anticipated. Mildew is causing injury to the barley. Leaf rust which was
first observed on April 12, following the unseasonably hot spell from April 6
to 8, inclusive, has not developed rapidly. The sulphur-dusting experiment
for the control of leaf rust is being handicapped by the frequent rains and
lack of warm weather.

Wheat seed inoculated with bunt spores in the seed-treatment experiment
is producing a yellow, stunted type of plant. A severe infection of bunt is
expected.

Some loose smut of barley is present in the varietal experiment, but
there is very little covered smut. Semesan- and ceresan-treated seed failed
to eliminate plants infected with loose smut. Barley seed sown at different
depths shows striking differences in the infection of both covered and loose
smuts. The results for 1929 on the depth of seeding barley and the occurrence of both smuts now appear to agree with those obtained in the past three
years.

Arlington Experiment Farm, Rosslyn (Corn Breeding, F. D. Richey)

Arlington Experiment Farm, Rosslyn (Cereal Smuts, V. F. Tapke, Acting in
Charge)

Arlington Experiment Farm, Rosslyn (Virus Diseases, H. H. McKinney)

NEW YORK

Cornell University Agricultural Experiment Station, Ithaca (Cereal
Breeding, H. H. Love)

HUMID MISSISSIPPI VALLEY AREA (South to North)

LOUISIANA

Rice Experiment Station, Crowley (Rice Agronomy, J. M. Jenkins)

Agricultural Experiment Station, Baton Rouge (Corn Breeding, H. F. Stoneberg)

MISSOURI

Agricultural Experiment Station, Columbia (Cereal Agronomy, L. J. Stadler)

TENNESSEE

Agricultural Experiment Station, Knoxville (Corn Breeding, L. S. Mayer)

IOWA

Agricultural Experiment Station, Ames (Oat Breeding, L. C. Burnett)

Agricultural Experiment Station, Ames (Corn Breeding, M. T. Jenkins)

Agricultural Experiment Station, Ames (Crown Rust of Oats, S. M. Dietz)

ILLINOIS

Funk Bros. Seed Co., Bloomington (Corn Root, Stalk and Ear Rots, J. R. Holbert)

INDIANA

Purdue University Agricultural Experiment Station, LaFayette (Corn Rots and Metallic Poisoning, ----------)

Purdue University Agricultural Experiment Station, LaFayette (Leaf Rusts, E. B. Mains)

WISCONSIN

Agricultural Experiment Station, Madison (Wheat Scab, J. G. Dickson)

MINNESOTA

Agricultural Experiment Station, University Farm, St. Paul (Wheat Breeding, K. S. Quisenberry, Acting in Charge)

Agricultural Experiment Station, University Farm, St. Paul (Stem Rust, E. C. Stakman)

Agricultural Experiment Station, University Farm, St. Paul (Flax Rust, H. A. Rodenhiser)

GREAT PLAINS AREA (South to North)

OKLAHOMA

Woodward Field Station, Woodward (Grain Sorghum and Broomcorn, J. B. Sieglinger)

KANSAS

Agricultural Experiment Station, Manhattan (Cereal Breeding, J. H. Parker) (April 27)

Director H. M. Bainer, of the Southwestern Wheat Improvement Association, of Kansas City, Mo., early in April made an automobile tour of the wheat belts of Kansas. Accompanying him on the 1,880-mile trip through 51 counties, were Prof. H. H. Laude, associate professor of agronomy of the Kansas State Agricultural College, and Mr. Pearson, of the Southwestern Milling Company.

The writer and Dean L. E. Call and Prof. S. C. Salmon, of the Kansas State Agricultural College, and Mr. E. C. Paxton, of the Division of Crop Statistics for Kansas, traveled with Mr. Bainer's party for certain periods of the trip. Personal inspection was made of a large number of fields along the route, and reports as to the condition of adjoining and sectional areas were solicited.

The following is an excerpt from Mr. Bainer's report on the trip, which began April 7 and ended April 13:

"As a whole, the present average condition of Kansas wheat is fully up to normal. While it is true that the south-central part of the State and some of the best wheat territory in the heart of the wheat belt is slightly below normal, this loss is fully balanced by the fine condition of the crop in the northern and northwestern parts of the State. There is an abundance of moisture everywhere both for the top soil and subsoil. Plenty of moisture [rain] and good weather from now on will bring out the late wheat and will help overcome the volunteer-wheat situation. With 12,173,000 acres of wheat sown in Kansas last fall, the present condition indicates that there will be considerable over 11,000,000 acres to harvest. A conservative estimate of yield, based on the present outlook of the Kansas crop, would place it at fully 150,000,000 bushels."

Agricultural Experiment Station, Manhattan (Corn Breeding, A. M. Brunson)

Agricultural Experiment Station, Manhattan (Wheat Foot Rots, Hurley Fellows)

Agricultural Experiment Station, Manhattan (Wheat Leaf Rust, C. O. Johnston) (April 30)

April has been a cool, rainy month, very favorable for the development of wheat but too cool for the rapid spread of rusts. There was considerable overwintering of leaf rust throughout central Kansas, but very little increase in the percentage of infection could be noted during the month. Rust is still confined to a few scattered uredinia on old leaves near the bases of the plants. Although the rust infection at present is small, it is widely distributed over the entire winter-wheat area of Kansas. It is not difficult to find uredinia in nearly every field. If the rainy weather should continue through May, there undoubtedly will be considerable leaf rust in the southern Great Plains.

The status of stem-rust is somewhat different. During the present season the writer has been unable to find this rust in Kansas. No report of its occurrence has been received.

Winter wheat in this area is in excellent condition. The crop is developing rapidly and making a great deal of top growth. If the present rainy weather continues, there will be considerable lodging in lowland fields. The plants are now entering the jointing stage.

Dr. H. B. Humphrey, of the Washington Office, and Mr. H. C. Murphy, of Ames, Iowa, were station visitors on April 9, 10, and 11, and Mr. Harry Ukkelberg, of University Farm, St. Paul, Minn., was a visitor on April 22 and 23. The latter very kindly made leaf-rust collections for the writer at various points in Kansas, Oklahoma, and Texas. These collections reveal an interesting situation in regard to leaf rust. There apparently is only a sprinkling of rust throughout central and southern Kansas and northern Oklahoma. A heavy infection already has developed around Oklahoma City in central Oklahoma, but there is only a sprinkling of rust in southern Oklahoma. There is another area of heavy infection around Sherman, Tex., but only a moderate infection in the vicinity of Forth Worth.

Dr. P. C. Mangelsdorf, on April 20, reported a very heavy infection of leaf rust in the nursery at College Station, and Mr. R. A. Hall reported on April 22 that many varieties in the leaf-rust nursery at Beeville, Tex., already had been killed by rust. The writer expects to visit these nurseries the second week in May.

Fort Hays Branch Experiment Station, Hays (Cereal Agronomy, A. F. Swanson

NEBRASKA

North Platte Substation, North Platte (Cereal Agronomy, G. F. Sprague)

NORTH DAKOTA

Agricultural Experiment Station, State College Station, Fargo (Flax Diseases, L. W. Boyle)

Dickinson Substation, Dickinson (Cereal Agronomy, R. W. Smith) (May 3)

Seeding at the Substation has proceeded without much interruption because of unfavorable weather, and the great part of it is done. In the vicinity of the Substation wheat seeding is nearly completed. Oats and barley are being sown. Reports indicate that about the usual acreage of spring wheat is being sown

At the Substation seeding of cereal varieties is completed with the exception of flax, proso, corn, a few head rows, and the date-of-seeding experiments. Early sown grain is emerging, germination having been somewhat retarded by cool weather.

More than 1,000 head rows were sown with bunt-inoculated seed. Most of these were hybrids of Hope wheat which will be in the 3rd and 4th generations this year; a few are of the 5th and 6th generations.

In the date-of-seeding smut experiment in which five varieties are sown with bunt-inoculated seed at 10-day intervals, a soil thermograph is being used to help correlate the soil temperature with the percentage of smut in the resulting crop. So far the soil doubtless has been cool enough for smut spores to germinate. Soil-moisture determinations also are being made, and, while the soil has not been wet, enough moisture probably has been present to insure a fair degree of smut infection.

The precipitation for April was only 0.60 of an inch; the mean temperature was about two degrees below normal.

Northern Great Plains Field Station, Mandan (Flax Breeding, J. C. Brinsmade, Jr.) (May 2)

The first seeding in the date-of-seeding-and-tillage experiment was made April 20. The plants are just emerging today.

The flax-sick soil nursery land was plowed and harrowed April 22. The land for the flax varietal plot and that for the clean-soil nursery were disked on the same date.

The second seeding in the date-of-seeding-and-tillage experiment coul not be made April 30 on account of rain, but was made on May 1.

A seeding of five new flax varieties, including one early variety, C. I. 473, two Argentine selections, C. I. Nos. 474 and 475, and two Argentir hybrids, C. I. Nos. 476 and 478, was made on May 1. The purpose is to in- crease the seed and compare early seeding of Argentine varieties with the regular seeding later in May.

Two interesting letters in regard to Argentine flax, accompanied by samples of seed, have been received to date.

Northern Great Plains Field Station, Mandan (Cereal Agronomy, E. R. Ausemus) (May 2)

Seeding of the varietal field and nursery plots of wheat, oats, and barley was completed on May 1. Weather conditions for the latter half of April were satisfactory for spring seeding. The weather continued dry for most of the time with an excellent rain on April 29 and 30, which should germinate all seed sown previously.

The wheat and oat varieties in the field plots were fully emerged toda May 2. The nursery material is beginning to emerge today.

Farmers have done most of their spring seeding of small grains. Seed- ing has been retarded because the land has been too wet to work in the lowe spots of the fields.

Minimum temperature for the last half of April, 30 degrees on April 2€ maximum, 73 degrees on April 29. The total precipitation was 1.75 inches; 0.63 of an inch of this fell on April 29 and 30.

MONTANA

Judith Basin Substation, Moccasin (Cereal Agronomy, B. B. Bayles) (J. L. Sutherland) (May 1)

The month of April has been cool and there has been very little preci tation. Freezing temperatures were recorded nearly every night of the mon a minimum of 7 degrees above zero was recorded on the 10th. The maximum t perature was 64 degrees on the 15th. The precipitation for April was 0.27 of an inch, which is 0.95 of an inch below the 21-year normal for this per

The dry weather has given opportunity for seeding the majority of the cereal plots. The first seeding was made on April 18, when plots of the different spring grains were sown as a part of the rate-and-date-of-seedir experiment. On April 22 and 23 the spring-wheat varietal plots were sown.

This test has been increased over that of last year and now 33 varieties
are being tested. The increase includes four promising selections from
the Marquis x Hard Federation cross and varieties which are being grown in
connection with the cooperative plot experiment with spring wheat. The
varietal plots of oats, which include two new selections of C. I. 357, were
sown April 25 The list of barley varieties, sown April 25, was not changed
materially from that of last year. Nursery seedings to date have been
limited to smut tests and a date-of-seeding experiment.

Farmers throughout the Judith Basin have made rapid progress with the
sowing of spring grains. The increased spring-wheat acreage promises to
balance the cut in fall seeding of winter wheat. The present season is
approximately a week earlier than that of last spring.

Some winterkilling has been recorded in the less winterhardy nursery
material, and a spotted injury is evident in the winter-wheat plots, owing
to the irregular snow covering.

WESTERN BASIN AND COAST AREAS (North to West and South)

IDAHO

Aberdeen Substation, Aberdeen (Cereal Agronomy, L. L. Davis)

Agricultural Experiment Station, Moscow (Stripe Rust, C. W. Hungerford)

WASHINGTON

Agricultural Experiment Station, Pullman (Cereal Breeding, E. F. Gaines)

OREGON

Sherman County Branch Station, Moro (Cereal Agronomy, D. E. Stephens)

CALIFORNIA

Biggs Rice Field Station, Biggs (Rice Agronomy, J. W. Jones) (May 1)

As a result of the dry winter and spring weather, work in the rice fields
this year was started much earlier than usual. Some rice land was plowed in
March, and plowing and seed-bed preparation were nearly completed by April 20.

A few commercial fields were sown the latter part of March and early in April, but the greater part of the rice acreage was sown and irrigated between April 10 and April 25, fully two weeks earlier than usual. A few fields sown and submerged in March are being reseeded, because of lack of stand.

Plowing at the Station was started on March 29 and completed on April 17. The varieties were sown from April 14 to 16; the nursery seeding was completed on April 21; and most of the plots were sown by April 25. Irrigation was begun on April 17.

There were several very cold nights early in April. The lowest temperature at the Station was 24 degrees F. on April 9. This frost caused a damage to the California fruit crops amounting to fifty to sixty million dollars. It was so cold that there was a thin sheet of ice on standing water. The maximum temperature for April was 84 degrees F. on the 27th.

The rice market remains about the same, prices ranging from $1.95 to $2.10 per hundred for paddy.

<u>University Farm, Davis</u> (Cereal Agronomy, G. A. Wiebe) [April 25]

Cereal crops in California will be short this year because of lack of rainfall. Precipitation is five inches below the normal for this time of year. Because of the cold winter there was abundant stooling, which is a serious handicap when coupled with a lack of moisture. It is doubtful if some of the plots will produce grain worth harvesting. Among the barley varieties in the plots, Vaughn and Atlas show the most promise. About half of the varieties have headed. This is somewhat later than last year. All varieties have a shorter straw this year.

On April 13 the writer made an official trip through the west side of the San Joaquin Valley. Where irrigation water was not available the grain, which had just headed, showed severe effects from lack of moisture. It is doubtful if a third of an average crop will be realized in this section.

The annual Cereal Day for the farmers of California will be held on May 24. On the following day the cereal experiments will be explained to the teachers of the agricultural high schools of California.

<u>Agricultural Experiment Station, Berkeley</u> (Cereal Smuts, F. N. Briggs)

BARBERRY ERADICATION PROGRESS

OHIO

<u>Ohio State University, College of Agriculture, Columbus</u>, J. W. Baringer
(April 30)

Our program of education on barberry eradication in the Ohio schools for the present school term was completed in April. All high schools and all sixth-grade city and village schools have been supplied with study material and teaching suggestions. In addition, all rural sixth grades in 50 counties have been reached in like manner.

April 1 marked the close of the Ohio lesson-plan contest on barberries and black stem rust, among instructors in vocational agriculture and instructors in normal schools. Some very interesting and worth-while ideas can be gleaned from the manuscripts submitted. First place in the State contest was awarded to Miss Ruth McMeen, principal and fourth-grade critic teacher at Ohio University, Athens. Her plan has been entered in competition with winning plans from 12 other States for the grand prize offered by The Conference for the Prevention of Grain Rust.

On April 7 pycnia were found on barberries by Mr. B. B. Beck at Hills and Dales Park near Dayton. This is the earliest date on which pycnial infection has ever been reported in Ohio. It probably is the earliest report on record for the entire barberry-eradication area. The earliest previous record for pycnial infection was April 11. In spite of the unusual earliness of the appearance of pycnia this year no aecia have been found in Ohio so far this spring. Frequent inspection of bushes on which pycnia were first noted has failed to disclose the presence of aecia. Intermittent low temperatures seemingly have been properly timed to retard aecial development.

The inspection in the latter part of April of several fields of winter wheat in central Ohio has furnished negative evidence on the overwintering of urediniospores of black stem rust in this vicinity.

On April 26 and 27, the writer conferred with teachers of botany and biology in several colleges and universities in Ohio while they were attending the annual meeting of the Ohio Academy of Science at Springfield. A set of wax models, depicting the various stages of the life cycle of black stem rust, prepared under the auspices of The Conference for the Prevention of Grain Rust, were being demonstrated for the purpose of obtaining expressions of opinion on the probable value of such models as helps in teaching barberry eradication to college students.

146

INDIANA

Purdue University College of Agriculture, LaFayette, W. E. Leer (May 2)

Field activities in barberry eradication were started on May 1. Messrs. Chance, Fosbrink, McCoy, Sharp, and Wright began a week's work in an area of escaped barberries in Henry County. Several teachers of vocational agriculture expect to bring their classes to this area to take part in a demonstration on finding and killing common barberries.

The intensive survey of Montgomery County will be started about May 8. It has been decided to work first in the area adjoining the major stream running diagonally through the county, because it probably can be most effectively surveyed in the early spring months.

Owing to the fact that nearly all of the rural grade schools and most of the rural high schools closed in March and April, educational activities in the schools have been discontinued until next fall.

MICHIGAN

Agricultural College, East Lansing, W. F. Reddy

WISCONSIN

Department of Agriculture, State Capitol Annex, Madison, R. M. Caldwell

ILLINOIS

Box 72, Post Office Building, Urbana, R. W. Bills

IOWA

Iowa State College, Ames, P. W. Rohrbaugh

MINNESOTA

Agricultural Experiment Station, University Farm, St. Paul, L. W. Melander (May 3)

The decision of the judges, who rated the manuscripts submitted in the teaching plan contest in Minnesota, was received this past week. The following were the prize winners:

First Prize $50.00 - Miss Myra Robinson, Box 30, Eveleth.

Second Prize $35.00 - R. S. Dunham, agronomist, Northwest School of griculture, Crookston.

Third Prize $15.00 - Della Henningsgard, Marietta.

Honorable Mention:
W. E. Dowdell, Bemidji   George H. Melbye, Eldred
Miss Clifford Everhart, Sauk Center   Hannah Okerlund, Renville
Mabel Erikson, Bemidji   Leo L. Knuti, Cloquet
W. G. Wiegand, Austin

The prize money was offered by the St. Paul Dispatch Pioneer Press. The contest was unusually keen. The quality of the 10 teaching plans presented was very high. Considerable State-wide publicity was given the barberry campaign through this contest. Numerous clippings were received from papers in all parts of the State.

Preparations are now being made for the annual weed conferences. Approximately 125 meetings will be held between May 15 and July 1. All of the township chairmen, in those counties which do not have duly appointed weed inspectors, are required by law to attend these meetings. Furthermore, the public will be invited to the meetings this year, so that the attendance perhaps will be more than double that of former years. The meetings will be handled in four circuits by four teams of speakers. On each circuit there will be a speaker to discuss the barberry-eradication problem. There will be a special meeting at Mahnomen, Mahnomen County. The grain dealers and business men of Mahnomen have asked that a special barberry and rust meeting be held in connection with the weed conference. At this meeting the barberry office intends to have a special program. In all probability there will be a large attendance.

Pycnial infection was found in two locations in Hennepin County on May 1 by Messrs. Cotter, Melander, and Rasmussen.

NEBRASKA

College of Agriculture, University Farm, Lincoln, A. F. Thiel

NORTH DAKOTA

Agricultural Extension Division, State College Station, Fargo, G. C. Mayoue (April 27)

The major activity in the barberry office in April has been the mailing of packets of study materials to schools and educational matter to the members of the North Dakota Retail Merchants Association, to agricultural extension agents, and to former barberry employees. All of the schools, including public and private grade and high schools of 16 counties have been supplied with packets containing bulletins, circulars, circular letters, specimens, plates, maps, charts, lesson plans, etc.

148

The packets intended for educational and publicity purposes contained circu^a
lar letter, a digest of the 1928 annual report, bulletins, specimens, maps,
and charts.

The State Leader and assistant have been making personal contacts with
all of the departments, particularly of botany and general science, in the
State University and the normal schools.

The lesson-plan contest sponsored by The Conference for the Prevention
of Grain Rust has just been completed. The judges of the State contest wer
the Dean of the School of Education at the North Dakota State College, the
State Superintendent of Public Instruction, Bismarck, and the County Super-
intendent of Schools, Cass County, Fargo. Mr. S. M. Thorfinnson, Smith-
Hughes instructor at Granville, was awarded first place; Mr. Earl Hendricks
Smith-Hughes instructor at Hazelton, second place; Russell B. Widdifield,
Smith-Hughes instructor at LaMoure, third place; and Mr. Marvin S. Kirk, .
Instructor in Agriculture at the Minot State Teachers College, fourth place
Messrs. Hendrickson and Widdifield are former barberry-eradication agents.

A regular course of training and instruction for applicants desiring
appointments on the barberry personnel for the coming season has been given
each Tuesday and Thursday evening since April 2. This training will be con
tinued on the same schedule for the month of May. The course will terminate
with field trips during the last two weeks of May.

The season has been backward to date. However, with favorable weather
for field operations, seeding of hard spring wheat will be nearly finished
by May 4, or about the same time as a year ago. The average date of beginning wheat seeding last year was April 9 for durum and April 8 for spring
wheat other than durum, three to four days earlier than the average beginning date this year, which is April 12 for both types of wheat. The presen
indications are that the wheat acreage will be less and the flax acreage
greater than that of last year.

MONTANA

State College of Agriculture, Bozeman, W. L. Popham

WYOMING

College of Agriculture, University of Wyoming, Laramie, W. L. Popham

COLORADO

Agricultural College, Ft. Collins, E. A. Lungren [May 7]

Copies of the progress report on the barberry-eradication campaign in
Colorado were sent recently to more than 2,000 farmers and cooperators.
Educational material has been sent to a large percentage of all the schools.
This has resulted in finding five properties containing mostly escaped bar-
berry bushes.

The State Leader inspected many fields in eastern Colorado in April and
found the condition of the grain to be about two weeks later than usual. At
that time he was unable to find any evidence of overwintering of stem or leaf
rust.

It is planned to begin second survey in Boulder County on June 1.

C E R E A L   C O U R I E R

Official Messenger of the Office of Cereal Crops and Diseases
Bureau of Plant Industry, U. S. Department of Agriculture
(NOT FOR PUBLICATION)

----

1. 21   No. 11
May 20, 1929
Personnel (May 11-20) and Field Station (May 1-15) Issue

PERSONNEL ITEMS

Mr. Wayne M. Bever, junior pathologist in the cooperative stripe rust
vestigations conducted at Moscow, Idaho, is making a six-weeks' trip in
ifornia, Oregon, Washington, and Idaho to get information concerning the
istribution of stripe rust and the conditions affecting local epidemics.
e also will visit cereal nurseries at Davis, Calif., Corvallis, Oreg., and
ullman, Wash., to take notes on varietal susceptibility of wheat and barley
o stripe rust.

Mr. C. H. Kyle, senior agronomist in corn investigations, left Washington
n May 18 for Tifton, Ga., to look after the corn in the cooperative experi-
ental plots. He wrote on May 19 that the corn looks well as a whole, al-
hough there are two rows nearly missing. F_1 is from 12 to 15 inches high.
he other corn is from 6 to 15 inches high. The old selfed lines of Garrick
ook better than they usually do. Nearly every kernel grew.

Garrick and Whatley are growing rapidly. It is difficult to tell which
as done better so far.

Some of the native corn in the vicinity is shoulder high and some early
arieties are tasseling. Oats are being harvested. Cantaloupes are in bloom.
otton and tobacco do not seem to have done much.

Mr. Kyle expects to go to Florence, S. C., after finishing his work at
ifton, and will be back in Washington about May 27.

This Office has been notified of the passing on May 11 of Mr. C. T. Nolan Chairman of the Flax Development Committee, of New York City, representing the paint, oil, and varnish manufacturers of the United States. Mr. Nolan, for more than 20 years, has been greatly interested in furthering investigations looking toward the improvement of flax varieties and their increased productio in the United States. Mr. Nolan's many friends among the agronomists in the D partment of Agriculture and in the flax-producing States of the middle Northwest will learn with deep regret of his passing.

Mr. John L. Richardson, agent in charge of barberry-eradication field pub licity, with headquarters in Minneapolis, arrived in Washington on May 20. While in Washington Mr. Richardson will summarize the progress that has been made in barberry-eradication publicity and will aid in outlining the publicity activities for the fiscal year ending June 30, 1930. He will remain in Washin ton about two weeks.

Mr. Roderick Sprague was appointed assistant pathologist, effective May 20, to assist Dr. Hurley Fellows, of Manhattan, Kans., in the investigation of foot rots of wheat that is being conducted in cooperation with the Kansas Agri cultural Experiment Station. The research is being conducted in Kansas, Orego and Washington, and to some extent in Colorado and Montana.

Mr. T. R. Stanton wrote on May 12 from Greenville, S. C., that his trip from Washington had been very interesting. In traveling through parts of the South he has noticed that the Fulghum oat seems to be replacing Red Rustproof (Red Texas, Appler, etc.) to a large extent. At Hartsville, S. C., Mr. Stanton visited the nursery of Mr. George J. Wilds, of the Pedigreed Seed Co. Mr. Wilds has a nursery of something like 10,500 rows of winter oats. This probably is the largest oat nursery ever grown in the South. In it there is some very promising material, especially in the F_4 generation of the cross Fulghum x Ferguson Navarro.

In general, oats are in excellent condition in that portion of the South through which Mr. Stanton has traveled. There has been very little winterkil ing. The cool spring has been favorable to oat production. Many excellent fields were seen along the route traveled by automobile from Florence to Gree ville.

Mr. G. A. Wiebe, assistant agronomist in charge of the cooperative cerea experiments at University Farm, Davis, Calif., is on a month's trip through t cereal-growing sections of California. Mr. Wiebe reports that it is very dry at Davis this spring and that oats on the Farm are likely to produce a poor yield.

VISITORS

Dr. H. L. Shantz, President of the University of Arizona, was an Office caller on May 14.

MANUSCRIPTS AND PUBLICATIONS

Galley proof of Farmers' Bulletin 1585 entitled "Varieties of Hard Red
Winter Wheat," by J. Allen Clark and Karl S. Quisenberry, was read on May 15.

The article entitled "The Occurrence of Strains Resistant to Leaf Rust i
Certain Varieties of Wheat," by C. O. Johnston, appears in the Journal of the
American Society of Agronomy 21 (5): 568-573. May, 1929. (Cooperation betwe
the department of botany and plant pathology of the Kansas State Agricultural
College and the Office of Cereal Crops and Diseases.)

The article entitled "Hetero-Fertilization in Maize," by George F. Sprag
appears in Science n. s. 69 (1794): 526-527. May 17, 1929. (Cooperation between Office of Cereal Crops and Diseases and the Nebraska Agricultural Exper
ment Station.)

UNITED STATES DEPARTMENT OF AGRICULTURE
Director of Personnel and Business Administration
Washington

May 16, 1929

CHIEFS OF BUREAUS AND OFFICES:

The following is quoted from a recent communication from the General Accounting Office:

It is noted on vouchers submitted to this office for preaudit by various bureaus of the Department of Agriculture, and also on vouchers submitted for post audit in the accounts of the Disbursing Clerk of the Department of Agriculture, that reimbursement is made on travel expense vouchers for payments by station employees for express charges on shipments received by them.

The Standardized Government Travel Regulations effective March 1, 1929, provide in paragraph 85 that shipments by express or freight of Government property, not classed as baggage and not admissible to the mails, should be made on Government bills of lading and that such charges must not be paid by the traveler. While it may at times be necessary to pay charges on shipments not made on Government bills of lading, it is suggested that such charges be billed by the express company on vouchers, rather than paid on travel expense vouchers. Charges of this nature are usually incurred at stations and it would appear possible and desirable to make payments on vouchers submitted by the express companies who furnish the services and such action is requested.

An additional reason for avoidance where possible of payments of express charges from private or advanced funds is that express shipments are now subject to land-grant deductions. This may not only mean suspension of charges on movements in the land-grant territory, but will impose on the employee the burden of collecting any disallowance from the express company.

(Sgd.)   W. W. Stockberger

Director.

FIELD STATION CONDITION AND PROGRESS

HUMID ATLANTIC COAST AREA (South to North)

GEORGIA

State College of Agriculture, Athens (Cereal Agronomy, R. R. Childs)

VIRGINIA

Arlington Experiment Farm, Rosslyn (Small Grain Agronomy, J. W. Taylor)

Arlington Experiment Farm, Rosslyn (Corn Breeding, F. D. Richey) (May 18)

The corn plots at the Arlington Experiment Farm were planted during the period from May 13 to 17, as weather permitted. The plantings include:

Yield comparisons of about 125 F_1 crosses among selfed lines of C. I. No. 119 (Boone County) corn selected for rough and smooth indentation and for numbers of kernel rows.

Yield comparisons of about 30 double crosses and 175 single crosses among the following selfed lines:

C. I. No. 165. 1 line from Mr. E. B. Brown's Texas variety, "U.S.Sel.165."
227. 8 lines from Chinese Bloody Butcher.
228. 9 lines from Lancaster Surecrop.
230. 1 line from "Australian Dent."
232. 1 line from St. Charles Yellow
390. 2 lines from a semi-prolific yellow dent.
540. Dr. J. R. Holbert's A and B lines.
549. Mr. H. A. Wallace's Illinois 2-ear.
--- 19 lines of yellow dent from Dr. M. T. Jenkins.
--- Nebraska 2 and 12 from Dr. T. A. Kiesselbach.

Yield comparisons (1) of the F_1 cross, C. I. No. 201 F x H, Line F (selfed 12 generations) and the cross back-pollinated 1, 2, 3, and 4 generations by Line F. (2) A similar comparison of 228, 6-5 x 4-8 through 4 generations of back pollinating to 4-8, and line 4-8 selfed 9 generations.

Plantings for continued selfing and selection in lines of the preceding C. I. numbers and plantings for obtaining F_1 crosses and double crosses. Plantings for back pollinating the third to the sixth time and for selfing following from two to five generations of selection in back-pollinated lines.

Miscellaneous genetic studies, including segregates from North American-South American crosses, and isolations of parallel strains differing in the A, C, R, B, and Pl genes.

Mr. C. H. Kyle has some 130 distinct inbred lines planted for continued selfing and study. Most of his experiments, which have been located at the Arlington Farm during the past several years, were transferred to the Georgia Coastal Plains Station at Tifton, Ga., where they will be carried in cooperation with the Georgia State Experiment Station. Mr. Kyle and Mr. Hammerly planted the plots at Tifton, comprising nearly five acres, April 10 to 15.

Arlington Experiment Farm, Rosslyn (Cereal Smuts, V. F. Tapke, Acting in Charge)

Arlington Experiment Farm, Rosslyn (Virus Diseases, H. H. McKinney)

NEW YORK

Cornell University Agricultural Experiment Station, Ithaca (Cereal Breeding, H. H. Love)

HUMID MISSISSIPPI VALLEY AREA (South to North)

LOUISIANA

Rice Experiment Station, Crowley (Rice Agronomy, J. M. Jenkins)

Agricultural Experiment Station, Baton Rouge (Corn Breeding, H. F. Stoneberg) (May 15)

The weather in January and February and the first half of March was cool and accompanied by heavy and frequent precipitation which prevented early field operations. Weather conditions have been ideal since March 15 for the preparation and planting of the experimental plots and for the emergence and early growth of the plants.

The corn experiments were planted April 3 to 30. The planting of inbred strains was spread out over a considerable period of time in order to give a longer season for hand-pollinating. It has been found from past experience that better results are obtained if experimental corn plots are not planted during the first favorable period in March but when the planting is delayed until after a period of unfavorable cool and wet weather which usually follows the first warm days in the spring.

A very good stand was obtained in the plots as the result of favorable weather conditions and because the depredations by birds and insects were less than in previous years. Corn planted early in April is now about two feet tall

TENNESSEE

Agricultural Experiment Station, Knoxville (Corn Breeding, L. S. Mayer)

MISSOURI

Agricultural Experiment Station, Columbia (Cereal Agronomy, L. J. Stadler)

OHIO

Agricultural Experiment Station, Wooster (Corn Investigations, M. T. Meyers)
ay 13)

Mr. J. T. McClure, associate in the corn-borer experiments cooperative be-
een the Office of Cereal Crops and Diseases, the Ohio Agricultural Experiment
ation, and the Ohio State University, and I visited Bono, Ohio, on May 11.
found things progressing very satisfactorily, although slowly. The first
antings at Bono, which were to have been made on May 10, were delayed by the
ceedingly heavy rains that occurred in that section of Ohio this spring. A
ek or so ago the canals were so high that it was impossible to pump into Lake
ie, and a considerable portion of the plot area was under water for some time.

Mr. J. S. Cutler, also agent of the Office in the corn-borer investigation,
ill leave Wooster for the Toledo area as soon as conditions permit to assist
r. L. H. Patch, of the U. S. Bureau of Entomology, in planting a series of corn-
)rer damage experiments.

Word from Mr. L. R. Jorgensen, agent of the Office at Columbus, indicates
iat the cooperative plantings there are going in somewhat ahead of schedule.
)nditions are much more favorable than at Bono.

IOWA

Agricultural Experiment Station, Ames (Oat Breeding, L. C. Burnett) (May 14)

So far, our planting is pretty well up to date. We are a few days behind
ith corn at the present time, and were about a week late with the variety plots
f oats a month ago.

Our early plantings, however, were put in on the 30th of March and we had
rerything in the ground before the 20th of April with the exception of the
arsery lots that were definitely listed for late seeding.

Agricultural Experiment Station, Ames (Corn Breeding, M. T. Jenkins)

Agricultural Experiment Station, Ames (Crown Rust of Oats, S. M. Dietz)

ILLINOIS

Funk Bros. Seed Co., Bloomington (Corn Root, Stalk and Ear Rots, J.R.H

INDIANA

Purdue University Agricultural Experiment Station, La Fayette (Corn Rot
and Metallic Poisoning, J. F. Trost, Acting in Charge) (May 16)

Dr. J. G. Dickson stopped here on May 8 on his return trip to Madison a
kindly agreed to supply us with culture of Penicillium and Giberella for cor
ing inoculation plots this year.

We made our first seedings at LaFayette on May 9 and 10. We also plant
at Bedford across the fertility plot series on May 10. Since that time we I
had general rains throughout the State and no further seeding can be attempt
until the end of the week. Soil temperatures generally are low enough to gi
a good test for seedling blights this year.

Purdue University Agricultural Experiment Station, La Fayette (Leaf Rus
E. B. Mains)

WISCONSIN

Agricultural Experiment Station, Madison (Wheat Scab, J. G. Dickson)

MINNESOTA

Agricultural Experiment Station, University Farm, St. Paul (Wheat Bree
K. S. Quisenberry, Acting in Charge)

Agricultural Experiment Station, University Farm, St. Paul (Stem Rust,
E. C. Stakman)

Agricultural Experiment Station, University Farm, St. Paul (Flax Rust,
H. A. Rodenhiser)

GREAT PLAINS AREA (South to North)

OKLAHOMA

Woodward Field Station, Woodward (Grain Sorghum and Broomcorn, J. B.
Sieglinger) (May 15)

The weather this spring has continued cool and fairly moist. Conditi
appear to have been right for wheat to develop rapidly, as it is heading a
present and there are indications of an early harvest. All but 10 of the
strains of winter wheat of C. O. Johnston's uniform leaf rust nursery are
headed at this date.

Threshing seed heads of grain sorghum and broomcorn is the main work at present.

Fruit prospects continue favorable.

Precipitation for April, 0.77 of an inch; for May to date, 1.39 inches. Minimum temperature for May to date, 35 degrees on the 1st, maximum for same period, 85 degrees on the 10th.

KANSAS

Agricultural Experiment Station, Manhattan (Cereal Breeding, J. H. Parker)

Agricultural Experiment Station, Manhattan (Corn Breeding, A. M. Brunson)

Agricultural Experiment Station, Manhattan (Wheat Foot Rots, Hurley Fellows)

Agricultural Experiment Station, Manhattan (Wheat Leaf Rust, C. O. Johnston) (May 13)

The following is a report of my observations on cereal rust so far on my southern trip. At College Station, Tex., an extremely heavy epidemic of both stem and leaf rust occurred in wheat and oats. Stem rust was much more severe than leaf rust, being so heavy that it was very difficult to make leaf-rust readings. Many varieties and hybrids were killed by stem rust and set no seed.

At Beeville, 100 miles east of San Antonio, we found an even more severe epidemic of stem rust in wheat. All varieties were short and many were entirely killed by rust. Leaf-rust readings were extremely difficult. Even the durums were heavily infected with stem rust, infection running as high as 40 per cent on Iumillo and 60 per cent on Vernal emmer. Einkorn had 40 per cent stem rust, but Webster showed only a trace, and Hope 5 per cent.

These two nurseries should have been visited 10 days ago, but it was impossible for me to get to them sooner if other nurseries were to be visited on the same trip.

The most interesting thing about the results in these nurseries is the origin of the rust. No wheat is grown within many miles of both stations and no infection seems to have been present last fall. Some wheat is grown about 100 miles west of Beeville.

Here at Denton there is considerable leaf rust but only a bare trace of stem rust. Wheat is well headed but still sufficiently green for considerable stem rust to develop. Conditions are favorable for rust at present, the past few days having been rainy and warm. In fact it rained four inches last night, and we are unable to get into the field for more than a scant survey today. Showers are continuing today.

I fear that Mr. Stanton and Mr. Murphy will be too late to see any oats in Texas. Most varieties are in full head now and will be dead ripe before the dates given in their itinerary. Oats already have been harvested at Colle Station. There was extremely heavy infection of both crown and stem rust on oats at that station.

It is my plan to proceed from here to Stillwater, Okla., although the whe there has been reported as late. If satisfactory notes can not be secured the now, I shall plan to make a second trip into Oklahoma and meet Mr. Murphy and Mr. Stanton.

Fort Hays Branch Experiment Station, Hays (Cereal Agronomy, A. F. Swanson

NEBRASKA

North Platte Substation, North Platte (Cereal Agronomy, G. F. Sprague) (May 16)

Corn planting was begun on May 14. The land for the varietal comparisons was listed in April and the ridges split just prior to planting. Small grains are growing nicely. Rye on summer fallow is about a foot high.

Many high schools in this section of the State have taken advantage of th fair weather to visit the Substation.

The maximum temperature for the period from May 1-15 was 90 degrees on Ma 14; minimum, 27 degrees on May 2. The total precipitation was 1.04 inches.

SOUTH DAKOTA

U. S. Forage-Crop Field Experiments, Redfield (Wheat Breeding, E. S. McFadden)

NORTH DAKOTA

Agricultural Experiment Station, State College Station, Fargo (Flax Diseases, L. W. Boyle)

Dickinson Substation, Dickinson (Cereal Agronomy, R. W. Smith) (May 15)

Temperatures below normal have prevailed for the greater part of the pas' two weeks. Minimum temperatures below freezing were recorded every morning o: the week ending May 10. A minimum of 14 degrees was recorded on May 6 and 7. The low temperatures combined with dry weather caused some injury to leaves o wheat, oats, and barley that had recently emerged. A shower of about a quart of an inch on the 10th helped to revive the injured grain so that no severe i: jury is apparent at this time.

Flax emerging during the coldest weather suffered less injury than in 1924, when May frosts followed by hot sunny days killed many flax plants that were emerging. The only hot day this month was the 13th, when the temperature was above 80 degrees during the afternoon. The warm spell was of short duration and last night a light rain set in, turning to snow. There are now about 2 inches of snow on the ground, making a total of 0.60 of an inch of precipitation for the month to date.

Corn planting, which usually begins before this time at the Substation, has been delayed waiting for warmer weather. If the condition of weather and soil permits, the last seeding in the date-of-seeding experiments with wheat, oats, barley, and emmer will be made tomorrow, and flax varieties probably will be seeded this week. Nursery seeding is completed with the exception of corn and proso and the date-of-seeding smut experiment.

Probably about the usual acreage of spring wheat has been sown in this district this spring. Apparently more spring plowing and less "stubbling in" than usual have been done. An increase in the use of tractors is noticeable. One type of outfit in use is a tractor drawing a 3-bottom plow and a small packer drill, plowing, packing, and seeding at one operation.

There is a prospect of an epidemic of grasshoppers in this district this summer according to Robert Shotwell, Government entomologist, who is cooperating with county agents in the Slope region of North Dakota in plans for combating the hoppers by destroying the eggs and poisoning the hoppers.

<u>Northern Great Plains Field Station, Mandan</u> (Flax Breeding, J. C. Brinsmade, Jr.) (May 17)

Continued cold weather during the first half of May has resulted in very slow growth of crops.

Freezing temperatures were recorded on eight of the 15 days. The minimum temperature was 20 degrees on May 5, and the maximum, 81 degrees on May 13. A temperature of 27 degrees was recorded for the night of May 14 and of 29 degrees for May 15.

Moisture conditions have continued satisfactory. A total precipitation of 0.81 of an inch was recorded for the first half of May. About two inches of snow covered the ground the morning of May 14. This melted slowly and nearly all of the moisture went into the ground.

Flax sown on April 21 in the date-of-seeding-and-tillage experiment was severely damaged by freezing temperatures early in May. The reduction in stand is about 50 per cent.

Flax sown on May 1 in the date-of-seeding-and-tillage experiment and the early seeding of new selections is coming up satisfactorily. Flax sown on May 7 in the classification nursery is just coming up.

Land was prepared on May 13 for the varietal and breeding nurseries.
Snow prevented seeding on May 14. In the afternoon of May 15, 540 17-foot ro
were seeded. This comprised the entire 9-row varietal nursery. High wind pr
vented further seeding May 16.

Flax sown on May 11 in the date-of-seeding-and-tillage experiment is not
yet coming up.

Northern Great Plains Field Station, Mandan (Cereal Agronomy, E. R. Ause
(May 17)

Cereal crops have been retarded in germination and g.....th by the excepti
ally low temperatures during the period May 2 to 7, inclusive. There were
freezing temperatures each night of this period with 20 degrees recorded as
the minimum. The continous freezing did some damage to wheat and oats which
had emerged previously. Light frosts occurred again on May 14 and 15.

The varietal barley plots sown on April 29 had emerged on May 10. All o
the nursery material had emerged by May 11.

There have been several days of high winds during the latter part of thi
period which have caused considerable soil blowing.

Farmers report damage to cereal crops from cut worms as well as from the
freezing temperatures. It is rather unusual for cut-worm damage to occur so
early in the spring.

MONTANA

Judith Basin Substation, Moccasin (Cereal Agronomy, B. B. Bayles) (Joe
L. Sutherland) (May 15)

The period of May 1 to 15 has been cool and backward and the precipitat
has been less than normal. The average maximum temperature for the above pe
was 55 degrees. An absolute maximum of 75 degrees was recorded on May 13, a
a minimum temperature of 20 degrees occurred during the night of the 7th.
Precipitation,--0.12 of an inch.

A strong wind on May 14 caused much soil blowing; the extent of the d
has not yet been determined.

The material seeded on the cereal project during the last two weeks inc
the spring wheat, oats, and barley nurseries, miscellaneous hybrid material
smut tests, flax variety plots, and the second date-of-seeding on the rate a
date experiment. Emergence of all grains has been very slow, 21 days being
required on the early seeded plots.

A great deal of interest has been shown in the rate-and-date-of-seeding plots of winter wheat within the last few days. This interest is due to the appearance of root rot in fields of winter wheat sown prior to September 1. Reports have been received of fields of winter wheat being plowed up and re-seeded to either flax, oats, or barley. Mr. W. L. Popham, in charge of the barberry-eradication work in Montana, visited the station on May 9 and 10. Mr. Popham was making a survey of wheat fields and reported that some fields in central Montana were infected with root rot. Plants from the plots of winter wheat sown on different dates were sent to Mr. H. E. Morris, pathologist at the Montana State College, Bozeman, for inspection in connection with this disease.

WESTERN BASIN AND COAST AREAS (North to West and South)

IDAHO

Aberdeen Substation, Aberdeen (Cereal Agronomy, L. L. Davis)

Agricultural Experiment Station, Moscow (Stripe Rust, C. W. Hungerford)

WASHINGTON

Agricultural Experiment Station, Pullman (Cereal Breeding, E. F. Gaines)

OREGON

Sherman County Branch Station, Moro (Cereal Agronomy, D. E. Stephens)

CALIFORNIA

Biggs Rice Field Station, Biggs (Rice Agronomy, J. W. Jones) (May 15)

The weather has been clear and temperatures have been sufficiently high for germination and growth of rice seedlings during the first half of May.

Station rice, grown by continuous submergence, is now emerging through the water, and apparently fairly good stands will be obtained, even though the rice was submerged considerably earlier than normal.

The varietal and nursery experiments, which are irrigated by alternate flooding and draining, have been irrigated three times and most of the rice has emerged with fairly good stands.

On many commercial fields the rice is now emerging through the water and apparently the stands will be as good as are usually obtained.

On May 4 Mr. G. A. Wiebe, in charge of the cooperative cereal experiment at Davis, visited the Station.

University Farm, Davis (Cereal Agronomy, G. A. Wiebe)

Agricultural Experiment Station, Berkeley (Cereal Smuts, F. N. Briggs)

BARBERRY ERADICATION PROGRESS

OHIO

Ohio State University, College of Agriculture, Columbus, J. W. Baringer

INDIANA

Purdue University College of Agriculture, LaFayette, W. E Leer (May 14)

Infected barberries were found on May 3 in the center of Spiceland, a town about 600 inhabitants in Henry County. About 10 per cent of the leaves on 13 large bushes were infected, while nearly 100 per cent of the leaves on several hundred seedlings showed infection. Most of the infection was in pycnial stage. However, several aecia were found discharging spores.

The science class of the Spiceland High School had an interesting field ip to the location. Dr. Millard S. Markle, Head of the Department of Biology, rlham College, came to collect rusted specimens for class use.

A barberry demonstration was placed at Purdue May 6 to 11, in connection th the annual Egg Show and Boys and Girls 4-H Club Round-Up.

MICHIGAN

Agricultural College, East Lansing, W. F. Reddy

WISCONSIN

Department of Agriculture, State Capitol Annex, Madison, R. M. Caldwell ay 13)

A very satisfactory response has been made to the educational activities the barberry-eradication campaign in Wisconsin this winter. High schools d normal schools and colleges have been very eager for materials for labory study of stem rust. At the present time, many of the rural grade schools the State are undertaking the study of rust in relation to the common barrry. Material for this study was supplied to one-third of the rural schools the State just at the time of the opening of the spring season.

Field activities were begun on a small scale on May 1, when three agents re stationed at Lake Geneva in Walworth County for resurvey in an area of caped barberries. The situation for finding bushes in dense brush is ideal this area at present and a marked contrast to the condition found there ring midsummer.

A written examination of applicants for field positions in barberry-eradication was held on May 4. A force consisting of 30 Federal and State agents will be placed in the field about June 19. Activities in second survey will be continued in Dane and Rock counties.

ILLINOIS

Box 72, Post Office Building, Urbana, R. W. Bills (May 9)

Six experienced field agents began operations in an area of escaped barberries near Sterling on May 7. This area was located by two rural school boy Lester Reecher and Carl Hackbarth, after they had learned how to identify barberry as a result of Mr. L. H. Corbin's visit to their school in December, in the interest of the National Rust Busters' Club. The two boys are the first members of the National Rust Busters' Club.

The area contains approximately 15 large bushes the largest being 20 feet in height. There also are many small bushes and hundreds of seedlings growing in a wooded pasture. Several hundred pounds of salt will be needed in the eradication of the bushes. It is hoped that one week will suffice to survey this area and eradicate the bushes.

Five more tips have been received from school children with applications for membership in the Rust Busters' Club during the past month, and three from school teachers and county agents.

Twenty additional field agents have been selected to begin work in June.

IOWA

Iowa State College, Ames, P. W. Rohrbaugh

MINNESOTA

Agricultural Experiment Station, University Farm, St. Paul, L. W. Melande

NEBRASKA

College of Agriculture, University Farm, Lincoln, A. F. Thiel (May 13)

The weather conditions in April were ideal for the germination of black spores and barberry infections. Cool, rainy weather was general. There shoul be heavy infections on the barberries if viable black spore material is available. Fifty bushes were examined last week near Louisville, Cass County, and no trace of rust could be found on any of these bushes.

Mr. H. H. Foster, who is assisting in the epidemiology studies in Nebraska and northern Kansas, found barberry infections on nine different properties last week. On two of these the infections were very heavy. On the remaining properties only a light infection was observed. The uredinial stage on grasses and grains has not been found to date. The weather conditions for May also have been favorable for the development of rust. Should these conditions continue there may be considerable rust in our cereal crops this year.

SOUTH DAKOTA

College of Agriculture, Brookings, R. O. Bulger

NORTH DAKOTA

Agricultural Extension Division, State College Station, Fargo, G. C. Mayoue

MONTANA

State College of Agriculture, Bozeman, W. L. Popham

WYOMING

College of Agriculture, University of Wyoming, Laramie, W. L. Popham

COLORADO

Agricultural College, Ft. Collins, E. A. Lungren

C E R E A L   C O U R I E R

Official Messenger of the Office of Cereal Crops and Diseases
Bureau of Plant Industry, U. S. Department of Agriculture
(NOT FOR PUBLICATION)

l. 21   No. 12

May 31, 1929
Personnel (May 21-31) and Project Issue

PERSONNEL ITEMS

Dr. J. R. Holbert, senior agronomist in charge of the cereal-disease
vestigations conducted in cooperation with Funk Bros. Seed Co., of Bloom-
gton, Ill., and the Illinois Agricultural Experiment Station, was in Wash-
gton on May 24 to confer with the Office pathologists regarding cooperative
vestigations.

Mr. C. H. Kyle, senior agronomist in corn investigations, returned on
ay 31 from Florence, S. C., where he found that the corn in the cooperative
xperiment plots had germinated well. The plants are making a satisfactory
rowth and there is a good stand. Insect damage is heavy, however. Nearly
very plant has been mutilated in some way. The early damage was done by the
ad worm or the southern corn rootworm. At the time of Mr. Kyle's visit the
reatest damage was being done by the billbug. This is working now and damage
ill continue for a few days.

Fifty plants were examined very carefully, and the larvae of the larger
orn stalk-borer were found on about 40 or 50 per cent of the plants.

The corn root aphis was present also although apparently it was doing no
reat damage.

Mr. H. H. McKinney, senior pathologist in charge of cereal-virus disease
investigations, left Washington on May 27 for a month's trip in Oregon, Wash-
agton, California, and Louisiana to investigate wheat foot rot and corn
osaic. Mr. McKinney will confer with officials of the agricultural experi-
ent stations in the States named.

Mr. T. R. Stanton, senior agronomist in charge of oat investigations, wrote from Columbus, Ga., on May 19 that he had been joined by Mr. H. C. Murphy at Experiment, Ga., where they examined the uniform crown-rust nursery. At Lovejoy, Ga., the 1,500-acre farm of the H. G. Hastings Seed Co., was visited. The large acreage of oats grown here is being harvested with a combine.

At Tifton, Ga., Messrs. Stanton and Murphy found a great deal of crown rust of oats; varieties such as Norton and Fulghum (Sel. No. 699-201 were completely destroyed. This year in south Georgia the strains of Red Rustproof appear to have been much more resistant than those of Fulghum.

VISITORS

Mr. Leon Margolin, Agricultural Economist, of Moscow, Russia, was a visitor in the Office on May 23. Mr. Margolin is interested in obtaining information on wheat breeding, as he is to be connected with the large experimental grain farm near Rostov.

Mr. Edward M. Tuttle, Editor in Chief of The Book of Rural Life, visited several of the members of the Office staff on May 22.

MANUSCRIPTS AND PUBLICATIONS

32 A brief manuscript entitled "Heterothallism in _Puccinia graminis_," by Ruth F. Allen, has been approved for publication in Phytopathology. This abstract will be presented by Dr. Allen before the meeting of the American Phytopathological Society at Berkeley, Calif., in June.)

33 A manuscript entitled "The Chemical Composition of Corn (_Zea mays_) Seedlings. Pt. I. The Isolation of Xylan and Cellulose from the Cell Walls. Pt. II. The Isolation of a Dextrin Similar to the Trihexosan Obtained by the Thermal Depolymerisation of Potato Starch," by Karl Paul Link, was approved on May 22 for publication in the Journal of the American Chemical Society.

34 A manuscript entitled "The Inheritance of Resistance to Bunt, Tilletia tritici, in White Odessa Wheat," by Fred N. Briggs, was submitted on May 24 for publication in the Journal of Agricultural Research.

Galley proof of Technical Bulletin 121, "Methods of Harvesting Grain Sorghums," by Martin, Reynoldson, Rothgeb, and Hurst, was read on May 23.

Galley proof of Farmers' Bulletin 1599 entitled "Scab of Wheat and Barley and Its Control," by J. G. Dickson and E. B. Mains, was read on May 25.

Page proof of Farmers' Bulletin 1583 entitled "Spring-Sown Red Oats," by T. R. Stanton and F. A. Coffman, was read on May 31.

WESTERN BRANCH OF THE AMERICAN SOCIETY OF AGRONOMY

The following letter has been received from Mr. H. W. Hulbert, Secretary of the Western Branch of the American Society of Agronomy, regarding the meeting to be held in July:

The final dates for the meeting of the Western Branch of the American Society of Agronomy to be held at Pullman, Washington, and Moscow, Idaho, have been set for July 15 to 17, inclusive.

The meetings will start on Monday, July 15, at 9:30 a.m. at the State College of Washington at Pullman. On Tuesday, after a short morning meeting, a visitation will be made of the Washington Experiment Station. This will be followed by a trip to Moscow later in the day where the work of the Idaho Station will be gone over. Tuesday afternoon a picnic has been planned at which the election of officers and such other business as may need to come up before the society can be transacted. The final day, July 17, will be held at Moscow and will consist of the regular program of papers.

It is hoped at this time that all the men who plan on presenting papers may signify their intentions at the very earliest opportunity. I would like very much to have the titles of all papers, together with the approximate length of time necessary for their presentation, sent me so that at least a tentative program can be outlined within the next two or three weeks. These papers may be along any line of agronomic investigation or results of investigations along related lines.

I believe that short papers are desirable. At the meetings of this branch of the society which I have attended, as well as those of the National Society of Agronomists, I find that it is the general consensus of opinion that lengthy papers, presenting in detail results of the methods of investigations, are less desirable from the average agronomist's standpoint. I believe that a short presentation of an investigation, followed by a comprehensive discussion will furnish us the most interesting program.

I hope to hear from you at your very earliest convenience in regard to any papers you may wish to present and assure you that both the State College of Washington and the University of Idaho are planning on making this three-day meeting an enjoyable and profitable one.

ANNOUNCEMENT

The following memorandum from Mr. H. E. Allanson, Assistant Chief of the Bureau of Plant Industry, to Dr. Ball may be of interest to some of the members of the field staff of this Office:

May 24, 1929

"As you probably know, Dr. Pennington, head of the Department of Pathology in the Syracuse University, recently died. I do not know just what salary this position carries, but probably a fairly good one. A friend of mine in Syracuse writes me that the University is interested in considering applicants for this vacancy. He has suggested that perhaps we have some individuals on our staff that we would be glad to see considered. It may be that there are men in your Office that in fairness to them should have the matter called to their attention so that they might, if they wish to do so, file an application with Syracuse University. Applications should be addressed to Dean F. F. Moon, Syracuse University, Syracuse, New York."

C E R E A L   C O U R I E R

Official Messenger of the Office of Cereal Crops and Diseases
Bureau of Plant Industry, U. S. Department of Agriculture
(NOT FOR PUBLICATION)

Vol. 21   No. 13

June 10, 1929
Personnel (June 1-10) and Field Station (May 16-31) Issue

PERSONNEL ITEMS

Mrs. Margaret P. Hazel, junior clerk-stenographer for Dr. A. M. Brunson
and Dr. J. H. Parker in the cooperative cereal experiments at Manhattan, Kans.,
resigned her position on June 7. The vacancy has been filled by the appointment of Miss Genevieve A. Johnson, effective June 3.

Miss Laura L. Huffine was appointed, effective June 3, as agent in the
Office of the State Leader of barberry eradication in Montana, with headquarters at Bozeman. Miss Huffine will take the place of Miss Marguerite
Marquis, who resigned on May 31, and will act as secretary-stenographer to
the State Leader.

Dr. H. B. Humphrey, principal pathologist in charge of cereal-rust investigations, left Washington on June 8 for Winnipeg, Canada, to attend the
meetings of the Canadian Society of Technical Agriculturists from June 11
to 14. Dr. Humphrey, who has been invited by the Canadian Society of Technical Agriculturists to attend these meetings at their expense, will give
two addresses entitled "Cereal Pests in Relation to Changes in Crop Practice," and "The Cereal Rusts and Their Control."

Dr. E. B. Mains, of La Fayette, Ind., came to Washington on June 5 to
confer with members of the Office staff and to take notes on leaf rust of
cereals at the Arlington Experiment Farm. Dr. Mains, who is agent in the
cooperative investigations conducted in cooperation with Purdue University
Agricultural Experiment Station, left on June 10 for Swannanoa, N. C., to
meet Dr. C. E. Leighty, principal agronomist in charge of eastern wheat
investigations. Together they will examine wheat fields and take notes on
the occurrence of leaf rust.

Mr. John L. Richardson, agent in charge of barberry-eradication field
publicity, with headquarters at Minneapolis, left Washington on June 5 to
return to his headquarters.

Mr. J. W. Taylor, associate agronomist in eastern wheat investigation
left Washington on June 6 for Blacksburg, Va., and Frederick, Md., to insp
fields of barley and wheat and to confer with officials of the State exper
ment stations. He will be gone about six days.

VISITORS

Dr. G. H. Cunningham, Director of the Imperial Plant Research Station
Palmerston North, New Zealand, was an Office visitor on June 10.

Dr. Germain Verplancke, Assistant Plant Pathologist of Belgium, Gemb
Belgium, conferred with members of the Office staff on June 10.

MANUSCRIPTS AND PUBLICATIONS

35 A manuscript entitled "Bacterial Streak Disease of Sorghums," by
Charlotte Elliott, was submitted on June 1 for publication in the Journal
f Agricultural Research.

Page proof of Farmers' Bulletin 1581 entitled "Oats in the North-
Central States," by T. R. Stanton and F. A. Coffman, was read on June 5.

Page proof of Farmers' Bulletin 1585 entitled "Varieties of Hard Red
Winter Wheat," by J. Allen Clark and Karl S. Quisenberry, was read on June 5.

The article entitled "Smuts and Rusts Produced in Cereals by Hypodermic
Injection of Inoculum," by Marion Griffiths Zehner and Harry B. Humphrey,
appears in the Journal of Agricultural Research 38 (11): 623-627, fig. 1.
June 1, 1929.

The Plant Rusts (Uridinales) by Joseph C. Arthur, Professor Emeritus of
Botany, Purdue University, and six collaborators, will be offered by the pub-
lishers, John Wiley and Sons, Inc., New York City, about July 1. The final
proof reading was done the latter part of May. The six collaborators in this
volume on the history, physiology, and taxonomy of the rusts are: F. D. Kern,
F. D. Fromme, E. B. Mains, C. R. Orton, H. S. Jackson, and G. R. Bisby. The
Office of Cereal Crops and Diseases gave valuable assistance in the preparation of the manuscript.

RECENT DECISION OF THE COMPTROLLER GENERAL

(A-26319)
8 Comptroller General 484
TRANSPORTATION--LAND-GRANT DEDUCTIONS--EXPRESS--SHIPMENTS

Under the reorganization plan of express service pursuant to which the Railway Express Agency, Inc., was organized to perform express service as an agency of participating railroads beginning March 1, 1929, charges for express services by such agency are subject to land-grant deductions the same as if the service by such agency were performed by the participating railroads subject to land-grant laws.

Note: No express charges should be paid in cash. Take Form 1034 voucher and submit to the Washington Office for direct settlement from the General Accounting Office. Use Government bills of lading to make all express shipments.

FIELD STATION CONDITION AND PROGRESS
HUMID ATLANTIC COAST AREA (South to North)

GEORGIA

State College of Agriculture, Athens (Cereal Agronomy, R. R. Childs)

VIRGINIA

Arlington Experiment Farm, Rosslyn (Small Grain Agronomy, J. W. Taylor)

Arlington Experiment Farm, Rosslyn (Corn Breeding, F. D. Richey)

Arlington Experiment Farm, Rosslyn (Cereal Smuts, V. F. Tapke, Acting in Charge)

Arlington Experiment Farm, Rosslyn (Virus Diseases, H. H. McKinney)

NEW YORK

Cornell University Agricultural Experiment Station, Ithaca (Cereal Breeding, H. H. Love)

HUMID MISSISSIPPI VALLEY AREA (South to North)

LOUISIANA

Rice Experiment Station, Crowley (Rice Agronomy, J. M. Jenkins)

Agricultural Experiment Station, Baton Rouge (Corn Breeding, H. F. Stoneberg)

TENNESSEE

Agricultural Experiment Station, Knoxville (Corn Breeding, L. S. Mayer) (June 1)

The interminable rains this season delayed planting somewhat, but all the experimental plots, including the selfed lines and crosses, were planted May 24. All but one of the regional test fields also have been planted. In May there was more than double the normal rainfall.

MISSOURI

Agricultural Experiment Station, Columbia (Cereal Agronomy, L. J. Stadler)

OHIO

Agricultural Experiment Station, Wooster (Corn Investigations, M. T. Meyers) (June 4)

The weather the past three weeks has been very favorable for corn plan ing in Ohio. The cooperative corn-breeding and agronomic experiments in th corn-borer area at Bono have gone in on schedule, with the exception of one small planting for May 10 which had to be dropped on account of the flooded condition of the area at that time. The first plantings were made May 22 and continued through until May 28, as the ground could be fitted. Some of the plants from the first plantings were appearing by June 1 and with the good condition of the soil the prospect looks bright for all the experiments at that place.

Planting at Columbus was completed several days ago and the plots are receiving their first cultivation.

Planting at Wooster is considerably delayed. The first plantings were made there about May 27 and much remained yet to be done after June 1.

IOWA

Agricultural Experiment Station, Ames (Oat Breeding, L. C. Burnett) (June 4)

Winter wheat is now starting to head. Probably the greater portion of the varieties in the nursery will be noted first head before the end of the week. Some of the barley varieties of the March 30 sowing will be in head also. Those sown two weeks later seem still to be nearly two weeks behind. I expect to make an inspection trip to the Mason City field within the next day or two. It is possible that there the behavior may not be as at Ames.

Agricultural Experiment Station, Ames (Corn Breeding, M. T. Jenkins)

Agricultural Experiment Station, Ames (Crown Rust of Oats, S. M. Diet

ILLINOIS

Funk Bros. Seed Co., Bloomington (Corn Root, Stalk and Ear Rots, J. F Holbert)

INDIANA

Purdue University Agricultural Experiment Station, LaFayette (Corn Ro and Metallic Poisoning, J. F. Trost, Acting in Charge)

Purdue University Agricultural Experiment Station, LaFayette (Leaf R E. B. Mains)

WISCONSIN

Agricultural Experiment Station, Madison (Wheat Scab, J. G. Dickson)

MINNESOTA

Agricultural Experiment Station, University Farm, St. Paul (Wheat Breeding, K. S. Quisenberry, Acting in Charge)

Agricultural Experiment Station, University Farm, St. Paul (Stem Rust, E. C. Stakman)

Agricultural Experiment Station, University Farm, St. Paul (Flax Rust, H. A. Rodenhiser)

GREAT PLAINS AREA (South to North)

OKLAHOMA

Woodward Field Station, Woodward (Grain Sorghum and Broomcorn, J. B. Sieglinger) (June 1)

The weather is cool and moist for this region. Wheat is headed. The prospects are good for an average yield on a slightly increased acreage. On May 31, Mr. C. O. Johnston of Manhattan, Kans., visited the Station and took notes on his uniform leaf rust nursery. Leaf rust was found on nearly all strains of wheat; only two showed any stem-rust infection.

The plots in the early date-of-seeding experiment with grain sorghums and broomcorn were seeded on May 24 and had emerged to good stands on May 31.

Maximum temperature for last half of May, 89 degrees on the 27th; minimum for same period, 47 degrees on the 19th. Precipitation for last half of May, 2.02 inches. Total for May, 3.41 inches.

KANSAS

Agricultural Experiment Station, Manhattan (Cereal Breeding, J.H.Parker)

Agricultural Experiment Station, Manhattan (Corn Breeding, A.M.Brunson)

Agricultural Experiment Station, Manhattan (Wheat Foot Rots, Hurley Fellows)

Agricultural Experiment Station, Manhattan (Wheat Leaf Rust, C. O. Johnston)

Fort Hays Branch Experiment Station, Hays (Cereal Agronomy, A. F. Swanson) (May 31)

The rainfall for May was slightly above normal and sufficiently well distributed to cause favorable growing conditions for all small-grain crops. At present wheat prospects are excellent wherever good tillage methods have been used in preparing the seed bed. Barley has done outstandingly well which can, perhaps, be attributed to a cool spring. On the other hand, oats have not responded so favorably as in other years.

The second seeding in the date-of-seeding experiment with sorghums has been completed. Excellent stands were secured on the first date of planting.

The Bankers' State Convention was held at Hays the week of May 20. About 1,500 visitors were present. The bankers were taken over the station and experimental fields from time to time during the session of the convention.

Preparation is being made to receive visitors who may attend the Corn-Belt Section of the American Society of Agronomy on Friday, June 14, at the Ft. Hays Branch Experiment Station. This should be an excellent year to study the agriculture of western Kansas under normal conditions, as well as the trend of the wheat-growing industry in the Great Plains region.

NEBRASKA

North Platte Substation, North Platte (Cereal Agronomy, G. F. Sprague)

SOUTH DAKOTA

U. S. Forage-Crop Field Experiments, Redfield (Wheat Breeding, E. S. McFadden)

NORTH DAKOTA

Agricultural Experiment Station, State College Station, Fargo (Flax Diseases, L. W. Boyle)

Dickinson Substation, Dickinson (Cereal Agronomy, R. W. Smith) (June 1)

Following a prolonged period of deficient rainfall, a wet spell set in about a week ago bringing numerous showers that have greatly improved the crop prospects. The total precipitation for the month of May was about 3.44 inches, which is an inch above the normal rainfall for the month.

Most of this rain fell during the past week. The heaviest rain was recorded on the 26th, when, following the downpour, the surface runoff caused a few itches to appear in the fields. Aside from this one rain there has been ractically no loss of rain from runoff.

The temperatures were below normal in May except for a hot spell following the 20th. The last killing frost occurred on May 20, with a minimum temerature of 24 degrees.

The seeding of cereal crops at the Substation is completed, except proso arieties in plots and date-of-seeding experiments.

As a whole the cereal crops are in excellent condition since the rain out somewhat below the usual height at the beginning of summer.

The cereal plots and nursery rows have been trimmed and the roads and alleys cultivated.

<u>Northern Great Plains Field Station, Mandan</u> (Flax Breeding, J. C. Brinsde, Jr.) (June 4)

Growth of crops has been slow during the last half of May on account of continued cool weather, but steady because of favorable moisture conditions.

Rains and frequent light showers have somewhat interfered with field operations. The rainfall for the last half of May was 1.87 inches. The total rainfall to date for the first five months of the year was 7.01 inches, which is about one and three-quarters inches more than the average for this period for the past 15 years.

Flax sown May 11 in the date-of-seeding-and-tillage experiment was up May 22 with a good stand. Flax sown May 20 emerged May 29. The fifth seeding was made May 31.

Seeding of the flax-breeding nursery was completed May 25. All flax seeded up to that date has emerged with satisfactory stands.

Weed growth was delayed on account of continued cold weather. Weeds are now very much in evidence.

The flax triplicated varietal plots were sown June 1. Many weeds were destroyed by disking just before seeding so that the plots should be comparatively clean this year.

Maximum temperature for the last half of May, 80 degrees May 24; minimum, 28 degrees May 19.

Northern Great Plains Field Station, Mandan (Cereal Agronomy, E. R.
Ausemus)

MONTANA

Judith Basin Substation, Moccasin (Cereal Agronomy, B. B. Bayles) (J
L. Sutherland) (June 1)

The temperatures continued warm from May 15 to 24. This period was
followed by a heavy rain of 1.61 inches on May 26 and 27. Although this
rain did not bring the total precipitation for the month up to average, fi
moisture conditions are excellent at present.

Work on the cereal project has been confined to the seeding of the re
mainder of the plots in the rate-and-date-of-seeding experiment and the tr
ming of plots and nursery rows.

Winter wheat seedings on the station have made a very favorable growt
and the prospects for this crop are excellent. Growth of spring grains ha
been retarded by cool, dry weather and dust storms, but with the present
moisture conditions these crops should improve rapidly.

A group of approximately 80 farmers from Judith Basin and Fergus coun
met at the station on May 24 to discuss the yellowing of early sown winter
wheat. After inspection of the winter-wheat plots sown on different dates
and with several types of drills, a general meeting was held in which Mr.
E. Morris, pathologist at the Montana State College, explained the differe
points in connection with this disease. Others present at the above meeti
were County Agents C. R. Mountjoy and Dan B. Noble.

An inspection of winter-wheat fields in the Judith Basin on May 25
indicated that fields seeded before September 1 were showing varying degre
of yellowing. It is very evident that the earliness of seeding has brougl
about this condition. The present moisture supply and growing weather ma;
serve to check the further development of this disease.

Montana Agricultural Experiment Station, Bozeman (LeRoy Powers) (Ma

Some injury from winterkilling has occurred in the winter wheat of t
Spring Hill community of Gallatin County. There are indications that dis
may have caused part of the injury. Very little winter injury occurred i
the winter wheat on the experiment station. Karmont and Montana 36 showe
some winterkilling in the plots, whereas Newturk came through with a 100
cent survival.

The early part of the week was cool and windy and there was no preci
tation. Seeding has progressed rapidly. All of the agronomic experiment
material has been planted. At present, moisture conditions are favorable
for maximum growth. However, if the warm weather continues without rain
newly seeded legumes and grasses will be injured.

(June 1)

The showers of the past week were favorable to the germination and emergence of the legumes and grass seedings which give promise of producing good stands. All crops made rapid growth during the past week.

Irrigation of winter wheat which had been delayed by rains was completed. The work of trimming the plots also was finished.

Owing to the favorable weather conditions since the early part of May, farmers have practically finished seeding small-grain crops.

Fourteen Russian agricultural delegates visited the station during the week and conferred with the head of the department concerning wheat production on a big scale.

WESTERN BASIN AND COAST AREAS (North to West and South)

IDAHO

Aberdeen Substation, Aberdeen (Cereal Agronomy, L. L. Davis) (May 27)

The spring at Aberdeen has been later than usual and unfavorable for spring seeding. The average minimum temperature for April was 30.4 degrees. The lowest was 19 degrees on April 10. Rain or snow was recorded on 15 days in April. Eight and one-half inches of snow fell on the 8th and 9th. The total rainfall for April was 1.78 inches as compared to an average of 0.91 of an inch for the last 17 years.

The month of May has been more favorable for spring work and plant growth. To date the average minimum temperature has been 35 degrees. One-half of an inch of rainfall has been recorded up to May 27.

The seeding of cereal plots was begun on April 15 and finished on the 17th. Nursery seeding was started April 18, and all the regular nursery seeding was finished by May 1. About 2,000 5-foot rows of oats were seeded in the first week of May. There has been an abundance of moisture and excellent stands have been obtained. To date no irrigation has been necessary.

Agricultural Experiment Station, Moscow (Stripe Rust, C. W. Hungerford)

WASHINGTON

Agricultural Experiment Station, Pullman (Cereal Breeding, E. F. Gaines)

OREGON

Sherman County Branch Station, Moro (Cereal Agronomy, D. E. Stephens)
(May 28)

Crop prospects in the Columbia Basin are daily growing worse because.
of continued dry weather. In many localities winter wheat is burning badly
and probably will be a total failure if the drought continues for 10 days or
two weeks longer. On the Station we shall have the nearest to a crop failure
that we have ever had. Turkey wheat on the tillage plots is badly in need of
moisture and it has not yet started to head. Soil-moisture determinations
indicate that the moisture in the soil is about down to the wilting point for
wheat. Spring grains are not suffering so much as the winter grains because
they are not quite so far advanced.

Spring grain has been injured severely by wireworms. In the field plots,
stands were thick enough so that yields probably will not be affected, but in
the nursery fully 25 per cent of the rows of spring grain show severe injury;
in most of these every plant has been killed by wireworms.

Fall-sown Federation wheat is heading. The early spring barley varieties
also have started to head.

The total precipitation for May was 0.31 of an inch, which was recorded
on five dates, 0.16 being the most received during any 24-hour period. The
total precipitation for the four months, February to May, inclusive, was only
1.57 inches.

The highest temperature recorded in the month of May was 86 degrees on
the 26th, and the lowest, 36 degrees on the 10th.

CALIFORNIA

Biggs Rice Field Station, Biggs (Rice Agronomy, J. W. Jones) (June 1)

Rice has emerged with fairly good stands, in the nursery and varietal
experiments at the station. In the fertilizer and depth-of-submergence
experiments, grown by continuous submergence, the rice is now nearly all
erect, and the stands range from fair to good.

The weather in May was reasonably favorable for the germination and
growth of rice. The maximum temperature was 96 degrees on May 21, the minimum, 42 degrees on May 5. The average maximum temperature for the month was
85.9 degrees, the average minimum, 49.8 degrees. The mean was 66.7 degrees.
The total evaporation was 7.021 inches. The highest average wind velocity
for a 24-hour period was 11.53 miles per hour.

On May 16, a group of merchants and bankers from nearby cities, who were being conducted about the county by the extension department, stopped at the station long enough for me to explain the work which is being conducted.

On the same day, Mr. Takashi Ishizuka, agriculturist in charge, for the Government General of Korea, with headquarters at Seoul, visited the station. Prof. E. J. Stirniman and Mr. M. R. Hurberty, of the University Farm, Davis, visited the Station on May 29.

University Farm, Davis (Cereal Agronomy, G. A. Wiebe)

Agricultural Experiment Station, Berkeley (Cereal Smuts, F. N. Briggs)

BARBERRY ERADICATION PROGRESS

OHIO

Ohio State University, College of Agriculture, Columbus, J. W. Baringer
(May 31)

The membership of the Ohio Grain Dealers' Association and the Ohio Millers' Association and a large list of leading farmers throughout the State were provided in May with information on the progress of the barberry-eradication campaign. The material mailed to them consisted of rust-loss posters, Farmers' Bulletins, and multigraphed summaries of the work in Ohio for 1928.

The selection of a crew of field men for the summer has been almost completed. One man has been working since May 1 on a labor basis on the proposition of bringing under control an outbreak of escaped barberries near Sullivan, Ashland County. The bushes in question were reported by a student of vocational agriculture in the Sullivan High School after the subject of common barberry and rust relationship had been studied in class. A second man will be added to the force on June 1 and three more will be placed in the field about the middle of June. On July 1 we expect our field force to number 30.

Pycnia on barberries were recorded on April 7 this year at Dayton. The first aecia reported for the State this year were found on May 6 near Dayton by Mr. B. B. Beck. It was noted that aecia did not form at all beneath many of the pycnia which appeared earliest at Dayton. Aecia developed relatively slow after the first appearance of pycnia. The weather of the latter part of April did not seem to be favorable for development of rust on barberries, but conditions have been more favorable in May. Rust was found on barberries near Sullivan, Ashland County, on May 10 (pycnia); near Auburn Corners, Geauga County, on May 10 (pycnia); near Hartsgrove, Ashtabula County, on May 10 (pycnia); near Rootstown, Portage County, on May 11 (pycnia); near Amherst, Lorain County, on May 14 (pycnia); near Toledo, Lucas County, on May 15 (aecia); near Sullivan, Ashland County, on May 20 (aecia); near Berlin Heights, Erie County, on May 23 (aecia); near Sherwood, Defiance County, on May 24 (aecia); near Lewisburg, Preble County, on May 24 (aecia); near Sidney, Shelby County, on May 24 (aecia); near Burton, Geauga County, on May 28 (aecia); and near Rootstown, Portage County, on May 28 (aecia). Collections of aecial material noted above have been sent to the University of Minnesota for physiologic-form determination.

Scores of wheat and rye fields in central, western, and northern Ohio were examined in May to obtain data on the probability of overwintering of urediniospores of Puccinia graminis and to observe the time of the first appearance of stem rust and leaf rust on grain. The overwintering evidence is negative. No new uredinia of stem rust have been found on grain or wild grasses in Ohio so far this spring.

Prospects for an excellent crop of wheat in Ohio this year are exceptionally bright. Weather conditions this spring have been ideal for profuse vegetative growth of small cereals. Some of the wheat is in the boot. Rye is blooming and oats is doing well.

INDIANA

Purdue University College of Agriculture, LaFayette, W. E. Leer (May 21)

That an effective barberry-educational campaign in the schools pays, is shown strikingly by two cases in Indiana.

Iris Graves, a pupil in the seventh grade at the Freedom (Indiana) school, last fall studied the characteristics of and the damage caused by barberry under the direction of her teacher, Clarence McBride. She told Mr. McBride that she thought that a barberry bush was growing in the orchard of her home. Mr. McBride sent some of the boys from the agriculture class to look for it, but they failed to find it. Then Iris brought in a branch of the suspected bush, which Mr. McBride identified as barberry and reported to the proper authorities. Later he took his agriculture class to the location as a class exercise, and the boys located many escaped bushes in the ravine below the orchard.

Another example is the work done by Helen Hawkins, an 8-year old pupil in the third grade of the Ellettsville (Indiana) school. Her teacher in agriculture, Mr. H. C. Weathers, had taught the barberry story in class. This pupil thought, from the description given in school, that some bushes which her parents had in the garden were barberries. She took a sample to Mr. Weathers, who identified it and reported it to the proper authorities.

Dr. D. M. Mottier, head of the department of botany at Indiana University, the State Leader, and two field agents examined these bushes on May 16 and found them infected with stem rust. The bushes near Freedom were only lightly infected, but the bushes near Ellettsville were literally plastered with rust. The immediate destruction of these bushes undoubtedly saved a large field of wheat only a few rods away from ruin by stem rust.

A barberry-eradication Service Medal from The Conference for the Prevention of Grain Rust has been recommended for each of these girls who have rendered a distinctive and valuable service to the campaign.

(May 31)

The following letter is an example of one of the many opportunities to carry on educational work through organizations other than schools:

"The lantern slides on barberry eradication were received a few days ago. I found them so much more complete in the information which they giv than I had expected, that I brought them to the attention of our local Izaac Walton League at our meeting that same evening. They were very much interested, and are anxious to use these slides at our next meeting which will be the first Tuesday evening of June, providing it will be possible t keep them until that time. You undoubtedly realize that the rural folks feel that this League is one interested only in hunting and thus tearing down the farmers' fences. Our local Chapter is attempting to branch out i as many fields as possible in which good may be done for the entire community, and the plan is to have this meeting at night and advertize same as widely as possible - bringing as many of the farmers in for it as will be possible. I feel that it will be much worth while in this community, and will possibly assist you as much in your program as any other thing which might be done in the community.

"I might add that our local president has written to the National hea quarters, telling them of our plan for the next meeting, and in this way i may be brought before other Waltonians in the National magazine published the organization."

(Signed) Liegh B. Freed
High School Instructor, North Man-
chester, Ind.

An attempt will be made this summer to work out a State educational p gram in cooperation with the Izaac Walton League of Indiana, which will be real value to both the League and the barberry-eradication campaign.

MICHIGAN

Agricultural College, East Lansing, W. F. Reddy

WISCONSIN

Department of Agriculture, State Capitol Annex, Madison, R. M. Caldw

ILLINOIS

Box 72, Post Office Building, Urbana, R. W. Bills

IOWA

Iowa State College, Ames, P. W. Rohrbaugh

188

MINNESOTA

Agricultural Experiment Station, University Farm, St. Paul, L.W.Melander

NEBRASKA

College of Agriculture, University Farm, Lincoln, A. F. Thiel

SOUTH DAKOTA

College of Agriculture, Brookings, R. O. Bulger (June 4)

The first infection on barberries in South Dakota this spring was found
n May 15 in the town of Scotland, Bon Homme County. One bush showed rather
eneral pycnial infection, and the aecia were just beginning to develop.
is is 13 days later than the earliest date on which the first infection has
ver been reported in this State; however, it is about an average date for
he past few years.

Aecial infection was general by May 31 as far north as Milbank, Grant
ounty. In fact, on this date the cluster cups were well developed and under
favorable weather conditions would have been dispersing spores in a few more
iays. Barberries in Deuel County showed heavy aecial infection on this date.
In general, seedlings are heavily infected this spring.

Uredinia of orange leaf rust can be found in spring-wheat fields as far
north as Grant County. Undoubtedly orange leaf rust is general over all of
?astern South Dakota. One report of red crown rust was received, but as no
specimen was included, a positive identification could not be made.

While only three field men are on the force at the present time, a total
of 49 bushes, and 136 seedlings has been found on four properties so far this
spring. One of these plantings was reported by a freshman in high school
after listening to a talk by Geo. M. Frandsen of this office. Mr. Frandsen
spoke before her biology class and before the general assembly of the high
school. Another planting was reported by a high school instructor, and two
plantings were reported by county agents.

The personnel for the present field season has been selected, and the
entire force of 19 men will be placed in the field on June 14.

NORTH DAKOTA

Agricultural Extension Division, State College Station, Fargo, G. C.
layoue (May 31)

The school for prospective field agents in barberry eradication continued through the month, meeting twice each week. Special instructions and lectures will be given to all appointees in the first week of June. They will meet in conference here at the College on June 29 for final instructions before going to their field stations. In addition to the regular schooling, these men have made several field trips. Twenty-one Federal appointments and two State appointments will have been made by July 1.

At present plans are being made for educational and publicity work in June and the first quarter of the next fiscal year. Demonstrations are being prepared for several county fairs to be held in June.

The North Dakota Retail Merchants' Association has requested a demonstration for its annual convention to be held in Bismarck June 9 to 12 and a demonstration is being prepared. The State Leader will attend the convention.

All members of the Retail Merchants' Association have been circularized with educational materials. The county agents have been provided with the latest available publicity material, including the summary of the 1928 annual report. This report also has been sent to State and College officials.

Illustrated lectures were given this month in several rural and town schools. An educational survey-information sheet has been completed by students of the country and town grades and high schools.

MONTANA

State College of Agriculture, Bozeman, W. L. Popham [June 4]

In May, Science teachers in all first, second, and third class high schools in Montana were furnished with material for a lesson on barberry-eradication and stem-rust control. The packages sent these instructors contained a teacher's guide for presenting the subject, Black Stem Rust Control, bulletins for reference material, a supplementary pamphlet, rusted straw and prepared slides for a laboratory exercise. Return cards for the use of pupils and teachers in reporting barberry locations also were included.

Actual field operations in barberry eradication began in Montana on June 3. At that time field agents Bartsch and Twilde were appointed and started survey in Flathead County. It is expected that by June 20 the entire crew will be in the field.

WYOMING

College of Agriculture, University of Wyoming, Laramie, W. L. Popham

COLORADO

Agricultural College, Ft. Collins, E. A. Lungren   (June 3)

During the month of May resurvey was conducted in Larimer and Weld counties in the areas where escaped barberries were found growing during the survey of 1927 and 1928. Five additional small barberries were found on this resurvey along the Poudre River in Larimer County. One was found near Greeley in Weld County. Pycnial infection was found on May 31 but no aecia were found.

Wheat is about two weeks later than usual, and no stem rust had appeared up to June 1.

Two men started second survey on June 1, and another will start June 7.

C E R E A L   C O U R I E R

Official Messenger of the Office of Cereal Crops and Diseases
Bureau of Plant Industry, U. S. Department of Agriculture
(NOT FOR PUBLICATION)

Vol. 21   No. 14
June 20, 1929
Personnel (June 11-20) and Field Station (June 1-15) Issue

PERSONNEL ITEMS

Mr. Burton B. Bayles, of Moccasin, Mont., who has been on leave without
pay since October 1, 1928, to engage in graduate study at the University of
Wisconsin, has completed the courses undertaken and has resumed his duties
as assistant agronomist in charge of the cooperative cereal-agronomy experiments at the Judith Basin Branch Station. Mr. Joe L. Sutherland has taken care
of the experiments during the period of Mr. Bayles' absence.

Mr. C. E. Chambliss, associate agronomist in charge of rice investigations, will leave on June 24 for Elsberry, Mo., to inspect the cooperative
rice field station at that place.

Mr. J. Allen Clark, senior agronomist in charge of western wheat investigations, left on June 20 for points in Illinois, Wisconsin, Minnesota, and
North Dakota, in the interests of wheat investigations.

Mr. F. A. Coffman, associate agronomist in oat investigations, will leave
on June 22 for Manhattan, Kans., to assist Dr. J. H. Parker and Mr. H. C.
Murphy, of Ames, Iowa, in harvesting cooperative crown-rust and other nurseries
at Manhattan.

Dr. Charlotte Elliott, associate pathologist, will leave Washington on
June 22 for Ames, Iowa, to make field studies of oat blast.

Dr. H. B. Humphrey, principal pathologist in cereal-rust investigations,
will leave Washington on June 27 for La Fayette, Ind., to make field studies
of cereal rusts.

Mr. Lynn D. Hutton will leave on June 21 for Blacksburg, Va., and adjace localities to study plants of Berberis canadensis that have escaped from cult vation, inspect rust locations in the vicinity of the barberry bushes, and tc establish similar locations for further observations. Mr. Hutton, who is pat ologist in charge of barberry eradication, also will make similar rust observ tions in Maryland, Pennsylvania, and New York. He will be accompanied throug out the trip by Dr. E. C. Stakman, of University Farm, St. Paul, Minn.

Mr. C. H. Kyle, senior agronomist in corn investigations, left Washingtc on June 15 for Tifton, Ga., to take notes on the condition of the cooperative experimental corn plots and to hand-pollinate corn.

Dr. C. E. Leighty, principal agronomist in charge of eastern wheat inves gations, returned to Washington on June 14 after an absence of six weeks in t interests of wheat investigations.

Mr. R. W. Leukel left Washington on June 15 for Manhattan, Kans., and No Platte and Lincoln, Nebr., to take notes on the occurrence of stinking smut o wheat and stripe disease of barley in the cooperative seed-treatment experime plots. Mr. Leukel also will collect diseased seed for future experiments.

The appointment of Mr. Marion T. Meyers, agent in corn-breeding investig tions cooperative with the Ohio Agricultural Experiment Station and the Ohio State University, was terminated on June 19.

Mr. M. N. Pope will leave Washington on June 23 for Columbus, Ohio, and Urbana, Ill., to make studies in the cooperative barley nurseries in these places. Mr. Pope is associate agronomist in barley investigations.

Mr. F. D. Richey, senior agronomist in charge of corn investigations, wi leave Washington on June 23 for Boston, Mass., to visit Bussey Institution, Harvard University, for conferences with officials in regard to certain maize problems.

Mr. T. R. Stanton, senior agronomist in charge of oat investigations, wr from Stillwater, Okla., on June 5 that he and Messrs. Murphy and Quisenberry made interesting visits at the Denton (Texas) Substation, at the U. S. Field S tion, Lawton, Okla., and at the Oklahoma Agricultural Experiment Station at Stillwater. At the latter place two days were spent in studying the varietie and strains of oats in the crown-rust and other nurseries. The spring-sown material was still a little green.

VISITORS

Mr. B. G. Lehman, representing John T. Lewis and Bros. Co., of Philadelphia, Pa., manufacturers of linseed oil and white lead, was an Office isitor on June 20.

Dr. T. K. Wolfe, formerly of the Virginia Agricultural Experiment Station, now editor of The Southern Planter, published in Richmond, Va., was n Office visitor on June 14.

MANUSCRIPTS AND PUBLICATIONS

37 A manuscript entitled "The Relation of Cereal Pests to Changes in Crop Practice," by H. B. Humphrey, was approved on June 11 for publication in Scientific Agriculture. [Canada] ·

38 A manuscript entitled "The Cereal Rusts and Their Control," by H. B. Humphrey, was approved on June 11 for publication in Scientific Agriculture. [Canada]

39 A manuscript entitled "Earliness in F_1 Barley Hybrids," by H. V. Har and Mary L. Martini, was approved on June 14 for publication in the Journal o: Heredity.

40 A manuscript entitled "Hygroscopic Moisture of Flaxseed and Wheat and Its Relation to Combine Harvesting," by A. C. Dillman, was approved on Ju 17. for publication in the Journal of the American Society of Agronomy.

41 A manuscript entitled "Varieties of Hard Red Spring Wheat," by J. All Clark, was submitted on June 18 for publication in the Farmers' Bulletin seri This manuscript is a revision of Farmers' Bulletin 1281.

42 A manuscript entitled "Factors Which Modify the Resistance of Wheat to Bunt, Tilletia tritici," by Fred N. Briggs, was approved on June 18 for pul lication in Hilgardia, official journal of the California Agricultural Experi ment Station.

43 A manuscript entitled "Synthetic Nutrient Solutions for Culturing Ustilago zeae," by Emery R. Ranker, was submitted on June 19 for publication in the Journal of Agricultural Research.

44 A manuscript entitled "A Mosaic of Wheat Transmissible to All Cereal Species in the Tribe Hordeae," by H. H. McKinney, was submitted on June 20 fo publication in the Journal of Agricultural Research.

Galley proof of Tech. Bul. 133 entitled "Flax Cropping in Mixture with Wheat, Oats, and Barley," by A. C. Arny, T. E. Stoa, Clyde McKee, and A. C. Dillman, was read on June 19.

Galley proof of Tech. Bul. 131 entitled "Spacing and Date-of-Seeding Experiments with Grain Sorghums," by John H. Martin and John B. Sieglinger et was read on June 19.

Technical Bulletin 120 entitled "Relation of Husk Covering to Smut of C Ears," by C. H. Kyle, was received from the Government Printing Office on J 12, bearing date of May, 1929.

Department Bulletin 1498 entitled "Distribution of the Classes and Var of Wheat in the United States," by J. Allen Clark, John H. Martin, Karl S. berry, John R. Hooker, C. E. Leighty, and Chester N. Dubois, was received fr the Government Printing Office on June 20, bearing date of May, 1929.

FIELD STATION CONDITION AND PROGRESS

HUMID ATLANTIC COAST AREA (South to North)

GEORGIA

State College of Agriculture, Athens (Cereal Agronomy, R. R. Childs)

VIRGINIA

Arlington Experiment Farm, Rosslyn (Small Grain Agronomy, J. W. Taylor)

Arlington Experiment Farm, Rosslyn (Corn Breeding, F. D. Richey)

Arlington Experiment Farm, Rosslyn (Cereal Smuts, V. F. Tapke, Acting in rge)

Arlington Experiment Farm, Rosslyn (Virus Diseases, H. H. McKinney)

NEW YORK

Cornell University Agricultural Experiment Station, Ithaca (Cereal Breeding, H. Love)

HUMID MISSISSIPPI VALLEY AREA (South to North)

LOUISIANA

Rice Experiment Station, Crowley (Rice Agronomy, J. M. Jenkins)

Agricultural Experiment Station, Baton Rouge (Corn Breeding, H.F.Stoneberg)

TENNESSEE

Agricultural Experiment Station, Knoxville (Corn Breeding, L. S. Mayer)

MISSOURI

Agricultural Experiment Station, Columbia (Cereal Agronomy, L. J. Stadler)

IOWA

Agricultural Experiment Station, Ames (Oat Breeding, L. C. Burnett)

Agricultural Experiment Station, Ames (Corn Breeding, M. T. Jenkins)

Agricultural Experiment Station, Ames (Crown Rust of Oats, S. M. Dietz)

ILLINOIS

Funk Bros. Seed Co., Bloomington (Corn Root, Stalk and Ear Rots, J.R.Hol

INDIANA

Purdue University Agricultural Experiment Station, LaFayette (Corn Rots
and Metallic Poisoning, J. F. Trost, Acting in Charge)

Purdue University Agricultural Experiment Station, LaFayette (Leaf Rusts
E. B. Mains)

WISCONSIN

Agricultural Experiment Station, Madison (Wheat Scab, J. G. Dickson)

MINNESOTA

Agricultural Experiment Station, University Farm, St. Paul (Wheat Breedi
K. S. Quisenberry, Acting in Charge)

Agricultural Experiment Station, University Farm, St. Paul (Stem Rust,
E. C. Stakman)

Agricultural Experiment Station, University Farm, St. Paul (Flax Rust,
H. A. Rodenhiser)

GREAT PLAINS AREA (South to North)

OKLAHOMA

Woodward Field Station, Woodward (Grain Sorghum and Broomcorn, J. B.
Sieglinger)

KANSAS

Agricultural Experiment Station, Manhattan (Cereal Breeding, J. H. Parker)
(June 8)

Rains have been frequent and heavy at Manhattan for the past two weeks.
Wheats in the nursery are badly lodged, and some very interesting differences
in lodging are to be observed in the variety plots at the Agronomy Farm. We
have taken one set of lodging notes in the nursery and must take another.
Prof. Throckmorton has had to call off Agronomy Field Day which was to have
been held today.

Leaf rust is abundant in our nursery and in the variety plots at the farm.
Mr. Johnston is cooperating with us in obtaining what I think will be a very
interesting set of notes.

The average estimate of the Kansas wheat crop for this year, as made by
a group of eight grain dealers and millers on their annual trip through the
Kansas wheat belt early in June, is 173,592,000 bushels.

Agricultural Experiment Station, Manhattan (Corn Breeding, A. M. Brunson)

Agricultural Experiment Station, Manhattan (Wheat Foot Rots, Hurley Fellows)

Agricultural Experiment Station, Manhattan (Wheat Leaf Rust, C. O. Johnston)
(June 17)

Dr. J. H. Parker and I have just returned from a visit to our nurseries
at Columbus, Kans. As far as leaf rust is concerned the trip was very disappointing. Wheat is very short and poor in that part of the State and most of
the leaves have already dried up. There is only a very small infection of leaf
rust in that section. I found a moderate amount of stem rust in several fields
in southeastern Kansas. The crop is nearly mature, however; in fact, we saw
many fields already in the shock. Therefore, there is no possibility of stem
rust doing any material damage there this year. There is plenty of inoculum
for a northward spread, however, and the wind has been blowing steadily from
the south for the past three days.

I have just received a letter from Dr. Peltier stating that he has found
stem rust as far north as Lincoln, Nebr. Wheat is still green in Nebraska and
it seems that there will be a moderate infection of rust in northern Kansas
and adjacent parts of Nebraska.

I expect to visit nurseries at Hays and at Lincoln the latter part of this
week.

Mr. Leukel will be here tomorrow. Mr. Quisenberry was here last week and
secured a fine set of notes on the uniform bunt nursery. I think Mr. Leukel
also will be able to secure valuable notes.

I have already reported to you the seriousness of leaf-blotch in the southern Great Plains. I made further observations in southeastern Kansas and find it very severe there also. I was able to secure a set of readings on varieties in the field plots here in Manhattan. Some interesting differences in susceptibility were found.

<u>Fort Hays Branch Experiment Station, Hays</u> (Cereal Agronomy, A. F. Swanson (June 15)

The last half of the meeting of the Corn-Belt Section of the American Society of Agronomy was held at Hays on June 14. The meeting opened at Manhattan on June 12 and continued until noon on June 13. On the afternoon of that day the visitors drove to Hays. They were invited to inspect the experiments on the Dry-Land Agriculture project which include methods of moisture conservation and seed-bed preparation and rotation and fertilizer studies. Later the visitors were taken over the Cereal project to note the varietal and nursery experiments and cultural methods. On the Forage project discussion centered largely on the re-establishment of alfalfa on old fields that had been abandoned.

In the afternoon of June 14 there was a demonstration of large power units and their application to the agriculture of western Kansas. Much interest was manifested in a small combine assembled at the Station for harvesting grain from experiment plots and successfully operated for two seasons.

On Saturday following the Agronomy meeting 200 farmers and wheat growers from 28 counties in Kansas came to the Station to study experiments in the growing of winter wheat.

Only 0.82 inch of rainfall has been recorded for the first 15 days of June. The season of wheat-ripening weather is at hand, and unless delayed by rain, harvest will be under way in a week. It is safe to predict that more than an average crop of small grains will be harvested in the Hays district. The prospects are favorable for a good crop in most of the wheat-growing sections of the State.

The best stands of sorghum ever produced on the Cereal project were made possible this year through an improvement in handling the seed bed. Most of this stand has been thinned to a desirable spacing distance between plants.

The following employees of the Office of Cereal Crops and Diseases were among those who came to Hays to attend the meeting of the Corn-Belt Section of the American Society of Agronomy:

Kansas: Dr. A. M. Brunson, Dr. Hurley Fellows, Mr. A. F. Swanson.

Iowa: Mr. A. A. Bryan, Prof. L. C. Burnett, Dr. M. T. Jenkins.

Oklahoma: Mr. J. B. Sieglinger.

Washington, D. C.: Mr. K. S. Quisenberry, Mr. T. R. Stanton.

NEBRASKA

North Platte Substation, North Platte (Cereal Agronomy, G. F. Sprague)

SOUTH DAKOTA

U. S. Forage-Crop Field Experiments, Redfield (Wheat Breeding, E. S.
dden)

NORTH DAKOTA

Agricultural Experiment Station, State College Station, Fargo (Flax
ases, L. W. Boyle) (May 22)

The weather during the first half of May has been comparatively cool and
re has been less than normal precipitation during this period. However, the
l is not so deficient in moisture as last season, in May, and the majority
the flax has germinated well but is slow in emergence apparently on account
the cool weather. This tardiness apparently has allowed the flax to avoid
ury by the frosts which have occurred in this vicinity lately.

(June 17)

The rainfall in the district immediately about Fargo has been especially
icient since the first of May and higher temperatures of late have caused
e heat canker to develop in nursery plantings of flax. Soil temperatures
ing the past ten days have been very favorable for the development of flax
t.

Dickinson Substation, Dickinson (Cereal Agronomy, R. W. Smith) (June 15)

Abundant rainfall and changeable temperatures have characterized the weather
the first half of June. It has rained on an average about every other day,
. a total of 2.86 inches has fallen since the beginning of the month. The nor-
. rainfall for the month is about 3.14 inches. The total precipitation for
9 since the first of January is about 4 inches above normal. This should more
in offset the extremely dry weather of last fall.

. The extreme western part of the State has received more rain, including a
/ violent downpours that flooded low areas and interfered with travel by wash-
; out grades on both railway and auto roads.

A recent trip to Fargo revealed the fact that, contrary to the usual condi-
n, the eastern part of the State was suffering from drought while the western
rt had an abundance of rain and too much in local areas. The drought in the
stern part probably is relieved by rain falling within the past few days.

Crops are in a very flourishing condition in this part of the State. Rains have stimulated the late seeding of flax. A small quantity is still being seeded although it is rather late for the crop to grow to maturity before time for killing frosts.

The Substation was recently visited by Dr. H. L. Walster, Dean of Agriculture at the State Agricultural College, and Mr. J. C. Russell, County Agent at Beach, N. Dak.

Mr. Robert Shotwell, Government entomologist, is making his headquarters at the Dickinson Substation while investigating the probability of injury fro grasshoppers and other insect pests in this area.

Northern Great Plains Field Station, Mandan (Flax Breeding, J. C. Brinsmade, Jr.) (June 17)

Growth of crops has been rapid as a result of high temperatures and favorable moisture conditions during the first half of June. The max mum temperatu for this period was 86 degrees on June 14; minimum 35 degrees on June 11; precipitation 0.72 of an inch, most of which fell on June 10 and 11.

Flax sown May 31 in the date-of-seeding-and-tillage experiment was up Jun 8. The final seeding was made June 10 and the plants are coming up today. Th flax varietal plots sown June 1 emerged June 10 with good stands.

Weeds are very abundant especially in plots sown May 11 and May 20. Weed. are unusually bad in grain fields around Mandan. Many fields are uniformly yellow with wild mustard.

Canker is very bad in the flax plots sown May 20. In the plot sown at the low rate of 16 pounds to the acre about 50 per cent of the plants are noticeabl girdled and about half of the girdled plants are broken off completely. Some canker is evident in plots sown May 10 and May 31 and in the varietal plots sov June 1, and more serious damage is probable if the present hot, dry, windy weather continues. Prompt cultivation has so far prevented serious damage fror canker in the flax nurseries.

First blooms appeared today in flax plots sown April 20 and in three rows in the classification nursery.

Fifteen flax varieties were sown June 10 in triplicated triple 24-foot rov for the purpose of studying the loss of bolls and seed from flax left standing during the fall and winter. The plants emerged today with good stands.

Leaf rust was found on wheat by Mr. Ausemus about a week ago, but it is still very scarce. No stem rust has been noted to date.

Mr. Ausemus left this morning on a trip to St. Paul and expected to be gor about a week.

Mr. Ralph W. Smith and his son Glenn, of Dickinson, visited the Station or June 12 while returning by auto from Fargo where the latter had just been graduated from the Agricultural College.

Northern Great Plains Field Station, Mandan (Cereal Agronomy, E. R. Ausemus)

MONTANA

Judith Basin Branch Station, Moccasin (Cereal Agronomy, B. B. Bayles)
e L. Sutherland) (June 16)

A heavy rain on June 1 and showers during the period from June 1 to 15 have
ntained a very favorable moisture condition in the fields of the Judith Basin.
total precipitation for the 15-day period was 1.07 inches. The maximum
perature was 81 degrees on June 9, while a low temperature of 34 degrees was
orded on the 4th.

Excellent growing conditions for the greater part of the two weeks have
sed all grain crops to make a very rapid growth. The yellowing, which was
y evident in fields of winter wheat a month ago, has been materially checked.
earlier fields of winter wheat in the Judith Basin are heading out and prom-
e to return good yields.

Mr. B. B. Bayles returned to the station on June 15 from Madison, Wis.,
ere he has been engaged in graduate study. He resumed his duties as assist-
agronomist in charge of the cooperative cereal agronomy experiments.

Mr. Oliver Lammers, student in agriculture at the Montana State College,
rived at the Station on June 16. Mr. Lammers will assist on the Cereal
oject during the summer months.

WESTERN BASIN AND COAST AREAS (North to West and South)

IDAHO

Aberdeen Substation, Aberdeen (Cereal Agronomy, L. L. Davis)

Agricultural Experiment Station, Moscow (Stripe Rust, C. W. Hungerford)

WASHINGTON

Agricultural Experiment Station, Pullman (Cereal Breeding, E. F. Gaines)
une 12)

Hybridizing is just beginning and smut counts can begin in about two weeks.
are five inches short on moisture and prospects for a normal crop are not
vorable at present. Wheat on some of the clay points will not even head out
less we get rain very soon.

OREGON

Sherman County Branch Station, Moro (Cereal Agronomy, D. E. Stephens)

CALIFORNIA

Biggs Rice Field Station, Biggs (Rice Agronomy, J. W. Jones)

University Farm, Davis (Cereal Agronomy, G. A. Wiebe)

Agricultural Experiment Station, Berkeley (Cereal Smuts, F. N. Briggs)

BARBERRY ERADICATION PROGRESS

OHIO

Ohio State University, College of Agriculture, Columbus, J. W. Baringer

INDIANA

Purdue University College of Agriculture, LaFayette, W. E. Leer (June 15)

The entire barberry field force of 13 men will be in the field June 17.
y will be engaged in the intensive second survey of Tipton, Hamilton, and
tgomery counties.

An occasional pustule of stem rust could be found on June 12, in nearly
ry field of wheat in the southern half of the State. An examination of a
ld of wheat near infected barberries in Monroe County showed   considerable
m rust in a very small area nearest the bushes. A few pustules of the rust
eady had passed into the telial stage, indicating that the rust had started
re some time ago.

In the fields of wheat examined during the past week, nearly 100 per cent
the plants were infected with leaf rust. In some fields the severity was
least 70 per cent, and in many fields it ran as high as 50 per cent. Leaf
st is bound to cause considerable damage in Indiana this year.

MICHIGAN

Agricultural College, East Lansing, W. F. Reddy

WISCONSIN

Department of Agriculture, State Capitol Annex, Madison, R. M. Caldwell

ILLINOIS

Box 72, Post Office Building, Urbana, R. W. Bills

IOWA

Iowa State College, Ames, P. W. Rohrbaugh

MINNESOTA

Agricultural Experiment Station, University Farm, St. Paul, L. W. Melander

NEBRASKA

College of Agriculture, University Farm, Lincoln, A. F. Thiel (June 15)

Eighteen field men started barberry eradication June 10. They stayed at Lincoln for a day and a half to take part in the barberry conference. Professor W. H. Brokaw gave a very interesting talk on "The Responsibility of Federal Employees to the Citizens of the State." Professor Brokaw emphasized the importance of being loyal to the institutions which they represent and their job. Dr. G. L. Peltier gave a lecture on the physiologic forms of stem rust and instructed the men in the identification of rust and the collection of specimens.

The systematic survey for common barberries was begun in Cuming and York counties. It was started in these counties last fall and is to be completed in the month of June. As soon as these counties are completed, Hall and Kearney counties will be surveyed.

A scattering of stem rust is general in the two southern tiers of counties. Rust still is very scarce and considerable time must be spent before a pustule is discovered. Leaf rust of wheat has developed quite rapidly during the past week. No epidemic of either leaf or stem rust is anticipated this year.

SOUTH DAKOTA

College of Agriculture, Brookings, R. O. Bulger

NORTH DAKOTA

Agricultural Extension Division, State College Station, Fargo, G. C. Mayoue

MONTANA

State College of Agriculture, Bozeman, W. L. Popham

WYOMING

College of Agriculture, University of Wyoming, Laramie, W. L. Popham

COLORADO

Agricultural College, Ft. Collins, E. A. Lungren

C E R E A L   C O U R I E R

Official Messenger of the Office of Cereal Crops and Diseases,
Bureau of Plant Industry, U. S Department of Agriculture
(NOT FOR PUBLICATION).

. 21   .No. 15

June 30, 1929
Personnel (June 21-30) and Project Issue

PERSONNEL ITEMS

Mr. C. E. Chambliss, associate agronomist in charge of rice investiga-
ons returned on June 29 from Elsberry, Mo.

Dr. Allan D. Dickson, agent in the cooperative cereal-disease experi-
nts conducted at Madison, Wis., who has been in Washington since February
gaged in physiological studies of cereals under the direction of Dr. A.
Hurd-Karrer, left on June 28 for Madison to resume his work on the chem-
cal phases of the barley scab problem.

Mr. A. C. Dillman, associate agronomist in charge of flax investigations,
eft Washington on June 30 for southeastern Kansas to visit flax-producing
ounties and to consult with officials of the Kansas Agricultural Experiment
tation at Manhattan. In July Mr. Dillman will study flax-classification nur-
eries at St. Paul, Minn., Mandan, N. Dak., and Bozeman, Mont.

Dr. Harold H. Flor, of St. Paul, Minn., has been appointed agent, effec-
ive July 1, to have charge of research on various phases of stinking smuts
f wheat to be conducted in cooperation with the Washington Agricultural Ex-
eriment Station at Pullman, Wash.

Dr. H. V. Harlan, principal agronomist in charge of barley investigations,
rote from Aberdeen, Idaho, on June 24, as follows: "We commenced to work on
ur genetic material the afternoon we arrived and there is much work to be
one. Dir. P. V. Cardon, of the Utah station, and Dir. William Peterson, of
e Extension Division, met us at the North Rim of the Grand Canyon and Direc-
or Cardon returned with us all the way to Logan. Climatic zones are crowded
own in southwestern Utah. I can't get over the surprise of hearing them say
i Hurricane: 'No, our strawberries are all gone in this section, but you
in get them in Toquerville.' Five or six miles, and apparently no change of
.titude. We visited the Branch Agricultural School at Cedar City and the
ections where the high altitude stations of Panguitch and Widtsoe are located.
here is not much doing in cereals south of the Levan ridge, the route we fol-
owed.

"While our work at Shaw's ranch in Idaho has been on a very small scale, I am still wedded to it as a high altitude spot. It has irrigation to eliminate features other than cold and a certainty of unfavorable conditions that I have not seen elsewhere."

Dr. A. G. Johnson, principal pathologist in charge of cereal-disease investigations, left Washington June 28 for Manhattan, Kans., to confer with Department and State experiment station officials regarding cooperative cereal-disease investigations.

Mr. H. H. McKinney, senior pathologist in charge of cereal-virus-disease investigations, returned on June 23 after a four weeks' trip in the Pacific Northwest and in Louisiana.

Some time was spent in the Columbia River Basin of Oregon and Washington studying a rosette disease in wheat which is associated with footrot. In general appearance this malady is indistinguishable from the mosaic-rosette present in wheat in Illinois and Indiana. However, no mosaic mottling was found associated with the footrot-rosette. Further study is necessary to determine the cause of this footrot-rosette. A specific virus may be the cause. However, it is possible that rosettes of the type under discussion may be due to fungi or even to nonparasitic factors.

In Louisiana, Mr. McKinney and Mr. Hugo Stoneberg, assistant agronomist in corn investigations, recorded data on about 50 selections of corn in connection with joint studies started in 1928 on types of mosaic symptoms and chlorophyll deficiency. This year the amount of mosaic infection on corn was unusually small in the vicinity of mosaic-diseased sugar cane on the bottom lands. There was one doubtful case of mosaic in the plots located on the uplands some distance from sugar cane. The reduced amount of disease in corn may be due to delayed activity of the insect vectors brought about by the late season.

It is too early to predict the outcome of these studies, but the evidence obtained this year indicates that several foliage characters may influence mosaic symptoms considerably. It appears also that these types are of a genetic nature. Some of the types of chlorophyll deficiency in selfed lines are indistinguishable from certain patterns of mosaic and other virus diseases of corn.

It is evident that an understanding of the virus diseases of corn depends to a large extent upon developing lines of corn that are genetically pure for characters affecting the mosaic symptoms. Some of the lines show unusually high susceptibility and others seem to show considerable resistance to mosaic.

Mr. M. N. Pope, associate agronomist in barley investigations, returned on June 28 from Columbus, Ohio, and Urbana, Ill., where he made studies of the cooperative barley nurseries. At both places the barley was in good condition.

Dr. E. R. Ranker, associate physiologist in corn-smut investigations, returned to Washington on June 24 after an absence of nine months in Chicago, where he had temporary headquarters at the University of Chicago while conducting research on his problem. Dr. Ranker consulted with specialists in the physiology of disease resistance of cereal plants, particularly corn, and carried on research in the laboratories of the University of Chicago, Northwestern University, and the University of Illinois.

Dr. E. C. Stakman, agent in the cooperative cereal-disease investigations conducted at University Farm, St. Paul, Minn., arrived in Washington on June 21 and left on the same day with Mr. L. D. Hutton, pathologist in charge of barberry eradication, for Blacksburg, Va., and adjacent localities to study the spread of stem rust from known locations of barberries and to compare forms of rust with those existing in the barberry area. Dr. Stakman returned to Washington en route to St. Paul to consult with Department officials regarding the studies made.

Mr. T. R. Stanton, senior agronomist in charge of oat investigations, returned to Washington on June 22 after an extended trip through the southern and southwestern States in the interest of oat investigations. Various experiments with oats were noted at experiment stations in North Carolina, South Carolina, Georgia, Alabama, Mississippi, Louisiana, Texas, Oklahoma, Kansas, Missouri, Tennessee, and Virginia. As about two-thirds of the trip was made by automobile, many fields of oats were inspected along the way.

In the cooperative experiments at the Coastal Plains Experiment Station, Tifton, some interesting notes were taken on the relative resistance of oats to crown rust. Norton, and Fulghum selection, C. I. No. 699-2011, in field plots at Tifton were virtually destroyed by crown rust. Ordinary Fulghum was badly infected. It probably will produce yields of only 25 bushels to the acre, or even less. Strains of Red Rustproof, on the other hand, showed high resistance and probably will produce yields of 50 to 60 bushels to the acre.

Several days were spent at A. and M. College, Miss., in assisting Dr. L. E. Miles in the selection of the most promising lines that are being grown in head rows, and in recording notes on the varieties in the cooperative uniform crown-rust nursery.

A study was made of the varieties in the cooperative crown-rust nurseries at Denton, Tex., Stillwater, Okla., and Manhattan, Kans., a few days being spent at each place.

Mr. Stanton attended the meetings of the Corn-Belt Section of the American Society of Agronomy. These meetings were held on June 12 and 13 at Manhattan and on June 14 at Hays. Both meetings were very interesting and profitable. There was an excellent representation of Corn-Belt agronomists and they were much interested in the extensive agronomic experiments. The results obtained in the various experiments were ably explained by members of the agronomic staff. The Kansas agronomists at both Manhattan and Hays, including President Farrell, Dean Call, and Superintendent Aicher, are to be congratulated on organizing and conducting such interesting and successful meetings. The excellent cooperative attitude and esprit de corps among members of the agronomic staff were commented on by several visiting agronomists.

One of the most interesting features of the program was the demonstration at Hays of wheat growing by use of large-scale machinery such as the two-bottom lister, the two-row ridge buster, the one-way disk or wheat-land plow, the combine, etc. The use of these machines has reduced the cost of wheat production in the Great Plains to a point where eastern farmers can no longer compete in growing the crop.

Dr. T. A. Kiesselbach, of the Nebraska Agricultural Station, invited the Corn-Belt agronomists to meet next year at Lincoln.

Mr. Stanton returned eastward from Kansas through Missouri, Tennessee, and Virginia. Oats at Columbia, Mo., were still very green, and there was no indication of crown rust. Specimens of crown rust were collected at Knoxville and Jackson, Tenn., and at Blacksburg, Va., and mailed to Mr. H. C. Murphy, Ames, Iowa. Some study also was made of the relative behavior of the same varieties of oats grown from both fall and spring seeding in the cooperative uniform crown-rust nursery at Knoxville, Tenn.

Ph. D. Degrees

The following employees of the Office were granted the Ph. D. degree from the University of Minnesota on June 17:

> Ralph U. Cotter, University Farm, St. Paul.
> H. H. Flor, Washington Agricultural Experiment Station, Pullman.
> Miss Helen Hart, University Farm, St. Paul.
> Paul D. Peterson, Arlington Experiment Farm, Rosslyn, Va.

M. N. Pope was granted the Ph. D. degree by the University of Maryland on June 11.

R. M. Caldwell was granted the Ph. D. degree in botany and plant pathology by the University of Wisconsin on June 24.

VISITORS

Countess Nandine Bombelles, Opeka-Vinica, via Varasdin, Jugo-Slavia, was an Office visitor on June 27. Countess Bombelles farms in her own country and is desirous of informing herself regarding the methods pursued in the United States Department of Agriculture.

Dir. P. V. Cardon, of the Utah Agricultural Experiment Station, was
n Office caller on June 21.

Prof. G. R. Hyslop, head of the department of farm crops, Oregon State
gricultural College and Agricultural Experiment Station, was an Office
isitor on June 27.

Dr. Eikichi Iso, assistant professor of the Taihoku Imperial University,
ormosa, Japan, was an Office visitor on June 26. Dr. Iso is the author of
eport No. 37 of the Department of Agriculture, Government Research Institute,
ormosa, Japan, entitled "Researches on the Formosan Rice Plants, with Special
eference to the Plant Breeding and Culture," a copy of which has been pre-
ented to this Office with the compliments of Dr. Kintaro Oshima, Director
f the Government Research Institute. This volume of 315 pages, published
n December, 1925, is entirely in Japanese, with the exception of an English
itle page.

Miss Anna M. Lute, seed analyst in charge of Seed Laboratory, Agricul-
ural College, Fort Collins, Colo., and Mrs. R. W. Cottle, of the Federal
eed Laboratory, Sacramento, Calif., conferred with T. R. Stanton on June
2 regarding the identification and germination of fatuoids and Avena fatua.

Prof. Tomosuke Nakashima, professor of plant pathology, Suigen Agricul-
ural College, Chosen, Japan, was an Office visitor on June 22.

Dr. Earl G. Sieveking, plant breeder associated with the Funk Bros.
eed Co., of Bloomington, Ill., called at the Office on June 22.

Dr. M. M. Wolf, formerly agronomist of the Kharkov Experimental Station,
ow the head of the Agricultural State Plan Commission in Moscow, consulted
ith Dr. Ball and others on June 26. Dr. Wolf, who has been visiting special-
sts in the Department of Agriculture for several days, expects to travel
ver the United States with some associates for two and one-half months, be-
inning July 1, to study large-scale methods of production of cereals, vege-
ables, and orchard crops, as well as rotation and tillage systems.

210

MANUSCRIPTS AND PUBLICATIONS

45 A manuscript entitled "Harvesting Flax with the Combine," by A. C. Dillman, has been approved for publication in the Department Yearbook of 1929.

46 A manuscript entitled "The Effect of a Seed Disinfectant on Grain and Straw Yields and Smut Control in Winter Barley," by J. W. Taylor and Marion Griffiths Zehner, was approved on June 27 for publication in the Journal of the American Society of Agronomy.

Galley proof of article entitled "The Influence of the Combine on Agronomic Practices and Research," by John H. Martin, for publication in the Journal of the American Society of Agronomy, was read on June 25.

The following nine articles written by members of the scientific staff of the Office appear in the U. S. Department of Agriculture Yearbook for 1928:

Flax Resistant to Wilt Developed at Experiment Stations, by A.C.Dillman.

Corn Breeding for Resistance to Cold Yields Good Results, by J. R. Holbert and W. L. Burlison.

Rust Epidemics of Local Areas Betray Barberries' Presence, by L.D.Hutton.

Seed-Borne Diseases of Cereals Succumb to Dust Fungicides, by R.W.Leukel.

Sorgo Known as Atlas Yields Well and Resists Lodging, by John H. Parker.

Broomcorn Harvesting at the Milk Stage Produces Best Brush, by J. B. Sieglinger.

Oat Varieties that Resist Smut Grown by Experimentation, by T. R. Stanton, F. A. Coffman, and V. F. Tapke.

Winter-Wheat Seeding Date in Great Plains Varies with Locality, by A. F. Swanson.

Corn Plants Dying Early May Reveal Potash Lack in Soil, by John F. Trost.

A brief letter entitled "The Synthetic Formation of Avena sterilis," by V. H. Florell, appears in the Journal of Heredity 20 (5): 227. May, 1929.

C E R E A L   C O U R I E R

Official Messenger of the Office of Cereal Crops and Diseases
Bureau of Plant Industry, U. S. Department of Agriculture
(NOT FOR PUBLICATION)

. 21   No. 16

July 10, 1929
Personnel (July 1-10) and Field Station (June 16-30) Issue

PERSONNEL ITEMS

Mr. E. R. Ausemus, assistant agronomist in charge of the cooperative
1all-grain investigations at the Northern Great Plains Field Station, Mandan,
Dak., since August 1, 1925, has been transferred to St. Paul, Minn., to
1ccéed Mr. K. S. Quisenberry, who has been temporarily in charge of the co-
)erative wheat-breeding experiments at the University Farm since the resigna-
.on of Dr. Olaf S. Aamodt on June 15, 1928. Mr. Ausemus was authorized to
:company Mr. J. Allen Clark, senior agronomist in charge cf western wheat in-
:stigations, to Winnipeg, Canada, early in July to consult experiment station
ficials about wheat breeding investigations.

Mr. Rayburn H. Bamberg was appointed agent, effective July 1, to have
1arge of the cereal pathology garden at the University Farm, St. Paul, Minn.
:. Bamberg was granted the M. S. degree from the University of Minnesota in
1ne.

Mr. J. Allen Clark, senior agronomist in charge of western wheat investi-
1tions, who left Washington on June 20 for an extensive trip in the interests
' his project, proceeded from Fargo, N. Dak., on July 1 in a Government-owned
1tomobile to inspect cooperative varietal and wheat breeding experiments at
5 cooperating stations in the spring-wheat States of Minnesota, North Dakota,
)uth Dakota, Montana, and Wyoming, and Canada. Mr. Clark also will confer
.th officials of agricultural experiment stations and with geneticists and
1eat breeders.

Mr. F. A. Coffman, associate agronomist in oat investigations, who went to Manhattan, Kans., on June 22 to make studies in and assist in the harvest of the cooperative crown-rust nurseries, left there on July 1 to visit agricultural experiment stations in Colorado and Nebraska. He will inspect cooperative oat experiments, consult with State and Federal officials located at or near agricultural experiment stations, and collect plant material for later study. Mr. Coffman also will go to Ames, Iowa, and to points in Ohio, Indiana, Michigan, and Illinois. He will return to Washington in September.

Mr. A. C. Dillman, associate agronomist in charge of flax investigations, wrote from St. Paul, Minn., on July 6 that in the flax-producing counties of southeastern Kansas farmers had been prevented by much wet weather from seeding as large an acreage as had been planned. The fields seen were in fairly good condition, however. Stands were almost uniformly too thin. It would seem that more satisfactory yields might be obtained by better seed-bed preparation and a somewhat heavier rate of seeding. At Manhattan, Mr. Dillman consulted with President Farrell and with Professors Throckmorton, Salmon, Laude, and others. Wheat is not doing so well as expected some time ago, especially in eastern Kansas. There has been too much rain. After making some studies in the flax plots and the nursery at University Farm, St. Paul, Mr. Dillman expected to go to Mandan, N. Dak., where the flax nursery was reported by Mr. Brinsmade to be in full bloom the first week in July.

Dr. Charlotte Elliott, associate pathologist, who has been making field studies of oat blast in the cooperative nursery at Ames, Iowa, expected to leave early in July for Manhattan, Kans., to make similar studies. Later Dr. Elliott will go to Aberdeen, Idaho, and Edmonton, Canada, in continuation of her work with oat blast. In the fall she will study bacterial diseases of so ghums in Texas.

Mr. V. C. Hubbard, agent in the cooperative cereal experiments at Manhat tan, Kans., since February 1, was transferred to Mandan, N. Dak., on July 1. He will succeed Mr. E. R. Ausemus in the conduct of the cereal-agronomy inves tigations that are being conducted at the Northern Great Plains Field Station Mr. Hubbard's title was changed on July 1 to Junior Agronomist.

Dr. H. B. Humphrey, principal pathologist in charge of cereal-rust inves tigations, who left Washington on June 21 for LaFayette, Ind., to make field studies of cereal rusts, went on July 1 to points in Minnesota to make simila studies. Dr. Humphrey also will go to North Dakota, South Dakota, Montana, Idaho, Washington, Oregon, and California, to continue his field studies and to confer with members of the field staff and officials of the agricultural experiment stations in the States named. Before returning to Washington abou the 10th of August, his itinerary will include Ames, Iowa, and Manhattan, Kan

Dr. A. G. Johnson, principal pathologist in charge of cereal-disease investigations, who left Washington on June 28 for Manhattan, Kans., went from the latter place to Bloomington, Ill., to consult with Dr. J. R. Holbert, of the Funk Bros. Seed Co. On July 7, Dr. Johnson expected to be at Madison, Wis., to confer with Dr. J. G. Dickson at the Wisconsin Agricultural Experiment Station, and on July 10 and 11 at LaFayette, Ind., to confer with Mr. J. F. Frost. Dr. Johnson will return to Washington on July 13.

Louis R. Jorgenson, agent in the corn-breeding investigations cooperative with the Ohio Agricultural Experiment Station and the Ohio State University, was granted the Ph. D. degree by the University of Minnesota on June 17.

Mr. R. W. Leukel, who left Washington on June 15 to make studies on the occurrence of stinking smut of wheat and stripe disease of barley in Kansas and Nebraska will make similar studies in Wisconsin, South Dakota, Minnesota, North Dakota, and Montana in July and the first part of August.

Mr. M. A. McCall, principal agronomist in charge of cereal-agronomy experiments, left Washington on July 4 for LaFayette, Ind., to inspect cooperative cereal experiments and to confer with Office and State station personnel. He also will go to Bloomington, Ill., and Madison, Wis. At the latter place he will remain until about August 15 to undertake research in wheat morphology in the laboratories of the University of Wisconsin.

Prof. Leo E. Melchers, of Manhattan, Kans., who went to Egypt in September, 1927, to make an agricultural survey for the Egyptian Ministry of Agriculture, has returned to the Kansas Agricultural College as head of the department of botany and plant pathology. He has been reappointed as agent in the cooperative investigations, beginning July 1. The appointment of Mr. Francis L. Smith, who acted as agent in Prof. Melchers' absence, was terminated on June 30.

Miss Marjorie M. Melching was appointed agent, effective July 1, to assist in the Office of the State Leader of barberry eradication at Fort Collins, Colo. She succeeds Miss Anne E. Kimball, whose resignation became effective on April 6.

Dr. John H. Parker wrote from Manhattan, Kans., on June 24 that a very severe wind and rain storm on the 17th had caused almost complete lodging of wheat, oats, and barley at the Station. It seemed possible, however, to get interesting notes on crown-rust infection of oats because a general epidemic had appeared in the rod-row plots as well as in the crown-rust nursery.

A large number of the strains included in the oat nursery this year are altogether too late to be of any value in Kansas and are very susceptible to crown rust as well. It therefore will be possible to discard a large number of lines.

On June 15, Dr. Parker and Mr. C. O. Johnston spent the entire day in the soft-red-winter-wheat breeding nursery at Columbus. The following day they visited three of the other experimental fields in southeastern Kansas at Parsons, Moran, and Fort Scott.

On June 19, Dr. Parker was at Hays with Mr. Swanson studying and taking notes on wheat, oat, and barley experiments, particularly the latter. Vaughn barley appears to be especially promising because of its earliness, stiff straw, and well-filled, solid heads.

At Manhattan a number of the early wheats in the nursery have been harvested, and in the next few days the wheat and barley harvest will be in full swing. Most varieties of oats still are green and probably will not be cut until the week of July 1.

Prof. S. C. Salmon has obtained interesting notes on stiffness of straw in his varietal plots on the Agronomy Farm. Plots of Kanred wheat were lodged from 80 to 90 per cent, while several of the new wheats--Oro, Kanred x Marquis, and Kanred x Hard Federation crosses, were down only five to 10 per cent.

Dr. M. N. Pope, associate agronomist in barley investigations, will leave Washington on July 12 for Ottawa, Canada, where he will study the barley nursery at the Central Experimental Farm. After spending three days there he will go to Ithaca, N. Y., Madison, Wis., St. Paul, Minn., and Brookings, S. Dak., to make studies in the barley nurseries at these places. In August, Dr. Pope will make combine-harvester studies in North Dakota and Minnesota.

Mr. Glenn S. Smith, of Dickinson, N. Dak., was appointed junior agronomist in charge of cooperative wheat experiments at the Langdon Substation, Langdon, N. Dak. Mr. Smith arrived at the Substation on June 30 and found everything in good condition. Rain was needed, however.

Mr. Marion A. Smith, former State Leader of barberry eradication in Iowa, was married on June 6 to Miss Josephine Busey, of Bloomington, Ill. Mr. and Mrs. Smith will be at home at 705 Arlington Court, Champaign, Ill.

Mr. T. R. Stanton, senior agronomist in charge of oat investigations, left Washington on July 8 en route to Morgantown, West Va., where he will make rust collections from the uniform crown-rust nursery which is being grown at that place. From Morgantown Mr. Stanton will proceed westward to LaFayette, Ind., Urbana, Ill., and Ames, Iowa. About one week will be spent at Ames in assisting in the harvest of the large cooperative oat nursery being grown at that station. From Ames he will proceed westward, making stops in Minnesota, the Dakotas, and Montana, reaching Aberdeen, Idaho, about August 1. There about three weeks will be spent in studying and recording data on oat varieties and hybrids. Returning eastward Mr. Stanton will make stops in Wyoming, Colorado, and Nebraska, reaching Washington about September 1.

Mr. Roy A. Weaver was appointed agent, effective July 1, to assist in the corn-disease investigations that are being conducted in cooperation with Purdue University Agricultural Experiment Station at LaFayette, Ind.

MANUSCRIPTS AND PUBLICATIONS

47 A manuscript entitled "Oats: The Fulghum Variety Winning Its Way,"
by T. R. Stanton and F. A. Coffman, was submitted on July 2 for publication
in the 1929 Yearbook.

48 A manuscript entitled "Stem Rust of Cereals: More Than '57' Physiologic Forms Exist," by M. N. Levine and E. C. Stakman, was submitted on July
9 for publication in the Department Yearbook for 1929.

Page proof of Tech. Bul. 121 entitled "Methods of Harvesting Grain Sorghums," by John H. Martin, L. A. Reynoldson, B. E. Rothgeb, and W. M. Hurst,
was read on July 6.

TRANSLATIONS

Averna-Saccá, R. O brusone de arroz. [The brusone disease of the rice.]
Bol. Agr. [Sao Paulo] 13: 291-302. 1912. (Translation by Theo. Holm, April,
1929.)

Voglino, Pietro. Ricerche intorno alla malattia del riso conosciuta col
nome di brusone. [Studies of the rice disease called "brusone."] Ann. R.
Accad. Agr. Torino 40 (1897): 143-146. 1898. (Translation by Theo. Holm,
April 10, 1929.)

The foregoing list of translations supplements the lists published in
earlier numbers of the Cereal Courier, as follows:

    Vol. 13: 12-15, 52, 69, 225-226. 1921.

        14: 38-39, 99-100. 1922.

        15: 11-13, 46-47. 1923.

        16: 16-18, 127. 1924.

        17: 62-63, 326-327. 1925.

        18: 4-5, 335. 1926.

        19: 16, 124-125. 1927.

        21: 116.   1929.

Copies of these translations are on file in the Library of the Bureau of
Plant Industry.

FIELD STATION CONDITION AND PROGRESS

HUMID ATLANTIC COAST AREA (South to North)

GEORGIA

State College of Agriculture, Athens (Cereal Agronomy, R. R. Childs)

VIRGINIA

Arlington Experiment Farm, Rosslyn (Small Grain Agronomy, J. W. Taylor)

Arlington Experiment Farm, Rosslyn (Corn Breeding, F. D. Richey)

Arlington Experiment Farm, Rosslyn (Cereal Smuts, V. F. Tapke, Acting in Charge)

Arlington Experiment Farm, Rosslyn (Virus Diseases, H. H. McKinney)

NEW YORK

Cornell University Agricultural Experiment Station, Ithaca (Cereal Breeding, H. H. Love) (July 3) (W. T. Craig)

Barley was sown here very late this spring owing to wet weather. Because of the unfavorable weather conditions barley is progressing very slowly. It is difficult to predict at this time when it will be in the milk stage, but probably it will be about the end of July or the first of August. Because of the wet spring which delayed seeding and the subsequent dry spell, the oats and barley experiments will be the poorest in many years.

HUMID MISSISSIPPI VALLEY AREA (South to North)

LOUISIANA

Rice Experiment Station, Crowley (Rice Agronomy, J. M. Jenkins)

Agricultural Experiment Station, Baton Rouge (Corn Breeding, H.F.Stoneberg)

TENNESSEE

Agricultural Experiment Station, Knoxville (Corn Breeding, L. S. Mayer)

MISSOURI

Agricultural Experiment Station, Columbia (Cereal Agronomy, L. J. Stadler)

IOWA

Agricultural Experiment Station, Ames (Oat Breeding, L. C. Burnett)

Agricultural Experiment Station, Ames (Corn Breeding, M. T. Jenkins)
e 28)

The cooperative corn experiments at Ames this year include

1. A selfing plot for the further inbreeding and selection of the lines
ng carried at this station. This plot contains 1728 ear rows.

2. A crossing plot of 459 rows. In this plot crosses are to be made
ch will be tested for yield next year.

3. A convergent improvement plot of 126 rows.

4. A yield test plot in which the following material is being compared
· yield:

F_1 crosses between inbred lines	499
Double crosses	18
Double-double crosses	4
F_1 crosses between inbred lines & varieties	76
Varieties	16
Total	613

5. A time-of-planting experiment with crosses. In this experiment 29
sses and 4 varieties are planted on two dates.

6. A comparison of level, furrow, and listed methods of planting.

The corn at the Agronomy Farm has been doing well in spite of the dry
ther. We had very little rain from planting time until June 26.

Agricultural Experiment Station, Ames (Crown Rust of Oats, S. M. Dietz)

ILLINOIS

Funk Bros. Seed Co., Bloomington (Corn Root, Stalk and Ear Rots, J.R.Holbert)

INDIANA

Purdue University Agricultural Experiment Station, LaFayette (Corn Rots and Metallic Poisoning, J. F. Trost, Acting in Charge)

Purdue University Agricultural Experiment Station, LaFayette (Leaf Rusts E. B. Mains) (June 20)

Leaf rust of wheat overwintered abundantly in the eastern wheat area. Overwintering at LaFayette was very abundant. Warm weather in late March and the first part of April favored the spread of the rust. Cool weather which has been prevalent until recently, checked the development and wheat was well headed before much rust appeared.

On a trip to Experiment, Ga., and Knoxville, Tenn., susceptible varietie showed 100 per cent of rust on May 23 to 24. Wheat was well advanced, and ea varieties showed signs of ripening. While the rust was prevalent, the maxim was reached late in the development of the wheat plant as the result of cool weather.

A similar situation was found on the Arlington Experiment Farm, near Was ington, D. C., June 6, and at Swannanoa, N. C., June 11. Susceptible varieti were heavily rusted, but early varieties were ripening.

Leaf rust was abundant at Vincennes, Ind., on June 18. Such susceptibl varieties as Poole showed 100 per cent of rust, and the leaves were prematur killed. Purkoff showed only a moderate infection of rust. A number of vari ties that have been found to rust severely in years when development of the disease was earlier, have shown only a moderate infection of rust this year.

The following information concerning leaf rust of wheat has been receiv from the barberry field agents. Mr. Baringer on June 1 reported that no lea rust was noted in fields examined in Ohio. About 2 per cent prevalence and less than 1 per cent severity were noted for central and western Ohio on Jun

On May 29, Mr. Leer found infected fields in the vicinity of Crawfordsv Ind. There was rapid development in northern Indiana on June 4 and 5. By J 15, about 100 per cent of the plants in southern Indiana were showing 50 to per cent of leaf rust. At this time wheat was in the milk stage.

On June 15, Mr. Bills reported leaf rust prevalent in southern Illinois while only a trace was showing in the northern part of the State.

On May 25, Mr. Caldwell reported a trace of leaf rust on wheat in Wisco By June 1, this had increased somewhat.

On June 4, Mr. Melander reported that leaf rust had not been found in t fields examined in Minnesota. On June 11 and 17 leaf rust was reported as 1

On May 25, Mr. Thiel reported finding a few scattered uredinia in Nebraska. On June 1, leaf rust was reported as developing very slowly. On June 8, considerable development for the previous week was reported. On June 15, uredinia were reported on all of the leaves of the wheat plant, the lower being most heavily infected, and the upper showing only a trace.

On May 25, Mr. Lungren reported that no leaf rust had been noted in Colorado. On June 8, a slight trace was reported for the southern part of the State.

WISCONSIN

Agricultural Experiment Station, Madison (Wheat Scab, J. G. Dickson)

MINNESOTA

Agricultural Experiment Station, University Farm, St. Paul (Wheat Breeding, K. S. Quisenberry, Acting in Charge) (June 21)

Crops have made satisfactory growth during the last three weeks. At present the winter-wheat plots and rod rows are fully headed. Some of the individually spaced hybrid material is still heading, being late because of thin stands due to winterkilling. Although stem-rust infection from artificial inoculation was noticed as early as May 25, development has not been fast. At the present time there is some stem rust in the winter wheat, and leaf rust is developing rapidly. There still will be time for an epidemic to develop if the weather does not turn off too hot and dry.

In the rust nursery, stem rust is present in the winter-wheat guard rows in small amounts. The earlier varieties of spring wheat are starting to head. Rows of Quality and Reward and some early foreign introductions are fully headed. These strains are heading very short. In some cases the straw is about a foot high.

Mr. E. R. Ausemus, of Mandan, N. Dak., visited University Farm on June 18 to 20, and Mr. B. B. Bayles, of Moccasin, Mont., spent June 11 here en route from Madison, Wis., to his headquarters.

The writer was away from St. Paul from May 28 until June 18, visiting stations in Texas, Oklahoma, Kansas, and Nebraska. Part of the trip through Oklahoma and Kansas was made by car with Mr. H. C. Murphy, of Ames, Iowa, and Mr. T. R. Stanton, senior agronomist in charge of oat investigations. In general, the wheat crop looked well at most of the places visited. Leaf rust was abundant on wheat at most of the stations. Stem rust was heavy on wheat at Denton, Tex., while farther north there was less infection. There was stem rust on susceptible, late varieties of wheat at Newton, Manhattan, and Hays, Kans., and at North Platte, Nebr.

At Denton, Manhattan, and Hays counts were taken on the uniform winter wheat bunt nursery. Some very interesting readings were obtained, as the infection was very heavy on the susceptible varieties.

While at Manhattan and Hays the writer attended the meetings of the Co Belt Section of the American Society of Agronomy. These meetings were well attended and very instructive. The meetings were so arranged as to give the visitors a good idea of the experimental work being done in Kansas as well some knowledge of wheat growing in the State.

Agricultural Experiment Station, University Farm, St. Paul (Stem Rust, E. C. Stakman)

Agricultural Experiment Station, University Farm, St. Paul (Flax Rust, H. A. Rodenhiser)

GREAT PLAINS AREA (South to North)

OKLAHOMA

Woodward Field Station, Woodward (Grain Sorghum and Broomcorn, J. B. Sieglinger) (June 18)

While summer weather was delayed it is here now without doubt. June t far has been hot and dry. This, in contrast with the cool, moist spring, m the present weather seem doubly severe.

Sorghum seeding has progressed according to schedule except that some the later seedings are awaiting rain.

The writer attended the meeting of the Corn-Belt Section of the Americ Society of Agronomy at Hays, Kans., on June 14, Crops at the Hays Station looked well, but between Woodward, Okla., and Hays, Kans., the percentage c cultivated land in winter wheat apparently is 95 per cent or more. On an average the wheat was in good condition and ripening fast. Along the route Oklahoma and southern Kansas wheat was ripe enough to bind on June 15, but is being left for the combine and header. The few fields of oats sown this year will produce a yield above the average.

Maximum temperature for the period from June 1 to 18, 104 degrees on t 10th and 103 degrees on the 11th; minimum for same period, 51 degrees on th 13th; precipitation, 0.16 of an inch in two showers.

(June 22)

Wheat in the vicinity of Woodward is ripening fast because of the hot, dry weather, and is being headed at this time.

(July 2)

The weather of the last half of June was hot and dry. Wheat harvest is well under way in the vicinity, and it appears as if about three-fourths of the crop is harvested. According to hearsay the yields vary from 6 to as high as 25 bushels per acre.

The last of the grain-sorghum experiments were seeded on June 25 and emerged in 5 days. Thinning is progressing rapidly, and at present the plots are making good growth.

Maximum temperature for the last half of June, 100 degrees on the 27th; minimum, 58 degrees on the 25th; precipitation, 0.42 of an inch on the 23rd; total precipitation for June, 0.58 of an inch.

. KANSAS

Agricultural Experiment Station, Manhattan (Cereal Breeding, J. H. Parker)

Agricultural Experiment Station, Manhattan (Corn Breeding, A. M. Brunson)
(July 2)

Corn is small and backward in eastern Kansas, and many fields are unusually weedy. The normal acreage probably will be reduced; it will require exceptionally favorable weather from now on to produce a good crop from the present acreage.

In June there was a continuation of the cool, wet weather of the spring months. Maximum temperature, 97 degrees on the 17th; minimum, 48 degrees on the 4th. The mean monthly temperature was 71 degrees as compared to a normal of 74.12 degrees. The total precipitation, recorded on 11 days, was 7.96 inches compared to a normal of 4.45 inches. The worst soil erosion in years has been caused by the heavy washing rains this spring.

The annual Agronomy Field Day, scheduled for June 8, had to be canceled at the last minute because of a very heavy rain the day before.

The summer meeting of the Corn-Belt Section of the American Society of Agronomy was held at Manhattan on June 12 and 13, and at Hays on June 14. More than 100 agronomists were in attendance. It was voted to accept the invitation of the University of Nebraska for the summer meetings next year.

Wheat in this section is nearly all cut, and threshing is starting. Early threshing returns are disappointing in many localities, and it is almost certain that the final production figures for the State will be materially below the June estimates. Scab is more prevalent than it has been in years.

Agricultural Experiment Station, Manhattan (Wheat Foot Rots, Hurley Fellows)

Agricultural Experiment Station, Manhattan (Wheat Leaf Rust, C.O.Johnston)

Hays Branch Experiment Station, Hays (Cereal Agronomy, A. F. Swanson)

NEBRASKA

North Platte Substation, North Platte (Cereal Agronomy, G. F. Sprague)
(June 29)

The period from June 15 to 30 has been characterized by hot, dry, windy
weather. Corn has wilted noticeably in the last few days. Oats are beginning
to show the effects of the drought. Wheat and barley still are in good condition
but would be greatly benefited by rain.

The Annual Field Day was held on June 27. About 500 people were in attendance and made the tour of the field plots. Dr. G. L. Peltier spoke on alfalfa
wilt and Prof. J. C. Russel talked on the fertility problems of central Nebraska.

The total evaporation for the period mentioned was 4.069 inches. The total
precipitation was 0.08 of an inch. The maximum temperature was 102 degrees on
June 29.

Washington visitors were Mr. K. S. Quisenberry on June 17 and Mr. R. W.
Leukel from June 26 to 29.

SOUTH DAKOTA

U. S. Forage-Crop Field Experiments, Redfield (Wheat Breeding, E. S.
McFadden)

NORTH DAKOTA

Agricultural Experiment Station, State College Station, Fargo (Flax
Diseases, L. W. Boyle)

Dickinson Substation, Dickinson (Cereal Agronomy, R. W. Smith) (July 1)

Early varieties of wheat, oats, and barley are beginning to head. The
dates of first heading are somewhat later than usual because of the unusually
cool temperatures that prevailed during May and most of June. Winter wheat is
scarcely any earlier in heading than spring varieties, because of the lack of
vigorous growth during dry weather last fall. Many of the new foreign barleys
are considerably earlier than any of our standard barley varieties.

A good rain will be needed in the near future in order to obtain good
yields this year from cereal crops.

The total precipitation for June was approximately three inches, or slightly below the normal for that month. All of this rain fell in the first half of the month, with the exception of a few very light showers. Therefore, the surface soil is now dry, although the crops are not suffering for lack of moisture. Last week a severe wind storm and some drifting of the soil bruised the leaves of crops to some extent. Some recently emerged flax fields in the vicinity were severely injured.

Northern Great Plains Field Station, Mandan (Flax Breeding, J. C. Brinsade, Jr.) (July 2)

Flax still looks very well in spite of very low precipitation in June. It is likely to suffer, however, unless we have rain soon.

Flax sown on May 20 and earlier in the date-and-rate-of-seeding-and-tillage experiment is in bloom. Nearly all the varieties in the classification nursery and many varieties in the regular varietal nurseries also are in bloom.

Wilt is developing rapidly in the flax-sick-soil nursery, and many rows of susceptible material already have died out completely.

Rust was found on flax June 21, the same date on which stem rust was first found on wheat. So far, however, there is very little rust in evidence.

A variety of white-flowered flax, which is grown to some extent by farmers in this locality, has proved completely susceptible to wilt. Four varieties of Argentine flax received from farmers have wilted to some extent but still show some resistance.

Northern Great Plains Field Station, Mandan (Cereal Agronomy, E. R. Ausemus) (July 2)

Cereal crops are beginning to suffer from lack of moisture. The precipitation for the last half of June was 0.27 of an inch. That for the first half was 0.72 of an inch, making a total of 0.99 of an inch. The normal rainfall for June is 3.60 inches. This makes a shortage of 2.01 inches for this month. Maximum temperature, 91 degrees on June 16; minimum, 40 degrees on June 24.

The earlier varieties are headed in the wheat, oat, and barley plots and in the nursery.

Stem rust was first found in the nursery on the border rows of Hard Federation wheat on June 21.

Mr. V. C. Hubbard arrived from Manhattan, Kans., on July 1 to take over the experiments with wheat, oats, and barley at this station.

MONTANA

Judith Basin Branch Station, Moccasin (Cereal Agronomy, B. B. Bayles)

WESTERN BASIN AND COAST AREAS (North to West and South)

IDAHO

Aberdeen Substation, Aberdeen (Cereal Agronomy, L. L. Davis) (July 2)

Weather conditions in June were favorable for plant growth. The avera maximum temperature for the month was 73.3 degrees, the highest being 94 de grees on June 28. The average minimum temperature was 43.5 degrees. The lowest temperature recorded was 23 degrees on June 3. This early June free caused considerable foliage injury in wheat and barley varieties, but no pe manent injury was noticed. Some very interesting varietal differences in foliage injury were noticed after this freeze.

Nearly all barley varieties are headed. Wheat and oat varieties are r heading.

The nursery was irrigated on June 7 and 23. Only one more irrigation be necessary to mature the crop.

Dr. H. V. Harlan arrived at the Substation on June 10, and has been ma numerous barley studies since that time.

Agricultural Experiment Station, Moscow (Stripe Rust, C. W. Hungerfor

WASHINGTON

Agricultural Experiment Station, Pullman (Cereal Breeding, E. F. Gain (July 1)

A rain of 2.4 inches about 10 days ago assures us of more wheat than had any reason to hope for when I wrote you on June 12. A local hail sto damaged the winter wheat somewhat but not seriously.

OREGON

Sherman County Branch Station, Moro (Cereal Agronomy, D. E. Stephens)

CALIFORNIA

Biggs Rice Field Station, Biggs (Rice Agronomy, J. W. Jones) (July 1)

Temperatures for the first half of June were below normal and for the second half above normal. From June 20 to 30, temperatures ranged from 10 to 108 degrees each day, except on the 28th, which was cool at 97 degrees. A precipitation of 1.36 inches was recorded in June. This, together with cloudy weather in the first half of the month, was distinctly beneficial t wheat and barley.

Rice on the station and on commercial fields is farther advanced than usual at this date. With favorable weather during the remainder of the season the yield should be satisfactory and the harvest early.

There is more water lily[1] (_Alisma plantago_) on the station plots and on commercial fields this year than in past years. However, the rice seems to be getting ahead of the weed during the hot weather. Plantain is now heading and should not make much more growth. In Colusa County water lily[1] (_Sagittaria latifolia_) is more abundant than plantain. Arrowhead is now in bloom and probably will not grow much more. Both plantain and arrowhead appear to be most troublesome in deep water where the stands of rice are thin.

The market for rough rice remains about the same, possibly a little stronger.

On June 22, E. A. Žemčužnikov, professor of plant physiology, Don College of Agriculture and Amelioration, Novocherkassk, Northern Caucasus, U.S.S.R. (Russia), visited the station.

[1] Water lily = term used by rice growers.

(July 5)

It continues very warm here. Except for one day, the temperature has been above 100 degrees since June 20.

University Farm, Davis (Cereal Agronomy, G. A. Wiebe)

Agricultural Experiment Station, Berkeley (Cereal Smuts, F. N. Briggs)

OHIO

Ohio State University, College of Agriculture, Columbus, J. W. Baringer
(June 30)

Considerable time in June was spent in bringing under control an area of
escaped barberries near Sullivan, Ashland County. The outbreak was reported
by a student of vocational agriculture in the local high school. About nine
tons of salt were required to complete the treating operation.

All field men who are to serve this summer on the barberry-eradication
force in Ohio have been selected. All the appointees will report on July 1
at Ashtabula where a two-day meeting will be held for a detailed discussion
of the barberry-eradication campaign. The history of the campaign will be reviewed in all its phases from the point of view of both the State and the
entire area. Several field men will read papers dealing with various aspects
of the problem at hand. Conferences will be held which will have to do with
the detailed discussion of plans for field activities in Ohio during the season of 1929.

The new colored posters which have been prepared by The Conference for
the Prevention of Grain Rust have arrived and are being sent to all postmasters
in the State to be posted on bulletin boards in post-office lobbies. It has
been several years since the postmasters in Ohio have been reached with any
barberry-eradication publicity material.

Stem rust of wheat was found in the following counties in June: Clermont,
Butler, Warren, Preble, Montgomery, Clark, Franklin, Delaware, Knox, Ashland,
Wayne, Portage, and Geauga. The first rust was found by Fremont Cowgill on
wheat near barberries at Lewisburg, Preble County, on June 13. In all probability some stem rust could be found in nearly all wheat fields in the State by
June 30. As far as observations have been made it seems that cases of severe
damage due to stem rust on wheat will be relatively few this year in Ohio. The
cutting of wheat is now in full swing in the southern part of the State.

In general, leaf rust on wheat seems to be heavier than usual this year.
In some local places leaf rust recently has been found to have completely
covered the leaves.

Stem rust has been reported on rye in Ashtabula County, but the report
has not been confirmed. Leaf rust on rye seems to be general, but on the
whole is not so severe as leaf rust on wheat.

The weather in June was for the most part conducive to the spread of rust
and also favorable for the development of small grain.

INDIANA

Purdue University College of Agriculture, La Fayette, W. E. Leer (July 1)

Considerable time is being spent in making a stem-rust collection for the study of physiologic forms. At the same time, the stem-rust situation in the State is being studied. A general epidemic of stem rust was found in the vicinity of Columbus. It covered an area of approximately 20 miles in every direction from Columbus. The prevalence was nearly 100 and the severity averaged about 20. In other parts of the State visited, it was difficult to find enough stem rust for a study of physiologic forms. It was often necessary to spend nearly 20 minutes in a field to collect 15 or 20 well-rusted stems.

The intensive survey of Tipton, Hamilton, and Montgomery counties is progressing nicely. In Montgomery County, four locations with five bushes have been found so far. No bushes have been found in either Tipton or Hamilton counties this year.

MICHIGAN

Agricultural College, East Lansing, W. F. Reddy

WISCONSIN

Department of Agriculture, State Capitol Annex, Madison, R. M. Caldwell (July 1)

The training school and conference for barberry-eradication field agents was held on June 19 and 20 prior to sending the men into the field. The first day was given over to the consideration of subject matter related to survey and eradication, review of fiscal regulations, and assignments and instructions. The second day was spent in the Black Earth area of escaped barberries where each squad was assigned to the survey of a block of barberry-infested woodland for practice in survey and eradication methods.

The field force numbers 31, of whom 27 are Federal employees and 4 State employees. Twelve new men have been added this year. Survey activities are being concentrated in Rock and Dane counties. Survey operations will be extended to Grant County later in the season in case the Rock County survey is completed.

In general, Wisconsin barberries have not been very heavily infected with stem rust this year. However, several spreads to grasses have been noticed thus far. One spread, found on May 18, is the earliest recorded occurrence of stem rust in this State.

At present, traces of stem rust are beginning to appear in fields where barberries are not known to exist.

ILLINOIS

<u>Box 72, Post Office Building, Urbana</u>, R. W. Bills (June 27)

Field operations are well under way. Six men covered an area of esca
barberries in Whiteside County the second week in May and have since conti
the second survey of Jo Daviess County. Twenty-one additional men have jc
the force since school closed in June. There are now 16 men in Jo Daviess
County. Squads are working on first survey in Monroe, Randolph, and Washi
ton counties. These counties will be completed early in July. Barberry t
have been found in each county.

The most heavily rusted bushes ever found in southern Illinois were 1
near Tilden, Randolph County, by T. O. Cutright on June 8. The bushes are
a road in the country and now form the center of an attractive roadside de
stration.

Weather conditions this spring have been favorable for rust developme
Leaf rust has been heavy in the southern counties, but stem rust has been
in developing. The first cases were reported on grains on June 16 when ru
was found in Marion County. Only traces of leaf rust have been found so f
in Jo Daviess County.

The second survey of Jo Daviess County will require much longer for c
pletion than was anticipated. Of the 124 square miles which remained for
second survey this spring, about 30 have been covered. Survey there shoul
be completed about September 1 according to latest estimates.

IOWA

<u>Iowa State College, Ames</u>, P. W. Rohrbaugh (June 17)

Fourteen additional barberry agents were put in the field on June 10,
making a total of 18 men. They are all stationed in Allamakee County wher
they will work most, if not all, of the summer. Barberries already have t
found in considerable number in several places. Three men eradicated 743
bushes and 1,798 seedlings in Green County in the period from May 1 to Jur

Several reports of what appear to be large areas of escaped barberrie
have been received in the office in the last two weeks from various parts
the State.

In general, the rust infection on barberry in Iowa this year is rathe
light.

MINNESOTA

Agricultural Experiment Station, University Farm, St. Paul, L.W.Melander
June 28)

The intensive survey was started on June 17, when nearly all of the agents
were sent to the field. Eight men each were assigned to Hennepin and Carver
counties, while six men will survey in Scott County. In all three counties
areas of escaped barberry bushes were located the first week. The bushes were
not numerous, but they were scattered one, two, or three to a wood lot. Only
an intensive survey would reveal locations of this kind. If bushes are found
in areas of this type throughout the season, a large number will be found and
eradicated before October 1.

The county agents of Scott and Carver counties are cooperating very closely
with the field men. County Agent Sheay, of Scott County, is sending out publicity every week to all of the papers in that county.

Nearly all of the annual weed meetings in all of the counties have been
held. Interest in both barberry eradication and weeds seems to be increasing.
Skepticism regarding the relation of common barberry to black stem rust seems
to be decreasing, especially among the farmers. The attendance at the meetings
was much larger than in previous years. Considerably more publicity regarding
these meetings was sent out and the newspapers were very responsive.

The annual progress report was favorably received. Approximately 6,000
copies were distributed. The Minneapolis Journal used it as the basis of a
very fine editorial. News articles regarding this report were sent out by the
Extension News Service at the University Farm. They gave articles to the
Associated Press, the United Press, and the Western Newspaper Union.

On June 18, at the request of the business men of Mahnomen, a special
barberry meeting was held in the Courthouse. As a result, so much enthusiasm
was aroused that the farmers in various townships will organize to look for
common barberry.

NEBRASKA

College of Agriculture, University Farm, Lincoln, A. F. Thiel

SOUTH DAKOTA

College of Agriculture, Brookings, R. O. Bulger (July 1)

An unusual find of barberries was reported last week from the town of
Beresford, Union County. County Agent L. C. Sayre, of Lincoln County, noticed
five small bushes while making an inspection of the yards in Beresford. He
reported these to the office and upon investigation the State Leader found 15
small bushes three years old that had grown from seed. The owner, Mrs. Andersen, had received the seeds from friends in Missouri, who claimed that they were
those of Japanese barberry.

However, the plants were clearly common barberries and had no resemblance to Japanese bushes. Mrs. Andersen had given several plants to her daughter, living on a farm five miles west of Beresford. These will be located and destroyed.

This is one instance clearly demonstrating the dangerous possibility of the State becoming reinfested with common barberry, through a medium which is not readily handled by quarantine. Education appears to be the only way to prohibit possibilities of this sort.

.Another planting of barberries was reported by a school boy in Turner County. He found two small bushes while picking asparagus. When the report was investigated, a number of other larger escaped bushes was found. It may lead to the finding of a considerable area of escaped bushes. The boy, Duane Cram, of Parker, Turner County, stated that he had learned to recognize common barberries in Minnesota, because there had been some on his father's farm near Worthington, Minn. He said that his class had spent nearly a week studying about the barberry and stem rust last winter in the Parker (S. Dak.) High School.

Spreads of stem rust from barberries have been noticed in two instances in South Dakota this spring. A school girl near Chamberlain, Brule County, reported a barberry bush heavily infected with the spring stage of stem rust. By June 27 stem rust had spread to nearby wheat and barley fields.

The squad of men working in Charles Mix County have been reporting unusually heavy stem rust in their territory. They are certain that there were barberries in the vicinity. A report has just been received that they found 10 heavily infected bushes and that there was a clear case of rust spread from them. This instance has not as yet been investigated in detail.

At present stem rust is light but general over most of eastern South Dakota. The infection occurs commonly on bread wheats and barley but not so generally on oats. Some damage may result to late crops.

NORTH DAKOTA

Agricultural Extension Division, State College Station, Fargo, G. C. Mayoue (June 29)

The field assistants of 1929 completed their course of training with a field trip on June 11. On the same day six men were placed on field survey along the Elm and Goose rivers in Traill County. All were placed along rivers because this is the best time of year to do that kind of work,- before there is a heavy growth of underbrush which makes survey progress very difficult.

The State Leader attended the State Convention of the Retail Merchants
Association at Bismarck on June 12. The special agent, Mr. Roberts, had an
attractive demonstration at Bismarck intended particularly for the merchants.
While in Bismarck the State Leader conferred with National and North Dakota
officers of the Farmers' Union.

The first rust on barberry was located in Grand Forks County on June 18.
Stem rust was found for the first time at Fargo on winter wheat. A trace of
leaf rust could be found June 8 on winter wheat, as well as on Ceres, Kota,
Marquis, and Ruby,- particularly on Ceres and Kota. Cool, dry weather during
June has retarded crop growth over the eastern half of the State, especially
throughout the Red River Valley, whereas crops west of the Missouri River are
in good growing condition for the most part, having had sufficient moisture
except for local areas where it has been dry.

Demonstrations are being made this week at the Lake Region Fair at Devils
Lake and at the Bottineau County Fair at Bottineau. According to reports both
of these demonstrations are attracting a lot of attention.

On June 29 the State Leader and the entire personnel, except those who
are busy with demonstration, will have a conference here at the College. All
the men will be ready to leave for their field assignments some time during
the forenoon of July 1.

Second survey will be conducted in Burke, Ward, and Bottineau counties,
and third survey in Traill County. Later in the season Sheridan County will
be second surveyed.

MONTANA

State College of Agriculture, Bozeman, W. L. Popham [July 2]

Intensive survey for barberry bushes is now being made in Montana in Flathead and Fergus counties. Four more field agents were appointed on July 1,
making a total of 10 now in the field. For the month of July the crew is
divided into two squads, a six-man squad working in Flathead County and four
men in Fergus. The survey this summer marks the beginning of intensive second
survey in Montana, and the type of work to be conducted in the future will de-
pend to some extent upon the bushes found this year.

During the past two weeks rural and small-town box holders in Flathead,
Fergus, and Judith Basin counties have been supplied with a circular letter,
bulletin, and return card. Arrangements are now under way whereby a mailing
list of about 800 farmers in Flathead County will receive a letter signed by
both their County Agent, Mr. J. Chester Paisley, and the State Leader in barberry eradication, dealing with the campaign. In this letter the attention of
property owners is called to the fact that an intensive survey for barberry
bushes is being made by agents of the United States Department of Agriculture
and that their county agent is in a position to supply interested people with
complete information pertaining to the work.

Miss Elizabeth Ireland, State Superintendent of Public Instruction, is cooperating with Mr. A. T. Peterson, Principal of the Beaverhead County High School in publishing "a course of study in agriculture" for eighth-grade pupils. Four thousand copies of the book are to be printed, and Miss Ireland has requested an equal number of each of Plates P-3, and P-4, to be inserted in the books when they are bound. These plates are to supplement an outlined lesson pertaining to the control of black stem rust. It is expected that in the next school term a copy of the book will be placed in the hands of each eighth-grade school teacher in the State.

WYOMING

College of Agriculture, University of Wyoming, Laramie, W. L. Popham [July 2]

An organized education program dealing with the barberry-eradication campaign is being conducted in Wyoming this summer. Mr. R. B. Bowden, who is on sabbatical leave from his regular position as director of publications for Montana State College, is conducting the program. Mr. Bowden is working with school officials, county agricultural extension agents, Smith-Hughes instructors, and daily and rural newspapers in getting before the people of the State the facts regarding the black-stem-rust control campaign.

In addition to the program outlined for the summer, arrangements are being made for further educational work with the high schools and grade schools of the State to be conducted in the coming school year.

COLORADO

Agricultural College, Ft. Collins, E. A. Lungren (July 1)

Second survey was conducted in Boulder County in June. Considerable publicity, such as window displays, posters, circular letters, and newspaper stories, also was made available.

The survey has been very thorough and rather difficult along the creeks. Many new properties were found in the town of Boulder which had been missed on the first survey. Several escaped bushes were found along the creeks. Light infection was found on all bushes in rural communities but no spread was apparent.

On July 1 a conference of all field men and college and station cooperators was held at the botany department of the Colorado Agricultural College. Survey, publicity, education, and extension activities were discussed.

C E R E A L   C O U R I E R

Official Messenger of the Office of Cereal Crops and Diseases
Bureau of Plant Industry, U. .S. Department of Agriculture
(NOT FOR PUBLICATION)

Vol. 21   July 20, 1929   No. 17
           Personnel (July 11-20) and Field Station (July 1-15) Issue

PERSONNEL ITEMS

Mr. J. Allen Clark, senior agronomist in charge of western wheat investigations, reported on July 18 from Havre, Mont., on the progress of his trip in
the spring-wheat area of the United States and Canada. Starting at St. Paul,
Minn., on June 27 Mr. Clark found crop conditions satisfactory at University
Farm, with plenty of moisture and but little or no rust infection except in the
rust nurseries. The plots were headed and in excellent condition.

On June 28, he visited the Southeast Station at Waseca, Minn., with Mr.
Quisenberry and Drs. H. K. Hayes and H. K. Wilson. The wheats were later there
than at St. Paul. Rust was found only on winter wheat.

At the North Dakota Station, Fargo, on July 1, evidence of drought was
apparent. The June rainfall had been lighter than for the previous 48 years.
The first infection of stem rust had been found on June 21, which was earlier
than the average initial infection for the previous 10 years.

On July 2 Mr. Clark started from Fargo in a Government-owned Ford truck
and visited the West-Central Station at Morris, Minn., on July 3. There wheat
and other crops also were in need of rain. The plots and nursery still were
in good condition, however. Stem rust could be found in the susceptible early
varieties of spring wheat.

At the South Dakota Station, Brookings, on July 4, stem rust was plentiful
on Supreme, Prelude, and other susceptible early varieties in the plots. Here
also crops were in need of rain, although little injury had occurred.

At the U. S. Cereal Field Experiments, Redfield, S. Dak., on July 5 and 6, drought had done much damage. The plot experiments were in fair condition, but the nursery was nearly gone, many strains having hardly headed. Most of the grain was not over a foot in height. Some F_3 spaced hybrid material for study of inheritance of stem-rust reaction still was in good condition, and with rain it probably would develop normally. Stem rust, which had started on susceptible border plants on June 20, was drying up rather than spreading.

At the Eureka Substation in South Dakota, and the Edgeley Substation in North Dakota, on July 6, drought also was in evidence. Fields along the route throughout this section were poor to fair, depending on cropping methods and local showers. Rain was needed badly to save the wheat. Oats and barley already were largely gone, but corn was in good condition.

Returning to Fargo, N. Dak., on July 7, it was found that light showers on the 3d and 6th had materially improved the condition of the wheat plots and nursery.

At the Northwest Station, Crookston, Minn., on July 8, the wheat experiments were in excellent condition and had not been affected by the drought. Only initial infections of stem rust could be found.

Dr. H. B. Humphrey joined Mr. Clark at Redfield, S. Dak., on July 6, and on the following day, Mr. E. R. Ausemus met them at Fargo, N. Dak., to travel to Crookston, Minn., Winnipeg and Morden, Manitoba, and Langdon, N. Dak. An interesting day was spent at the University of Manitoba, Winnipeg, July 9, in going over the experiments in the Rust Research Laboratory and the varietal and breeding experiments in the field. Wheat on the College farm was in good condition, but farther west in the Province wheat was affected by drought. There was stem rust on susceptible early varieties, and the Laboratory had had evidence of a spore shower on June 17, about 10 days before the first field infections were noted.

On July 9 a stop was made at the station at Morden, Man., where it had been very dry. The wheat experiments still were in fair condition, however. Rust was developing about as at Winnipeg. A large breeding nursery was being grown there for Dr. C. H. Goulden, of the Rust Research Laboratory at Winnipeg. The Morden station is located in a section often severely affected with stem rust, and the Dominion investigators are cooperating closely at the two stations.

At the Langdon Substation, North Dakota., on July 10, plot and nursery experiments were found in fair condition because of having been grown on fallow. Wheat on grain land or even on corn land was severely hurt by drought, and rain was needed badly. The crops, especially durum wheat, were late. This is largely a durum-wheat area, and late seeding is commonly practiced.

On July 11, at the North Dakota Station, Fargo, improvement was noted in the condition of crops, but a heavy infection of stem rust was present on susceptible varieties in both plots and nursery. No such infections were found in commercial fields in the vicinity of Fargo. Much of the wheat from Fargo westward to Valley City was of the Ceres variety and it was relatively free from rust. In Marquis fields only initial infections could be found and rust was only slightly more plentiful than in the previous week. Loose smut was generally present in all fields, especially in Ceres wheat, but as much as 7 per cent was recorded by Dr. Humphrey in a field of Marquis.

On July 12 and 13, at the Northern Great Plains Field Station, Mandan, N. Dak., the nursery and plot experiments still were in good condition, but rain was needed. Stem rust, which had first been noted on June 21, was rapidly becoming general throughout the nursery from a heavy infection on border plants of Hard Federation. A heavy infection of stem rust was assured on F_3 material studied for inheritance of stem-rust reaction, involving five crosses between the resistant and susceptible varieties, Hope, Marquillo, Ceres, and Red Bobs.

Going west in North Dakota on July 13, evidence of stem rust disappeared gradually and none could be found in the experiments at the Dickinson Substation, in North Dakota. The crops were much later there than at Mandan, but the drought was not so severe.

At the Hettinger Substation, North Dakota, on July 14, plot experiments were found in good condition in spite of drought. Only a trace of stem rust was noted on the most susceptible varieties.

On July 15 the party traveled from Hettinger back to Dickinson and on to the Williston Substation. An improvement in crop conditions was noted northward and they were excellent at Williston, where there was no evidence of rust. The varieties were grown on fallow, and the absence of rain had not affected them yet, although wheat on cropped land was beginning to burn.

Going westward in Montana on July 16 and 17, crop conditions rapidly deteriorated. From Culbertson to Malta the crops were largely destroyed by drought, with the exception of those on fallow. Conditions improved near Havre. At the Northern Montana Substation, the plot experiments on fallow were in good condition. Oats and barley were standing the drought better than wheat. This condition was the reverse of that in the Dakotas. The wheat nursery at Havre, which was seeded earlier and at a thicker rate than the plots, was badly burned and only the early wheats had attained normal height. It is expected that a real test for drought resistance with hybrid selections will be obtained at this station and this is greatly desired.

Mr. H. S. Garrison, assistant agronomist in corn investigations returned from Tifton, Ga., on July 13 after spending 10 days in helping Mr. Kyle in pollinating and taking notes in the cooperative corn plots.

Mr. Austin G. Goth was appointed agent, effective July 16, to assist in the cereal-breeding experiments that are being conducted in cooperation with the Kansas Agricultural Experiment Station at Manhattan.

Dr. H. B. Humphrey, principal pathologist in charge of cereal-rust investigations, who left on June 21 for an extended trip in the West, sent the following summary of his observations for the period from June 28 to July 14:

At La Fayette, Ind., there was relatively little stem rust but an almost ideal epiphytotic of leaf rust of wheat on both winter and spring varieties. Dr. E. B. Mains will be able to get fairly conclusive data on the behavior of those varieties and hybrids on which some information already has been obtained from the La Fayette and Manhattan nurseries.

At the University Farm, St. Paul, the rusts had not yet developed to any extent. Therefore, after an inspection of Mr. Rodenhiser's flax-rust nursery, Dr. Humphrey went to Ames to inspect the cooperative crown-rust nursery at Iowa State College with Dr. S. M. Dietz and Mr. H. C. Murphy. The nursery gives greater promise of real results this year than were obtained in 1928 and the results probably will equal those of 1927, the best crown-rust year so far experienced. From a trace to 20 per cent severity of crown-rust infection was found all the way from Ames to Waterloo via a route through Ft. Dodge, Sheldon, and Rock Rapids, Iowa; Luverne, Minn.; and Sioux Falls, S. Dak. Stem rust of oats, barley, and wheat was seen in nearly all fields inspected but never more than a trace.

At Redfield, S. Dak., on July 6 Dr. Humphrey joined Mr. J. Allen Clark to make a tour of the stations where this Office is conducting cooperative research. In the Dakotas there is urgent need of rain. At Redfield and elsewhere in that part of South Dakota, wheat is heading at 6 to 12 inches in height and is badly burned. In the Red River Valley and at Dickinson, N. Dak., crops are in fair to good condition and of uneven development, varying from the heading stage to the early dough stage. At no point except at Brookings, S. Dak., and Fargo, N. Dak., was there found in the nurseries more than a trace of stem rust. Leaf rust is general but not severe. At Dickinson there is little more than a trace on the most susceptible varieties, and stem rust apparently is entirely lacking. No rust has been seen on oats since leaving Fargo. Unless there is a marked change in conditions, there will be no more stem rust this year than in 1928.

Dr. A. G. Johnson, principal pathologist in charge of cereal-disease investigations, returned to Washington on July 17 after visiting the cooperative cereal-disease experiments at Manhattan, Kans., Bloomington, Ill., Madison, Wis., and La Fayette, Ind.

Mr. C. H. Kyle, senior agronomist in corn investigations, returned to Washington on July 18. He was at Tifton, Ga., from June 16 to July 16, during which time he hand-pollinated about 10,000 ears of corn in the cooperative experiments. General notes were obtained on all breeding lines. Those segregating from crosses between primary selfed lines are of unusual interest. The corn in the experimental plots looks very well.

Mr Kyle was at Gainesville, Fla., on July 17 to inspect the corn-breeding work at the Florida Agricultural Experiment Station. About 15 acres are devoted to corn experiments at this Station. The selfed lines are just getting under way, but many of them have special interest because they are from little-known varieties of Florida.

Dr. C. E. Leighty, principal agronomist in charge of eastern wheat investigations, left on July 17 for Ithaca, N. Y., to inspect cooperative cereal experiments and to confer with cooperators and officials of the Cornell Agricultural Experiment Station. He will return to Washington about July 24.

Dr. J. H. Martin will leave Washington on July 28 for St. Paul, Minn., Fargo, N. Dak., and Hardin, Mont., to make a study of the windrow method of harvesting small grains. Dr. Martin, who is agronomist in charge of grain sorghum and broomcorn investigations, will later proceed to Sacaton, Ariz., to conduct physiological experiments with grain sorghums at the U. S. Field Station. He also will go to California, New Mexico, Texas, Oklahoma, Kansas, Nebraska, and Colorado to inspect and study grain-sorghum experiments and confer with experiment station officials. Before returning to Washington about the middle of October he will study broomcorn conditions in the vicinity of Mattoon, Ill.

Dr. V. F. Tapke, pathologist in cereal-smut investigations, will leave Washington on July 25 for the Aberdeen Substation, Aberdeen, Idaho, to harvest and take notes on wheat, oats, and barley used in studies on cereal smuts. He will be away about a month.

Mrs. Marion Griffiths Zehner, associate pathologist in cereal-smut investigations, left Washington on July 20 for Brookings and Redfield, S. Dak., where she will take notes on cereals grown in cooperative cereal-smut nurseries at the South Dakota Agricultural Experiment Station and at the U. S. Cereal Field experiments. Mrs. Zehner will make similar studies in Minnesota at the University Farm, St. Paul, in North Dakota at the Agricultural Experiment Station, Fargo, the Northern Great Plains Field Station, Mandan, and the Dickinson Substation, Dickinson, in Montana at the Agricultural Experiment Station, Bozeman, and at the Northern Montana Substation, Havre, and in Washington at the Agricultural Experiment Station, Pullman. Mrs. Zehner will be away until the end of August.

VISITORS

Mr Philip F. Nieukirk, General Purchasing Agent·of the Campbell Soup Company, was an Office visitor on July 16. He brought some additional information on Patna rice which he had obtained from U. S. Consular officers in India, and again expressed the willingness of his Company to be of any possible service in making laboratory or factory tests of rice for soup-making purposes.

Rev. A. D. Luckhoff, from Stellenbosch, Cape Town, South Africa, was a visitor on July 16. He has been traveling in the United States as a representative of the Government of the Union of South Africa, studying methods of land reclamation and colonization, in which he was greatly facilitated by representatives of the Department of the Interior.

MANUSCRIPTS AND PUBLICATIONS

49 A manuscript entitled "Stem Rust of Wheat: Fooling the Rust with Sulphur Dust," by E. C. Stakman and Lee H. Person, Jr., was submitted on July 11 for publication in the Department Yearbook for 1929.

Galley proof of Tech. Bul. 136 entitled "Breeding Hard Red Winter Wheats for Winter Hardiness and High Yield," by Karl S. Quisenberry and J. Allen Clark, was read on July 15.

Page proof of Farmers' Bulletin 1599 entitled "Scab of Wheat and Barley and Its Control," by James G. Dickson and E. B. Mains, was read on July 20.

On July 15 there was received in this Office a copy of the book entitled "The Plant Rusts (Uredinales)." by Joseph C. Arthur, in collaboration with F. D. Kern, C. R. Orton, F. D. Fromme, H. S. Jackson, E. B. Mains, and G. R. Bisby, 446 p., 186 figs. 1929. New York: John Wiley & Sons, Inc. London: Chapman & Hall, Limited. (Cooperation with the Office of Cereal Crops and Diseases.)

FIELD STATION CONDITION AND PROGRESS

(All experiments except those conducted at the Arlington Exper·

Farm, Rosslyn, Va., are in cooperation with State agricult

experiment stations or other agencies.)

HUMID ATLANTIC COAST AREA (South to North)

GEORGIA

State College of Agriculture, Athens (Cereal Agronomy, R. R. Childs

VIRGINIA

Arlington Experiment Farm, Rosslyn (Small Grain Agronomy, J. W. Tayl
(July 16)

Harvesting of the small grains was finished before July 1. Threshin
operations are under way and well advanced considering the date. On the
the 1928-1929 year at the Arlington Experiment Farm was an unsatisfactory
for experimental results. Plant-lice injury or outright killing in the f
necessitated discarding one series of barley plots in the varietal experi
Disked land seeded to fall-sown oats produced a heavy crop of weeds which
ially reduced the yields. The excessive spring rains encouraged heavy ve
tive growth and diseases, especially in wheat.

Because of the unfavorable weather in June and the appearance of dis
the later-maturing wheat varieties ripened too early. Straw, rachis, and
were exceptionally brittle at harvest time, and shattering of grain or lo
heads was excessive. Finally, the Angoumois moth has severely injured th
in the field. The yield of wheat and oats will be below the average and
rye and barley slightly above the average.

The grain yields of the varieties of fall-sown barley grown in singl
acre plots are shown in the following table:

eties grown in single 40th-acre plots compared

1929

Variety Yield (Bu. per acre)	Check Yield (Bu. per acre)	Gain or loss of variety compared to check (Bu. per acre)
65.0	51.6	+ 13.4
61.6	51.6	+ 10.0
51.5	51.6	.1
45.3	46.8	. 1.5
49.2	53.2	. 4.0
47.1	53.0	. 5.9
46.7	53.0	. 6.3
40.7	47.3	. 6.6
44.2	53.0	. 8.8
37.8	46.8	. 9.0
47.3	56.3	. 9.0
37.5	46.8	. 9.3
36.9	47.3	- 10.4
36.5	47.3	- 10.8
31.3	46.8	- 15.5
34.0	53.0	- 19.0
26.3	53.2	- 26.9
22.9	53.2	- 30.3
21.3	53.2	- 31.9
51.0	----	----

Esaw, a selection from Nakano Wase, was highest in grain yield but wa
closely followed by the Mechanical Mixture lot. The former selection has
the highest yielding variety in the four years it has been under experimen
It apparently carries the covered-smut resistance of the Nakano Wase but n
the resistance to loose smut. Esaw is a short-awned variety and stands up
well. The Beardless strains, namely, No. 5 and No. 6, shattered badly. T
came through the winter in excellent condition but apparently the spring w
was very unfavorable for it.

The seed of the fall-sown barley varieties were dusted with Ceresan.
varieties also were sown with untreated and with Semesan-treated (liquid) :
The grain yields are shown in the following table:

Acre yields from 40th-acre plots of winter barley sown with untreated
Semesan-treated, and Ceresan-treated seed, 1929

Variety	C.I.No.	Untreated Seed (Bu.per acre)	Semesan-treated Seed (Bu.per acre)	Ceresan-treated Seed (Bu.per acre)
Wisconsin Winter	2159	46.7	50.0	51.7
Orel	351	27.1	35.0	36.5
Tennessee Winter	3543	34.4	36.5	31.3
Esaw	----	54.6	61.8	65.0
Average	----	40.7	45.8	46.1

The untreated plots contained unusually low percentages of both smuts,
and the comparative merits of Semesan and Ceresan as a seed treatment for t
control of smuts can not be obtained. Both treatments reduced significantl
the percentage of loose smut in all varieties but Esaw.

Scarified and covered-smut inoculated seed of 14 barley varieties gave
24.4 per cent of covered smut as compared to 4.9 per cent for scarified un-
inoculated seed. Those varieties which have shown little covered smut in t
field tests were resistant to covered smut when dehulled and inoculated.

Arlington Experiment Farm, Rosslyn (Corn Breeding, F. D. Richey)

Arlington Experiment Farm, Rosslyn (Cereal Smuts, V. F. Tapke, Acting
Charge)

Arlington Experiment Farm, Rosslyn (Virus Diseases, H. H. McKinney)

NEW YORK

Cornell University Agricultural Experiment Station, Ithaca (Cereal Breed-ng, H. H. Love)

HUMID MISSISSIPPI VALLEY AREA (South to North)

LOUISIANA

Rice Experiment Station, Crowley (Rice Agronomy, J. M. Jenkins)

Agricultural Experiment Station, Baton Rouge (Corn Breeding, H. F. toneberg)

TENNESSEE

Agricultural Experiment Station, Knoxville (Corn Breeding, L. S. Mayer)

MISSOURI

Agricultural Experiment Station, Columbia (Cereal Agronomy, L. J. Stadler)

IOWA

Agricultural Experiment Station, Ames (Oat Breeding, L. C. Burnett)

Agricultural Experiment Station, Ames (Corn Breeding, M. T. Jenkins)

Agricultural Experiment Station, Ames (Crown Rust of Oats, S. M. Dietz)

ILLINOIS

Funk Bros. Seed Co., Bloomington (Corn Root, Stalk and Ear Rots, J. R. Holbert) (July 16)

Our pollination work is started. Dr. Sieveking has a number of men out detasseling today. We are putting on a few shoot bags this afternoon.

INDIANA

Purdue University Agricultural Experiment Station, La Fayette (Corn Rots and Metallic Poisoning, J. F. Trost, Acting in Charge) (July 13)

Mr. M. A. McCall, of the Washington Office, was here on July 5, and Dr. A. G. Johnson spent July 10 and 11 at La Fayette. Dr. J. R. Holbert of Bloomington, Ill., came on July 11 and went over some of the field plots with Dr. Johnson, Mr. R. R. St. John, Mr. G. M. Smith, and the writer. Mr. T. R. Stanton, of the Washington office, also was here for part of the time.

On July 12, on invitation of Dr. Holbert, the party went to Bloomington to see some of Dr. Holbert's field experiments. The party returned the same day to La Fayette as Mr. St. John was to begin detasseling Early Yellow dent strains and Mr. Smith expected to start hand pollination on Golden Bantam corn.

Mr. Smith went to Windfall, Ind., on July 11 with Director Skinner, and Mr. Laurenz Greene and Dr. H. D. Brown, of the Department of Horticulture, to attend a meeting of the Seed Committee of the Indiana Canners' Association. They received favorable reports on the improved stands and uniformity of growth in the hybrid strains which Mr. Smith supplied this year to representative canners for comparison with the best commercial seed stocks now available. The canners are much interested in the evident possibility of improving the quality of their product by the use of these disease-resistant hybrid strains.

Purdue University Agricultural Experiment Station, La Fayette (Leaf Rusts, E. B. Mains)

WISCONSIN

Agricultural Experiment Station, Madison (Wheat Scab, J. G. Dickson)

MINNESOTA

Agricultural Experiment Station, University Farm, St. Paul (Wheat Breeding, K. S. Quisenberry, Acting in Charge)

Agricultural Experiment Station, University Farm, St. Paul (Stem Rust, E. C. Stakman)

Agricultural Experiment Station, University Farm, St. Paul (Flax Rust, H. A. Rodenhiser)

GREAT PLAINS AREA (South to North)

OKLAHOMA

Woodward Field Station, Woodward (Grain Sorghum and Broomcorn, J. B. Sieglinger) (July 17)

Grain sorghums and broomcorn are growing rapidly. Within the next few days they will be cultivated and in excellent condition. The work of thinning is finished and the roadways have been trimmed. At present stands are being counted.

Wheat has been harvested in the vicinity of Woodward, but farther to the east and southeast considerable wheat remains to be combined.

The weather of the first half of July was hot. The drought has been broken, however. Maximum temperature for the first half of July, 99 degrees on the 15th; minimum, 58 degrees on the 3d; precipitation, 2.76 inches.

KANSAS

Agricultural Experiment Station, Manhattan (Cereal Breeding, J. H. Parker)

Agricultural Experiment Station, Manhattan (Corn Breeding, A. M. Brunson)

Agricultural Experiment Station, Manhattan (Wheat Foot Rots, Hurley Fellows) (June 26)

This has been a banner year for wheat diseases in Kansas and Oklahoma, from the standpoint of foot-rot and allied diseases. Holminthosporium, take-all, and wheat scab have taken a heavy toll from the farmer.

Wheat scab has been found in Kansas in previous years but never to any great extent. This year, however, it is not uncommon to find 5 per cent loss in many fields. I have observed wheat fields following corn where 70 per cent of the heads were blighted. The infestation extends across the entire State of Kansas and south as far at least as Oklahoma City. However, the eastern half of Kansas has received the greatest losses. No doubt the high humidity after heading has made possible this severe infestation.

Take-all this year is more severe than has been noted before. Not only is its distribution wider but also it is more severe in the localities where it has been present before. I have noticed some very peculiar things with respect to take-all this year. Fields which have been in wheat 20 years and free from take-all suddenly flare up with a high per cent of the disease. On the other hand, an occasional field known to have take-all severely for several years suddenly becomes free of it and produces good wheat, while fields in the immediate vicinity are badly diseased.

The most severe infestation from take-all is in Rice, Reno, and Stafford counties. Here one may travel for miles without finding a field free from it. However, it is present throughout the central tier of counties in Kansas and Oklahoma south to Kingfisher. Grant County in Oklahoma is the only place from which take-all has been reported before.

The breaking over of wheat culms at the nodes has been a frequent source of trouble in Oklahoma and Kansas for several years. A white and partially filled head accompanies the buckled culm. In 1929 this trouble has greatly increased. In south central Kansas some fields have as high as 90 per cent of the culms broken over. This trouble is causing large losses in the best wheat region of central Oklahoma. Plants which have fallen show the lower nodes to be blackened or browned entirely through the tissue. The broken nodes, however, are usually above the diseased ones. Isolation and inoculation have shown that Helminthosporium probably is the causal organism.

<u>Agricultural Experiment Station, Manhattan</u> (Wheat Leaf Rust, C. O. Johnston)

<u>Hays Branch Experiment Station, Hays</u> (Cereal Agronomy, A. F. Swanson)

NEBRASKA

<u>North Platte Substation, North Platte</u> (Cereal Agronomy, G. F. Sprague)
(July 15)

Owing to dry weather all grain is ripening earlier than was expected, considering the lateness of the season. Some of Dr. Harlan's barley importations were harvested on July 3. None of these appeared equal to those grown in our regular nursery. Smyrna selections were cut July 6 and the other nursery rows were harvested July 8. The first winter wheats to be harvested were those in the winter-hardiness nursery. Early Blackhull ripened July 6. The entire winter-wheat nursery except some hybrid selections sent out by Dr. J. H. Parker, were harvested by July 15.

The first oats were cut on July 10, and the nursery rows were completed on the 15th. Grasshoppers have done some damage to the oats nursery, biting the kernels off the panicle. They apparently show a decided preference for the Richland variety. Oat varieties, except Ferguson and Markton, were cut July 13. The first and second seeding of oats and barley and the first seeding of rye in the date-of-seeding experiment were cut on the same day.

Barley varieties were cut on July 15. The nursery material is ripening in excellent sequence from the standpoint of harvesting. Of the spring wheats only Prelude has ripened. Winter wheat varieties will be ready for the binder in two or three days, and most of the spring-wheat varieties will follow soon.

Only 0.38 of an inch of precipitation was recorded for the period from July 1 to 15. In contrast, the evaporation totaled 3.869 inches. The maximum temperature of 99 degrees was recorded on July 13.

SOUTH DAKOTA

U. S. Cereal Field Experiments, Redfield (Wheat Improvement, E. S. Fadden)

NORTH DAKOTA

Northern Great Plains Field Station, Mandan (Cereal Agronomy, V. C. Hubbard) (July 15)

The weather of the past 10 days has been very favorable for the development of leaf and stem rusts. Infection in the wheat nursery is developing rapidly.

Several local showers since July 10 have removed the cereals from immediate danger of burning. The heaviest shower amounted to 0.32 of an inch. The total rainfall for the first half of the month was 1.04 inches. The maximum temperature was 98° on July 12 and the minimum was 48° on July 9.

Visitors at the station for the first half of July were Mr. J. Allen Clark, Dr. H. B. Humphrey, and Mr. Frank Rupert. Mr. E. R. Ausemus has left for University Farm, St. Paul, Minn., to take charge of the cooperative wheat breeding experiments.

Northern Great Plains Field Station, Mandan (Flax Breeding, J. C. Brinsade, Jr.) (July 16)

The dry weather of June has continued during the first half of July. Local showers in the past week, amounting to about one inch of precipitation, have temporarily averted serious damage to flax. A temperature of 100° today, accompanied by a hot wind from the south, is likely to cause serious damage to crops. The dry weather has cut short the blossoming period of all flax. Flax sown on May 20 and earlier in the date-of-seeding-and-tillage experiment is through blooming. Flax sown on May 1 and earlier was through blooming July 10, and is beginning to turn.

Flax rust has developed very little since it was first found on May 21.

Wilt has continued to develop. Rows of Reserve, Damont, and Newland in the flax-sick-soil nursery are nearly all dead. In Linota, Rio, and most of the other wilt-resistant varieties there is hardly any wilt.

Mr. A. C. Dillman arrived at Mandan on July 13.

<u>Dickinson Substation, Dickinson</u> (Cereal Agronomy, R. W. Smith) (July 12)

Dry weather has prevailed during the past four weeks, only light showers having fallen in that time. The only rain this month was 0.30 of an inch on July 6.

Temperatures have been somewhat below normal most of the time since spring work began. Cool weather in June and part of July has helped to offset the lack of moisture in the soil. The maximum temperature was 95 degrees on July 11.

Crops are suffering somewhat for lack of moisture, as shown by the drying up of the lower leaves. Most cereal crops are heading out somewhat shorter than usual.

Early varieties of wheat, oats, and barley are now fully headed, and late varieties are heading. Crops began heading later than usual but are developing rapidly now owing to hotter weather and lack of moisture.

A small percentage of leaf rust is present. It was first noticed on July 6 on susceptible varieties in the rust nursery. No stem rust has yet been see

The Substation was visited early in the month by Dr. C. F. Marbut and Dr. T. D. Rice, of the U. S. Bureau of Chemistry and Soils. Mr. J. A. Clark and Dr. H. B. Humphrey are expected tomorrow.

<u>Agricultural Experiment Station, State College Station, Fargo</u> (Flax Diseases, L. W. Boyle)

<u>Langdon Substation, Langdon</u> (Wheat Improvement, G. S. Smith) (July 15)

This is the first report on small-grain experiments at Langdon, the writer having taken over his duties on July 1. Both the durum-wheat nursery and the wheat varietal plots were found in very good condition, in spite of the fact that the rainfall in June was less than half the average amount.

The nursery is heading rapidly now but will not be fully headed for another week. The plots, having been sown earlier, are nearly all fully headed. The precipitation for the first half of July was but 0.13 of an inch. If rain does not come soon, the nursery will be injured. Crops around the country are in bad shape.

The Substation is in the heart of the durum-wheat area, so that the cereal experiments are mainly with durum wheats, although a portion of the nursery is made up of some common wheats on which Dr. L. R. Waldron has been working. The main activity now is the making of crosses.

Visitors at the Substation since the first of July have been Mr. J. Allen Clark, Dr. H. B. Humphrey, Mr. E. R. Ausemus, and Mr. T. E. Stoa.

MONTANA

Judith Basin Branch Station, Moccasin (Cereal Agronomy, B. B. Bayles)

WESTERN BASIN AND COAST AREAS (North to West and South)

IDAHO

Aberdeen Substation, Aberdeen (Cereal Agronomy, L. L. Davis)

Agricultural Experiment Station, Moscow (Strip Rust, C. W. Hungerford)

WASHINGTON

Agricultural Experiment Station, Pullman (Cereal Breeding, E. F. Gaines)

OREGON

Sherman County Branch Station, Moro (Cereal Agronomy, D. E. Stephens)

CALIFORNIA

Biggs Rice Field Station, Biggs (Rice Agronomy, J. W. Jones) (July 15)

Temperatures during the first half of July have been very favorable for
e development of the rice crop. On commercial fields the crop looks as well
it did last year at this time. Water lilies (Alisma plantago and arrowhead)
e thick on the low ground in many commercial fields. On such spots good
ands of rice are seldom obtained. Good stands of rice tend to check the
owth of these weeds.

On the Station a few of the real early maturing varieties are beginning
head. Early varieties are jointing and nearing the booting stage. Mid-
ason varieties have hardly started to joint.

The Station rice is making fairly good growth, and the yields should be
out normal or above.

The rice market is a little stronger and indications are that the carry-
er will be much less than for last year. Should this be the case, prices
ould advance.

The acreage sown to rice in California this year is estimated to be 95,000
res, compared with 133,000 for last year.

University Farm, Davis (Cereal Agronomy, G. A. Wiebe)

Agricultural Experiment Station, Berkeley (Cereal Smuts, F. N. Briggs)

BARBERRY ERADICATION PROGRESS

OHIO

Ohio State University, College of Agriculture, Columbus, J. W. Baringer

INDIANA

Purdue University College of Agriculture, La Fayette, W. E. Leer (July 19)

Mr. Stanley Castell, publicity agent in Indiana, is now giving a series of ctures and demonstrations at the 21 boys-and-girls-club camps in the State. ile so far only a few camps have been visited, the interest has been unusual. ve bushes of both common and Japanese barberry, as well as rusted straw and riveled grain, are being used in connection with this educational program.

Stem rust varied from almost zero in the extreme southern part of the ate to 100 per cent prevalence and a severity of 25 per cent in three areas cated near Columbus, Newcastle, and Columbia City. For the State as a whole, em rust could not be described as being more than a trace. Damage to wheat om stem rust probably will not exceed one-half of one per cent. At present, em rust is not heavy enough on either oats, rye, or barley to cause injury.

So far this year, 162 bushes, 861 seedlings, and 102 sprouting bushes ve been found in Indiana.

MICHIGAN

Agricultural College, East Lansing, W. F. Reddy

WISCONSIN

Department of Agriculture, State Capitol Annex, Madison, R. M. Caldwell uly 16)

Survey in Rock County is being conducted this season in territory where ore are few barberry bushes. However, the need for very careful search of e wooded areas becomes more apparent, as large single bushes occasionally e discovered where least expected. It seems that all portions of Rock County e infested with barberries and that bushes may be found in any tract of land the county.

Survey at Black Earth, Dane County, has reached the margin of the very heavily barberry-infested region which centers about the abandoned Bell nursery where common barberry bushes originally were planted.

Weather conditions this season have been almost ideal for stem-rust development. Stem rust became generally prevalent on barley, oats, and wheat during the last week of June, appearing as a trace in almost all fields examined. Since that time the development has been very rapid owing to frequent rains and high humidity. If humid conditions continue it is probable that rust will be severe.

At present the severity of infection on barley and oats is estimated at about 10 to 15 per cent and the prevalence at 100 per cent. Early oats are in the soft-dough stage while late oats are in the milk stage. Barley kernels are approaching the hard-dough stage. Rye is ripening with little stem rust in general. However, rye has been found quite heavily rusted in the vicinity of barberries. The uniform rust outbreak, as found on oats and barley, was absent in case of rye. A large acreage of rye is being grown in central Wisconsin.

ILLINOIS

Box 72, Post Office Building, Urbana, R. W. Bills

IOWA

Iowa State College, Ames, P. W. Rohrbaugh

MINNESOTA

Agricultural Experiment Station, University Farm, St. Paul, L.W.Melander

NEBRASKA

College of Agriculture, University Farm, Lincoln, -----------------------

SOUTH DAKOTA

College of Agriculture, Brookings, R. O. Bulger

NORTH DAKOTA

Agricultural Extension Division, State College Station, Fargo, G. C. Mayoue

MONTANA

State College of Agriculture, Bozeman, W. L. Popham

WYOMING

College of Agriculture, University of Wyoming, Laramie, W. L. Popham

COLORADO

Agricultural College, Ft. Collins, E. A. Lungren

C E R E A L   C O U R I E R

Official Messenger of the Office of Cereal Crops and Diseases
Bureau of Plant Industry, U. S. Department of Agriculture
(NOT FOR PUBLICATION)

.. 21   No. 18
July 31, 1929
Personnel (July 21-31) and General Issue

PERSONNEL ITEMS

Mr. C. H. Kyle, senior agronomist in corn investigations, will leave
hington about August 4 to spend about seven weeks in Georgia, Alabama,
iisiana, Mississippi, Tennessee, and South Carolina, in harvesting, se-
:ting, drying, fumigating, packing, shipping, and recording data on corn
wn on cooperative experiment plots at various places in these States.
Kyle also will consult with officials of the agricultural experiment sta-
ns in the interested States.

Dr. Roderick Sprague, who was appointed assistant pathologist on May 20
assist Dr. Hurley Fellows, of Manhattan, Kans., in the cooperative investi-
ion of foot rots of wheat, has been assigned permanent headquarters at
allis, Oreg., at the Oregon Agricultural Experiment Station, to continue
research, particularly in the region of The Dalles.

Dr. Sprague received the degree of Doctor of Philosophy from the Uni-
sity of Cincinnati in June, 1929.

Mr. T. R. Stanton, senior agronomist in charge of oat investigations,
te on July 28 from Dickinson, N. Dak., that since leaving Washington, D. C.,
July 8 he had visited agricultural experiment stations in West Virginia,
iana, Illinois, Iowa, South Dakota, Minnesota, and North Dakota. There was
crown-rust infection in the special crown-rust nursery that is being grown
Morgantown, W. Va. Therefore no leaf specimens were collected for forward-
to Mr. H. C. Murphy at Ames, Iowa. Oats and other cereals in the vicinity
Morgantown, as well as in the experiment plots on the station, were in good
dition.

At the experiment station at La Fayette, Ind., the new smut-resistant selections from crosses of Markton on Victory and Idamine were in good condition. However, most of these strains probably will be too late for best results under conditions in central Indiana. The behavior of these strains was similar at Urbana, Ill.

In Illinois there evidently is renewed interest in oats owing to the great reduction in the 1929 barley acreage as the result of the severe scab epidemic of last year. There also is some interest in the use of dehulled oats for feeding purposes. Some elevators and mills are installing dehullers for custom work.

At the Iowa experiment station, Ames, several of the new selections resulting from the large head-row nursery grown in 1928 appear very promising. Those from the Hajira and Kherson varieties were outstanding. One of the smut-resistant selections from the Markton X Sixty-Day cross showed unusual standing ability for any early oat. Some of the Edkin selections also were very promising. Owing to the heavy rains on July 13 and 14, the later oat varieties probably will outyield the earlier sorts at Ames. Corn, while slightly late, is uniform and generally promising.

At the U. S. Cereal Field Experiments at Redfield, S. Dak., crops had been severely damaged by dry weather. Early oats had been harvested. Midseason varieties were ripening prematurely and will make very low yields.

At the South Dakota station, Brookings, Mr. Stanton was pleased to find that Mr. Matthew Fowlds had made marked progress in his oat-breeding experiments during the past few years. In addition to developing many strains of hull-less oats which are resistant both to stem rust and smut, he has some very promising material of the Kherson type which has the smut resistance of Markton and the stem-rust resistance of Richland. There is every reason to believe that some valuable new oat strains will result from Mr. Fowlds' work at Brookings.

At University Farm, St. Paul, Minn., crops were in fair to good condition in spite of the dry weather.

In North Dakota crops generally are in poor condition owing to continuous dry weather. During the past week higher temperatures have been recorded than for several years, resulting in severe crop injury.

Mr. Harland Stevens was appointed agent, effective July 24, to assist in the cereal experiments that are being conducted at Manhattan, Kans., in cooperation with the Kansas Agricultural Experiment Station, under the direction of Dr. J. H. Parker. Mr. Stevens succeeds Mr. Vincent C. Hubbard, whose transfer to Mandan, N. Dak., to have charge of the cereal experiments at the Northern Great Plains Field Station, became effective on July 1.

Mr. and Mrs. Houston Lowe Gaddis, of Marshall, Va., were Office visitors on July 24. Mrs. Gaddis is·an enthusiastic farmer, much interested in barley. Several years ago she obtained seed of the Arlington Awnless barley from Messrs. Wood and Sons, of Richmond, Va. For several years she has practiced mass selection of the best heads and now her entire acreage is sown with this better seed. She says that she gets an average of a little more than 30 bushels to the acre, and feeds the entire product to hogs and other farm animals.

Mrs. Gaddis is interested now in making a comparative test of Tennessee Winter barley or any other good winter strain. Her experience ·is that spring barleys do not do very well under the conditions of her farm in Fauquier County, Virginia, at about 700 ft. elevation.

Prof. G. R. Hyslop, head of the department of·farm crops, Oregon State Agricultural College, called at the Office on July 30 to inspect samples of scabbed wheat, oats, and barley in connection with grading such material. Prof. Hyslop will be in or around Washington for the next two and one-half months in connection with grain grading studies.

Mr. J. Warren Kinsman, Vice-President ·of the Bayer-Semesan Company, Inc., 105 Hudson Street, New York City, and Dr. W. H. Tisdale, of the E. I. du Pont de Nemours and Company, Inc., of Wilmington, Del., were in the Office on July 23 to discuss their future plans for the production of cereal seed disinfectants. Mr. Kinsman also is associated with the sales division of the dyestuffs department of the du Pont de Nemours and Company, Inc., of Wilmington.

Dr. E. D. Merrill, dean of the college of agriculture and director of the agricultural experiment station of the University of California, was a visitor in the Office on July 30. Dr. Merrill recently was elected director of the New York Botanical Garden.

Mr. Gordon K. Middleton, of the crop improvement and seed certification division, of the North Carolina State College, and Mr. J. B. Cotner, professor of agronomy, of the same institution, were Office visitors on July 30. They had motored up from North Carolina on their way to Cornell University, Ithaca, N. Y., where they expect to complete their theses in plant breeding, looking toward obtaining the degree of Doctor of Philosophy.

MANUSCRIPTS AND PUBLICATIONS

50 A manuscript entitled "The Value of Physiologic-Form Surveys in the Study of the Epidemiology of Stem Rust," by E. C. Stakman, M. N. Levine, and J. M. Wallace, was approved on July 22 for publication in Phytopathology.

The article entitled "Bulked-Population Method of Handling Cereal Hybrids by V. H. Florell, appears in the Journal of the American Society of Agronomy 21(7): 718-724. July, 1929. (Cooperation between the Office of Cereal Crops and Diseases and the department of agronomy of the California Agricultural Experiment Station, University Farm, Davis, Calif.)

The article entitled "Effect of Date of Seeding on Yield, Lodging, Maturi and Nitrogen Content in Cereal Varietal Experiments," by V. H. Florell, appear in the Journal of the American Society of Agronomy 21(7): 725-731, fig. 1. Ju 1929. (Cooperation between the Office of Cereal Crops and Diseases and the division of agronomy of the California Agricultural Experiment Station.)

The article entitled "The Influence of the Combine on Agronomic Practices and Research," by John H. Martin, appears in the Journal of the American Socie of Agronomy 21(7): 766-773. July, 1929. (These investigations were conducted by the Bureaus of Agricultural Economics, Plant Industry, and Public Roads, of the U. S. Department of Agriculture, in cooperation with the agricultural experiment stations of Texas, Oklahoma, Kansas, Nebraska, Montana, North Dakota South Dakota, Minnesota, Illinois, Indiana, Pennsylvania, Virginia, and Georg

C E R E A L   C O U R I E R

Official Messenger of the Office of Cereal Crops and Diseases
Bureau of Plant Industry, U. S. Department of Agriculture
(NOT FOR PUBLICATION)

----

1. 21   No. 19

August 10, 1929
Personnel (Aug. 1-10) and Field Station (July 16-31) Issue

PERSONNEL ITEMS

Dr. Charlotte Elliott, associate pathologist, wrote on August 2, from
Great Falls, Mont., that she had just finished making oat-blast counts at the
Aberdeen (Idaho) Substation and was on her way to Edmonton, Alberta. The oats
at the Aberdeen Substation were very fine, as usual.

Mr. H. S. Garrison, assistant agronomist in corn investigations, will leave
Washington about August 20 for Tifton, Ga., and Florence, S. C., to assist Mr.
J. H. Kyle in harvesting, selecting, drying, fumigating, packing, shipping, and
recording data on corn grown in cooperative experiment plots. He will return to
Washington about September 20.

Mr. F. D. Richey, senior agronomist in charge of corn investigations, will
leave Washington about August 14 to visit various places in Florida, Georgia,
Alabama, Mississippi, and Tennessee in the interests of cooperative corn investigations. He will be in the field about three weeks.

Mr. John B. Sieglinger, agronomist in charge of the grain-sorghum and broomcorn experiments at the U. S. Dry-Land Field Station, Woodward, Okla., was
authorized to attend Farmers' Week of the Oklahoma Agricultural Experiment Station at Stillwater, Okla., from August 13 to 16, and to present a paper on
'Grain Sorghums for Western Oklahoma."

VISITORS

Mr. Constantine Apostolides, of the Haytian Pineapple Co., Cap-Haitien, Haiti, was an Office visitor on August 5.

Mr. Tranquilino G. Fajardo, of the Philippine Islands, who has been in the United States for a period of years, engaged in graduate study at different universities, was an Office visitor on August 7. He has just completed his graduate study in plant pathology and botany at the University of Wisconsin for his doctorate. Mr. Fajardo was on the rolls of this Office for the summer months in 1924 when assisting Dr. C. W. Hungerford, of the University of Idaho, in cooperative investigations of stripe rust. He received the M. S. degree from that institution in 1924. During the school year of 1928-29, Mr. Fajardo was with Prof. H. P. Barss, of the Oregon Agricultural College, assisting in plant pathology.

Dr. James G. Horsfall, of the New York State Agricultural Experiment Station, Geneva, N. Y., was an Office visitor on August 3.

MANUSCRIPTS AND PUBLICATIONS

51 A manuscript entitled "Barley Scab. Farmers Use Scabbed Grain Safely
d Profitably," by James G. Dickson, was submitted on August 8 for publication
the Department Yearbook for 1929.

Galley proof of article entitled "Sulphur Dusting for the Prevention of
em Rust of Wheat," by E. B. Lambert and E. C. Stakman, for publication in
ytopathology, was read on August 3; page proof read on August 9.

Galley proof of article entitled "Influence of Varietal Resistance, Sap
idity, and Certain Environmental Factors on the Occurrence of Loose Smut in
eat," by Victor F. Tapke, for publication in the Journal of Agricultural Re-
arch, was read on August 6.

Galley proof of article entitled "Concerning Heterothallism in Puccinia
aminis," by Ruth F. Allen, for publication in Science, was read on August 7.

Galley proof of article entitled "Relation of Leaf Acidity to Vigor of
heat Grown at Different Temperatures," by Annie M. Hurd-Karrer, for publication
n the Journal of Agricultural Research, was read on August 8.

The article entitled "The Development of Disease-Resistant Strains of Corn,"
y James R. Holbert and James G. Dickson, appears in the Proceedings [4th] of
he International Congress of Plant Sciences [Ithaca] 1: 155-160. 1929. (Co-
peration between the Office of Cereal Crops and Diseases and the Funk Bros.
eed Co., and the Wisconsin Agricultural Experiment Station.)

The article entitled "Breeding Wheat for Disease Resistance," by C. E.
eighty, appears in the Proceedings [4th] of the International Congress of
lant Sciences [Ithaca] 1: 149-153. 1929.

The article entitled "Occurrence of the Zonate-Eyespot Fungus Helmintho-
porium giganteum on Some Additional Grasses," by Charles Drechsler, appears
n the Journal of Agricultural Research 39 (2): 129-135, pls. 1-6. July 15,
929. (Dr. Drechsler formerly was a member of the staff of the Office of Cereal
rops and Diseases.)

Page proof of Technical Bulletin 133, "Flax Cropping in Mixture with Wheat,
ats, and Barley," by A. C. Arny, T. E. Stoa, Clyde McKee, and A. C. Dillman, was
ead on August 5.

FIELD STATION CONDITION AND PROGRESS

(All experiments except those conducted at the Arlington Experiment Farm, Rosslyn, Va., are in cooperation with State agricultural experiment stations or other agencies.)

HUMID ATLANTIC COAST AREA (South to North)

GEORGIA

State College of Agriculture, Athens (Cereal Agronomy, R. R. Childs)

VIRGINIA

Arlington Experiment Farm, Rosslyn (Small Grain Agronomy, J. W. Taylor) (August 7)

The yields of winter oats for the 1928-29 crop year were below average, judging by the plot results. Two series of the varietal oat test were grown on a seed bed prepared by disking, and weed competition was great. On the seed bed prepared by plowing weeds were not a yield factor and excellent grain yields resulted. The bushel weight of the oats were unusually high, varying from 35 to 39 pounds. As usual the variety Lee produced the heaviest grain.

Eight of the 10 varieties or selections of winter oats outyielding Culberson, the check, are Arlington selections. The Fulghum selection, 699-202, appears to be a high yielding type in mild winters like the past one. It is considerably hardier, however, than the true Fulghum and Kanota types.

Average yield of winter-oat varieties grown in triplicated 40th-acre plots, compared with that of check plots, at Arlington Experiment Farm in 1929

Variety	C. I. No.	Yield (Bu. per acre)	Yield Check plot (Bu. per acre)	Gain or loss of variety compared to check (Bu. per acre)
Selection	699-202	45.1	34.7	+10.4
Randolph	2275	48.8	39.3	+ 9.5
Custis	2041	40.4	34.3	+ 6.1
Selection	1001-D1-2B	44.5	39.3	+ 5.2
Red Rustproof	1815	42.0	37.4	+ 4.6
Jackson	2276	38.0	34.7	+ 3.3
Fulghum Selection	699-2011	42.0	39.3	+ 2.7
Lee	2042	35.6	34.3	+ 1.3
Winter Turf	541-4	35.4	34.3	+ 1.1
Hatchett	838	39.9	39.3	+ .6
Winter Turf	431	34.4	34.7	- .3
Bicknell	206-155	36.4	37.4	- 1.0
Fulghum	708	33.8	34.7	- 1.1
Culberson	273-I-14	35.9	37.4	- 1.5
Kanota	839	31.7	37.4	- 5.7
Culberson[1]	273	36.8	----	----

[1] Average yield of 14 check plots.

The comparative rank in grain yield of 10 varieties of winter oats ob_
ained by the exclusion or inclusion of the two border rows of each plot are
iven in the following table. The standing of the varieties was but slightly
ffected by discarding the border rows.

Rank of 10 varieties of winter oats grown in triplicated 40th-acre plots
hen yields are based on entire plot as compared to yields with border rows
iscarded, at Arlington Experiment Farm, 1929

Variety	C.I.No.	Rank with border rows	Rank without border rows
Selection	699-202	1	1
Custis	2041	2	2
Red Rustproof	1815	3	3
Winter Turf	541-4	4	6
Jackson	2276	5	4
Lee	2042	6	5
Fulghum	708	7	9
Winter Turf	431	8	7
Bicknell	206-155	9	8
Kanota	839	10	10

Winter wheat yields, although below average, were better than expected.
he rainfall for the crop year totaled 49.23 inches, or approximately 8 inches
bove normal. A total of 16.2 inches fell in April, May, and June,- almost 5
nches above the average for these months. Straw growth was heavy, but hardly
ny lodging occurred.

The Purplestraw. type was the highest in yield for 1929. Four varieties
r selections in the triplicated series outyielded the check (Purplestraw) two
f which, Wheat-Rye 10 and Dixie, approach Purplestraw in type. Nittany, as
sual, was the outstanding bearded variety.

Average yield of winter-wheat varieties grown in triplicated 40th-acre plot~
ompared with that of the check variety, at Arlington Experiment Farm, 1929

Variety	C.I.No.	Yield (Bu.per acre)	Yield, check plots (Bu. per acre)	Gain or loss of variety compared to check (Bu. per acre)
Wheat-Rye 10	----	34.0	30.1	+3.9
Dixie	----	32.8	30.4	+2.4
Nittany	6882	32.3	30.4	+1.9
Forward	6691	30.5	30.1	+ .4
Orlando	----	29.8	30.1	- .3
Purplestraw	1957	30.4	30.7	- .3
Wheat-Rye 16-1A	----	29.6	30.4	- .8
Fulcaster	1945	29.1	30.1	-1.0
Dietz	1981	28.8	29.9	-1.1
Mammoth Red	2003	29.5	30.7	-1.2
Fulcaster	6162	28.8	30.1	-1.3
Red Wonder	5780	29.5	31.0	-1.5
Fultz	1923	29.3	31.0	-1.7
Illini Chief	5406	28.2	30.1	-1.9
Poole	3489	27.6	29.9	-2.3
Poole	1979	27.1	29.9	-2.8
Shepherd	6163	27.2	30.4	-3.2
Missouri Bluestem	1912	26.8	31.0	-4.2
Red Rock	5976	25.1	30.1	-5.0
Leap	4823	23.6	29.9	-6.3
Tennessee Giant	1744	22.1	30.7	-8.6
Purplestraw 1/	1915	30.4		

1/Average of 19 check plots.

Yield of winter-wheat varieties grown in single 40th-acre or 80th-acı
plots, compared with that of check variety, at Arlington Experiment Farm,

Variety	Yield (Bu. per acre)	Gain or loss of variety pared to check (Bu. per a
Purplestraw (Selection)	36.0	+ 4.7
Trumbull	31.7	0
Nigger	26.5	- 1.9
V. P. I. No. 112	24.7	- 2.3
Berkeley Rock	24.5	- 2.5
Gladden	28.4	- 3.3
Currell	25.0	- 3.4
Fulhard	26.2	- 5.1
Valley x Grandprize	22.7	- 8.6
Kawvale	20.2	-11.1

Average yield of winter-wheat varieties in duplicate 40th-acre plots,
pared with that of the check variety, at Arlington Experiment Farm, 1929

Variety	C.I.No.	Yield (Bu. per acre)	Gain or loss of variety co to check (Bu. per acre)
Stoner	2980	32.0	+ 1.9
Harvest Queen	6883	32.9	+ 1.4
Brown Fife	1933	31.9	+ .8
China	180	31.2	- .3
Dawson	6162	29.2	- .9
Rod Row 115	----	27.5	- 2.6
Red Rock (Selection)	----	30.6	- 2.8
Purkoff	----	27.8	- 4.8
Potomac	1733	26.0	- 6.6
Michikoff	----	23.6	- 7.9
Jersey Fultz	5774	21.7	- 9.8
Kanred	5146	13.4	-19.2

Arlington Experiment Farm, Rosslyn (Corn Breeding, F. D. Richey)

Arlington Experiment Farm, Rosslyn (Cereal Smuts, V. F. Tapke, Actin
Charge)

Arlington Experiment Farm, Rosslyn (Virus Diseases, H. H. McKinney)

NEW YORK

Cornell University Agricultural Experiment Station, Ithaca (Cereal B
H. H. Love)

HUMID MISSISSIPPI VALLEY AREA (South to North)

LOUISIANA

Rice Experiment Station, Crowley (Rice Agronomy, J. M. Jenkins) (August 3)

Some commercial fields of rice are well advanced and will be ready for harvest by the first week in August. The percentage of early maturing rice appears o be much less in this vicinity than it was last year. In some cases, it would eem that Fortuna has been seeded in place of earlier varieties. Early seeded ields of Fortuna are beginning to mature.

Weeds are very abundant in most fields, especially red rice. For some reaon red rice seems more abundant than it has been for several years. This peraps is due to rather dry summer weather for the past several years. Heavy rains t seeding time also may have something to do with the abundance of red rice, by ausing germination along with the seeded crop. Heavy rains at seeding time are esponsible for the abundance of sedges and grasses in many of the fields.

The rains at seeding time also caused many grassy plots on the station. rasses and sedges, seed of which is even now present, germinated along with the rice. This condition is especially noticeable in certain fertilizer plots and in continuous check plots. The flooding rains of May also scattered seeds throughout certain low areas on the station.

All soybean and cotton plots have been thoroughly cultivated, two to three times during the month.

Blister beetles were unusually abundant in July. It has been several years since they have appeared in such numbers. By dusting with sodium fluosilicate, 12 to 14 large groups were killed in the soybean plots. Frequent rains in July seemed to be favorable for the development of this insect.

Agricultural Experiment Station, Baton Rouge (Corn Breeding, H. F. Stoneberg) (August 1)

The hand-pollinating season began on June 20 and ended July 15. Approximately 500 cross-pollinations and 5,000 self-pollinations were made. The weather conditions were ideal for the work.

The weather this year has been very favorable for the growth and development of the corn plant. Strains that have been inbred for 11 years and which were brought to Louisiana six years ago have produced larger and more vigorous plants this year than in any previous year since they were moved to Baton Rouge. This may be due to the favorable weather conditions that have prevailed. There has been plenty of moisture at all times, and the average maximum temperatures have been considerably lower than for the previous years. The latter fact may have had something to do with the better growth. The maximum temperatures have been above 90 degrees on 12 days only during the last two months and have not exceeded 93 degrees.

The recording of notes on the plants and ear-rows is now in progress.

The fifth annual session of the American Institute of Cooperation is being held at the Louisiana State University, July 29 to August 8. It is a session of unusual importance because of the greater interest in cooperatives since the enactment of the farm relief bill, and because of the addresses by members of the Federal Farm Board outlining the policies of the board.

TENNESSEE

Agricultural Experiment Station, Knoxville (Corn Breeding, L. S. Mayer)

MISSOURI

Agricultural Experiment Station, Columbia (Cereal Agronomy, L. J. Stadler

OHIO

Ohio State University, Columbus (Corn Breeding, L. R. Jorgenson) (August

Corn pollination at Columbus is nearly completed. The biggest day was Sunday, August 4, when about 2,700 pollinations were made. There remain only abo 300 self pollinations and a few miscellaneous crosses in the sweet-corn crossin plot. This should be completed by the 10th. Data on silking are being taken i the various experiments.

IOWA

Agricultural Experiment Station, Ames (Oat Breeding, L. C. Burnett)

Agricultural Experiment Station, Ames (Corn Breeding, M. T. Jenkins)

Agricultural Experiment Station, Ames (Crown Rust of Oats, S. M. Dietz)

ILLINOIS

Funk Bros. Seed Co., Bloomington (Corn Root, Stalk and Ear Rots, J. R. Ho

INDIANA

Purdue University Agricultural Experiment Station, LaFayette (Corn Rots a Metallic Poisoning, J. F. Trost, Acting in Charge)

Purdue University Agricultural Experiment Station, LaFayette (Leaf Rusts, E. B. Mains)

266

WISCONSIN

Agricultural Experiment Station, Madison (Wheat Scab, J. G. Dickson)

MINNESOTA

Agricultural Experiment Station, University Farm, St. Paul (Wheat Breeding,
K. S. Quisenberry, Acting in Charge)

Agricultural Experiment Station, University Farm, St. Paul (Stem Rust,
E. C. Stakman)

Agricultural Experiment Station, University Farm, St. Paul (Flax Rust,
H. A. Rodenhiser)

GREAT PLAINS AREA (South to North)

OKLAHOMA

Woodward Field Station, Woodward (Grain Sorghum and Broomcorn, J. B. Sieglinger) (August 3)

The weather of the last half of July was dry and hot. Sorghums will need
rain soon. The heat and drought have hastened the heading and development of
some of the early varieties of the early seedings.

At present bagging heads for seed is in progress. Several crosses also
have been made.

Maximum temperature for July, 105 degrees on the 17th; minimum for same
period, 64 degrees on the 20th and 25th. Precipitation, 0.39 of an inch in tw
showers on the 17th and 18th.

KANSAS

Agricultural Experiment Station, Manhattan (Cereal Breeding, J. H. Parker)
(August 5)

All of our nursery threshing was completed on August 1, and we are now busy
summarizing data, making individual plant selections of F_4 wheat crosses, taking
notes on grain quality, etc.

The following data on yields of hard red winter and soft red winter wheats
grown in triplicated plots at the Agronomy Farm were obtained by Prof. S. C.
Salmon, who has charge of plot experiments. Data also are included of yields
of some new varieties grown in single plots.

Average yield of winter-wheat varieties grown in triplicated plots at Agronomy Farm, Manhattan, Kans., 1928-29

Variety	Kansas No.	Yield	P.E.$_m$
Hard Red Winter			
Fulhard	2593	28.9	$\pm$1.63
Kanred x Hard Federation	2627	26.4	$\pm$0.20
Tenmarq Selection	2637	25.0	$\pm$2.28
Tenmarq	439	24.3	$\pm$2.28
Kanred x Marquis	2638	22.8	$\pm$1.21
Prelude x Kanred	2628	22.1	$\pm$0.11
Kanred x Marquis	2644	20.2	$\pm$1.40
Blackhull	343	18.1	$\pm$2.11
Oro	495	18.0	$\pm$0.81
Early Blackhull	483	17.4	$\pm$0.33
Kanred x Hard Federation	2625	17.3	$\pm$1.21
Superhard	470	16.8	$\pm$1.07
Kanred (checks)	2401	14.8	$\pm$0.44
Kharkov	382	14.2	$\pm$0.51
Turkey	570	12.8	$\pm$0.23
Kharkov (Hays No. 2)	2659	12.2	$\pm$0.55
Newturk	2536	11.4	$\pm$0.18
Soft Red Winter			
Kawvale	2593	29.5	$\pm$1.78
Fulcaster	317	26.9	$\pm$1.17
Nebraska No. 28	34	24.3	$\pm$1.39
Michigan Wonder	500	23.5	$\pm$2.24
Currell	501	19.9	$\pm$0.66
Harvest Queen	19	19.6	$\pm$0.92
Kanred (checks)	2401	16.5	$\pm$1.03

Average yield of new wheat varieties grown in single plots at the Ag Farm, Manhattan, Kans., 1928-29

Variety	Kansas No.	Yield	P.E.$_m$
Kanred x Marquis	2642	34.2	
Do	2640	30.7	
Do	2647	30.3	
Cooperatorka	499	27.7	
Kanred x Marquis	2639	23.8	
Kanred x Hard Federation	2650	23.4	
Kanred x Marquis	2641	21.9	
Illini Chief x Kanred	2655	21.7	
Prelude x Kanred	2652	21.4	
Kanred x Marquis	2645	21.1	
Illini Chief x Kanred	2656	21.0	
P1066-1 x Super	2654	20.9	
Kanred x Marquis	2643	20.7	
Red Hull	487	19.8	
Illini Chief x Kanred	2657	19.3	
Eagle Chief	498	19.1	

Continued)

Variety	Kansas No.	Yield	P.E.$_m$
Kanred x Marquis	2646	17.8	
Prelude x Kanred	2653	16.9	
Kanred x Hard Federation	2648	15.7	
Do	2651	14.0	
Kanred (checks)	----	13.7	$\pm$0.61
Kanred x Hard Federation	2649	12.9	

Agricultural Experiment Station, Manhattan (Corn Breeding, A. M. Brunson)

Agricultural Experiment Station, Manhattan (Wheat Foot Rots, Hurley Fellows)

Agricultural Experiment Station, Manhattan (Wheat Leaf Rust, C. O. Johnston)

Fort Hays Branch Experiment Station, Hays (Cereal Agronomy, A. F. Swanson) July 30)

Harvesting, threshing, recleaning, and weighing of grain from the varietal nd nursery plots have been completed.

The following yields of winter wheat were obtained from fall-listed and fal- ow land:

Variety	C.I.No.	Average 2-plots on fall-listed land	Average 2-plots fal-lowed land
Early Blackhull	----	19.0	33.6
Superhard	8054	13.7	30.8
Prelude x Kanred (Kans. 2623)	----	15.6	26.8
Blackhull	6521	18.8	28.7
Fulhard	----	13.8	29.6
Kawvale	----	13.1	27.9
Tenmarq	----	15.2	24.8
Nebraska No. 28	----	14.0	24.8
P1068 x Preston(Kans.444)	----	12.1	24.0
Fulcaster	5471	11.3	24.2
Miracle (Eagle Chief-Okla)	----	12.3	21.3
Kanred	5146	12.7	20.0
Newturk	6935	12.1	19.8
Nebraska No. 6	6245	12.7	18.8
Nebraska No. 60	6250	12.1	19.0
Kharkof Hays No. 2	6686	11.1	19.8
Oro	8220	12.7	17.9
Harvest Queen	6199	10.6	19.0
Local Ellis Co. Turkey	----	9.6	19.2
Turkey	1558	10.2	18.5
Kharkof	1442	10.0	17.9

The varietal experiment of winter wheat on fall-listed land was seeded November 15, after the first seeding of September 27 had been discarded in ord to destroy an excessive volunteer growth.

In another experiment on fall-listed land seeded on September 27 and wher volunteer wheat was not a factor, the following yields were obtained from an average of 8 replications for five well-known varieties of Kansas wheat.

Variety	Yield (Bu. per acre)
Blackhull	28.4
Tenmarq	25.4
Kanred	22.6
Kharkof Hays No. 2	21.9
Ellis County Local Turkey	20.4

The following yields of oats were obtained from three replicated plots of each variety:

Variety	C.I.No.	Yield (Bu. per acre)
Fulghum Selection H. C. 713	----	65.9
Kanota	839	64.6
Burt x Sixty Day	727	62.8
Burt 916	2054	62.0
Red Rustproof Tex. 118-2	----	60.4
Fulghum	708	59.4
Burt	293	52.3
Richland	787	48.1
Iogold	2329	42.2
Kherson	459	36.4

The yields of Richland, Iogold, and Kherson are the average of two plots only. These three varieties were greatly injured by the hot drying winds of June 15, 16, and 17 which caught the varieties in a tender critical stage of growth. The third series of plots for the last named varieties were so badly lodged, tangled, and shriveled that the yields obtained from them were not included in the calculations.

The following yields of barley were obtained from three replicated plots of each variety:

Variety	C.I.No.	Yield (Bu. per acre)
Pryor	2359	53.1
White Smyrna	195	52.1
Club Mariout	261	50.0
Vaughn	1367	49.6
Flynn	1311	49.0
Preston	1348	48.4
Stavropol H. C. 249	----	47.2
Huntington	4110	46.9
Francis	4109	46.2
Colby Local Stavropol	----	42.9
Coast	690	34.9

The yields of wheat on the project and throughout this section were reduced / the hot winds of June 15, 16, and 17, from what would have been an above-ormal prospect.

The total rainfall for July was seven inches and the weather was relatively ool and ideal for corn growth. Yesterday and today hot winds prevailed and hile row crops are not yet suffering a good rain will soon be needed.

Farmers are making good progress in getting wheat ground ready, but there s considerable complaint about the excessive stubble covering the ground.

NEBRASKA

North Platte Substation, North Platte (Cereal Agronomy, G. F. Sprague)

SOUTH DAKOTA

U. S. Cereal Field Experiments, Redfield (Wheat Improvement, E. S. McFadden)

NORTH DAKOTA

Northern Great Plains Field Station, Mandan (Cereal Agronomy, V. C. Hubbard) (August 1)

Dry hot weather has brought on an early harvest. The greater number of the varieties in the spring-wheat nursery are ripe and are being harvested. All of the barley, six of the oat varieties, and two varieties of wheat from plots have been harvested.

Stem rust is surprisingly abundant in spite of the dry weather. Varietal differences are easily noticeable.

Washington visitors at the Station since July 15 have been Messrs. T. R. Stanton and F. A. Coffman.

Mr. Wallace Butler, of San Antonio, Tex., also was here to make rust readings on the uniform wheat and oat nursery.

Northern Great Plains Field Station, Mandan (Flax Breeding, J. C. Brinsmade, Jr.) (August 1)

The weather of the last half of July has been exceptionally dry and hot. Temperatures of 100 degrees and over were recorded on five days for this period. The maximum temperature was 108 degrees on July 26 and the minimum, 52 degrees on July 17 and 28. The total precipitation for this period was 0.21 of an inch. The total precipitation for July was 1.16 inches, which is less than half the average for the month for the past 15 years.

The blooming period of flax was greatly shortened because of the dry, ho:
weather, and flax is ripening very rapidly. Flax sown on April 20, May 1, an
May 11 in the date-and-rate-of-seeding-and-tillage experiment, and two early
varieties sown on May 1, were harvested July 29, just 10 days earlier than fl;
sown on the same dates in 1928, and just one month earlier than in 1927. Fla:
plots sown on May 20 are nearly ready to harvest. Fifteen early varieties in
the triplicated triple-row nursery were harvested on July 30.

Grasshoppers are unusually abundant. Poison bran distributed July 29
already has had a noticeable effect in reducing their numbers.

Rust on flax developed very little in July. Burbank flax, which is extremely susceptible, is only moderately infected in the May 25 seeding, and
almost rust-free in the June 10 seeding.

Dickinson Substation, Dickinson (Cereal Agronomy, R. W. Smith) (July 31)

The weather in July was unusually hot and dry, especially during the latt
half of the month. There were 13 days in July when the maximum temperature wa
above 90 degrees. On the 26th and 27th the maximum was 101 and 106 degrees,
respectively, the latter being the highest temperature recorded at the Substation since 1919.

The precipitation for the month was 0.54 of an inch, which is nearly two
inches below normal for this month at Dickinson. There has been no rainfall
except light showers since June 14.

Because of the drought and extreme heat crops are ripening somewhat prematurely and grain yields will be light in this section of the State. Some
yields will be fairly good where grain was sown on summer fallow or corn land

Early varieties of oats and barley at the Substation have been harvested
also the rye plots. Early spring-wheat varieties are now ripe and several wi
be harvested this week. Harvest in this section will become general by the
first of next week.

Some of the official visitors at the Substation in July were Dr. C. F.
Marbut and Dr. T. B. Rice, of the Bureau of Soils and Chemistry, Mr. S. H.
Hastings, of the Office of Western Irrigation Agriculture, Supt. J. M. Stephe
of the Mandan Field Station, Supt. Dan Hansen and Mr. A. E. Seamans, of the
Huntley (Montana) Field Station, Dr. H. B. Humphrey, Mr. J. A. Clark, Mr. T.
Stanton, Mr. F. A. Coffman, Mr. R. W. Leukel, and Mr. V. C. Hubbard.

On July 27 about 30 auto loads of farmers and their families, accompani
by Floyd Garfoot, County Agent of Slope County, drove up from Amidon to visi
the Substation. After having their picnic dinner the crowd assembled in the
machine shed where seats had been prepared for the occasion. After brief ta
on the work of the Substation by Supt. Moomaw and the cereal man, the farmer
were shown over the Substation in two groups and the experiments were explai
in detail.

Much interest was shown in the various experiments and numerous questions were asked and answered. The farmers showed special interest in varieties of grain and forage crops, the crossing of wheat varieties for disease resistance, the growing of crested wheat grass, and the use of the duck-foot cultivator for tillage and as a substitute for the plow in summer-fallowing.

Other county agents who brought delegations of farmers from neighboring counties to visit the Substation in July were J. C. Russell from Beach, Golden Valley County, N. Dak., and M. P. Ostby from Wibaux in Wibaux County, Mont.

Agricultural Experiment Station, State College Station, Fargo (Flax Diseases, L. W. Boyle) (July 30)

As yet rust and pasmo have not appeared in the flax-disease plots here this season, which has been exceptionally dry. At present the accumulated deficiency is over seven inches below the average precipitation. This is in marked contrast with the exceptionally wet season of last year when both pasmo and rust were very prevalent.

The continued drought and high temperatures of late are causing flax to ripen more quickly than usual. The flax, however, has developed surprisingly well in view of the dry season, apparently drawing on the reserve soil moisture left from last season.

Langdon Substation, Langdon (Wheat Improvement, G. S. Smith) (August 1)

The nursery, being clean and on fallow, still looks very well, and the varietal plots probably will produce fair yields.

Crops in this vicinity are developing slowly, and the early seeded grain is dried up past much hope of recovery. An occasional field of barley is being cut, and some crops are being plowed under. A good rain still would be of much benefit in filling the later grain.

The rainfall for the month totaled 1.46 inches. Several days have been extremely hot, here as well as elsewhere. The maximum temperature was 98 on July 26.

The work of the Office of Cereal Crops and Diseases at this station consists of maintaining varietal experiments of 16 common and 7 durum wheat varieties, and a nursery of 1,433 rows, besides the rust nursery and uniform smut nursery. The main nursery is made up partly of hybrid material and partly of foreign introductions, mostly durums, because more durum is grown here than in any other section.

The writer also has charge of the local combine study in standing loss for small grains, carried on by the State agronomy department.

MONTANA

Judith Basin Branch Station, Moccasin (Cereal Agronomy, B. B. Bayles)
(August 1)

All winter wheat on the station, with the exception of late dates of see
ing, has been cut and threshing of the winter nursery is nearly finished.

Montana has experienced the driest and hottest growing season since 1919
The rainfall for June was 1.86 inches as compared with a normal of 3.23 inche
and that for July was 0.62 of an inch as compared to a normal of 1.82 inches.
The rainfall for July was recorded on the 6th and 7th and was followed by thr
weeks of unusually hot weather accompanied by drying winds. Winter wheat in
central Montana was far enough along so that it will produce fair yields.
Spring wheat was just heading at that time and the yields probably will be
greatly reduced.

The damage from Helminthosporium this year will be less than in 1928. H
ever, early seeded fields of winter wheat show considerable injury from disea
and during a recent survey, by Dr. Hurley Fellows, Helminthosporium was found
in nearly all fields of both winter and spring wheat in the Judith Basin and i
south-central Montana.

The Judith Basin Farmers' Picnic Association held its annual picnic at th
station on July 25. A count at the gate showed that 4,500 persons attended.
Talks were given by Governor Erickson, Representative Scott Leavitt, Chancello
Brannon, and Director Linfield.

Official visitors at the Station in July have included Mr. J. A. Clark,
Dr. H. B. Humphrey, Mr. F. A. Coffman, Office of Cereal Crops and Diseases, a
Dr. Hurley Fellows, of Manhattan, Kans., and Messrs. H. E. Morris and P. A.
Young of the Montana Experiment Station.

Montana Agricultural Experiment Station, Bozeman (LeRoy Powers) (August

In recent years farmers of some of the more favorably located winter-whe
sections of Gallatin County have sustained considerable loss due to covered s
even though copper carbonate was used to treat the seed. Figures from the te
minal inspection of carload wheat receipts from Bozeman show that there has t
a steady increase in the number of cars grading smutty from 12.4 to 43.3 per
cent during the period 1923 to 1927, inclusive. For the first half of the cr
year 1928, the percentage of cars grading smutty was 44. These figures were
taken from data compiled by E. G. Boerner, Marion Griffiths Zehner, and F. C.
Meier, of the U. S. Department of Agriculture. The data emphasize the need i
determining the resistance to covered smut possessed by existing wheat variet
as well as the importance of work tending to develop varieties more resistan
this disease.

The following table gives the results of tests on resistance of winter-
wheat varieties to covered smut collected from the Spring Hill Community of
Gallatin County where infection is severe.

Resistance of winter-wheat varieties to stinking smut[1] seed covered with
smut and planted in single rod rows, Bozeman, Mont., 1928-29

Variety or Hybrid	Mont. No.	Per cent of smutted heads		Average
		1928	1929	1928-29
Hard Federation x Hussar	54	0.5	0.4	0.5
Ridit	38	1.0	0.2	0.6
Turkey x Florence	52	0.8	1.0	0.9
Cooperatorka	49	0.4	1.6	1.0
N. N. 487	56	2.2	3.2	2.7
Minturki	10	3.6	2.6	3.1
Albit	44	7.6	0.2	3.9
C. I. 8033	64	8.0	0.0	4.0
(Turkey x Florence) x				
(Turkey x Hybrid 128)	55	6.1	2.0	4.1
Oro	68	6.8	2.0	4.4
Berkeley Rock	25	15.6	6.0	10.8
C. I. 8045	66	24.6	2.0	13.3
Kanred Selection 1	--	8.4	24.4	16.4
Stepinatschka	51	13.2	22.2	17.7
Iowa 1946	8	31.4	8.6	20.0
Turkey x Minhardi	79	25.8	19.0	22.4
Nebraska No. 60	5	44.2	11.0	27.6
N. N. 488	57	56.0	8.2	32.1
Jones Fife	16	40.4	32.2	36.3
Superhard	45	44.8	31.8	38.3
Newturk	33	40.6	36.2	38.4
Turkey	4	46.0	31.0	38.5
Hostianum	47	58.2	27.8	43.0
Karmont	7	60.8	27.6	44.2
Hybrid 128	14	57.3	33.6	45.5
Blackhull	9	55.2	37.4	46.3
Kanred	2	43.4	50.4	46.9
N. N. 497	58	75.0	21.8	48.4
Montana No. 36	36	55.6	44.0	49.8
Ukrainka	50	51.4	48.4	49.9
Kharkof	3	55.2	46.2	50.7
Lutescens	48	72.4	30.0	51.2
N. N. 509	63	84.6	23.0	53.8
N. N. 511	67	70.6	32.2	51.4
Eureka x Minhardi	75	82.2	31.8	57.0
N. N. 507	62	84.8	38.0	61.4
N. N. 504	61	90.6	32.8	61.7
Homer	46	55.6	68.4	62.0
N. N. 502	60	88.0	36.6	62.3
Minhardi x Minturki	73	85.0	41.4	63.2
N. N. 500	59	84.8	49.8	67.3
Minhardi	13	97.2	40.2	68.7
C. I. 8040	65	89.6	48.4	69.0
Smutless	70	----	0.2	----
Kanred x Minhardi	80	----	10.0	----
Minard x Minhardi	78	----	11.4	----
Minred K	71	----	11.4	----

[1] Tilletia levis used for inoculum was collected from the Spring
Hill Community of Gallatin County.

(Continued)

Variety or Hybrid	Mont. No.	Per cent of smutted heads 1928	1929	Average 1928-29
Kawvale	77	----	14.0	----
Super	15	----	35.4	----
Mystery	72	----	49.0	----
Early Blackhull	76	----	55.0	----

WESTERN BASIN AND COAST AREAS (North to West and South)

IDAHO

Aberdeen Substation, Aberdeen (Cereal Agronomy, L. L. Davis)

Agricultural Experiment Station, Moscow (Stripe Rust, C. W. Hungerford)

WASHINGTON

Agricultural Experiment Station, Pullman (Cereal Breeding, E. F. Gaines)

OREGON

Sherman County Branch Station, Moro (Cereal Agronomy, D. E. Stephens)
(July 31)

The weather for June and July in eastern Oregon was unseasonably cool, and
there was little precipitation in the Columbia Basin region. Eastern Umatilla
County and the Blue Mountain section received enough rainfall in June to be of
material benefit to crops. The total rainfall at Moro for June was only 0.62
of an inch, the greatest for any one day being 0.19 of an inch. The highest te
perature recorded in June was 94 degrees on the 24th, and the lowest 34 degree
on the 3rd. There was no precipitation in July and no hot weather until the e
of the month. The highest temperature for the month was 101 degrees on the 30'
and the lowest 44 degrees on the 11th.

Harvest operations are in full swing in the Columbia Basin of eastern Ore
In Sherman County, farmers are reporting yields of winter wheat of from 15 to
bushels per acre. Threshing started on the Station on July 29. We are using
new No. 2 Ellis Keystone thresher with wind stacker.

The following table, compiled by Mr. J. F. Martin, presents the results o
a varietal trial for resistance to bunt of a number of wheats grown on the Pen
ton Field Station. The seed of these varieties was inoculated with a mixture
smut of several physiologic forms obtained from the 1928 nurseries.

at varieties inoculated with a mixture of
forms and grown on the Pendleton Field

	Sel.No.	Smutted Heads	Total Heads	Smut (Per cent)
	----	19	685	2.8
	----	19	623	3.0
rence)	947	9	243	3.7
	----	30	510	5.9
rence)	946	27	424	6.4
	935	35	526	6.7
	----	63	756	8.3
	----	47	556	8.5
	932	36	425	8.5
	43	80	713	11.2
	933	79	684	11.5
	934	69	536	12.9
	----	47	345	13.6
	----	138	652	21.2
	1009	111	251	44.2
	----	324	620	52.3
	----	199	379	52.5
	1015	134	239	56.1
	----	333	505	66.0
	1013	178	263	67.7
	950	200	295	67.8
	960	277	400	69.3
	----	348	501	69.5
	1011	224	320	70.0
	993	155	220	70.5
	----	498	688	72.4
	994	287	394	72.8
	----	472	636	74.2
	1005	233	309	75.4
	957	282	372	75.8
	955	336	432	77.8
	----	592	758	78.1
	952	247	315	78.4
	954	270	341	79.2
	----	494	622	79.4
	----	554	690	80.3
	----	584	714	81.8
	953	378	458	82.5
	----	473	570	83.0
	998	339	408	83.1
	995	346	416	83.2
	----	569	680	83.7
	997	372	444	83.8
	1004	299	354	84.5
	951	323	379	85.2
	956	412	474	86.9
	----	343	394	87.1
	----	612	700	87.4
	1003	351	391	89.8
	----	630	681	92.5
	----	---	---	95.0

CALIFORNIA

Biggs Rice Field Station, Biggs (Rice Agronomy, J. W. Jones) (July 31)

The weather during the last half of July has been reasonably favorable for the development of the rice crop in California. The condition of the crop, however, is not so good as it was last year at this time, and indications are that the average yield per acre will be considerably less than that of last year.

On commercial fields 1600 and Onsen sown in April are now heading, and with normal temperatures for the next 50 days some of these fields will be ready to harvest by September 15 or 20. The Caloro variety, though sown earlier this spring than usual, probably will not mature any earlier than usual, or about October 4.

Very early maturing varieties at the Station are nearly fully headed, early varieties are starting to head, and the midseason varieties are jointing. Yields at the Station will be much lower this year than they were last season which was a very favorable year for high yields.

The rice market has advanced considerably in the past three weeks. Rice is now being sold by the Rice Growers'Association on a basis of $2.45 per hundred for No. 1 paddy, an advance of about 45 cents a hundred during the past two weeks.

On July 26, Mr. E. L. Adams, President of the California Rice Growers' Association, and Hon. Clarence F. Lea, M. C., visited the Station. Prof. G. A. Studentsky, of the Samara Agricultural Institute, Moscow, Russia, also was a visitor in July.

University Farm, Davis (Cereal Agronomy, G. A. Wiebe)

Agricultural Experiment Station, Berkeley (Cereal Smuts, F. N. Briggs)

BARBERRY ERADICATION PROGRESS

OHIO

Ohio State University, College of Agriculture, Columbus, J. W. Baringer
uly 29]

On July 1 and 2 a training school was held at Ashtabula for barberry-eradi-
tion field agents. Twenty-seven agents were present. All but three are agents
o have had previous experience in Ohio, and a special field trip was arranged
r these three. The men were divided into four crews, three having seven agents
ch and the fourth crew six. The entire field force has worked all through July
Ashtabula County in an attempt to hasten the completion of the first survey in
e State. It seems now that the first survey will be finished some time between
ust 10 and August 15, possibly earlier. The territory is very difficult from
e standpoint of survey progress. Second growth woodlots are numerous. There
a generous number of slashings. Thick woods are plentiful and there are many
amps. It is a region where barberries were introduced early, and the birds
ve done their part in scattering seeds. Several patches of escaped barberry
hes are being found.

When the first survey has been completed it is planned to transfer the en-
ire field force to Preble County, where it will push forward the second survey
iich was started there last year.

In July much of the State was covered by the State Leader by automobile for
ie purpose of collecting samples of leaf and stem rust of small grains. These
amples are to be used in studies of physiologic forms of rust and to obtain in-
ormation on the general status of stem rust in Ohio. Stem rust on wheat was
meral, and in many favorably situated fields throughout the State the rust be-
ame moderate to heavy just before harvest. However, in many fields where the
;em rust was heavy the grain seemed to have filled fairly well, an indication
iat the rust came too late to cause as much loss as might have been the case if
pening of the grain had been delayed a few days. Generally speaking, wheat
i four or five counties in the northwest corner of Ohio was hardest hit by stem
ist this year. In some fields in this section quite a bit of shriveling re-
ilted.

As far as barley is concerned the status of stem rust is about the same as
i wheat.

No stem rust has been found on rye, and only a little has been observed on
its.

Leaf rust on wheat and oats was general and severe in most parts of Ohio
iis year. Leaf rust on barley and rye was general but not heavy.

Nearly all grain, with the exception of oats, has been cut, and oats cutting
; in progress in the southern and central part of the State.

Colored barberry posters are being sent to all banks in Ohio.

On Thursday, July 25, the State Leader talked on barberry eradication to the Rotary Club at Jefferson.

INDIANA

Purdue University College of Agriculture, LaFayette, W. E. Leer (July 30

The educational program which is being carried on in connection with the boys' and girls' club camps in Indiana this summer is proving very much worth while. The following letter was received from a camp director:

"I have the pleasure to report that the instruction given by Mr. Stanley Castell at Camp Hoosier last week was well received and bore fruit.

"Thursday morning while hunting specimens for a nature study class, a camper, Raymond Baird of Vevay, Ind., (Switzerland County) found a common barberry bush at the northwest corner of the Phi Gamma Delta house which is nearly opposite Hanover gymnasium. The identification of the bush was directly due to Mr. Castell's demonstration."

(Signed) W. R. Beall,
Camp Director."

The success of an educational program of this nature depends to a very large degree on the personnel in charge of such a program. Mr. Castell has proved his ability in this connection.

MICHIGAN

Agricultural College, East Lansing, W. F. Reddy (July 22)

Common barberry bushes were only moderately infected in Michigan this sp No early spreads of stem rust to grains or grasses were observed. At present there are only a few pustules on scattering stalks of grain. The rust that h been seen has come too late to do severe damage.

Thirty-six field men are employed this season. Intensive first survey i being conducted in Leelanau and Antrim counties. There is much waste and cut over land in these counties. Unfortunately the early settlers planted barber bushes. These early plantings are responsible for thousands of bushes growin in areas of escapes.

WISCONSIN

Department of Agriculture, State Capitol Annex, Madison, R. M. Caldwell

ILLINOIS

Box 72, Post Office Building, Urbana, R. W. Bills   (July 23)

Twenty-seven field agents are carrying on the barberry survey in Illinois. eventeen men are engaged in an intensive survey of Jo Daviess County and will omplete it about September 1. Ten men are conducting a modified-intensive irst survey in southern Illinois. Monroe County has been completed. Randolph, ashington, and Perry counties are being covered, with Jefferson and Franklin ext in order.

Three properties, all in the city of Waterloo, were found in Monroe County. o rural plantings were found. Scouts in Washington, Randolph, and Perry coun- ies have found an average of four properties in each county.

Wheat has escaped injury from black stem rust this year. Oats are less ortunate. While early oats in western Illinois escaped heavy infection, the ate oats are being injured by rust which was found on July 18 to vary from a race to 50 per cent severity.

All of the grain is harvested and threshing is well under way in southern Ilinois.

IOWA

Iowa State College, Ames, P. W. Rohrbaugh

MINNESOTA

Agricultural Experiment Station, University Farm, St. Paul, L. W. Melander July 30)

The staging of barberry demonstrations at 4-H club camps is beginning to roduce results. So far this year three boys from different counties have ound barberries as a result of these demonstrations. Rudolph Longen, a club oy, brought a specimen to the camp at Hokah, Houston County. This resulted n the finding of two planted and two escaped bushes. Harvey Svoboda, a Scott ounty boy, found an escaped barberry bush on the edge of Jordan and reported t to the scouts. Alfred Jessen, a 4-H member from Pipestone County, sent a pecimen of barberry from that county. All three boys stated that they had earned to recognize common barberry at 4-H club camps.

The second survey is progressing slowly in Carver, Scott, and Hennepin counties in which there is considerable timber. The underbrush is dense in many places. The most interesting phase of the intensive survey is that we find escaped bushes the origin of which is difficult to ascertain. This has happened in all of the counties in which we are working. We are hoping to complete Carver County by August 15.

NEBRASKA

College of Agriculture, University Farm, Lincoln, B. F. Dittus, Acting in Charge.

SOUTH DAKOTA

College of Agriculture, Brookings, R. O. Bulger

NORTH DAKOTA

Agricultural Extension Division, State College Station, Fargo, G. C. Mayo (July 30)

Field agents are working in Traill, Burke, and portions of Ward and Bottineau counties. The communities in which they are working are evidencing a good spirit of cooperation. Business men particularly are assisting the agents with publicity and personal contacts.

Demonstrations were made at the leading fairs, including the State fairs at Grand Forks and Fargo, the Lake Region Fair at Devils Lake, the Northwest State Fair at Minot, and the Missouri Slope Fair at Mandan, in addition to county fairs at Stanley, Flaxton, and Langdon. Several leads to probable barberry plantings were secured through these demonstrations.

Definite stem-rust spreads from barberries have not been found to date this season. However, barberries have been found in local areas where the rust spreads of last season indicated near-by sources of infection. At present, field agents are working in areas where the outbreak of infection points to bar berries.

The drought, particularly of June and July, extending over the entire State with the exceptions of local areas, has done a great deal of damage to the crop The very high temperature accompanied by wind has caused the grain to ripen from one to two weeks earlier than under normal conditions. As a result, wheat harvest has been started in many places over the State, especially through the Valley and in the central districts.

There is a general spread of stem rust over the State except for the north-
st quarter, where it is difficult to find more than a trace. The rust infec-
on varies depending on local showers and drought. All of the early grain will
cape without any material injury, whereas all the later grain, representing
proximately 5 to 10 per cent of the total acreage of small grains, could re-
ive a lot of damage with favorable rust weather.

MONTANA

State College of Agriculture, Bozeman, W. L. Popham (July 30)

Barberry-eradication activities this season have taken the form of an in-
nsive survey of two escaped areas. Six men are attempting to clean up at
ast all fruiting bushes in the vicinity of the north end of Flathead Lake, in
athead County. The spread of barberry bushes in this particular instance is
nown to extend over the greater part of four sections of hilly and timbered
nd. Just how much farther is not known, as definite boundaries of the area
ave not been established.

In Fergus County the survey of timbered areas along the Judith River is
roving to be a very difficult task, because of the heavy growth of underbrush.
his escaped area was unknown until this year, and is so located that it could
ot have been responsible for severe rust losses in seasons when temperature
nd moisture conditions were favorable for the development of rust.

Very little cereal rust of any kind has been reported in either Montana or
yoming this season. Weather conditions in the spring were not favorable for
ust development on barberry bushes, and the resulting scarcity of local inocu-
m, together with the lack of moisture during the growing season, has prevented
ust from developing to any extent in either State. During the past week a
race of leaf rust has been reported from central and western Montana, and
tripe rust again has appeared on Crail Fife wheat in Gallatin and Flathead coun-
ies. No stem rust has been reported this season.

WYOMING

College of Agriculture, University of Wyoming, Laramie, W. L. Popham

COLORADO

Agricultural College, Ft. Collins, E. A. Lungren (August 1)

In July, second survey progressed favorably in Adams and Arapahoe counties.
wo new areas of escaped bushes were found in Arapahoe County, the largest be-
ng just outside of Farmont cemetery southeast of Denver. Evidently these bushes
ame from the seeds of those which were taken out of the cemetery on the first
urvey. Many new rural and city properties also were found. In only one case
as there difficulty in removing the bushes.

Two large Berberis vernae and 750 cuttings were found in a nursery just east of Englewood. Fortunately, these were destroyed before they were distributed and sold.

There has been very little stem rust this year, and leaf rust was lighter than in 1928. Only a trace of each can be reported. In some fields of late spring wheat stem rust was heavier but not sufficient to cause injury. Oats and barley escaped rust almost entirely.

Weather conditions this year have not been entirely favorable for rust infection. However, many local showers have prevailed throughout the month. Barberry infections were light, and so far it has not been possible to determine any definite spreads. However, in one case in Adams County rust appeared heavier near the places where light infection appeared on the barberries.

In the two counties now being surveyed, window displays are being used extensively, and the newspapers are constantly reporting the progress of the survey. Circular letters also have been sent out to all rural-box holders. One radio talk was given over KOA at Denver. The State Leader also gave a talk to the Colorado Smith-Hughes teachers at their annual conference.

C E R E A L   C O U R I E R

Official Messenger of the Office of Cereal Crops and Diseases
Bureau of Plant Industry, U. S. Department of Agriculture
(NOT FOR PUBLICATION)

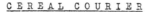

Vol. 21   No. 20
August 20, 1929
Personnel (Aug. 11-20) and Field Station (Aug. 1-15) Issue

PERSONNEL ITEMS

Dr. James G. Dickson, agent in the cooperative cereal disease investigations that are being conducted at Madison, Wis., arrived in Washington on
August 12 to confer with Department officials on barley scab matters. He
left for Madison on August 14.

Dr. H. B. Humphrey, principal pathologist in charge of cereal-rust investigations, returned to Washington on August 17 from an extensive trip in the
central and western States. While in the field he covered much of the spring-
wheat area with Mr. J. Allen Clark, by automobile, and obtained considerable
valuable information on rusts, smuts, and other cereal diseases. He visited
nearly all of the experiment stations and substations in Minnesota, North
Dakota, South Dakota, and Montana.

Leaving Montana, Dr. Humphrey visited Moscow, Idaho, where he conferred
with Department workers concerning stripe rust research. He also visited
Pullman, Puyallup, and other points in Washington; Corvallis, Oreg., and Davis,
and Berkeley, Calif.

Returning from Berkeley, he stopped for a conference with Messrs. Parker,
Johnston, and Mains at Manhattan, Kans., relative to leaf rust investigations;
and at Ames, Iowa, for consideration of the current year's results in crown-
rust investigations and of future research plans.

Dr. Humphrey then went to St. Paul, Minn., where he had opportunity to
review the results of the past season's stem-rust studies and to consider with
Doctors Stakman and Levine, and others, projected plans and manuscripts bearing directly on stem rust of wheat. He returned direct to Washington from St.
Paul.

Dr. A. G. Johnson, principal pathologist in charge of cereal-disease
investigations, left Washington August 15 for Mobile, and Bay Minette, Alabam
to inspect corn for a bacterial disease that has been occurring in that secti
for the past two seasons. He returned on August 17.

Mr. M. A. McCall, principal agronomist in charge of cereal agronomy, who
has been at the University of Wisconsin for several weeks engaged in research
on wheat morphology, will return to Washington on or about August 26.

Dr. V. F. Tapke, pathologist in cereal-smut investigations, returned to
Washington on August 17 from Aberdeen Substation, Aberdeen, Idaho, where he
has been harvesting and taking notes on wheat, oats, and barley used in studi
on cereal smuts. Dr. Tapke reports that his experiments at Aberdeen were sat
isfactory, and also, that the season at that Station was successful.

VISITORS

Maj.-Gen. E. A. Kreger, Judge Advocate General of the Army, was an Offi
visitor on August 19.

Dr. W. H. Tisdale, of the E. I. Du Pont de Nemours and Co., Inc., Wilmi
ton, Del., was an Office visitor on August 19.

MANUSCRIPTS AND PUBLICATIONS

52 A manuscript entitled "The Inheritance, Interactions, and Linkage
elations of Genes Causing Yellow Seedlings in Maize," by Merle T. Jenkins and
. A. Bell, was approved on August 12 for publication in Genetics.

The article entitled "Smuts and Rusts Produced in Cereals by Hypodermic
Injection of Inoculum," by Marion Griffiths Zehner and Harry B. Humphrey,
appears in the Journal of Agricultural Research 33 (11): 623-627, fig. 1.
June 1, 1929.

The article entitled "Moisture Content of Flaxseed and Its Relation to
Harvesting, Storage, and Crushing," by A. C. Dillman and R. H. Black, appears
in the Journal of the American Society of Agronomy 21 (8): 818-831, fig. 1.
August, 1929.

The article entitled "Dehiscence of the Flax Boll," by A. C. Dillman,
appears in the Journal of the American Society of Agronomy 21 (8): 832-833,
fig. 1. August, 1929.

FIELD STATION CONDITION AND PROGRESS

(All experiments except those conducted at the Arlington Experiment Farm, Ros
lyn, Va., are in cooperation with State agricultural experiment stations or
other agencies.)

HUMID ATLANTIC COAST AREA (South to North)

GEORGIA

State College of Agriculture, Athens (Cereal Agronomy, R. R. Childs)

VIRGINIA

Arlington Experiment Farm, Rosslyn (Small Grain Agronomy, J. W. Taylor)

Arlington Experiment Farm, Rosslyn (Corn Breeding, F. D. Richey)

Arlington Experiment Farm, Rosslyn (Cereal Smuts, V. F. Tapke, Acting in
Charge)

Arlington Experiment Farm, Rosslyn (Virus Diseases, H. H. McKinney)

NEW YORK

Cornell University Agricultural Experiment Station, Ithaca (Cereal Breed
ing, H. H. Love) (F. P. Bussell) (August 9)

Each year the acreage of fields of cereals entered for inspection stead
increases. This year there were 2,760 acres of wheat, oats, and barley ente
and while the amount of corn to be entered is yet unknown, it will be consid
able. This is all of varieties recommended by us as the result of careful e
perimental work.

I think one feature of the whole matter is quite significant and that i
the changed attitude of the seed trade regarding varieties of field seeds.
near as I can figure it they are coming to realize that seed is a speciality
and not a commodity and the experiment stations have been mainly responsible
for bringing them to the realization of this fact. As I meet the men in the
trade I am conscious that they no longer look upon Experiment Station men as
white-collared paper farmers but as specialists who are doing something help
to their business.

HUMID MISSISSIPPI VALLEY AREA (South to North)

LOUISIANA

Rice Experiment Station, Crowley (Rice Agronomy, J. M. Jenkins)

Agricultural Experiment Station, Baton Rouge (Corn Breeding, H. F. toneberg)

TENNESSEE

Agricultural Experiment Station, Knoxville (Corn Breeding, L. S. Mayer)

MISSOURI

Agricultural Experiment Station, Columbia (Cereal Agronomy, L. J. Stadler)

OHIO

Ohio State University, Columbus (Corn Breeding, L. R. Jorgenson)

IOWA

Agricultural Experiment Station, Ames (Oat Breeding, L. C. Burnett)

Agricultural Experiment Station, Ames (Corn Breeding, M. T. Jenkins)

Agricultural Experiment Station, Ames (Crown Rust of Oats, S. M. Dietz)

INDIANA

Purdue University Agricultural Experiment Station, LaFayette (Corn Rots and Metallic Poisoning, J. F. Trost, Acting in Charge)

Purdue University Agricultural Experiment Station, LaFayette (Leaf Rusts, E. B. Mains)

ILLINOIS

Funk Bros. Seed Co., Bloomington (Corn Root, Stalk and Ear Rots, J. R. Holbert)

WISCONSIN

Agricultural Experiment Station, Madison (Wheat Scab, J. G. Dickson)

MINNESOTA

Agricultural Experiment Station, University Farm, St. Paul (Wheat Breeding, E. R. Ausemus) (August 17)

Harvest of nearly all of the small grains in the plots and rod rows has been completed and threshing is now in progress. There was very little stem rust present in either of these experiments.

In the rust nursery there was a heavy epidemic of leaf rust but stem rust was not so prevalent. Some very good data was secured on leaf rust resistance on the different varieties grown this year. Plants resistant to leaf rust in the individually spaced hybrid material tagged early in the season have been examined for stem rust and black chaff resistance and selections made for continuation in the experiments next year.

Mr. K. S. Quisenberry, who has been acting in charge of the work at University Farm during the past year, left for Montana on August 1, to take care of his winter wheat studies. Recent visitors at the Station have been Dr. H. B. Humphrey and Mr. A. C. Dillman of the Office of Cereal Crops and Diseases.

Agricultural Experiment Station, University Farm, St. Paul (Stem Rust, E. C. Stakman)

Agricultural Experiment Station, University Farm, St. Paul (Flax Rust, H. A. Rodenhiser)

GREAT PLAINS AREA (South to North)

OKLAHOMA

Woodward Field Station, Woodward (Grain Sorghum and Broomcorn, J. B. Sieglinger) (August 17)

A good rain followed by several showers from the 5th to the 10th improve prospects for good sorghum and broomcorn yields. Since this rainy period, th crops have made rapid growth and heading has progressed rapidly.

At present the main work is bagging heads. This will continue for the next two weeks.

Crops are looking better here than farther east, as the writer observed
n a trip to Stillwater on the 12th.

Maximum temperature, 107 degrees on the 5th; minimum for the same period,
9 degrees on the 14th; precipitation 1.93 inches, 1.5 inches of which occurred
n the 5th, and the remainder, 0.43 of an inch, in four showers.

KANSAS

Agricultural Experiment Station, Manhattan (Cereal Breeding, J. H. Parker)

Agricultural Experiment Station, Manhattan (Corn Breeding, A. M. Brunson)

Agricultural Experiment Station, Manhattan (Wheat Foot Rots, Hurley Fellows)

Agricultural Experiment Station, Manhattan (Wheat Leaf Rust, C. O. Johnston)

Fort Hays Branch Experiment Station, Hays (Cereal Agronomy, A. F. Swanson)

NEBRASKA

North Platte Substation, North Platte (Cereal Agronomy, G. F. Sprague)
(August 15)

It is feared that there will not be much corn except under irrigation.
We have had about two inches of rain since June 1. The dry-land corn is hold-
ing on remarkably well and may still make something if we have rain.

Corn pollination has been completed. My genetic material and one crossing
block were under irrigation and prospects are for a good set of seed. Under
dry conditions we do not expect to get much.

SOUTH DAKOTA

U. S. Cereal Field Experiments, Redfield (Wheat Improvement, E. S. McFadden

NORTH DAKOTA

Northern Great Plains Field Station, Mandan (Cereal Agronomy, V. C. Hubbard
(August 17)

The 1/50th-acre plots of wheat, oats, and barley have been threshed but as
yet yield and test weight data for each of the varieties has not been calculated.
Threshing of the rod row plots was started on August 17.

291

Messrs. J. Allen Clark and E. R. Ausemus spent from August 3 to 9 here taking stem rust notes on some F$_3$ crosses of Hope, Ceres, Marquillo, and Red Bobs. Other visitors at the Station since July were Messrs. Harlan Sumner, Karl S. Quisenberry, Glenn S. Smith, L. R. Waldron, J. H. Martin, and Mrs. Marion Griffiths Zehner.

Northern Great Plains Field Station, Mandan (Flax Breeding, J. C. Brins made, Jr.) (August 17)

Hot, dry weather has continued during the first half of August, except for a few exceptionally cool nights. The maximum temperature was 97 degrees on August 15 and the minimum 36 degrees on August 13; precipitation 0.61 of inch. The precipitation during the last half of July was 0.25 of an inch in stead of 0.21 of an inch as previously reported. This includes 0.04 of an i which occurred the night of July 31. Slight frost was reported the night of August 13 in the river valleys and coulees, but caused no serious damage.

Eleven early flax varieties were harvested on July 29. Bison and Buda and the later varieties are not yet ready to harvest. Flax plots from the first four dates of seeding and varieties sown on May 1 were threshed on August 16, but yields are not available as the seed has not yet been cleaned

Dickinson Substation, Dickinson (Cereal Agronomy, R. W. Smith) (August

Harvest is nearly completed at the Substation and the threshing of rot tion plots of wheat began today. Harvest in this section is nearing comple and some threshing has been done. A few combines are in operation in the v ity of Dickinson.

Dry weather has prevailed so far this month, as in July. A few light showers have occurred bringing only a few hundredths of an inch of moisture The maximum temperature has been in the nineties a few days this month with the minimum in the forties a few times.

The dry weather is favorable to the operation of combines which are m numerous in the State and County than in any previous year.

Some of the official visitors this month so far have been: Mrs. M. G Zehner, Dr. John H. Martin, and Messrs. J. Allen Clark, K. S. Quisenberry, V. C. Hubbard from the Office of Cereal Crops and Diseases; Mr. Wallace Bu who took notes on the rust nursery; and Dr. L. R. Waldron and Prof. Eikenb from the North Dakota Experiment Station and Agricultural College.

Agricultural Experiment Station, State College Station, Fargo (Flax Diseases, L. W. Boyle)

Langdon Substation, Langdon (Wheat Improvement, G. S. Smith) (August 15)

Four of the 23 wheat varieties tested here have been harvested, and the remainder will be ready to cut by the end of this week or the first of next. The hard red spring wheats in the nursery will be ready for harvest in three or four more days. The oat varieties have all been harvested.

The rainfall for the past two weeks has been 0.72 of an inch. The grain in this region, being so much later than in the rest of the State, seems to have given the rust more time to develop. At present infection is rather general. In the rust nursery all but one or two varieties show more than a trace and range as high as 70 per cent infection. A slight frost on the 13th killed what prospects we had for corn.

During the first week of the month, the writer went by automobile west from Langdon through the northern part of the State, and south through Minot to Dickinson, thence to Mandan to visit the field station there, and returned to Langdon by going to the east and then north. From about 50 miles west of Langdon through Bottineau County and south to about 100 miles southwest of Minot the crops looked very good in general. At Dickinson the drought had had some effect and at Mandan grain was dried out rather badly. However, from a short distance east of Mandan up through the Carrington and Devil's Lake districts there had been a good amount of precipitation apparently and crop conditions were promising. One fact which was rather noticeable on this trip was the line of demarcation between durum and hard red spring wheats. West and north of Minot the wheat was largely durum, with a little Ceres and an occasional field of Marquis, but from there south, the change to Marquis was rather sudden. A short distance east of Bismarck the same difference was noted.

On August 9 the writer made another trip to Morden, Manitoba, which is some 60 miles north and east of Langdon. Although crops about the country are a failure, some of the rotations which have been conducted for several years look very good. Mr. Brachy, who is in charge of the field work, said that they had had but four inches of precipitation since March.

MONTANA

Judith Basin Branch Station, Moccasin (Cereal Agronomy, B. B. Bayles)

WESTERN BASIN AND COAST AREAS (North to West and South)

IDAHO

Aberdeen Substation, Aberdeen (Cereal Agronomy, L. L. Davis) (August 15)

Harvesting of the cereal nursery was completed on August 14. Excellent weather enabled harvesting of the varieties as they became ripe. There were no diseases present or injurious insects to damage the crop. The weather conditions have been such that ripening was not hastened and complete filling of the crop resulted.

On August 5, Mr. T. R. Stanton and the writer visited the experime station at Logan, Utah. Considerable wheat work is being carried on at both genetic and varietal testing. The oats and barley nurseries conta some new and promising varieties. Mr. Stanton made a careful study of number of smut-resistant oat hybrids.

The trip was made through the Rockland Valley where Kanred and Tur are grown almost entirely on the dry farms. The crop in the valley thi is only fair, few fields yielding more than 10 bushels per acre.

Agricultural Experiment Station, Moscow (Stripe Rust, C. W. Hunger

WASHINGTON

Agricultural Experiment Station, Pullman (Cereal Breeding, E. F. G

OREGON

Sherman County Branch Station, Moro (Cereal Agronomy, D. E. Stephe (August 12)

We have finished threshing all our field plots and are now threshi nursery. Our yields, like those of the farmers, were disappointing. I our winter wheats yielded less than 15 bushels to the acre, and our sp wheats still less. Our spring barley was fairly good, and the oats yie more pounds per acre this year than winter wheat.

CALIFORNIA

Biggs Rice Field Station, Biggs (Rice Agronomy, J. W. Jones)

University Farm, Davis (Cereal Agronomy, G. A. Wiebe)

Agricultural Experiment Station; Berkeley (Cereal Smuts, F. N. Br

BARBERRY ERADICATION PROGRESS

OHIO

Ohio State University, College of Agriculture, Columbus, J. W. Baringer

INDIANA

Purdue University College of Agriculture, LaFayette, W. E. Leer (August 15)

The intensive survey of Tipton County will be completed on August 17, and the intensive survey of Hamilton County should be completed by September 7. It will be impossible to complete more than one-third of Montgomery County this year. The heavy underbrush in the woods and the rank weed growth along the banks of the many streams have greatly retarded the work in Montgomery County. Unfortunately, the hardest part of the County is yet to be worked. Eight men have been in Montgomery County nearly all summer.

Considerable time is being devoted to the building of the barberry demonstration for the Indiana State Fair which will be held from August 31 to September 7. The barberry demonstration is to be one of the feature attractions in the Purdue University building this year. A jail is being built. The common barberry, having been convicted of spreading black stem rust to the small grains and sentenced to die by Judge Plant Pathology, will be in the death cell waiting execution by treatment with salt or kerosene.

MICHIGAN

Agricultural College, East Lansing, W. F. Reddy

WISCONSIN

Department of Agriculture, State Capitol Annex, Madison, R. M. Caldwell

ILLINOIS

Box 72, Post Office Building, Urbana, R. W. Bills

IOWA

Iowa State College, Ames, P. W. Rohrbaugh

MINNESOTA

Agricultural Experiment Station, University Farm, St. Paul, L.

NEBRASKA

College of Agriculture, University Farm, Lincoln, B. F. Dittus Charge

SOUTH DAKOTA

College of Agriculture, Brookings, R. O. Bulger

NORTH DAKOTA

Agricultural Extension Division, State College Station, Fargo,

MONTANA

State College of Agriculture, Bozeman, W. L. Popham

WYOMING

College of Agriculture, University of Wyoming, Laramie, W. L.

COLORADO

Agricultural College, Ft. Collins, E. A. Lungren

****

C E R E A L   C O U R I E R

Official Messenger of the Office of Cereal Crops and Diseases
Bureau of Plant Industry, U. S. Department of Agriculture
(NOT FOR PUBLICATION)

Vol. 21   No. 21

August 31, 1929
Personnel (Aug. 21-31) and General Issue

PERSONNEL ITEMS

Dr. C. R. Ball, principal agronomist in charge, will leave Washington
on September 4. He will go to Illinois, Indiana, Iowa, Kansas, Nebraska, New
Mexico, Oklahoma, and Ohio to confer with Station officials, inspect cooperative experiments, and study recent developments in grain sorghum and winter
wheat production in the southern Great Plains area. Dr. Ball will be in the
field for about one month.

Mr. F. A. Coffman, associate agronomist in oat investigations, who has
been in the field since June 22, reported on August 21 as follows:

Since leaving Washington, official stops have been made at Federal and
State experiment stations in the following States: Kansas, Colorado, Nebraska,
Iowa, Wisconsin, Minnesota, North Dakota, Montana, and Idaho. All stations
were visited just prior to or during harvesting operations. Generally, cereal
crop prospects had suffered severely. Yields in many sections were below average. Probably Colorado and North Dakota were most seriously in need of moisture. In both States crops were spotted and in some sections not worth harvesting for grain. Conditions in most of the States visited have been reported
on previously by other members of the Office staff.

Mr. Stanton and I arrived at Bozeman, Mont., on the same day. We traveled
together from Bozeman to Aberdeen, Idaho, reaching there the morning of July 31.
Because of the late arrival of spring weather here crops have not reached maturity as early as usual. This delayed us to some extent in getting started
but has permitted us to take care of the material as fast as it was ready for
attention. In some previous seasons we have been troubled with plants becoming
ripe before we could take all the notes we desired.

In this section crop prospects seem up to the average despite unfavorable early spring conditions. The farmers are greatly heartened over the prospects of a good price for potatoes. Last season prices were ruinously low and some fields of potatoes were never dug. Wheat and barley threshing is now well started and yields are as high as usual. · The alfalfa seed prospects seem very good. This is one of the greatest alfalfa-seed-producing sections in the United States.

All of the members of the Washington Office soon will have completed their seasons' work here and left for Washington. Dr. Charlotte Elliott left on August 1 for Canada. Dr. V. F. Tapke left on August 9, en route to Washington. Dr. H. V. Harlan, Mrs. Harlan, their two boys, and Miss Mary L. Martini left on August 16, en route to Washington via Wyoming, Colorado, and Kansas. Mr. Stanton and I will leave en route to Washington on August 21. Mr. Stanton expects to make stops in Wyoming, Nebraska, and Iowa, and I expect to stop en route in Wyoming, Colorado, and Kansas.

Since Mr. Stanton arrived he has been very busy in harvesting and taking data on a viability nursery containing rows of all the oat varieties accessioned by the Office of Cereal Crops and Diseases to date, of which seed is available. One of the objects of this nursery is to obtain for future use viable seed of all varieties.

Most of the time since my arrival has been spent studying 10 hybrids for the inheritance of kernel characters. Some 12,000 to 15,000 plants are being studied individually. In addition to these, special studies, we have studied and made selections from several hundred hybrids for sowing at this and other stations. Weather conditions have been ideal for field work this season and we have had less trouble even than usual from that source.

Mr. R. W. Leukel, associate pathologist, left Washington on August 30 to visit a farmer near Clinton, Maryland, to inspect his oats, and to secure smut-infested seed for experiments.

Dr. H. H. Love, of Cornell University, who is now in Nanking, China, in connection with the cooperative work carried on by an agreement between the International Education Board, the University of Nanking, and Cornell University, writes under date of July 25 that the work there is progressing very favorably. A portion of his letter follows:

"We do not have all the facilities we could use and our land might be closer and more adapted to experimental work and yet, with our cooperative stations in addition to our own, we have a wonderful chance. We have been busy with our summer conference. I expected about 20-25 to register and 53 did register. Besides we had 20 visitors. I gave a lecture a day for the first seven days, then two a day after that. I had three afternoon laboratories a week. Needless to say, I have not added any extra flesh. It ends tomorrow. I closed my work this morning expecting to go to Shanghai to meet Mrs. Love but just before I started word came that the boat had been delayed more than one day by storms, so will go down tomorrow night.

"We are now getting ready to weigh our wheat for sowing. We have a lot of interesting looking things. Hope they hold up. Some of them are 50 to 100 per cent better than the check and the check is nine per cent better than the farmers' varieties. These new ones are too good, I will admit, and will not continue to hold up so high. I do have hopes that some of them will go 20 per cent better than the check. I have started a collection of several hundred sorts of wheat to America."

Mr. Marion T. Meyers has been appointed field assistant, effective August 19, in corn-borer research at Wooster and Bono, Ohio.

Mr. F. D. Richey, senior agronomist in charge of corn investigations, returned to Washington on August 30 after a two weeks' field trip in the southeastern States.

Mr. T. R. Stanton, senior agronomist in charge of oat investigations, returned to Washington on August 29 after an extended field trip throughout the north-central and northwestern States in the interests of oat investigations. After spending one week at Ames, Iowa, where he assisted in harvesting and recording data on the extensive oat breeding nursery in progress at that Station, he proceeded westward through Minnesota, the Dakotas, and Montana, arriving at Aberdeen, Idaho, on July 31. While at Aberdeen, he assisted in harvesting and recording data on the oat breeding and varietal classification nurseries conducted in cooperation with the Idaho Agricultural Experiment Station. During August 4 and 5, Mr. Stanton made a brief side trip from Aberdeen by automobile to Logan, Utah, to inspect experiments with oats and to confer with officials of the Utah Agricultural Experiment Station. He was accompanied by Mr. Loren L. Davis of the Aberdeen Substation. From Aberdeen, Mr. Stanton returned eastward making stops in Wyoming, Nebraska, and Iowa.

VISITORS

Prof. Wallace W. Brookins, Head of the Department of Agronomy at the Panhandle Agricultural and Mechanical College, Goodwell, Okla., was an Office visitor on August 30 to discuss graduate study and especially international fellowships in agronomy.

Mr. George L. Fawcett, pathologist, Sugar Experiment Station, Tucuman, Argentina, visited the Office and the virus disease laboratory at Arlington Experiment Farm, Rosslyn, Va., on August 27. Mr. Fawcett is especially interested in developing methods for studying sugar cane mosaic.

MANUSCRIPTS AND PUBLICATIONS

52 A manuscript entitled "Cultural Characteristics of Physiologic Forms of Spacelotheca Sorghi," by C. H. Ficke and C. O. Johnston, was approved on August 30 for publication in Phytopathology.

Page proof of article entitled "Breeding Hard Red Winter Wheats for Winter Hardiness and High Yield," by Karl S. Quisenberry and J. Allen Clark, was read on August 24.

Farmers' Bulletin 1581, entitled "Oats in the North-Central States," by T. R. Stanton and F. A. Coffman, was received from the Government Printing Office on August 20 bearing date of June, 1929.

A brief note entitled "The Synthetic Formation of Avena Sterilis," by V. H. Florell, appears in the Journal of Heredity, under Correspondence, 22 (5): 227. May, 1929.

B. P. I. Memo. 443   August 22, 1929

MEMORANDUM FOR HEADS OF OFFICES

Gentlemen:

In a number of cases recently the question has been raised
by the offices as to the permissibility of employment in the field
of relatives by members of our staff, particularly where the con-
templated employment is of a temporary character. Generally speaking, the Bureau is unwilling to authorize the employment of family
connections, temporary or otherwise, except to meet an emergency.
Long experience has clearly shown that such employment frequently
leads to criticism alike of the employee concerned and of the Department.

Hereafter no employee of the Bureau is authorized under his
Letters of Authorization to employ members of his family or close
relatives where he has any supervision, direct or indirect, over
the individuals concerned. Should a case develop where an emergency exists apparently justifying this type of employment, appropriate recommendations should be submitted through the head of
office to the Chief of Bureau for consideration.

Whenever an appointment is recommended by an office of the
Bureau where the appointee is a relative of another member of
the office with which he will be associated or of anyone having
a supervisory relationship to the employee, full information as
to the relationship and the conditions under which the appointee
will work should be included in the recommendation. Appointments
will be recommended only where it is entirely clear that no com-
plications prejudicial to the service are likely to result.

Very sincerely,

(Signed) WM. A. TAYLOR
Chief of Bureau.

C E R E A L   C O U R I E R

Official Messenger of the Office of Cereal Crops and Diseases
Bureau of Plant Industry, U. S. Department of Agriculture
(NOT FOR PUBLICATION)

----

ol. 21   No. 22

September 10, 1929
Personnel (Sept. 1-10) and Field Station (Aug. 16-31) Issue

PERSONNEL ITEMS

Dr. C. R. Ball, principal agronomist in charge, was unable to make the trip mentioned in the Cereal Courier of August 31 to inspect grain sorghum and wheat experiments and production in the South Plains area. He has been authorized to attend the meetings of the Joint Committee on European Corn Borer Research at Toledo, Ohio, and surrounding territory during the period from September 25 to 27. He expects also to inspect cooperative corn investigations in Illinois and Indiana.

Mr. A. C. Dillman, associate agronomist in charge of flax investigations, returned to Washington on September 3.

Mr. Colburn C. Fifield has been given appointment, effective September 3, as associate baking technologist. He will conduct, in cooperation with the Grain Division of the Bureau of Agricultural Economics, extensive baking investigations with the different classes and numerous varieties of wheat in order to determine the suitability and adaptability of these wheats for specific baking purposes. Mr. Fifield, who is a native of Minnesota, was granted the B. A. degree by Macalester College of St. Paul, Minn., in 1924. He also specialized in baking and milling chemistry at the Dunwoody Evening School, and has taken part-time post-graduate work at the University of Minnesota. He was employed for three years as chemist by the Atkinson Milling Company. He was research assistant under Dr. R. A. Gortner, Chief of the Division of Agricultural Biochemistry of the University of Minnesota, from March, 1927, to June 30, 1929, and thereafter until his appointment in the Office of Cereal Crops and Diseases he was instructor in the same division.

Dr. H. V. Harlan, principal agronomist in charge of barley investigations, returned to Washington on September 3.

Mr. M. A. McCall, principal agronomist in charge of cereal agronomy inves tigations, returned to Washington on September 3.

Mr. F. D. Richey, senior agronomist in charge of corn investigations, was authorized on September 3 to go to the New Jersey Agricultural Experiment Sta tion, Brunswick, N. J., and the Carnegie Institution at Cold Spring Harbor, N. to make a study of corn breeding and genetic experiments. Mr. Richey also has been authorized to attend the meetings in late September of the Joint Committe on European Corn Borer Research at Toledo, Ohio, and in surrounding territory. These meetings will be held on September 25, 26, and 27. He expects also to inspect cooperative corn investigations in Ohio and Illinois.

Mr. Reed Walker, who was appointed in September, 1928, as junior chemist in connection with the breeding and genetic experiments of the western wheat project of this Office, was transferred to the Food Research Division of the Bureau of Chemistry and Soils, effective September 3.

Mrs. Marion Griffiths Zehner, associate pathologist in cereal-smut invest gations, returned to Washington on September 8.

VISITORS

Mr. Takashi Ishizuka, agriculturist in charge, the Government-General of Chosen, Industrial Bureau, of Keijo, Japan, was an Office visitor on September 3. Mr. Ishizuka conferred with Mr. C. E. Chambliss regarding rice culture in the United States.

Mr. V. K. Rosental, a member of the Board of Directors of the Grain Trust Corporation, Moscow, Russia, and Mr. Timothy O. Beresney, of Teacher's College, Columbia University, New York City, interpreter, were Office callers on Septem ber 7 to get information and publications on combine harvesters. These gentle men are members of a group of Russians who have been traveling this summer through the agricultural areas of the United States.

Mr. Jacq. P. F. Sellschop, 17 Market St., Pretoria, South Africa, a gradu student at the University of Illinois, visited the Office on September 3. Mr. Sellschop conferred with the corn-project personnel and inspected corn experi- ments. He expects to return to South Africa shortly.

MANUSCRIPTS AND PUBLICATIONS

54 A manuscript entitled "A Cytological Study of Heterothallism in Puccinia graminis," by Ruth F. Allen, was submitted on September 9 for publi tion in the Journal of Agricultural Research.

Galley proof of Farmers' Bulletin 1607 entitled "The Nematode Disease o Wheat and Rye," by R. W. Leukel, was read on September 4.

The article entitled "The Relation of Cereal Pests to Change in Crop Pr tice," by H. B. Humphrey, appears in Scientific Agriculture [Canada] 9 (12): 783-791. August, 1929.

FIELD STATION CONDITION AND PROGRESS

(All experiments except those conducted at the Arlington Experiment Farm, Rosslyn,
Va., are in cooperation with State agricultural experiment stations or other
agencies.)

HUMID ATLANTIC COAST AREA (South to North)

GEORGIA

State College of Agriculture, Athens (Cereal Agronomy, R. R. Childs)

VIRGINIA

Arlington Experiment Farm, Rosslyn (Small Grain Agronomy, J. W. Taylor)

Arlington Experiment Farm, Rosslyn (Corn Breeding, F. D. Richey)

Arlington Experiment Farm, Rosslyn (Cereal Smuts, V. F. Tapke, Acting in
Charge)

Arlington Experiment Farm, Rosslyn (Virus Diseases, H. H. McKinney)

NEW YORK

Cornell University Agricultural Experiment Station, Ithaca (Cereal Breeding,
H. H. Love) (W. T. Craig) (August 28)

The oat and barley tests this year were the poorest in many years because
of a very wet spring followed by a dry June and July.

The soft-winter-wheat conference held at Ithaca, on July 18, principally to
bring the millers of New York State together to discuss the winter-wheat situation and to learn what we are doing at Cornell to meet the demand for a better
soft winter wheat, was well attended. A very remarkable interest and appreciation was shown by them in our wheat work from inspecting the plots of standing
grain just ready for harvest and information given from lectures and discussions.

Dr. C. E. Leighty, of the Office of Cereal Crops and Diseases, attended this
meeting of the millers of New York State and later helped with some of the wheat
work out in the State.

Dr. M. N. Pope of the Office of Cereal Crops and Diseases, Dr. M. N. Levine, iversity Farm, St. Paul, Minn., were visitors in August.

The wheat test this year was very good. While the yields were rather low ie stand was uniformly good.

The red-kerneled sorts continue to outyield the white-kerneled sorts. How-er, a large number of the later white-kerneled hybrid selections tested this ear in the 5- and 2-row tests have yields from three to five bushels better han the check, Forward.

The following table shows the yield per acre in bushels and the gain or oss over the check, Forward, of 20 of the highest yielding sorts out of 68 ed-kerneled varieties, and 20 of the highest yielding sorts out of 51 white-erneled varieties tested in the ten-row test this year.

Variety	Yield (Bu. per acre)	Gain or loss over check
Red-kerneled Sorts		
320a3-16 (1027a1-8-6-12 x Hybrid No. 86)	31.7	8.6
254a1-9-12 (Dietz 105-5 x Gold Coin 129-65)	28.7	5.3
320ar11-3 (Hybrid No. 86 x 1027a1-8-6-12)	27.9	5.1
320ar15-3	29.5	4.9
320ar15-1	29.8	4.8
319ar6-19 (Hybrid No. 86 x 1185a1-73-1)	29.5	4.7
324a4-6 (Japan Bearded x Early Arcadian)	28.9	4.7
319a2-3 (1185a1-73-1 x Hybrid No. 86)	27.2	4.6
320ar10-17	29.7	4.5
319a4-64	29.6	4.5
133-115 State Selection	28.9	4.5
320a9-1	26.9	4.5
319a4-3	26.7	4.2
320ar11-20	29.4	3.9
320ar12-12	29.2	3.8
320a13-17	28.4	3.8
320a13-19	26.6	3.7
320a9-4	26.2	3.6
320ar10-10	28.4	3.4
320a13-14	28.3	3.4
White-kerneled Sorts		
245a1-105-3 (Dawsons' Golden Chaff 507-8 x Honor)	27.3	.7
245a1-105-2	27.5	.5
245a1-101-19	27.8	.1
254a1-101-15 (Dietz 105-5 x Gold Coin 129-65)	26.0	.1
311a5-8 (1185a1-73-1 x Honor)	28.3	- .2
245a1-101-15	27.5	- .5
245a1-101-14	25.8	- .5
Honor	25.8	- .9
319a3-27 (1185a1-73-1 x Hybrid No. 86)	27.0	-1.0
253a1-35-14 (Dietz 105-5 x Honor)	27.8	-1.5
311a3-3	28.4	-1.6
319ar6-20 (Hybrid No. 86 x 1185a1-73-1)	26.0	-1.7
319a4-21	26.1	-1.9
319a4-13	25.9	-2.0

(Continued)

Variety	Yield (Bu. per acre)	Gain or loss over check
White-kerneled Sorts (Cont'd)		
251a1-7-3 (Forward x Gold Coin 129-65)	26.2	-2.0
311a8-10	26.1	-2.1
311a6-5	26.3	-2.3
319ar6-36	26.3	-2.3
311a4-5	26.4	-2.4
311a4-10	26.1	-2.5

HUMID MISSISSIPPI VALLEY AREA (South to North)

LOUISIANA

Rice Experiment Station, Crowley (Rice Agronomy, J. M. Jenkins) (September

The appearance of the rice plots on the Station has improved during the past month, and there are indications of much better yields in some instances than were expected in July. The leaf-spot disease also found in commercial fields has been noted in all plots. In some areas it was very conspicuous as early as June, and it has continued to spread from these badly infested areas, causing the plants to assume a very unhealthy and stunted appearance. This disease has been noted nearly every year, but has never been so widespread and abundant before in the history of the Station.

Weather conditions in August were much the same as in July, and approached closely the records for the same month last year.

The temperature extremes were somewhat less than those of August, 1928, although the average was about the same. The rather constant high temperatures with practically no real cloudy days in the month, seems to have had a detriment effect upon the late maturing commercial rices. The indications are that the average yield from these rices will be low. During the month a large number of commercial fields were inspected, and in every case some kind of leaf-spot disease was noted. In some fields large areas appeared greatly reduced in growth by this disease. In nearly all fields of Blue Rose rice most of the lower leaves have died. This disease was noted in early spring and it has continued to spread during the summer. The infestation seems greater in the presence of grass. The early maturing rices were attacked but the disease did not make much headway before maturity.

Most of the commercial fields of Fortuna were harvested in August. Good erage yields were expected. The increase in the acreage of this variety over at of last year is very marked. In the vicinity of Crowley there were only ree or four fields last year, while this year there are nearly 20. Eight or en farmers have requested inspection of their fields of Fortuna and instruction s to the proper time to begin harvest. One of these was a miller of Beaumont, ex, who has 200 acres of Fortuna. The popularity of this variety is increasng. The station already has had requests for more seed than it will produce. ne request for 3,000 pounds of Fortuna seed was from Argentina. In past years here have been other requests from South America for rather large quantities f seed of this variety.

The blister beetle appeared frequently on soybeans during the month of ugust but was quickly destroyed by dusting with sodium fluosilicate. Early n the month the "grass worm" was noted on Otootan soybeans. This insect inreased and spread until by the end of the month nearly all fields were infected. ome fields have been completely stripped of foliage, and unless something happens to check them, the bean crop will be almost a loss. It seems that this insect appeared first in the southeastern part of the State and moved westward. Beans in the vicinity of New Iberia have been killed by them, and a farmer east of the Station had them on his beans in alarming numbers before they were noticeable on the Station beans. The Entomologist has found sodium fluosilicate very effective in destroying them; however, it is too expensive, as the entire field has to be dusted. This worm has been present in limited numbers every year, but never before in the history of the Station has it been sufficiently abundant to cause any concern.

The following have been recent visitors at the Station:

Mr. Cotton, of the U. S. Bureau of Entomology;

Mr. Takashi Ishizuka, Agriculturist in charge, The Government-General of Chosen, Keijo, Japan;

Mr. G. H. Banks, Asst. Director, Rice Branch Station, Stuttgart, Ark.;

Mr. F. C. Green, Director, Cornstalks Products Co., New York City;

The Cuban representative of the International Harvester Company, and the representative of the Case Machine Company, of Dallas, Texas.

Agricultural Experiment Station, Baton Rouge (Corn Breeding, H. F. Stoneberg)

TENNESSEE

Agricultural Experiment Station, Knoxville (Corn Breeding, L. S. Mayer)

MISSOURI

Agricultural Experiment Station, Columbia (Cereal Agronomy, L. J. Stadler)

OHIO

Ohio State University, Columbus (Corn Breeding, L. R. Jorgenson)

IOWA

Agricultural Experiment Station, Ames (Oat Breeding, L. C. Burnett)

Agricultural Experiment Station, Ames (Corn Breeding, M. T. Jenkins) (August 31)

Hand pollinating was started on July 16 and completed on August 19. Approximately 12,000 selfs and 9,000 cross pollinations were made. As far as the hand pollinating is concerned, this has been one of the most success- ful seasons since the work was started in 1922. There was plenty of moisture in the soil during the time that the corn was tasseling and silking, and there seemed to be less than the usual difference in time of tasseling between the early and the late-maturing lines. The bulk of the pollinations was made over a much shorter period than usual.

We are now busily engaged taking records on the inbred lines and the yield experiments with crosses. This work is progressing very satisfactorily and should be completed some time next week.

Mr. T. R. Stanton stopped in Ames on the 26th on his way back to Washington. While here he looked over our corn breeding experiments.

Agricultural Experiment Station, Ames (Crown Rust of Oats, S. M. Dietz)

ILLINOIS

Funk Bros. Seed Co., Bloomington (Corn Root, Stalk and Ear Rots, J. R. Holbert)

INDIANA

Purdue University Agricultural Experiment Station, LaFayette (Corn Rots and Metallic Poisoning, J. F. Trost, Acting in Charge)

Purdue University Agricultural Experiment Station, LaFayette (Leaf Rusts, E. B. Mains)

WISCONSIN

Agricultural Experiment Station, Madison (Wheat Scab, J. G. Dickson)

MINNESOTA

Agricultural Experiment Station, University Farm, St. Paul (Wheat Breeding, R. Ausemus)

Agricultural Experiment Station, University Farm, St. Paul (Stem Rust, C. Stakman)

Agricultural Experiment Station, University Farm, St. Paul (Flax Rust, A. Rodenhiser)

GREAT PLAINS AREA (South to North)

OKLAHOMA

Woodward Field Station, Woodward (Grain Sorghum and Broomcorn, J. B. Sieg-inger)

KANSAS

Agricultural Experiment Station, Manhattan (Cereal Breeding, J. H. Parker)

Agricultural Experiment Station, Manhattan (Corn Breeding, A. M. Brunson)

Agricultural Experiment Station, Manhattan (Wheat Foot Rots, Hurley Fellows)

Agricultural Experiment Station, Manhattan (Wheat Leaf Rust, C. O. Johnston) August 27)

Much of the time in July and August has been spent in harvesting and thresh-ng the 1929 Manhattan leaf-rust nursery. We have just finished threshing, 1,300 -foot rows of winter wheat and 210 rows of spring wheat. The seed is very light nd of poor quality owing to extremely heavy infections of Septoria leaf-spot and cab. A few of the earlier hybrid selections produced a fair quality of seed. bout 1,000 of the 1,300 winter wheats grown were hybrid selections representing ore than 40 crosses. The F_1 generation of 19 crosses was grown in the nursery s well as in the greenhouse. It is planned to have a large sowing of space-lanted F_2's for study in 1930.

August has been very hot and dry. These conditions have caused considerable injury to corn and sorghums. The ground for the 1930 leaf-rust nursery
has been plowed but is in very poor condition. Considerable labor will be required to get it in shape for sowing.

The data collected on the reaction of varieties and hybrids of wheat to
leaf rust and other diseases in 1929 are being compiled, and some very interesting things are being brought to light. The yields of varieties of winter wheat
in 40th-acre plots at the agronomy farm are particularly interesting when the
percentage of leaf rust and leaf blotch are considered. These data are given
in the following table.

Average yield, per cent of leaf rust, and per cent of leaf blotch of
winter-wheat varieties grown in triplicated plots at the Agronomy Farm, Manhattan, Kans., 1928-29

Variety	Kansas No.	Yield	Leaf rust (Per cent)	Leaf blotch[a] (Per cent)
Hard Red Winter				
Fulhard	2593	28.9	86.6	T
Kanred x Hard Federation	2627	26.4	T+	56.6
Tenmarq Selection	2637	25.0	16.6	10.0
Tenmarq	439	24.3	15.0	8.3
Kanred x Marquis	2638	22.8	T-40	23.3
Prelude x Kanred	2628	22.1	T	86.6
Kanred x Marquis	2644	20.2	T-40	30.0
Blackhull	343	18.1	71.6	56.6
Oro	495	18.0	80.0	13.3
Early Blackhull	483	17.4	43.3	53.3
Kanred x Hard Federation	2625	17.3	70.0	38.3
Superhard	470	16.8	53.5	55.0
Kanred (checks)	2401	14.8	55.0	68.7
Kharkov	382	14.2	80.0	26.6
Turkey	570	12.8	83.3	31.6
Kharkov (Hays No. 2)	2659	12.2	80.0	18.3
Newturk	2536	11.4	88.3	8.3
Soft Red Winter				
Kawvale	2593	29.5	T	20.0
Fulcaster	317	26.9	63.3	T+
Nebraska No. 28	34	24.3	60.0	8.3
Michigan Wonder	500	23.5	63.3	T+
Currell	501	19.9	90.0	6.6
Harvest Queen	19	19.6	83.3	T+
Kanred (checks)	2401	16.5	30.0	80.0

[a] Per cent of upper leaves killed by Septoria tritici.

There can be no question that both these diseases were limiting factors
the yield of wheat at Manhattan this year. It will be noted that among the
d red winter varieties the highest yielding all except Fulhard had consider-
e resistance to leaf rust. That variety was highly resistant to leaf blotch
toria tritici) although heavily rusted. As a consequence the leaves re-
ned green on Fulhard while on many other varieties they were dried up by
f blotch.

Among the soft red winter varieties Kawvale was outstanding for resistance
leaf rust and also was high yielding. In general, the soft red winter varie-
es seemed to be less severely injured by leaf blotch than the hard red winters.
th Fulhard and Kawvale have been extensively tested in leaf-rust experiments,
d Fulhard is the direct result of those experiments. Although it does not
ve resistance to leaf rust, it apparently has considerable tolerance to that
sease.

Several new varieties were tested in single 40th-acre plots for the first
me in 1929. Some of these were highly resistant to leaf rust and leaf blotch.
e data given in the following table bring out this point quite clearly. It
interesting to note that the highest yielding strains are resistant to leaf
st. Cooperatorka, a Russian variety, is very susceptible to leaf rust but
sistant to leaf blotch. It also is resistant to bunt.

Average yield, per cent of leaf rust, and per cent of leaf blotch of new
eat varieties grown in single plots at the Agronomy Farm, Manhattan, Kans.,
28-29

Variety	Kansas No.	Yield	Leaf rust (Per cent)	Leaf blotch[a] (Per cent)
anred x Marquis	2642	34.2	T+	15
Do	2640	30.7	T+	40
Do	2647	30.3	T+	T+
ooperatorka	499	27.7	90	5
anred x Marquis	2639	23.8	T	20
anred x Hard Federation	2650	23.4	80	5
anred x Marquis	2641	21.9	10	15
llini Chief x Kanred	2655	21.7	60	10
relude x Kanred	2652	21.4	T+	90
anred x Marquis	2645	21.1	5	25
lini Chief x Kanred	2656	21.0	60	25
066-1 x Super	2654	20.9	60	20
nred x Marquis	2643	20.7	70	40
d Hull	487	19.8	90	50
lini Chief x Kanred	2657	19.3	70	10
gle Chief	498	19.1	10-60	20
nred x Marquis	2646	17.8	T-60	40
elude x Kanred	2653	16.9	T+	90
nred x Hard Federation	2648	15.7	80	20
Do	2651	14.0	70	10
nred (checks)	----	13.7	45	65
nred x Hard Federation	2649	12.9	80	5

a/
Per cent of upper leaves killed by Septoria tritici.

Fort Hays Branch Experiment Station, Hays (Cereal Agronomy, A. F. Swans(

NEBRASKA

North Platte Substation, North Platte (Cereal Agronomy, G. F. Sprague)
[August 31]

A rain of 2.50 inches was recorded on August 28. It fell in a very shoi
time with a heavy run off. For the most part this rain came too late to hel;
corn, except for an occasional field which was planted late.

Varietal corn plots on the table land will be total failures. Inbreds
stood the drought somewhat better, and some selfed and crossed ears will be
obtained. Corn under irrigation suffered very little from the drought and
there are indications of a heavy yield. Three double crosses obtained from M
F. D. Richey look very promising.

Land is being prepared for fall seeding. It is hoped that early seeding
of winter wheat will result in a heavy fall growth and tend to reduce the inj
from soil blowing in the spring.

SOUTH DAKOTA

U. S. Cereal Field Experiments, Redfield (Wheat Improvement, E. S. McFa

NORTH DAKOTA

Northern Great Plains Field Station, Mandan (Cereal Agronomy, V. C. Hubb
(September 2)

All threshing was completed on August 22. Yields were excellent, consi
ing the dryness of the season. Only 7.43 inches of rain were recorded during
the growing season, April 1 to August 31, as compared with 11.66 inches, the
average for the 15-year period from 1914 to 1928, inclusive. Of this year's
rainfall, 4.43 inches fell in April and May.

Crops need rain badly. There was 0.2 of an inch of precipitation in th
period from August 16 to 31, inclusive. The maximum temperature was 101 deg
on August 24 and the minimum 46 degrees on August 22.

Nearly all varieties produced grain that was from 80 to 90 per cent pl
The following yields of wheat, oats, and barley were obtained from 50th-acre
plots grown at the Northern Great Plains Field Station in 1929.

C. I. No.	Yield (Bu. per acre)
6900	16.7
8004	16.2
8018	15.9
7370	15.5
8384	15.5
8385	14.5
5878	14.3
3641	14.0
6607	13.8
8082	13.2
----	12.7
6887	12.5
8178	11.1
8182	11.0
7287	12.6
1440	12.1
8383	12.0
3320	11.2
6519	10.9
5296	9.8
2329	34.4
2027	29.7
165	27.5
2344	26.5
2345	24.1
----	22.0
2053	21.9
560	17.2
493	13.9
2343	12.4
134	10.6
845	9.0
---	4.4a/
936	20.8
531	20.8
---	20.7
926	19.6
1120	16.8
----	16.7
182	16.7
959	15.0
---	11.3

tacked Twentieth Century much more vigorously than they
eties.

314

Northern Great Plains Field Station, Mandan (Flax Breeding, J. C. Brinsmade, Jr.)

Dickinson Substation, Dickinson (Cereal Agronomy, R. W. Smith) (August 31)

Warm, dry weather has prevailed most of the time since early in July up to the present time. The maximum temperature passed the 100 degree mark three times this summer. The maximum temperatures on July 26, July 27, and August 23 were 101, 106, and 102 degrees, respectively. The mean maximum temperature for August was 86.6 degrees, and the mean minimum, 48.3 degrees. Most of the days were sunny and hot, but the coolness of the nights kept the mean temperature for the month down to 67.5 degrees which is only about one degree above normal. The precipitation for the month was 0.09 of an inch.

Threshing at the Substation has progressed without interruption from unfavorable weather and is now nearly finished with the exception of part of the hybrid nursery and a few miscellaneous plots. Threshing in this vicinity is making good progress. The work of harvesting in this locality was divided among binders, headers, and combines, with a small number of the latter in this (Stark) county.

Yields reported from threshing vary from low to fairly good, depending upon local rainfall, variety of grain, and previous tillage or cropping. Some report light weight wheat and others fairly good in test weight. The highest yield of wheat from the rotation plots was 21.9 bushels per acre from Marquis sown on summer fallow. Other rotations yielded less and a few as low as 8 bushels.

Yields from the varietal plots of spring wheat are given in the following table. The varieties were sown on corn land. A few of the durums tested as much as 60 pounds, while most of the hard red wheats weighed less than 58 pounds per bushel. The early varieties were more nearly mature than the later ones when seriously affected by the drought, hence the former gave the highest yields, contrary to the usual results.

Mr. J. Allen Clark and Mr. K. S. Quisenberry arrived at the Substation on August 24. Mr. Quisenberry remained until August 26.

Acre yields of spring-wheat varieties grown on corn land in quadruplicated 1/56th-acre plots at the Dickinson Substation in 1929[a]/

Group and Variety	C. I. No.	Yield (Bu. per acre)
Hard Spring		
Quality	6607	14.5
Reward	8182	13.3
Ruby	6047	12.5
Garnet	8181	12.0
Supreme	----	10.5
Marquis x Kota (1656.85)	----	10.1
Reliance	7370	10.1
Ceres	6900	10.0
Montana King	----	10.0
Renfrew	----	9.3
Marquis x Kota (1656.97)	8005	9.2
Marquis	3641	9.1

[a]/ These figures are subject to slight changes when checked for final

Group and Variety	C. I. No.	Yield (Bu. per acre)
rd Spring (Continued)		
Marquis x Kota (1656.84	8004	8.8
Marquillo	6887	8.5
Kota	5878	8.3
Preston	3081	8.3
Progress	6902	8.1[b/]
Reliance Selection No. 22	----	7.6
Do No. 16	----	7.3
Haynes Bluestem	2874	7.2
Power Fife	3697	6.4
Hope	8178	6.2
Red Fife	3329	6.0
Hurdsfield	----	5.5[b/]
rum		
Pentad	3322	8.8
Kubanka	1440	8.4
Do Selection No. 132	----	8.0
Nodak	6519	7.8
Mondak	7287	7.6
Mindum	5296	7.6
Akrona	6881	7.5
Monad	3320	7.5

[b/]
Only two plots.

Agricultural Experiment Station, State College Station, Fargo (Flax Diseases, L. W. Boyle)

Langdon Substation, Langdon (Wheat Improvement, G. S. Smith) (August 31)

The nursery harvest is nearly completed, and the varietal plots will be threshed the first week in September, weather permitting.

Excellent weather has prevailed during the harvest season, with a few very hot days. The rainfall for the month of August has totaled 1.21 inches, coming in six or eight small showers.

Threshing in the vicinity is just fairly under way. Yields in general probably will be slightly better than anticipated at an earlier date.

Messrs. J. Allen Clark and K. S. Quisenberry spent August 27 and 28 at the Substation taking stem-rust notes on F_2 crosses of Nodak, Mindum, Pentad, Akrona, and Kubanka 132. Dr. L. R. Waldron, of the North Dakota Agricultural College, was a visitor also.

316

MONTANA

Judith Basin Branch Station, Moccas'n (Cereal Agronomy, B. B. Bayles)

Montana Agricultural Experiment Station, Bozeman (LeRoy Powers)

WESTERN BASIN AND COAST AREAS (North to West and South)

IDAHO

Aberdeen Substation, Aberdeen (Cereal Agronomy, L. L. Davis) (September

The first killing frost occurred on September 4. Late potatoes and alfa: seed were the only two crops injured to any extent.

Plot threshing was completed on August 24, and nursery threshing on Septe ber 5.

The following yields were obtained from the barley varietal plots.

Variety	C. I. No.	Yield (Bu. per acre)
Ezond	----	95.2
Trebi	936	89.3
Smyrna	4580	88.2
Horn	926	86.2
Hannchen	531	85.4
Arequipa	1256	84.7
Smyrna	910	84.2
Flynn	1311	82.3
Beldi	2777	81.5
Meloy	1176	79.5
Alpha	959	70.3
Foust	4579	67.1
Orel	351	63.5

The yields are the average of four plots, two of which were 1-40 acre an two were 1-93 acre.

Agricultural Experiment Station, Moscow (Stripe Rust, C. W. Hungerford)

WASHINGTON

Agricultural Experiment Station, Pullman (Cereal Breeding, E. F. Gaines)

<u>Agricultural Experiment Station, Pullman</u> (Stinking Smuts of Wheat, H. H.
r) [August 31]

The following summary was prepared by Drs. H. H. Flor and E. F. Gaines on
pletion of the July, 1929, survey for stinking smut of wheat in eastern and
tral Washington. The survey showed large variations in severity. Bunt was
st severe in the winter-wheat region of eastern Washington. It was not severe
spring wheat. In the fields of winter wheat examined, Ridit was outstanding
being almost free from smut while Hybrid 128 was the most heavily attacked.

The summary of the results of the survey follows:

Variety	Time sown	Number fields examined	Average per cent of smut
Hybrid 128	Fall	5	26.5
Triplet	Do	3	7.0
Fortyfold	Do	5	6.6
Albit	Do	2	3.5
Coppei	Do	1	3.0
Turkey	Do	6	1.8
Ridit	Do	4	T
Federation	Spring	5	0.6
Bluestem	Do	5	0.1
Jenkin	Do	4	T
Dicklow	Do	3	T
Marquis	Do	1	T
Thompsons Club	Do	1	T
Hybrid 128	Do	1	T

Each collection was examined microscopically for the prevalence of <u>Tilletia</u>
itici and <u>T. levis</u>. Several other Washington collections also were examined
d are included in the following summary of the results:

Collections having <u>Tilletia tritici</u> alone	31
Collections having <u>Tilletia levis</u> alone	4
Collections mixed	27
Collections mixed <u>Tilletia tritici</u> predominant	21
Collections mixed <u>Tilletia levis</u> predominant	5
Collections mixed evenly	1
Total collections examined	62

<u>Tilletia tritici</u> occurred in much greater abundance than <u>T. levis</u>. In fact
ly on Albit and Turkey was <u>T. levis</u> predominant. In every collection of every
her variety <u>T. tritici</u> predominated.

OREGON

<u>Sherman County Branch Station, Moro</u> (Cereal Agronomy, D. E. Stephens)

CALIFORNIA

<u>Biggs Rice Field Station, Biggs</u> (Rice Agronomy, J. W. Jones)

<u>University Farm, Davis</u> (Cereal Agronomy, G. A. Wiebe)

Agricultural Experiment Station, Berkeley (Cereal Smuts, F. N. Briggs)

BARBERRY ERADICATION PROGRESS

OHIO

Ohio State University, College of Agriculture, Columbus, J. W. Baringer August 31)

Early in August the entire crew of barberry-eradication field agents completed the first survey for barberries in Ashtabula County. This event marked the completion of the first survey in the State.

All of the agents were thereafter placed on second survey in Preble County. Two townships of Preble County were covered by second survey in 1928. At this time there are less than two townships left in Preble County to be covered by second survey, and this phase of the program has been started in Montgomery County.

Only the intensive method of procedure is being employed on the second coverage. For the most part few barberries have been discovered in those townships of Preble County so far second-surveyed, with the exception of Harrison Township. A number of farms in this region were found to be infested with escaped common barberries when the first survey was made. In this same general vicinity several barberries were discovered this year on near-by farms where they had never been noted before. In addition, several bushes of considerable size and many small ones were recorded on rechecking properties where previous eradication attempts were only partially successful.

INDIANA

Purdue University College of Agriculture, LaFayette, W. E. Leer (August 31)

The field force is being broken up at this time because of resignations. Eight men are returning to their teaching positions and six will be returning to school about September 12. It now appears that only three or four men will be working after September 7. Mr. I. Lester McCoy, who was in charge of the educational work in the high schools last winter, will be available again for that type of work this year, and will start the school campaign about October 1.

A barberry demonstration has been prepared in the center of the Purdue University building at the Indiana State Fair and gives promise of being the center of attraction in the building.

The intensive survey of Tipton County was completed on August 16, and the intensive survey of Hamilton County should be finished within a week or 10 days. Since the beginning of the campaign, 608 bushes have been found in Tipton County.

MICHIGAN

Agricultural College, East Lansing, W. F. Reddy

WISCONSIN

Department of Agriculture, State Capitol Annex, Madison, R. M. Caldwell

ILLINOIS

Box 72, Post Office Building, Urbana, B. W. Bills (September 3)

Since the beginning of the field season, Monroe, Randolph, Washington, an
Perry counties have been completed on first survey, and it is expected that
Jefferson, Wayne, Edwards, and Wabash will be completed by September 15, when
the force will be reduced because of the beginning of the school year. The re
maining force will complete the second survey of Jo Daviess County and the fir
survey of White, Hamilton, and possibly Franklin counties. This will leave th
11 southernmost counties of Illinois unsurveyed at the close of this year.

More than 100 barberry bushes have been destroyed on first survey thus fa
a few of them being enormous bushes. One bush found in Edwards County was reported to have been brought from New England and planted 100 years ago. Scout
ing for escaped bushes near plantings in southern Illinois this year has been
fruitless.

At the Illinois State Fair a 20-foot booth was used for the barberry-erad
cation demonstration with the "death cell" as the center of attraction. Hundr
of people stopped and both of the attendants were kept busy all during the fai
talking to the people. Smaller demonstrations have been used at the fairs in
Franklin, Jefferson, Edwards, White, and Jo Daviess counties and demonstratior
will be prepared for the fairs in Wabash and Perry counties the first two week
in September.

A great deal of interest is being shown by people in all of the southern
counties. The fine cooperation which the scouts are receiving is very largel
due to the intensive educational program which was carried out during the pas
winter.

IOWA

Iowa State College, Ames, P. W. Rohrbaugh

MINNESOTA

Agricultural Experiment Station, University Farm, St. Paul, L. W. Meland

NEBRASKA

<u>College of Agriculture, University Farm, Lincoln</u>, B. F. Dittus, Acting in arge

SOUTH DAKOTA

<u>College of Agriculture, Brookings</u>, R. O. Bulger

NORTH DAKOTA

<u>Agricultural Extension Division, State College Station, Fargo</u>, G. C. Mayoue ugust 31)

One of the outstanding local rust epidemics was found the last week of July etween Bismarck and Wilton in Burleigh County, indicating quite definitely a ocal source of infection. The field agents who made a more extensive study of hat rust spread found that it extended northwest across the Missouri River and nto Oliver County.

In the course of the systematic survey for barberries, one of the largest 'inds of this season was discovered two miles west of the Missouri River and pproximately three miles southeast of Washburn. The bushes, which had been lanted in 1891, were heavily infected and also were carrying a moderate crop f berries. Many seedlings were found near the bushes. The fact that the bushes ere bearing seeds leads one to believe that a considerable number of seedlings ay be found along the Missouri River, particularly within a few miles of the riginal barberry location. Agents at this time are doing some work along the issouri River in that area.

In addition to the field work which is being done in Burleigh County, agents lso are working in portions of Traill, Burke, Logan, and LaMoure counties. chool children in the areas which have been and are being surveyed are more nterested than in previous years in the destruction of the barberries. Their nterest undoubtedly can be attributed to the educational work which has been arried on in the schools.

MONTANA

<u>State College of Agriculture, Bozeman</u>, W. L. Popham

WYOMING

<u>College of Agriculture, University of Wyoming, Laramie</u>, W. L. Popham

COLORADO

Agricultural College, Ft. Collins, E. A. Lungren (September 4)

Second survey was completed in Arapahoe and Adams counties during the month of August. A portion of Denver County also was second-surveyed, which leaves only a small part to be surveyed.

Since January 1, 2,093 barberry bushes, sprouting bushes, and seedlings have been found on all surveys in the counties covered this season. Light infection was found on the majority of the bushes, and some spreads were apparent. Two large areas of escapes were found. Their locations were ideal for large spreads.

There was very little rust in the State this year, only a trace appearing on all grains but rye, on which no rust could be found. The rust damage can be reported only as a trace.

C E R E A L   C O U R I E R

Official Messenger of the Office of Cereal Crops and Diseases
Bureau of Plant Industry, U. S. Department of Agriculture
(NOT FOR PUBLICATION)

----

ol. 21   No. 23
September 20, 1929
Personnel (Sept. 11-20) and Field Station (Sept. 1-15) Issue

PERSONNEL ITEMS

Mr. J. Allen Clark, senior agronomist in charge of western wheat inves-
igations, returned to Washington on September 12 after an absence of nearly
hree months in the field. Mr. Clark devoted his summer largely to an inspection of the enlarged cooperative hard-spring-wheat breeding and testing
experiments conducted at the following stations: St. Paul, Waseca, Morris,
and Crookston, Minn.; Fargo, Edgeley, Langdon, Mandan, Dickinson, Hettinger,
and Williston, N. Dak.; Brookings, Highmore, Eureka, Redfield, Newell, and
Ardmore, S. Dak.; Bozeman, Moccasin, Havre, and Huntley, Mont.; and Sheridan
and Archer, Wyo. By using a Government-owned car, Mr. Clark was able to visit
all of these stations. Almost all of these official stops were made on schedule, and some of the stations were visited two and three times. Temporary
headquarters were at Fargo, N. Dak.

In addition to these stations, Mr. Clark visited the agricultural experiment stations at Madison, Wis., and Winnipeg and Morden, Manitoba, Canada, the
substation at Gillette, Wyo., and the new Central Great Plains Field Station
now being established at Cheyenne, Wyo.

Considerable time was spent at the U. S. Cereal Field Experiments, Redfield, S. Dak., at the Northern Great Plains Field Station, Mandan, N. Dak.,
and at the Langdon Substation, Langdon, N. Dak., in making studies of the inheritance of stem-rust reaction in certain wheat crosses. At the Montana
Agricultural Experiment Station, Bozeman, Mr. Clark studied the inheritance
of awnedness in a series of wheat crosses, and, in cooperation with Mr. LeRoy
Powers, the inheritance of bunt reaction in other wheat crosses.

Miss Serena A. Collings was appointed junior stenographer, effective September 18, to succeed Mrs. Edna T. Basart as assistant in the office of the
State Leader of barberry eradication in Iowa. Mrs. Basart resigned her position on August 7.

Dr. A. G. Johnson, principal pathologist in charge of cereal-disease investigations, left Washington on September 21 to inspect cooperative cereal-disease experiments and to confer with State and Federal officials in Indiana, Illinois, Missouri, Arkansas, Kansas, and Wisconsin.

Miss Mary L. Martini, assistant botanist in barley investigations, returned to Washington on September 4 upon completion of extensive field studies of barley in Arizona and Idaho.

Mr. Karl S. Quisenberry, associate agronomist in western wheat investigations, returned to Washington on September 16 after being away since June, 1928. From September 1, 1928, until August 1, 1929, Mr. Quisenberry was acting in charge of the cooperative wheat breeding experiments at University Farm, St. Paul, Minn. In June, Mr. Quisenberry made a trip through Texas, Oklahoma, Kansas, and Nebraska, visiting stations where cooperative experiments with winter wheats are being conducted.

Upon leaving St. Paul on August 1, of this year, Mr. Quisenberry visited field stations in North and South Dakota and Montana in the interests of winter-wheat investigations. At Dickinson, N. Dak., the winter-wheat nursery was found to be a total failure owing to severe winterkilling and dry weather. The yields of the winter-wheat plots were very satisfactory, however. Mr. Quisenberry reports that at Moccasin, Mont., crops were generally poor because of continued dry, hot weather. Winter wheat on the Station farm and on farms in the Judith Basin was below average, while spring wheat was a total failure in many cases. While at Moccasin, Mr. Quisenberry packeted and mailed to 29 stations in northern United States and Canada seed for the Uniform Winter Hardiness nurseries.

While at Bozeman, Mont., Mrs. Marion Griffiths Zehner, associate pathologist in cereal-smut investigations, and Mr. Quisenberry put up and inoculated seed for ten Uniform Winter Wheat Smut nurseries.

Returning from Bozeman to Washington, D. C., Mr. Quisenberry traveled by Government-owned car from Fargo, N. Dak., to Manhattan, Kans. He reports that between St. Paul, Minn., and Manhattan, Kans., corn fields looked well and farmers were preparing the ground for fall crops. There had been rain throughout most of the area traversed.

VISITORS

Mr. Donald G. Fletcher, Secretary of The Conference for the Prevention of Grain Rust, Minneapolis, Minn., and Dr. E. C. Stakman, agent in the cooperative cereal-disease investigations conducted at University Farm, St. Paul, Minn., called at the Office on Saturday, September 14. They were on their way home from New York City, where they had attended a meeting of the International Automobile Chamber of Commerce on invitation to present the story of barberry and stem rust to that organization.

Dr. Sewall Wright, of the University of Chicago, was an Office visitor on September 16. He conferred with Messrs. J. Allen Clark and F. D. Richey on inheritance studies of wheat and corn.

MANUSCRIPTS AND PUBLICATIONS

55 A manuscript entitled "Varietal Resistance of Spring Wheats to Bunt,"
y W. E. Brentzel and Ralph W. Smith, was submitted on September 7 for publi-
ation as a cooperative bulletin by the North Dakota Agricultural Experiment
tation.

The article entitled "Sulphur Dusting for the Prevention of Stem Rust of
heat," by E. B. Lambert and E. C. Stakman, appears in Phytopathology 19 (7):
31-643, fig. 1. July, 1929. (Cooperative investigations between the Minneota Agricultural Experiment Station and the Office of Cereal Crops and Diseases.

Georgia State College of Agriculture Ext. Div. Bul. 355 entitled "Fall
own Oats for Georgia," by R. R. Childs, bearing date of November, 1928, has
een received. (Cooperation between the Extension Division of the Georgia
tate College of Agriculture and the Office of Cereal Crops and Diseases.)

The note entitled "A Cereal Nursery Seeder," by G. A. Wiebe, appears in
he Journal of the American Society of Agronomy 21 (8): 863-864, figs. 1-2.
ugust, 1929.

A revised edition [October, 1928] of Ill. Agr. Expt. Sta. Circ. 284
ntitled "A Program of Corn Improvement," by C. M. Woodworth, has been received.
(In cooperation with Office of Cereal Crops and Diseases.)

The article entitled "Distribution of Anthocyan Pigments in Rice Varieties,"
by Jenkin W. Jones, appears in the Journal of the American Society of Agronomy
21 (9): 867-875. September, 1929. (Contribution from the Office of Cereal
Crops and Diseases in cooperation with the California Agricultural Experiment
Station.)

The article entitled "Correlations between Seed Ear and Kernel Characters
and Yield of Corn," by Arthur M. Brunson and J. G. Willier, appears in the
Journal of the American Society of Agronomy 21 (9): 912-922. September, 1929.
(Joint contribution from the Office of Cereal Crops and Diseases and the Kansas
Agricultural Experiment Station.)

The article entitled "Influrence of Varietal Resistance, Sap Acidity, and
Certain Environmental Factors on the Occurrence of Loose Smut in Wheat," by
Victor F. Tapke, appears in the Journal of Agricultural Research 39 (5): 313-
339, figs. 1-4. September 1, 1929.

The article entitled "Relation of Leaf Acidity to Vigor in Wheat Grown at
Different Temperatures," by Annie M. Hurd-Karrer, appears in the Journal of
Agricultural Research 39 (5): 341-350, figs. 1-2. September 1, 1929.

The brief paper entitled "The Water Content of Wheat Leaves at Flowering
Time," by Annie M. Hurd-Karrer and J. W. Taylor, appears in Plant Physiology
4 (3): 393-397, fig. 1. July, 1929. (Received September 16.)

Farmers' Bulletin 1585 entitled "Varieties of Hard Red Winter Wheat," by
J. Allen Clark and Karl S. Quisenberry, was received on September 18, bearing
date of June, 1929.

FIELD STATION CONDITION AND PROGRESS

(All experiments except those conducted at the Arlington Experiment Farm, Rosslyn, Va., are in cooperation with State agricultural experiment stations or other agencies.)

HUMID ATLANTIC COAST AREA (South to North)

GEORGIA

State College of Agriculture, Athens (Cereal Agronomy, R. R. Childs)

VIRGINIA

Arlington Experiment Farm, Rosslyn (Small Grain Agronomy, J. W. Taylor)

Arlington Experiment Farm, Rosslyn (Corn Breeding, F. D. Richey)

Arlington Experiment Farm, Rosslyn (Cereal Smuts, V. F. Tapke, Acting in Charge)

Arlington Experiment Farm, Rosslyn (Virus Diseases, H. H. McKinney)

NEW YORK

Cornell University Agricultural Experiment Station, Ithaca (Cereal Breeding, H. H. Love)

HUMID MISSISSIPPI VALLEY AREA (South to North)

LOUISIANA

Rice Experiment Station, Crowley (Rice Agronomy, J. M. Jenkins)

Agricultural Experiment Station, Baton Rouge (Corn Breeding, H. F. Stoneberg)

TENNESSEE

Agricultural Experiment Station, Knoxville (Corn Breeding, L. S. Mayer)

MISSOURI

Agricultural Experiment Station, Columbia (Cereal Agronomy, L. J. Stadler)

OHIO

Ohio State University, Columbus (Corn Breeding, L. R. Jorgenson)

IOWA

Agricultural Experiment Station, Ames (Oat Breeding, L. C. Burnett)

Agricultural Experiment Station, Ames (Corn Breeding, M. T. Jenkins)

Agricultural Experiment Station, Ames (Crown Rust of Oats, S. M. Dietz)

ILLINOIS

Funk Bros. Seed Co., Bloomington (Corn Root, Stalk and Ear Rots, J. R. bert)

INDIANA

Purdue University Agricultural Experiment Station, LaFayette (Corn Rots d Metallic Poisoning, J. F. Trost, Acting in Charge)

Purdue University Agricultural Experiment Station, LaFayette (Leaf Rusts, B. Mains)

WISCONSIN

Agricultural Experiment Station, Madison (Wheat Scab, J. G. Dickson)

MINNESOTA

Agricultural Experiment Station, University Farm, St. Paul (Wheat Breeding, R. Ausemus)

Agricultural Experiment Station, University Farm, St. Paul (Stem Rust, C. Stakman)

Agricultural Experiment Station, University Farm, St. Paul (Flax Rust, A. Rodenhiser)

GREAT PLAINS AREA (South to North)

OKLAHOMA

Woodward Field Station, Woodward (Grain Sorghum and Broomcorn, J. B. Sieglinger) (September 16)

From present appearances the yield of the grain sorghums and broomcorn on the Station will be slightly better than it was in 1928.

A group of 25 investigators, making a tour in the interests of grain-sor ghum experimentation and production, visited the Station on Tuesday afternoo September 10. From Woodward they went to Chillicothe, Tex., where Substatio No. 12 of the Texas Agricultural Experiment Station was inspected on Septembe 11. On September 12 the substations at Spur and Lubbock were visited. On September 13 the experiments at the Tucumcari (N. Mex.) Field Station were inspected, and on September 14 the party visited the U. S. Dry-Land Field Sta tion at Dalhart, Tex., and the Panhandle Agricultural Experiment Station at Goodwell, Okla.

The sorghums at Dalhart probably will produce the highest yields of any seen on the trip. The largest acreage of grain sorghums was seen between Lub bock and Farwell, Tex. About one half of it was devoted to dwarf hegari, the remainder to Dwarf milo and Blackhull kafir.

So far this month 3.99 inches of rain have been recorded on two dates. This is favorable for a good seed bed for winter wheat wherever tillage has been done.

Maximum temperatures for first half of September, 103 degrees on the 1st minimum, 44 degrees on the 10th.

KANSAS

Agricultural Experiment Station, Manhattan (Cereal Breeding, J. H. Parke

Agricultural Experiment Station, Manhattan (Corn Breeding, A. M. Brunson

Agricultural Experiment Station, Manhattan (Wheat Foot Rots, Hurley Fell

Agricultural Experiment Station, Manhattan (Wheat Leaf Rust, C. O. Johns

Fort Hays Branch Experiment Station, Hays (Cereal Agronomy, A. F. Swanso

NEBRASKA

North Platte Substation, North Platte (Cereal Agronomy, G. F. Sprague)
(August 16)

The following yields were obtained from the plot experiments with spring
wheat at the North Platte Substation in 1929.

Class and Variety	C. I. No.	Yield (Bu. per acre)
Hard Red Spring		
Reliance	7370	17.7
Marquillo	6887	17.5
Ceres	6900	16.0
Marquis	3641	15.6
Reward	8182	15.4
Progress	6902	14.7
Supreme	8026	14.3
Java (Kearney Co.)	----	14.3
Garnet	8181	14.1
Hope	8178	13.0
Kota	5878	11.2
Durum		
Kubanka	1440	14.9
Nodak	6519	14.6
Mindum	5296	14.5
Akrona	6881	14.3
White		
Quality	6607	13.0

SOUTH DAKOTA

U. S. Dry-Land Field Station, Ardmore (O. R. Mathews) (Office of Dry-
Land Agriculture) (September 16)

After Mr. Dillman's visit to the Ardmore Field Station on July 25 the
weather continued very hot and dry. The flax yields were so exceedingly low
that they were meaningless.

The flax had to be mowed. Even though it was gathered up clean, the total
weight was only about 20 pounds to the plot. The grain yields varied from 0 to
4 pounds to the plot. All yields were so low that it was thought best to consider them total failures. The most that can be said is that the Argentine
varieties were slightly less drought-resistant than the others. Rio was a
total failure on all replications and Commercial Argentine was very little
better. Linota produced the highest yield, but its average yield was only 2
bushels to the acre.

U. S. Cereal Field Experiments, Redfield (Wheat Improvement, E. S.
McFadden)

NORTH DAKOTA

The following yields were obtained from the spring-wheat varieties grown in plot experiments at Edgeley in 1929.

Class and Variety		C. I. No.	Yield (Bu. per acre)
Hard Red Spring			
Kota x Marquis	1656.85	8385	21.8
Do	1656.84	8004	20.0
Ceres		6900	17.6
Hope		8178	17.6
Reliance		7370	17.3
Marvel		8876	16.5
Marquillo		6887	16.2
Kota		5878	15.9
Reward		8182	15.7
Ruby		6047	15.3
Marquis		3641	15.3
Whiteman		8379	15.1
Montana King		8878	13.7
Garnet		8181	12.3
Supreme		8026	10.7
Durum			
Kubanka No. 132		8383	21.5
Pentad (D-5)		3322	21.0
Mindum		5296	20.0
Monad (D-1)		3320	19.5
Kubanka		1440	18.9
Bol. 211		----	16.5
Nodak		6519	16.2
Bol. 216		----	15.7
Akrona		6881	14.9
White			
Quality		6607	10.5

Agricultural Experiment Station, State College Station, Fargo (Flax Diseases, L. W. Boyle)

Northern Great Plains Field Station, Mandan (Cereal Agronomy, V. C. Hubbard) (September 16)

The agronomic data for the triplicate and single-rod rows of wheat repli cated three times have been computed. The percentage of stem rust and the yield per acre of 20 of the highest yielding varieties and strains from each nursery are as follows:

Percentage of stem rust and yield per acre of wheats grown in triplicate od rows replicated three times at Mandan, N. Dak., in 1929

Variety or Strain	C. I. or Hybrid No.	Stem rust (Per cent)	Yield (Bu. per acre)
eliance	7370	28.3	26.3
anred x Marquis	N.33	35.0	25.7
eliance Selection	B-8-11-22	32.6	24.8
Apollo	Sask. 1850	23.3	24.8
Reliance Selection	----	23.3	24.5
Marquis x Kota	8385	8.3	24.5
Kota-Hard Federation x Kanred-Marquis	A-1-20-3-1	25.0	24.0
Marquis x Kota	1656.178	16.6	23.8
Kanred x Marquis	8018	25.0	23.5
Marquillo x Kanred-Marquis	II-21-7	8.3	23.5
Kanred x Marquis	B-9-14-42	48.3	23.3
Do	B-9-14-24	40.0	23.2
Marquis x Kota	8004	15.0	22.9
Ceres	6900	18.3	22.5
Marquis	3641	43.3	22.3
Reliance Selection	B-8-11-7	18.3	22.2
Kota-Hard Federation x Kanred-Marquis	C-1-19-1-24	18.3	21.8
Marquillo x Marquis	II-22-4	11.6	21.8
Reliance Selection	B-8-11-16	21.6	21.5
Marquis x Kota	1656.84	6.6	21.5

Percentage of stem rust and yield per acre of wheats grown in single rod rows replicated three times at Mandan, N. Dak., in 1929

Variety or Strain	C. I. or Hybrid No.	Stem rust (Per cent)	Yield (Bu. per acre)
Hope x Ceres	A-1-8	6.6	29.3
Kota-Hard Federation x Kanred-Marquis	A-1-52-1	23.3	28.3
Do	B-1-20-2	33.3	28.2
Marquis-Emmer x Kanred-Marquis	A-7-12	5.0	27.7
Hope x Ceres	A-5-11	5.0	27.3
Do	A-4-43	5.0	26.8
Kota-Hard Federation x Kanred-Marquis	A-2-45-1	21.6	26.3
Hope x Ceres	A-2-20	5.0	26.3
Do	A-2-10	6.6	26.0
Kota-Hard Federation x Kanred-Marquis	A-1-5-1	25.0	25.5
Hope x Ceres	A-1-10	8.3	25.5
Kota x Webster	H-123-25	16.6	25.2
Kota-Hard Federation x Kanred-Marquis	B-2-4-1-1-2	46.6	24.7
Do	A-2-45	28.3	24.7
Marquis x Kota	1656.47	10.0	24.5
Hope x Ceres	A-4-34	11.8	24.5
Do	A-4-49	6.6	24.5
Do	A-5-5	10.0	24.5
Marquis	3641	43.3	24.3
Kota-Hard Federation x Kanred-Marquis	A-3-4-2-10	33.3	24.2

A Uniform Winterhardiness nursery consisting of 30 varieties, was sown on September 9. The seed bed was in good condition though the soil was very dry, and on September 16 no signs of germination were evident.

Northern Great Plains Field Station, Mandan (Flax Breeding, J. C. Brinsmade, Jr.) (September 16)

The weather of the first half of September has been generally cloudy and cool, except that on September 1 a temperature of 103 degrees was recorded. Maximum temperature for this period was 103 degrees on September 1; minimum, 32 degrees on September 5. There was slight frost injury to tender garden plants but no complete killing.

The precipitation for this period was 0.37 of an inch.

The yields of flax varieties sown on May 1 (South Field) are as follows:

Variety	C. I. No.	Yield (Bu. per acre)	P. E.
Selection of C. I. 119	474	8.0	.1
Selection 167-254	475	8.0	.2
Siberia No. 206	473	7.9	.2
Selection of Hybrid 19 x 112	478	7.5	.4
Selection of Hybrid 167 x 179	476	7.4	.3
N. D. R. 114	13	7.0	.2

Average yields of 11 varieties already threshed (Main Field) range from 3.7 for Chippewa to 4.9 for Redwing.

Flax sown June 10 in the date-and-rate-of-seeding-and-tillage experiment, and the late varieties in the triplicated varietal plots sown June 1, were harvested on September 10. Most of the plots still had many green bolls on that date. These plots are not yet dry enough to thresh.

In the date-and-rate-of-seeding-and-tillage experiment, flax sown on May 1 produced the highest yields of the plots already threshed. A complete report of plot yields will be made when all yields are available.

Dickinson Substation, Dickinson (Cereal Agronomy, R. W. Smith) (September 16)

All cereal threshing at the Substation has been completed for the season. Yields have been tabulated only for spring-wheat varieties grown in replicated plots and in triplicated 3-row blocks. Yields for the latter are presented in the following table, the varieties being arranged in order of average yield. The percentages of smutty heads for these same varieties grown in a separate nursery from smut-inoculated seed also are given. The yields of other varieties grown in single rows and triplicated single rows have not yet been computed.

The winter-wheat nursery, consisting of 1,119 17-foot rows and 210 8-foot rows, was sown on September 14. The ground is too dry for the germination of the seed and has been in that condition most of the time for the past two months. Half an inch of rain fell in the first week of September. If the wheat had been sown at that time germination would have occurred but the plants would soon be dying for lack of moisture to continue their growth unless more rain fell in the near future.

The 12 varieties of corn and six different strains of Northwestern dent
e harvested this morning. The first killing frost was recorded on Septem-
6, about a week earlier than usual, and put an end to further development
the corn crop. The early varieties of flint and semident were fairly well
ured, but late varieties again failed to mature.

The maximum temperature for the month so far has been 100 degrees on the
; minimum, 26 degrees on the 8th.

Yields of spring-wheat varieties grown in triplicated 3-row blocks, and
rcentages of smutty heads obtained from the same varieties grown in a sep-
ate nursery from seed inoculated with bunt on the Dickinson Substation in
29[1]/

	: Acre yield : :(Bu. per acre):	Bunt (Per cent)
ta x Webster H-209	19.6	78.5
ollo	17.7	14.0
liance Selection 64	17.6	36.5
rquis x Kota (1656.84)	17.3	42.0
liance Selection 22	17.1	18.0
rquis x Sunset	16.9	21.0
rquis x Kota (1656.44)	16.5	31.0
liance Selection 16	16.3	12.0
arquis x Kanred B9-11-50	16.0	24.0
eres (Average of checks)	16.0	59.1
arquis x Kota (1656.48)	15.8	36.0
eliance	15.6	6.0
arquis x Kota (1656.175)	15.5	28.0
Do (1656.178)	15.5	60.0
-44	15.5	1.0
eward	15.3	34.0
arnet	15.0	15.0
arquis (Average of checks)	14.9	27.0
Lanet	14.8	43.0
arquis x Kota (1656.90)	14.8	56.0
Do (1656.85)	14.7	58.0
eliance Selection 7	14.2	21.0
arquis x Kota (1656.118)	14.0	78.0
ardsfield	14.0	45.0
roesus	13.7	61.0
ontana King	13.7	19.0
(ota-Hard Federation)x(Kanred-Marquis) A3-3-3-2	13.6	47.0
uality	13.5	10.0
arquis x Kanred II-17-40	13.3	18.0
enfrew	13.3	16.0
arquis x Kota (1656.123)	13.2	20.0
arquis x Kanred B9-14-42	13.0	32.0
arquis x Kota (1656.125)	12.8	60.0
ota	12.5	39.8
ota x Webster H-178	12.5	33.0
ota x Kanred B11-1-1	12.4	10.4
xminster	12.3	13.5
ota x Kanred B2-1-7	12.0	2.5
(ota-Hard Federation)x(Kanred-Marquis) 6-4	11.8	36.9
ope	10.9	0.0

[1]/The bunt used was a mixture of _Tilletia levis_ and _T. tritici_.

Langdon Substation, Langdon (Wheat Improvement, G. S. Smith) (Septembe

The first half of September has been characterized by cool and cloudy weather. Four or five light frosts have been recorded with temperatures a low as 27 degrees. The heaviest rain of the summer (1.12 inches) fell on September 3. Otherwise the season has been excellent for threshing and ha permitted the farmers of this community to complete their threshing earlie than usual. Crop yields in this region are fair and somewhat better than a cipated earlier in the summer.

The nursery threshing is just well under way at this station. The wi hardiness nursery, seeded on September 7, is germinating but because of the cool weather has not yet emerged.

Following are the yields of the wheat varieties grown at this station season. These varieties were grown on 1/60th acre plots replicated three

Class and Variety	C. I. No.	Yield (Bu. per acre)
Hard red spring		
Kota x Marquis 1656.84	8004	33.2
Reliance	7370	32.0
Ceres	6900	29.7
Kota x Marquis 1656.85	8085	29.5
Marquis	3641	29.5
Hope	8178	29.2
Supreme	8026	28.3
Marquillo	6887	27.7
Kota	5878	27.3
Garnet	8181	27.2
Reward	8182	26.3
Brownhead	----	25.7
Montana King	8878	25.3
Ruby	6047	24.7
Durum		
Monad	3320	28.2
N. D. R. 216	----	28.0
Kubanka	1440	27.8
Nodak	6519	27.2
Mindum	5296	25.3
Akrona	6881	25.3
Kubanka 132	8383	25.2
White		
Quality	6607	25.0
Axminster	8195	23.2

MONTANA

Northern Montana Branch Station, Havre (M. A. Bell) (Office of Dry-Land griculture) (September 16)

Mr. M. A. Bell, assistant agronomist, has reported the yields of nine arieties of flax grown in triplicate 1/40th-acre plots in 1929. The yields re shown in the following table, with the annual and average yields for the ive-year period, 1925 to 1929, inclusive.

Annual and average yields of flax varieties at Havre, Mont., 1925 to 929, inclusive

Variety	C. I. No.	Annual Yields in Bushels per Acre					
		1925	1926	1927	1928	1929	Average
Reserve	19	9.6	0.0	13.8	11.9	5.5	8.2
Linota	244	9.3	0.0	14.0	10.8	4.3	7.7
Stark	185	7.0	0.0	14.0	10.8	6.2	7.6
Newland	188	8.6	0.0	13.0	10.5	4.2	7.3
N. D. R. 52	275	7.3	0.0	12.4	10.4	4.5[1]/	6.9
N. D. R. 114	13	7.9	0.0	11.4	9.2	4.5	6.6
Winona	179	7.5	0.0	11.6	9.5	4.5	6.6
Bison	389	---	---	----	11.4	6.7	---
Buda	326	---	---	----	----	4.8	---
Commercial Argentine	488	---	---	----	----	6.9	---

[1]/Yield interpolated.

Judith Basin Branch Station, Moccasin (Cereal Agronomy, B. B. Bayles)

WESTERN BASIN AND COAST AREAS (North to West and South)

IDAHO

Aberdeen Substation, Aberdeen (Cereal Agronomy, L. L. Davis)

Agricultural Experiment Station, Moscow (Stripe Rust, C. W. Hungerford)

WASHINGTON

Agricultural Experiment Station, Pullman (Cereal Breeding, E. F. Gaines)

Agricultural Experiment Station, Pullman (Stinking Smuts of Wheat, H. H. Flor)

OREGON

<u>Sherman County Branch Station, Moro</u> (Cereal Agronomy, D. E. Stephens)
(September 16)

The weather in eastern Oregon continues dry, very dry, there having be
no precipitation of consequence in the Columbia River Basin area for many r
The total rainfall at Moro for the 6-month period, March 1 to August 31, wa
only 1.88 inches. The total precipitation for the crop year, August 1, 19?
to September 1, 1929, was 8.07 inches. The first half of September has be
dry and unseasonably warm. Some soaking rains are needed to make condition
favorable for sowing winter wheat, as fallow ground is dry to a depth of al
10 inches.

The following tables present the yields obtained this year in our var?
experiments with wheat, barley, and oats. In the tables the varieties are
arranged in their seeding order, the earliest-maturing varieties appearing
first.

Yields of winter-wheat varieties grown at Moro, Oreg., in 1929

Variety	Nursery No.	C. I. No.	Average (Bu. per acre
Turkey	----	1571	16.9
Hybrid 128	----	4512	16.5
Hybrid 128 x Fortyfold	1997A4-3-2-2	----	16.1
P1068 x Preston	----	8244	15.8
Fortyfold x Federation	----	8247	15.8
Argentine	----	1569-2	15.7
Kanred	----	5146	14.9
White Odessa	----	4655	14.5
Fortyfold Selection 54	----	----	14.4
Oro	----	8220	14.4
Kharkof	----	8249	14.4
Local Turkey	----	4429	14.0
Ridit	----	6703	13.9
Arcadian x Hard Federation	----	8246	13.4
Albit	----	8275	13.3
Arcadian x Hard Federation	979	----	12.4
Fortyfold Selection 29	----	----	12.1
Federation	----	4734	12.1
Fortyfold Selection 43	----	----	11.6
Average			14.3

Yields of spring-wheat varieties grown at Moro, Oreg., in 1929

Variety	C. I. No.	Average (Bu. per acre)
Hard Federation	4733	12.6
White Federation	4981	12.3
Baart	1697	11.7
Hard Federation Selection 71	----	10.4
Hard Federation Selection 31	----	10.2
Baart x Federation	8254	9.7
Hard Federation Selection 79	----	9.6
Onas	6221	9.2
Federation	4734	8.7
Baart x Federation	8252	8.6
Marquis	4158	8.1
Pacific Bluestem	4067	8.1
Hard Federation Selection 82	----	7.6
Average		9.8

Yields of spring-barley varieties grown at Moro, Oreg., in 1929

Variety	C. I. No.	Average (Bu. per acre)
Trebi	936	34.9
Peruvian	925	32.5
Flynn	1311-1	31.5
Arequipa	1256	30.0
Club Mariout	261	30.0
Coast	4117	28.5
Pryor	2359	27.5
Meloy	1176	26.4
Pryor	1429	24.3
Chevalier	1419	21.7
Average		28.7

Yields of spring-oat varieties grown at Moro, Oreg., in 1929

Variety	C. I. No.	Average (Bu. per acre)
Three Grain	1950	49.4
Western Wonder	1951	46.7
Siberian	635	46.2
Swedish Select	134-1	45.2
Richland	787	45.0
Iogold	2329	41.7
Markton	2053	41.1
Sixty-Day	165-1	39.4
Madrid	603	37.3
Average		43.6

CALIFORNIA

Biggs Rice Field Station, Biggs (Rice Agronomy, J. W. Jones) (August 3

The weather in August has been very favorable for the development of the
rice crop. Temperatures have been normal or above, and the humidity has beer
higher than normal. The rice crop has headed very quickly and from four to
five days earlier than usual.

Near Butte City a few small fields that were sown very early last sprinq
have been cut, threshed, and sold. The highest price paid for this new crop
rice was $3.05 per hundred for the Onsen variety.

Most of the commercial fields sown to Onsen and 1600, early maturing
varieties, are being drained now, and the harvesting of these varieties will
start about September 12. The Caloro variety on commercial fields is fully
headed now and with favorable ripening weather will be ready to harvest by tl
end of September.

On the Station the very early maturing varieties are ripe, the early mai
ing varieties are starting to ripen, and the midseason varieties are fully
headed· The Station crop is not so good as it was last year. It is believec
that the average acre yield for the State will be considerably less than it v
in 1928.

On August 22 four Russian professors visited the Station for a short tir

(September 15)

The weather is very warm now, and the rice crop is ripening rapidly. A
rice on the Station is drained, with the exception of that in the nursery. I
vest probably will start on the 25th.

The Annual Rice Day held at Richvale and at the Station last Friday was
well attended. About 75 farmers were present at the Station to inspect the
different lines of work.

University Farm, Davis (Cereal Agronomy, G. A. Wiebe).

Agricultural Experiment Station, Berkeley (Cereal Smuts, F. N. Briggs)

TEXAS

U. S. San Antonio Field Station, San Antonio (I. M. Atkins, Assistant
Superintendent, Office of Western Irrigation Agriculture) (August 22)

Mr. Atkins has reported yields of flax varieties and yields from the
date-of-seeding experiments for the crop year 1928-29. The varietal plots
were seeded on December 26 and 27, 1928, and the seedlings emerged with fair
to good stands within two weeks. On February 9 and 10, minimum temperatures
of 21 and 20 degrees F. were recorded followed by freezing temperatures for
several days. Stands were reduced to approximately 25 to 60 per cent of the
stands previous to the cold period. The surviving plants branched freely,
however, and fairly good yields were obtained.

Acre yields of flax varieties grown in triplicate 1/10-acre plots at an Antonio, Tex., in 1929

Variety	C. I. No.	Final Stand (Thousands per acre)	Yield (Bu. per acre)
Rosquin	109	252	15.9
Morteros	107	198	14.5
Rio (Long 79)	280	174	12.2
N. D. R. No. 114	13	177	11.9[1]
N. D. R. No. 720	318	164	11.2
Linota	244	156	11.0
Selection 4-1	260	125	10.3
Redwing	320	122	7.8
Bison	389	96	7.7
Winona	179	129	6.2

[1] Average of ten check plots.

Acre yields of N. D. R. No. 114 flax grown in single 1/10-acre plots in a date-of-seeding test at San Antonio, Tex., 1928-29

Date of seeding	Final stands	Date ripe	Yield (Bu. per acre)
December 4, 1928	Good	May 10	9.5
December 26, 1928	Good	May 14	8.8
January 22, 1929	Good	May 25	1.6[1]
February 23, 1929	Good	June 20	4.0

[1] Low yield due to loss in shock.

BARBERRY ERADICATION PROGRESS

OHIO

Ohio State University, College of Agriculture, Columbus, J. W. Baringer

INDIANA

Purdue University College of Agriculture, LaFayette, W. E. Leer
(September 14)

The intensive survey of Hamilton County was finished on September 11.
Since the beginning of the campaign, 2,668 bushes have been found in Hamilton
County. Of this number 2,043 were planted while 625 were escaped bushes.

A barberry demonstration was placed in the Purdue Building at the Indiana
State Fair for the period from August 31 to September 7. It was by far the
most successful barberry demonstration that has ever been prepared for the
Indiana State Fair. The two newspaper clippings indicate that the "jail" was
successful in arousing the curiosity of the newspaper reporters. The following is a quotation from the Indianapolis Star dated September 3:

"GRAPHIC FAIR EXHIBIT

"About 5,000 persons passed through the 'Condemned to Die' cell hourly
in the Purdue building at the Indiana State Fair yesterday afternoon. These
were the figures kept by Wayne E. Leer, in charge of the barberry-eradication
campaign in Indiana. Leer has in the 'cell,' which has every appearance of a
prison, a display showing common barberry, which spreads black stem rust of
wheat. An excellent example of the growing plant was in the cell behind a
second iron-bar door, awaiting execution."

On the following day the Indianapolis News published the following note:

"Purdue University brings home its fight against the common barberry
plant in grim fashion. In a barred, cell-like structure in the center of
the Purdue building is found a living specimen of the common barberry. It
stands alone in a 'death cell.' That has been made realistic. Around it
are placards telling of the havoc wrought to grain by pests harbored by the
plant."

MICHIGAN

Agricultural College, East Lansing, W. F. Reddy

WISCONSIN

Department of Agriculture, State Capitol Annex, Madison, R. M. Caldwell

ILLINOIS

Box 72, Post Office Building, Urbana, R. W. Bills   (September 18)

Twelve field men are now in the field. Four are completing the second
urvey of Jo Daviess County and eight are continuing the first survey in
outhern Illinois. The survey of Hamilton and White counties is to be started
his week.

Twenty-seven leads on barberry bushes were received at the Illinois State
air during the period from August 17 to 24. Many of them have been investi-
ated and found correct. Mr. L. R. Davis and Mr. J. W. Weber eradicated five
ushes at the East Moline State Hospital, in Rock Island County, one at the
rphans' Home at Carthage, Hancock County, and a hedge at Delavan, Tazewell
ounty. They also eradicated nine escaped bushes in Mercer County, which were
eported by Robert Bryant, student of vocational agriculture at the Joy High
chool.

IOWA

Iowa State College, Ames, P. W. Rohrbaugh

MINNESOTA

Agricultural Experiment Station, University Farm, St. Paul, L. W. Melander
(September 10)

The intensive survey has been successful this year. Carver County has
been completed, and it is hoped to finish Hennepin County this fall, with the
exception of the corporate limits of Minneapolis. The weather in August was
very dry and hot. The survey, therefore, was not hindered by rainy weather.
This meant much in the maximum utilization of field help. It is planned to
cut the field force to six men by September 21. If the survey of Hennepin
County is completed early in October, an area of escaped barberries in Scott
County may be surveyed after the heavy frosts. This area consists of dense
underbrush and can be surveyed effectively only after the leaves have fallen.

The barberry demonstration at the Minnesota State Fair has further emphasized two things. In the first place, the general public seemed to be more
interested than ever. Groups of people frequently would stop at the booth and
some member would begin to tell his companions about barberry spreading black
stem rust to grains and grasses. In the second place, it was found possible
to interest boys and girls in barberry eradication if the proper stimulus were
used, which was to arouse interest in the National Rust Busters Club. Attractive pledge cards with colored strings, supplied by The Conference for the
Prevention of Grain Rust, were given to the boys and girls. On one side of
these cards is inscribed the following: "I hereby promise to look for and report all Common Barberry Bushes. A full life membership in the N. R. B. C.
and a beautiful bronze medal will be mine as soon as I report a property having
Common Barberry to the Barberry Eradication Office, University Farm, St. Paul,
Minnesota." As a result, at least five locations of common barberry were reported by boys who will receive the N. R. B. C. medals. One of these medals
and an enlarged colored picture of the medal were displayed in the barberry booth

NEBRASKA

College of Agriculture, University Farm, Lincoln, B. F. Dittus, Acting
in Charge

SOUTH DAKOTA

College of Agriculture, Brookings, R. O. Bulger [September 10]

The intensive survey for common barberries which was started last year
in Grant County was completed in August. There were found 77 bushes and 101
seedlings on 16 different properties. While the number of bushes found is not
great, the number of properties exceeds those reported on the first survey.
Many of these properties contained only a few or single bushes growing wild
in planted and natural groves.

The second survey of Douglas County was completed the week of August 24.
No bushes were found on this survey. Ten plantings of barberries were found
in Charles Mix County, the survey of which is only a little over half completed. Considerable spring wheat is grown in these three counties.

People in general are giving their hearty cooperation. There are a few
exceptions, and these are largely due to the lack of a proper understanding
of the purpose of eradication. There are more people in favor of the work now
than in previous years.

One planting of barberries was found in Platte, Charles Mix County, as
a result of educational work. A freshman high school girl had learned about
stem rust and the barberry in her classes. When our field men arrived at
Platte, she informed them that she knew where there were some small bushes.
She gave the location and two small sprouts about two inches high were found.
The owner had been keeping them cut off with a lawn mower. However, there
were large crowns in the ground which would have resulted in large bushes if
they had been allowed to grow. These two bushes undoubtedly would not have
been found for many years if they had not been reported by this girl.

Nearly 600 barberry bushes and seedlings have been found in South Dakota
so far this year.

NORTH DAKOTA

Agricultural Extension Division, State College Station, Fargo, G. C. May

MONTANA

State College of Agriculture, Bozeman, W. L. Popham [September 11]

Barberry survey activities in Montana will be suspended the last week
n September. The work during the entire season has been with areas of
scaped barberries in Fergus and Flathead counties. Neither of these counties
as been completed, but it is expected that the survey in them will progress
ore rapidly next year now that the areas of escaped bushes are cleared.

As a part of the educational work pertaining to the control of stem rust
n Montana and Wyoming arrangements have been made to place a demonstration
t five, and perhaps six, of the leading fairs in these two States. The fairs
ncluded in the itinerary are: Central Montana Fair, Lewistown, Mont.,
idland Empire Fair, Billings, Mont., Wyoming State Fair, Douglas, Wyo.,
astern Montana Fair, Miles City, Mont., and Montana State Fair, Helena, Mont.
automatic delineascope and a set of models, supplied by The Conference for
the Prevention of Grain Rust, are proving very valuable assets to the demonstration.

WYOMING

College of Agriculture, University of Wyoming, Laramie, W. L. Popham

COLORADO

Agricultural College, Ft. Collins, E. A. Lungren

C E R E A L   C O U R I E R

Official Messenger of the Office of Cereal Crops and Diseases
Bureau of Plant Industry, U. S. Department of Agriculture
(NOT FOR PUBLICATION)

Vol. 21   No. 24

September 30, 1929
Personnel (Sept. 21-30) and General Issue

PERSONNEL ITEMS

Dr. Jonas J. Christensen, agent in the epidemiology studies conducted in cooperation with the Minnesota Agricultural Experiment Station, University Farm, St. Paul, since April, 1922, resigned his position on September 30 to accept a John Simon Guggenheim Memorial Fellowship for a year's study in Europe.

Mr. V. H Florell, formerly in charge of cereal agronomy experiments at the University Farm, Davis, Calif., who has been on leave of absence since April 1, 1929, engaged in graduate study at the University of California, came to Washington on September 27 to conduct research in greenhouse and laboratory on the cytology and genetics of interspecific and intergeneric hybrids of the genera Triticum and Secals.

Mr. M. A. McCall, principal agronomist in charge of cereal agronomy, left Washington on September 30 to visit points in Missouri, Kansas, Oklahoma, California, Oregon, Washington, Idaho, Montana, South Dakota, Minnesota, and Wisconsin to confer with officials of agricultural experiment stations and Office personnel concerning cooperative investigations. Mr. McCall will be in the field about a month.

Mr. H. H. McKinney, senior pathologist in charge of cereal-virus-disease investigations, will leave Washington on October 1 for Granite City and Urbana, Ill., and St. Louis, Mo., to make fall seedings of wheat in connection with mosaic experiments and to confer with officials of agricultural experiment stations and office personnel in regard to cooperative investigations. Mr. McKinney will be in the field for a week.

Dr. Emery R. Ranker, associate physiologist in corn-smut investigations since April, 1926, resigned his position on September 30 to engage in personal study and research at Northwestern University.

345

MANUSCRIPTS AND PUBLICATIONS

56 A manuscript entitled "Unusual Crossing in Oats at Aberdeen, Idaho," by F. A. Coffman and G. A. Wiebe, was approved on September 26 for publication in the Journal of the American Society of Agronomy.

57 A manuscript entitled "Breeding Wheats Resistant to Bunt by the Back-Cross Method," by Fred N. Briggs, was approved on September 30 for publication in the Journal of the American Society of Agronomy.

Galley proof of article entitled "Mosaic Diseases in the Canary Islands, West Africa, and Gibraltar," by H. H. McKinney, for publication in the Journal of Agricultural Research, was read on September 25.

Reading of page proof of Technical Bulletin 96 entitled "Yields of Barley in the United States and Canada, 1922-1926," by H. V. Harlan, L. H. Newman, and Mary L. Martini, was finished on September 30.

Page proof of Technical Bulletin 131 entitled "Spacing and Date-of-Seeding Experiments with Grain Sorghums," by John H. Martin and John B. Sieglinger, et al., was read on September 30.

An article entitled "Progress in Barberry Eradication," by R. M. Caldwell, appears in Wisconsin State Department of Agriculture Biennial Report for 1927 and 1928 (Wis. Dept. Agr. Bul. 98), p. 119-124; illus. March, 1929.

An article entitled "Barberry Eradication: Rust Losses Reduced Since Beginning of Barberry Eradication," by [R. M. Caldwell], appears in Wisconsin Horticulture 19 (12): 376-377, illus. August, 1929.

U. S. Dept. Agr. Tech. Bul. 136 entitled "Breeding Hard Red Winter Wheats for Winter Hardiness and High Yield," by Karl S. Quisenberry and J. Allen Clark, has been received, bearing date of September, 1929.

The brief article entitled "Concerning Heterothallism in Puccinia graminis, by Ruth F. Allen, appears in Science 70 (1813): 308-309. September 27, 1929.

C E R E A L   C O U R I E R

Official Messenger of the Office of Cereal Crops and Diseases
Bureau of Plant Industry, U. S. Department of Agriculture
(NOT FOR PUBLICATION)

----

ol. 21   No. 25

October 10, 1929
Personnel (Oct. 1-10) and Field Station (Sept. 16-30) Issue

PERSONNEL ITEMS

Mr. Clyde C. Allison was appointed agent, effective October 1, to assist in the research on the epidemiology of black stem rust that is being conducted in cooperation with the Minnesota Agricultural Experiment Station at St. Paul. Mr. Allison will succeed Dr. J. J. Christensen who resigned on September 30. Mr. Allison was granted the B. S. degree by the University of Minnesota in 1928. During the year 1928-1929 he was a student at the University of Halle in Germany.

Dr. C. R. Ball, principal agronomist in charge, returned to Washington on October 3. He visited points in Illinois and Indiana in the interests of cooperative corn investigations. He attended the meetings of the Joint Committee on European Corn Borer Research from September 25 to 27.

Mr. B. B. Bayles, assistant agronomist in charge of the cooperative cereal-agronomy experiments at the Judith Basin Substation, Moccasin, Mont., has been authorized to go to Madison, Wis., for the winter months to conduct research in the greenhouse and laboratories of the University of Wisconsin. Mr. Bayles will return to Moccasin about the middle of March.

Dr. Charlotte Elliott, associate pathologist, returned to Washington on September 29 after visiting stations in Iowa, Kansas, Texas, Idaho, and Alberta.

At Manhattan, Kans., 81 inbred strains of sorghum in Mr. C. O. Johnston's plots were sprayed with suspensions of two bacterial organisms which cause leaf spots. The inoculations were made to determine varietal differences in susceptibility to the two diseases. Bacterium andropogoni produced no infection on 24 strains, heavy infection on 4, moderate infection on 9, and only slight infection on the other 44 strains. Inoculations with the other unnamed organism produced only slight infection in 6 strains. There was very little natural infection with this second organism at Manhattan or at Hays this season.

At Chillicothe, Tex., experiments were carried on to determine the cause of a destructive milo disease. Hypodermic injections with sterile water and with four bacterial organisms were made on about 300 plants, some in the open field and some inside a cage built to exclude chinch bugs. Typical symptoms of the disease have been induced by inoculations with bacteria, and observations in both Texas and Kansas indicate that the organism lives over in the soil.

At Ames, Iowa, Aberdeen, Idaho, and Edmonton, Alberta, Mr. Stanton's Oat Classification Nursery of 140 strains and varieties was used for making counts of varietal differences in percentages of blast under varying environmental conditions. At Edmonton all varieties appeared to develop more open panicles, and long-season varieties such as Coast Black showed the influence of the longer days in heading out with the other late varieties. Percentages of blast at Edmonton were higher than had been expected.

Mr. C. H. Kyle, senior agronomist in corn investigations, returned to Washington on September 26. In the corn-breeding experiments at Tifton, Ga., Baton Rouge, La., Knoxville, Tenn., and Florence, S. C., a good crop of corn had been produced, and trends in the work were unusually well defined.

Many new corn-breeding lines of the second and third selfed generation from crosses between primary selfed lines were studied at Tifton, Ga. It became evident from these studies that obvious deleterious factors of the primary parent lines would be avoided by the selection of some of the new lines and that, in some of these, desirable characteristics of the primary parent lines would be recovered and combined, thereby improving the stability of the breeding material.

Five F_1 crosses between selfed lines of the Garrick variety averaged from 6 to 42 per cent more ear corn than the parent variety on the Pee Dee Experiment Station at Florence, S. C. The same crosses produced from 21 to 46 per cent more corn than the Creole variety on the State Experiment Station at Baton Rouge, La. Both yield tests were in agreement as to the least productive and most productive crops.

Dr. John H. Martin, agronomist in charge of grain sorghum and broomcorn investigations, wrote from Woodward, Okla., on October 1 that in a 3,000-mile tour of the grain-sorghum region excellent crops were seen in some sections, especially in the western portion of the Texas Panhandle. The best crops on the field stations were seen at Dalhart, Tex., and at Hays, Kans. Crops in the vicinity of Spur, Tex., were very poor owing to drought and hail.

Beaver milo, the new extra-dwarf straightneck variety, seems to be rather promising this season. An extremely early yellow milo produced at Woodward gives promise of outyielding all other varieties for grain at Akron, Colo., and Colby, Kans. This strain is a hybrid between Dwarf Yellow milo and Early White milo and is able to mature where the ordinary milos seldom do.

Rains in September throughout the southern Great Plains have encouraged
he seeding of winter wheat. Most of the land already has been seeded, and
uch of the wheat is up now. Good stands of volunteer wheat are being left
n some fields. Present prospects are for a large production of wheat in this
egion next year. Considerable land in southeastern Colorado has been sold,
roken, and sown to wheat in recent years.

Furrow drills have become very popular in this region this year. Most
f the new drills sold this fall have been of this type. Several of the leading implement manufacturers are making furrow drills.

Mr. F. D. Richey, senior agronomist in charge of corn investigations, returned on October 7, having attended the meetings of the Joint Committee on
European Corn Borer Research from September 25 to 27.

The appointment of Joe L. Sutherland, agent in the cooperative cereal experiments at the Judith Basin Substation, Moccasin, Mont., was terminated on
August 31. Mr. Sutherland has accepted a fellowship in the agronomy department of the Iowa State College.

Mr. Isadore L. Wolk was appointed junior chemist, effective October 1, to
take the place of Mr. Reed Walker in making nitrogen determinations on wheats
from the breeding nurseries, in cooperation with the Bureau of Chemistry and
Soils. Mr. Wolk was graduated this year from the School of Chemistry of the
University of Minnesota.

MANUSCRIPTS AND PUBLICATIONS

58 A manuscript entitled "Growth Habit and Yield in Wheat as Influenced by Time of Seeding," by B. B. Bayles and J. F. Martin, was approved on October 1 for publication in the Journal of the American Society of Agronomy.

Galley proof of revision of Farmers' Bulletin 1162 entitled "Proso, or Hog Millet," by John H. Martin, was read on October 5.

Reading of galley proof of article entitled "Correlation Studies with Inbred and Crossbred Strains of Maize," by Merle T. Jenkins, for publication in the Journal of Agricultural Research, was finished on October 9.

Galley proof of Farmers' Bulletin 1611 entitled "Oats in the Western Half of the United States," by T. R. Stanton and F. A. Coffman, was read on October 10.

Farmers Bulletin 1583 entitled "Spring-Sown Red Oats," by T. R. Stanton and F. A. Coffman, bearing date of June, 1929, was received on October 1.

October 10, 1929

. P. I. Memo. 451

MEMORANDUM TO HEADS OF OFFICES

Gentlemen:

I quote below in its entirety a memorandum just received from Dr. Stockberger, Director of Personnel and Business Administration. This is self-explanatory. Will you kindly see that Dr. Stockberger's memorandum is called to the attention of all members of your staff who may have occasion to perform travel on official Government business?

"The General Accounting Office in a recent communication has drawn attention to the occurrence in vouchers of this Department of 'numerous instances of employees using transportation requests for personal travel while away from their official stations, taking leave en route or prior to return to official stations on completion of their duty, returning to headquarters by a circuitous route.' The communication cites Paragraph 20 of the Standardized Government Regulations providing that 'transportation requests must not be used for personal travel.'

"It is important that employees dismiss the idea, which has probably been responsible for some of these instances, that roundabout travel for personal reasons between points in an official itinerary is not to be deemed personal travel. The provision in the Standardized Regulations is categorical. It is based not only on the fundamental impropriety of using the Government requests for personal travel but on the fact that such use throws upon both the Department and the General Accounting Office the burden of auditing, settling, and paying additional transportation accounts. You are therefore requested to reach as nearly as possible the entire personnel of your bureau with request that cognizance be taken of the regulation in question and that it be strictly observed in future."

Very sincerely,

(Signed) WM. A. TAYLOR

Chief of Bureau.

351

October 8, 1929

B. P. I. Memo. 452

MEMORANDUM TO HEADS OF OFFICES

Gentlemen:

There has been a marked tendency throughout the field to make more payments in cash under Letters of Authorization since advances of funds have been made by the Government. It is important that cash payments be held to an absolute minimum, particularly in the vicinity of field stations or at points where we are conducting work. Whenever it is possible to do so, vouchers should be secured and submitted to the Washington office for payment by check. This applies particularly to all purchases and to the employment of labor. Whenever it is possible to do so, labor should be appointed and payments made by check from Washington.

Please see that this matter is brought to the attention of all of our men in the field who have occasion to make expenditures. As their vouchers are submitted, please see that they are carefully reviewed from this standpoint, and explanations required wherever the circumstances justifying cash payments are not obvious. A rigid policy of payment by voucher should be enforced, with cash payments made only where payment by voucher is clearly impracticable.

Very truly yours,

(Signed) WM. A. TAYLOR

Chief of Bureau.

FIELD STATION CONDITION AND PROGRESS

(All experiments except those conducted at the Arlington Experiment Farm,
Rosslyn, Va., are in cooperation with agricultural experiment stations or
other agencies.)

HUMID ATLANTIC COAST AREA (South to North)

GEORGIA

State College of Agriculture, Athens (Cereal Agronomy, R. R. Childs)

VIRGINIA

Arlington Experiment Farm, Rosslyn (Small Grain Agronomy, J. W. Taylor)

Arlington Experiment Farm, Rosslyn (Corn Breeding, F. D. Richey)

Arlington Experiment Farm, Rosslyn (Cereal Smuts, V. F. Tapke, Acting in
Charge)

Arlington Experiment Farm, Rosslyn (Virus Diseases, H. H. McKinney)

NEW YORK

Cornell University Agricultural Experiment Station, Ithaca (Cereal Breeding, H. H. Love) (W. T. Craig)

HUMID MISSISSIPPI VALLEY AREA (South to North)

LOUISIANA

Rice Experiment Station, Crowley (Rice Agronomy, J. M. Jenkins)

Agricultural Experiment Station, Baton Rouge (Corn Breeding, H. F. Stoneber

TENNESSEE

Agricultural Experiment Station, Knoxville (Corn Breeding, L. S. Mayer)

MISSOURI

Agricultural Experiment Station, Columbia (Cereal Agronomy, L. J. Stadler)

OHIO

Ohio State University, Columbus (Corn Breeding, L. R. Jorgenson)

IOWA

Agricultural Experiment Station, Ames (Oat Breeding, L. C. Burnett)

Agricultural Experiment Station, Ames (Corn Breeding, M. T. Jenkins)

Agricultural Experiment Station, Ames (Crown Rust of Oats, S. M. Dietz) (H. C. Murphy)

ILLINOIS

Funk Bros. Seed Co., Bloomington (Corn Root, Stalk and Ear Rots, J. R. Holbert)

INDIANA

Purdue University Agricultural Experiment Station, LaFayette (Corn Rots and Metallic Poisoning, J. F. Trost, Acting in Charge)

Purdue University Agricultural Experiment Station, LaFayette (Leaf Rusts, E. B. Mains)

WISCONSIN

Agricultural Experiment Station, Madison (Wheat Scab, J. G. Dickson)

MINNESOTA

Agricultural Experiment Station, University Farm, St. Paul (Wheat Breeding,
. R. Ausemus) (October 8)

We seeded our winter wheat at St. Paul from September 5 to 10 and it is up
ow with good uniform stands. We have completed the threshing of the winter and
pring wheat and are very busy at the present time summarizing the records for
he annual report. In addition all of the material has been gone over in the
ust nursery and we are now making plans for next year's work.

Agricultural Experiment Station, University Farm, St. Paul (Stem Rust,
. C. Stakman)

Agricultural Experiment Station, University Farm, St. Paul (Flax Rust,
. A. Rodenhiser)

GREAT PLAINS AREA (South to North)

OKLAHOMA

Woodward Field Station, Woodward (Grain Sorghum and Broomcorn, J. B.
Sieglinger)

KANSAS

Agricultural Experiment Station, Manhattan (Cereal Breeding, J. H. Parker)
(September 27)

Seeding of the winter-wheat nursery of about 2,500 rod rows began on September 20 and was finished on September 26. The Columbia planter was used for
part of the operation. Emergence has been quicker and more uniform than in
the rows sown in furrows opened by hand.

Today we are beginning the seeding of some 1,500 rows of space-planted F_3
and F_5 crosses.

A nursery has been sown at Colby. A nursery of soft red winter wheat will
be seeded at Columbus on October 5.

Agricultural Experiment Station, Manhattan (Corn Breeding, A. M. Brunson)

Agricultural Experiment Station, Manhattan (Wheat Foot Rots, Hurley Fellows

Agricultural Experiment Station, Manhattan (Wheat Leaf Rust, C. O. Johnston

Ft. Hays Branch Experiment Station, Hays (Cereal Agronomy, A. F. Swanson)

NEBRASKA

North Platte Substation, North Platte (Cereal Agronomy, G. F. Sprague
(September 30)

Twenty-eight winter-wheat varieties were seeded in the varietal plots
September 16. Two of these had not previously been tested in field plots.
Nebraska No. 50 was obtained from Lincoln, and a Beloglina selection was a
vanced from the nursery because of its resistance to bunt in the smut nur

The winter-wheat nursery was seeded on the 18th, with the exception of
600 head selections which were sown the next day. The head selections are
crosses made at North Platte but grown at Moccasin, Mont., the past three
seasons.

The uniform smut nursery and the irrigated smut nursery have not yet
seeded as it was thought best to wait until the soil temperature was favor
for infection. Through the courtesy of Prof. H. O. Werner, of the Departi
of Horticulture of the Nebraska College of Agriculture, two soil thermogra
were available. These should provide an interesting study of the relation
temperature to bunt infection.

Precipitation has been negligible, although there has been considerab
cloudiness for the past week.

SOUTH DAKOTA

U. S. Dry-Land Field Station, Ardmore (O. R. Mathews) (Office of Dr
Land Agriculture) (October 1)

The following yields were obtained from triplicate plot experiments
spring wheat at Ardmore in 1929.

Class and Variety	C. I. No.	Yield (Bu. per acre)
Hard Red Spring		
Hope	8178	10.3
Reliance	7370	9.2
Kota	5878	8.3
Supreme	8026	8.1
Marquillo	6887	7.0
Ceres	6900	6.9
Reward	8182	6.7
Marquis	3641	5.8
Durum		
Kubanka	1440	10.3
Peliss	1584	10.3
Nodak	6519	8.3
Acme	5284	7.8
Mindum	5296	6.9

U. S. Cereal Field Experiments, Redfield (Wheat Improvement, E. S. McFadden) (September 24)

There has been little to report so far from this station except continued dry weather. This has been the driest growing season on record at this station.

Harvesting and threshing of both field plots and nursery rows have been completed for some time on the station, and yields are now being computed. As might be expected, due to abnormal conditions throughout the season, our varietal yield data this year will appear somewhat upside down when compared with average yields over a series of years. The Iogold oat which has been outstanding in yield heretofore was outyielded by several other varieties this year. Odessa barley, which has the highest average yield of all varieties of barley on all of the State stations, was outyielded by White Smyrna, a variety that seldom gives high yields in eastern South Dakota. Ceres wheat was outyielded by Quality, and Hope wheat was near the bottom of the list. The durum wheats as a class were outyielded by the bread wheats, which is exceptional for eastern South Dakota.

Wheat diseases, particularly rust, scab, and black chaff, were of very minor importance here this year. No data of much value on reaction of the wheat varieties to these diseases were obtained. Stem rust made an early appearance, having been first observed on June 20, but due to lack of moisture it failed to develop normally. A peculiarity about stem rust this year was that it was more abundant on the leaves than on the stems.

Considerable data were obtained this year on resistance to loose and stinking smut and on resistance to frost injury. Reliance and Mindum were outstandingly resistant to frost, while Marquillo and Hope proved to be peculiarly susceptible.

Notes on shattering on the outside rows in the triple rod row nursery have just been completed. The percentage of shattering varied from zero for Hope and H-44 to 50 per cent for Ruby and Preston. The wheats had stood for two months after ripening.

The winter-wheat nursery, consisting of 390 rows, was seeded on September 13 following a light rain, and emerged on September 18 with good uniform stand. The winter wheat plots, consisting of 10 varieties replicated three times, were sown on September 19 and are beginning to emerge today. We experienced a real sensation in the form of a light rain of 0.27 of an inch today.

Had it not been for a good supply of subsoil moisture to start with this spring, crops would have been a complete failure. However, in spite of the prolonged drought, yields of wheat on good soils in this section are close to the average. Marquis made from 6 to 12 bushels an acre and Ceres from 10 to 14 bushels. A small field of Hope wheat grown on corn ground about two miles south of the station made a little better than 20 bushels an acre, which is the highest yield I have heard reported for this section this year. Wheat, in general, is of good quality although somewhat shriveled where grown on gumbo soils. The protein content is running exceptionally high.

NORTH DAKOTA

Hettinger Substation, Hettinger (C. H. Plath) [October 1]

Yields of the spring-wheat varieties grown in triplicated 1/50-acre plots at Hettinger in 1929.

Class and Variety	C. I. No.	Yield (Bu. per acre)
Hard Red Spring		
Kota x Marquis 1656.84	8004	32.3
Supreme	8026	31.8
Ceres	6900	30.0
Marquis 10B	----	29.5
Kota x Marquis 1656.85	8385	29.1
Marquis	3641	26.9
Marquis Sask. No. 7	----	26.1
Montana King	8378	25.9
Reliance	7370	25.8
Marquis (Mitchell)	----	25.5
Kota	5878	24.4
Marvel	8876	23.9
Ruby	6047	23.0
Hope	8178	23.0
Garnet	8181	22.7
Reward	8182	22.6
Bolley 209	----	21.5
Marquillo	6887	20.8
Durum		
Pentad	3322	26.6
Bolley 216	----	25.4
Kubanka	1440	21.6
Nodak	6519	20.0
Mindum	5296	19.7

Dickinson Substation, Dickinson (Cereal Agronomy, R. W. Smith) (Oct

Rainy weather prevailed in the last week in September, supplying 1.1 inches of rain. The total precipitation for the month was 1.67 inches. will insure the germination of the winter grain in plots and nursery.

The cleaning of grain varieties is in progress. Duplicate samples f milling and baking experiments have been prepared for sending to Fargo an Washington. These consist of 32 varieties of spring wheat. Samples of 1 varieties of winter wheat have been prepared for milling at Washington.

Data on the acre yields obtained from the replicated plots of winter and rye and from the flax varieties are presented in the following table.

Acre yields obtained from duplicated 40th-acre plots of winter wheat sown in standing corn in the fall of 1928 at the Dickinson Substation

Variety	C. I. No.	Yield (Bu. per acre)
---------	8030	14.5
Beloglina	1543	14.2
---------	8033	13.4
Minturki	6155	12.7
---------	8028	12.4
Turkey	1571	11.4
---------	8034	11.3
Karmont	6700	11.1
Kharkof	1583	10.6
Buffum No. 17	3330	9.3

Acre yields of rye varieties sown in duplicate 56th-acre plots in grain stubble in the fall of 1928 at the Dickinson Substation

Variety	C. I. No.	Yield (Bu. per acre)
N. S. 2148	----	11.2
N. D. R. No. 9	----	10.8
German rye	----	10.8
N. S. 2147	----	10.3
Dakold	----	9.5
Prolific Spring Rye	----	7.2

Acre yields of flax varieties grown in triplicated 56th-acre plots at the Dickinson Substation

Variety	C. I. No.	Yield (Bu. per acre)
N. D. 40084	----	7.5
Linota	244	6.1
N. D. 40046	---	5.7
Newland	---	5.6
Rio (Long 79)	280	5.4
Buda	326	5.2
Bison	389	4.8
-----	383	4.8
-----	473	4.7
Redwing	320	4.2
-----	474	3.9
N. D. R. 114	13	3.2
N. D. R. 52	8	2.6

Northern Great Plains Field Station, Mandan (Cereal Agronomy, V. C. Hubbard)

Northern Great Plains Field Station, Mandan (Flax Breeding, J. C. Brinsmade, Jr.) (October 2)

The weather has been generally cool and cloudy during the last half of September. It was almost continuously cloudy and rainy nearly every day of the second week of this period. The total precipitation for this period was 1.19 inches, all of which was recorded from September 22 to 28, inclusive.

The first severe killing frost occurred the night of September 17, when a temperature of 25 degrees was recorded. The maximum temperature was 78 degrees on September 22 and the minimum 25 degrees on September 17.

The late flax plots so far have been too wet to thrash but should be in condition to thresh after a short period of clear, dry weather.

All of the flax plant selection material has been threshed. About 700 5-foot rows of late material still remain to be threshed.

Some flax rust developed late in the season but not enough to make rust notes of much value in genetic investigations. Rust was bad on all check rows of Burbank flax but was not noted on many rows of less susceptible varieties which, however, are usually severely infected. In the F_4 material from the cross Rio x Burbank grown from plants most severely rusted in 1928 no plant was noted so severely rusted as any of the Burbank plants.

Agricultural Experiment Station, State College Station, Fargo (T. E. Stoa) (October 2)

The following yields were obtained from the spring-wheat varieties grown in triplicate plot experiments at Fargo, in 1929

Class and Variety		C. I. No.	Yield (Bu. per acre)
Hard Red Spring			
Kota x Marquis	1656.84	8004	34.6
Do	1656.48	----	34.4
Do	1656.85	8385	33.7
Do	1656.97	8005	33.6
Reliance		7370	31.9
Kota x Marquis	1656.118	----	31.8
Ceres		6900	31.2
Marquis		3641	29.3
Hope		8178	29.2
Preston		3081	28.4
Kota		5878	28.2
Marquillo		6887	28.1
Whiteman		8379	28.1
Reward		8182	27.8

Class and Variety	C. I. No.	Yield (Bu. per acre)
Hard Red Spring (continued)		
Garnet	8181	27.2
Bolley 132	----	26.7
Progress	6902	26.7
Marvel	8876	26.5
Ruby	6047	26.3
Power	3697	26.2
Brownhead	----	25.4
Montana King	8878	25.1
Supreme	8026	24.2
Durum		
Bolley 216	----	34.9
Mindum	5296	34.6
D-46	----	34.4
Kubanka	1440	33.8
Kubanka Selection 132	8383	33.8
Akrona	6881	33.3
Pentad	3322	32.2
Nodak	6519	31.3
Algerian (Bruns)	----	31.0
Mohad	3320	30.9
Bolley 211	----	28.1
White		
Quality	6607	27.2
Axminster	8195	26.6

Agricultural Experiment Station, State College Station, Fargo (Flax Diseases, L. W. Boyle)

Langdon Substation, Langdon (Wheat Improvement, G. S. Smith)

MONTANA

Agricultural Experiment Station, Bozeman (J. E. Norton) [October 1]

Yields obtained from spring-wheat varieties grown in triplicate 1/40-acre plots and irrigated once at Bozeman in 1929

Class and Variety	Mont. No.	C. I. No.	Yield (Bu. per acre)
Hard Red Spring			
Reliance Selection 16	---	----	79.6
Reliance	582	7370	74.2
Kitchener	525	4800	69.1
Marquillo	611	6887	68.7
Supreme	531	8026	67.6
Hope	600	8178	66.7
Marquis 10B	511	----	64.4
Marquis	---	3641	63.1
Ceres	578	6900	62.2
Reward	588	8182	53.3

Class and Variety (continued)	Mont. No.	C. I. No.	Yield (Bu. per acre)
White			
Federation	503	4734	76.9
Baart	523	1697	72.5
Durum			
Mindum	607	5296	65.1
Kubanka	520	1440	61.1
Nodak	637	6519	57.3

The following additional varieties and new hybrid selections increased from Mr. Clark's cooperative nursery were grown in triplicate 1/120-acre plots at Bozeman in 1929

Class and Variety	Mont. No.	Nursery No.	C.I. No.	Yield (Bu. per acre)
Hard Red Spring				
Kanred x Marquis (B-9-11-50)	---	33	----	81.3
Reliance Selection 22	---	17	----	77.3
Marquis x Hard Federation	---	708	----	76.7
Do	---	705	----	76.0
Kanred x Marquis (B-9-14-42)	---	41	----	76.0
Marquis x Hard Federation	---	666	----	74.0
Do	---	673	----	74.0
Marquis	513	---	----	66.0
Champlain	583	---	4782	66.0
Marquis x Hard Federation	---	657	----	65.3
University 222	577	---	----	64.0
Renfrew	576	---	8194	63.3
Kota	516	---	5878	62.7
Marquis x Hard Federation	---	653	----	62.0
Marquis 10B	511	---	----	61.3
Triumph	530	---	6795	60.7
Montana King	586	---	8878	60.0
White				
Dicklow	506	---	3663	81.3
Hybrid J.	590	---	----	72.0
Hard Federation	502	---	4733	55.3
Durum				
Mondak	581	---	7287	76.7

Huntley Field Station, Huntley (Office of Western Irrigation Agriculture) (A. E. Seamans) [September 28]

Cooperative varietal experiments with spring wheat were grown at Huntley for the first time this year. The varieties were grown in triplicate plots on bean land, under irrigation and on dry land. The yields obtained are presented in the following table.

Class and Variety	C. I. No.	Yield (Bu. per acre)
	Irrigated Land	
Hard Red Spring		
Champlain	4782	65.9
Reliance	7370	62.5
Hope	8178	54.8
Marquillo	6887	54.4
Ceres	6900	53.3
Supreme	8026	52.4
Marquis	3641	51.4
Reward	8182	46.7
Durum		
Nodak	6519	60.1
Kubanka	1440	59.6
Mindum	5296	59.6
	Dry Land	
Hard Red Spring		
Reward	8182	10.8
Kota	5878	7.5
Ceres	6900	7.2
Supreme	8026	7.0
Marquis 10B	----	6.8
Marquis	3641	6.3
Hope	8178	6.0
Marquillo	6887	5.8
Reliance	7370	5.0
Champlain	4782	4.0
White		
Hard Federation	4733	10.3
Federation	4734	7.3
Durum		
Mindum	5296	7.0
Acme	5284	6.7
Peliss	1584	6.5
Nodak	6519	4.0
Kubanka	1440	3.5

Judith Basin Branch Station, Moccasin (Cereal Agronomy, B. B. Bayles)
September 30)

The precipitation for September was 2.41 inches as compared with a normal
of 1.62 inches. The precipitation for the crop season, April 1 to August 31,
was 5.21 inches as compared with the normal of 10.06 inches. In only one other
year since the station was established has the seasonal precipitation been
lower. In 1919 it was 3.29 inches.

Spring grain yields in general were very low in Montana while winter wheat
yields were excellent. Even though this fall the weather was very dry until
September 21, a larger acreage of winter wheat was seeded than last fall. Several farmers in the Judith Basin, who did not seed because of the dryness of
the soil in the first 20 days of September, plan to seed this week.

Nearly all threshing in central Montana has been completed except on a few fields in the foothill sections which were cut with the binder.

Yields from the varietal and date-of-seeding experiments with cereals a presented in the following tables.

Yields of winter-wheat varieties grown at Moccasin, Mont., in 1929. [Average of four plots, two on alfalfa ground and two on fallow.]

Variety	C. I. No.	Yield (Bu. per acre)
Minhardi x Minturki	8034	26.2
Newturk	6935	26.0
Kharkof (Hays No. 2)	6686	25.7
Nebraska No. 60	6250	24.9
Kharkof	1583	24.6
Oro	8220	24.3
Minturki x Beloglina-Buffum	8033	24.3
Eureka x Minhardi	8036	23.7
Kanred x Minhardi	8040	23.7
Montana No. 36	5549	23.7
Kanred	5149	23.5
Turkey	6152	23.2
Beloglina	1543	23.1
Karmont	6700	23.0
Minard	6690	22.5
Turkey	1558	21.9
Kharkof Selection	6938	21.2
Kanred x Minessa	8045	21.1
Single Plots		
Kanred x Minhardi	8042	25.8
Kanred x Minhardi Nursery No. 125	----	25.2
De Kalb (Local Turkey)	----	22.7
Minhardi x Minturki	8215	22.3

Average yields of 4 plots of Karmont wheat sown on stated dates at Mocca sin, Mont., in 1929

Date Seeded	Furrow Drill Spring Survival	Yield (Bu. per acre)	Test Weight	Ordinary Drill Spring Survival	Yield (Bu. per acre)	Test Weig
July 16	78	0	----	--	----	----
July 30	89	0.3	51.5	--	----	----
August 13	99	8.4	55.9	--	----	----
August 30	100	23.8	61.3	95	20.2	60.
September 11	100	31.1	60.3	97	30.9	60.
September 24	100	23.0	59.0	---	----	---
October 8	100	15.2	57.3	---	----	---
October 20	100	17.8	57.1	---	----	---
November 5	100	15.8	57.2	---	----	---

The spring survival does not give an index to the stand at harvest.
It gives the percentage of plants alive when growth started in the spring,
while in the early seedings, plants continued to die until June. When the
writer returned to Moccasin on June 15 nearly all plants on the July 16 and
30 seedings were dead or at least in a very weakened condition.

Yields of spring-wheat varieties grown in 2 plots on alfalfa fallow and
2 on cereal fallow at Moccasin, Mont., in 1929

Variety	Nursery No.	C. I. No.	Yield (Bu. per acre)
Hard Red Spring			
Marquis x Hard Federation	456	----	14.5
Do	666	----	13.8
Red Bobs Selection 25	---	----	13.6
Marquis x Hard Federation	657	----	13.5
Do	653	----	12.7
Red Bobs Selection 32	---	----	12.5
Kota x Marquis (1656.84)	---	8004	12.5
Kanred x Marquis (B-2-14-20)	11	----	12.5
Reward	---	8182	12.4
Marquis	---	3641	12.3
Marquis x Hard Federation	378	----	12.3
Do	402	----	12.1
Kanred x Marquis	33	----	12.0
Do	37	----	11.7
Red Bobs Selection 51	---	----	11.6
Reliance	---	7370	11.5
Supreme	---	8026	11.4
Kanred x Marquis (B-9-14-42)	41	----	11.0
Marquis 10B	---	----	10.6
Reliance Selection (pure for rust form 17)	---	----	10.5
Power	---	3697	10.2
Ceres	---	6900	10.1
Hope	---	8178	9.3
Marquillo	---	6887	8.4
Reliance Selection 22	17	----	9.4 (2 plots)
Durum			
Mindum	---	5296	11.9
Nodak	---	6519	11.3
Mondak	---	7287	11.1
Peliss Selection 14	---	----	10.5
Kubanka	---	1440	9.9
White Spring			
Baart	---	1697	15.3
Hard Federation	---	4733	13.2
Federation	---	4734	12.7

Yields of oat varieties grown in 2 plots on alfalfa fallow and 2 on cereal fallow at Moccasin, Mont., in 1929

Variety	C. I. No.	Yield (Bu. per acre)
Markton	2053	27.4
-------	357-168[a]	27.1
-------	357-112[a]	26.8
Iogold	2329	25.6
Silvermine	714	23.7
Sixty-Day	165	22.7
Lincoln	738	22.6
Alexander	1592	22.5
Victory	742	22.1
Green Russian Selection	2343	20.9
Banner	751	20.2
Swedish Select	134	17.9

[a] Selection from the unnamed variety, C. I. No. 357.

Yields of barley varieties grown in 2 plots on cereal fallow and 2 plots on alfalfa fallow at Moccasin, Mont., in 1929

Variety	C. I. No.	Yield (Bu. per acre)
Meloy Selection 3	4656	23.6
Coast	626	20.8
Arequipa	1256	19.4
Hurst	1304	19.3
Trebi	936	18.8
Hannchen Selection	---	18.3
Mechanical Mixture	4115	17.4
Horn	926	17.0
Composite Cross	4116	16.5
White Smyrna	195	16.0
Faust	4579	15.8
Himalaya	620	13.5
Hannchen	531	13.2

Yields of flax varieties grown in 3 plots on alfalfa land fallow at Moccasin, Mont., in 1929

Variety	C. I. No.	Yield (Bu. per acre)
Rio	280	2.5
Bison	389	2.2
Redwing	320	2.1
Linota	244	1.9
Newland	188	1.6
Selection 8-4	189	1.6
Selection 64-6	191	1.3
Stark	185	1.3
N. D. R. 114	13	1.2
Selection 167-254	475	1.3 (single plot)
Siberian No. 206	473	1.3 (single plot)

Yields from a rate-and-date-of-seeding test with six varieties of spring wheat are summarized in the following table to give a varietal comparison. Each yield is the average of 3 plots sown on each of three dates.

Variety	Yield (Bu. per acre)
Supreme	11.9
Ceres	11.6
Hard Federation	11.6
Marquis	9.7
Reliance	9.6
Mondak	8.9

North Montana Substation, Havre (M. A. Bell) [October 7]

The following yields were obtained from the spring-wheat varieties and hybrid strains grown in 1/50-acre plots at Havre in 1929

Class and Variety	Nursery No.	C. I. No.	Yield (Bu. per acre)
	(Triplicate plots)		
Hard red spring			
Reward	----	8182	23.1
Marquis x Hard Federation	657	----	22.5
Do	653	----	21.7
Do	666	----	21.1
Kota x Marquis 1656.84	----	8004	20.3
Supreme	----	8026	19.5
Ceres	----	6900	19.2
University 222	----	----	19.2
Kanred x Marquis	----	7372	17.8
Marquis	----	3641	17.0
Marquillo	----	6837	16.7
Power	----	3697	16.4
Reliance	----	7370	16.1
Kota	----	6248	16.1
Montana King	----	8878	15.3
Kitchener	----	4800	15.3
Hope	----	8178	14.2
Renfrew	----	8194	13.9
Durum			
Peliss	----	1584	19.7
Mindum	----	5296	17.5
Akrona	----	6881	17.5
Kubanka	----	1440	17.0
Nodak	----	6519	16.4
White			
Baart	----	1697	22.5
Federation	----	4734	20.0

Class and Variety	Nursery No. (Single Plots)	C. I. No.	Yield (Bu. per acre
Hard Red Spring			
Marquis x Hard Federation	649	----	22.5
Do	399	----	21.7
Do	673	----	20.0
Do	674	----	20.0
Do	377	----	19.2
Marquis (Average of 6 checks)	---	3641	19.2
Marquis x Hard Federation	421	----	19.2
Do	393	----	18.3
Do	395	----	18.3
Do	676	----	16.7
Do	670	----	16.7
Do	736	----	15.8

WESTERN BASIN AND COAST AREAS (North to West and South)

IDAHO

Aberdeen Substation, Aberdeen (Cereal Agronomy, L. L. Davis) (Septembe

The following yields were obtained from the oat varieties grown in plot at Aberdeen this year.

Variety	C. I. No.	Yield
Markton	2053	157.3
Vietto	2010	151.5
Golden Rain	1718	151.4
Idamine	1834	150.8
Abundance	2038	145.6
Crown	2022	140.9
Victory	2020	140.4
Swedish Select	1627	136.2
Triumph No. 20	1793	135.7

The yields are the average of four plots, two of which were 1/40-acre and two 1/93-acre.

Besides the strains grown in replication, the F_6 crosses of Markton x Idamine, Markton x Victory, Silvermine x Markton and Iogren x Markton were grown in a single 1/93-acre plot. A large number of selections was made fro these crosses by Mr. Stanton, Mr. Coffman, and the writer, to grow in head r in 1930.

Agricultural Experiment Station, Moscow (Stripe Rust, C. W. Hungerford)

WASHINGTON

Agricultural Experiment Station, Pullman (Cereal Breeding, E. F. Gaines)

Agricultural Experiment Station, Pullman (Stinking Smuts of Wheat,' H.H.Flor

· OREGON

Sherman County Branch Station, Moro (Cereal Agronomy, D. E. Stephens)

CALIFORNIA

Biggs Rice Field Station, Biggs (Rice Agronomy, J. W. Jones) (October 1)

The weather in September was very favorable for the ripening of rice. The crop, owing to earlier seeding last spring and favorable ripening weather, is about a week earlier than usual. Most of the early maturing varieties on commercial fields have been harvested and threshed. The quality of the early varieties is not so good as it should be. A good deal of the Caloro variety was ready to harvest by September 25, the earliest date that this variety has ever ripened. Harvesting of the Caloro variety is well under way now, whereas normally we are just about ready to start cutting.

The station plots are all harvested and threshing will be started the last of this week, fully a week earlier than usual.

Price prospects are better this fall than they have been for the past two years. The early rice threshed is selling for from $2.50 to $3.00 per hundred.

University Farm, Davis (Cereal Agronomy, G. A. Wiebe)

Agricultural Experiment Station, Berkeley (Cereal Smuts, F. N. Briggs)

BARBERRY ERADICATION PROGRESS

OHIO

Ohio State University, College of Agriculture, Columbus, J. W. Baringer
(September 30)

The usual barberry-eradication demonstration was held in connection with
the Ohio State Fair the last week in August. This year's demonstration seemed
to attract more interest than those of previous years. Eagerness to learn the
identity of common barberries through acquaintance with their outstanding characteristics seemed to be the principal concern of visitors.

Demonstrations also were placed at the Preble County Fair and at the
Williams County Fair in September.

The second survey of Preble County and the resurvey of old locations were
completed in September of this year.

The second survey of four townships in Montgomery County was completed in
September, and considerable work was done in checking old locations and in making a second survey in the city of Dayton.

Two men with a 1½-ton truck and plenty of salt were busily engaged in September destroying barberries in various parts of Ohio, which were found as a
result of leads on barberry locations received from miscellaneous sources in
the past few years.

The number of field agents decreased rapidly in September. Many of them
resumed their studies at various colleges and universities. Seven field agents
will be kept at work in October.

Indoor barberry-eradication posters will be mailed to railway express
agents to be placed on bulletin boards or on the walls of railway stations.
Outdoor barberry-eradication posters were placed at all principal road inter-
sections in the territory which has been covered by second survey this year.

INDIANA

Purdue University College of Agriculture, LaFayette, W. E. Leer (September.

On the intensive survey in Hamilton, Tipton, and Montgomery counties, 2 escaped bushes on 2 properties, 5 planted bushes on 4 properties, and 1 sprouting
bush had been found up to September 30.

In areas of escaped barberries outside of these three counties, 196 bushes
have been found this year.

Approximately 40 per cent of Montgomery County has been surveyed so far.
Two field men will continue with the intensive survey of Montgomery County as
long as weather will permit.

The reports on the educational work conducted last winter indicate that
the program was well received and much worth while. Mr. McCoy is now working
on a similar program for the high schools in the fall, winter, and early spring.
It is planned to visit every high school in the State during the next four
years. The schools are being worked on a county basis. Every high school in
a county is visited before leaving that particular county. A lantern-slide
lecture is to be given to each school assembly and to special classes wherever
possible. Literature on the common barberry and black stem rust will be left
at each school.

MICHIGAN

Agricultural College, East Lansing, W. F. Reddy

WISCONSIN

Department of Agriculture, State Capitol Annex, Madison, R. M. Caldwell

ILLINOIS

Box 72, Post Office Building, Urbana, R. W. Bills

IOWA

Iowa State College, Ames, P. W. Rohrbaugh

MINNESOTA

Agricultural Experiment Station, University Farm, St. Paul, L. W. Melander

NEBRASKA

College of Agriculture, University Farm, Lincoln, B. F. Dittus, Acting in
Charge

SOUTH DAKOTA

College of Agriculture, Brookings, R. O. Bulger (September 25)

With the beginning of the school season the field force in barberry eradication was reduced to four men. They are working in Charles Mix County and probably will complete the second survey this fall.

Over 700 bushes and seedlings have been reported in South Dakota this year. Most of these were found in four different counties. One find of over 200 bushes was the result of educational work. Earlier in the season a high-school boy had reported two small barberries on a farm in Turner County. A clean-up squad was sent down there to investigate, and over 200 escaped bushes were found on this and near-by farms.

Last week a nine-year-old school boy reported a purple-leaved barberry in the city of Platte. He had studied about the barberry and stem rust at school in the spring. This is the fifth planting of barberries in this State that has been reported by school children since spring.

The territory has been gone over rather slowly this summer owing to the topography. A large number of creeks and wooded ravines were evident. In addition to barberries, three rattlesnakes were found along the Missouri River in Charles Mix County. One of these was captured alive and will be turned over to the zoology department of the State College.

NORTH DAKOTA

Agricultural Extension Division, State College Station, Fargo, G. C. Mayoue

MONTANA

State College of Agriculture, Bozeman, W. L. Popham

WYOMING

College of Agriculture, University of Wyoming, Laramie, W. L. Popham

COLORADO

Agricultural College, Ft. Collins, E. A. Lungren (October 1)

The educational activities started early in September. A complete list of the 1929 school teachers in Colorado is being compiled. When completed, educational materials and a list of available bulletins will be mailed to all teachers of biology, science, and agriculture of grade and high schools in the State.

C E R E A L   C O U R I E R

Official Messenger of the Office of Cereal Crops and Diseases
Bureau of Plant Industry, U. S. Department of Agriculture
(NOT FOR PUBLICATION)

----

ol. 21   No. 26

October 20, 1929
Personnel (Oct. 11-20) and Field Station (Oct. 1-15) Issue

PERSONNEL ITEMS

Mr. Nelson E. Jodon was appointed junior agronomist, effective October 1, to assist in the cooperative cereal investigations conducted at the North Platte Substation, North Platte, Nebr. He has immediate charge of the plot and nursery experiments with corn and small grains. Mr. Jodon was granted the B. S. degree by the University of Nebraska in June, 1929. Mr. George F. Sprague, who has had charge of the experiments at North Platte for several years, has been transferred to the Arlington Experiment Farm, near Washington, D. C., to conduct corn investigations, under the direction of Mr. F. D. Richey. Mr. Sprague reported for duty in the Washington Office on October 17.

Dr. J. H. Martin, returned to agronomist in charge of grain sorghum and broomcorn investigations, returned to Washington on October 17 after an extended trip in the grain-sorghum and broomcorn area.

The appointment of Miss Dorothy M. McKnew, typist in this Office since April 21, was terminated on October 20.

Mr. Glenn S. Smith, junior agronomist in charge of the cooperative wheat experiments at the Langdon Substation, Langdon, N. Dak., has been granted leave of absence without pay from October 1, 1929, to March 31, 1930, inclusive, to engage in graduate study at the Kansas State Agricultural College.

Mr. Hugo Stoneberg, assistant agronomist in the cooperative corn investigations conducted at Baton Rouge, La., met with a serious automobile accident early in October while en route from New Orleans to Baton Rouge. The car he was driving overturned on the road near Hammond, La., and his left arm was crushed. He was taken to a hospital in New Orleans, where it was found necessary to amputate the arm. Mr. Stoneberg returned to his headquarters at Baton Rouge on October 12.

Chester N. DuBois, formerly junior scientific aid of this Office, now with the Trunk Line Association of New York City, was a caller on October 12.

Dr. Mary E. Reid, who has been conducting physiological studies on the effect of nitrogen-carbohydrate ratio on plant growth at the University of Wisconsin, at the Boyce Thompson Institute for Plant Research, Inc., and at Yale University, was a visitor in the Office on October 17. Dr. Reid has some very interesting results from growing wheat and other plants from kernels containing smaller and larger quantities of nitrogen, respectively, in atmospheres containing larger and smaller percentages, respectively, of carbon dioxide.

Mr. Marion A. Smith, of Champaign, Ill., a former employee of this Office, who is in the third year of a Crop Protection Institute fellowship at the University of Illinois, was an Office visitor on October 16. Mr. Smith was en route to New Brunswick, N. J., to attend a meeting of the fellowship committee at the New Jersey Agricultural College.

MANUSCRIPTS AND PUBLICATIONS

59 A manuscript entitled "Methods of Eradicating Rhamnus Species Suscep-
ible to Puccinia coronata Corda," by S. M. Dietz and L. D. Leach, was submitted
n October 17 for publication in the Journal of Agricultural Research.

60 A manuscript entitled "Experiments on the Effect of Fungicidal Dusts
on the Rate of Seeding and Their Relation to Drill Injury," by R. W. Leukel,
was submitted on October 17 for publication as a Technical Bulletin of the Department series.

61 A manuscript entitled "Heritable Characters of Maize--Rootless," by
Merle T. Jenkins, was approved on October 17 for publication in the Journal of
Heredity.

Galley proof of article entitled "The Cereal Rusts and Their Control," by
H. B. Humphrey, for publication in Scientific Agriculture, was read on October 1

Page proof of Farmers' Bulletin 1607 entitled "The Nematode Disease of
Wheat and Rye," by R. W. Leukel, was read on October 18.

The article entitled "Grain Free from Mixture Worth All the Effort of
Growing It," by V. H. Florell, appears in the Farm and Orchard Magazine Section
of the Los Angeles Sunday Times of June 23, 1929.

U. S. Dept. Agr. Technical Bulletin 121 entitled "Methods of Harvesting
Grain Sorghums," by John H. Martin, L. A. Reynoldson, B. E. Rothgeb, and W. M.
Hurst, was received on October 12 bearing date of August, 1929. (In coopera-
tion with the Kansas and Oklahoma agricultural experiment stations.)

Farmers' Bulletin 1599 entitled "Scab of Wheat and Barley and Its Control,"
by James G. Dickson and E. B. Mains, was received on October 17, bearing date of
September, 1929.

FIELD STATION CONDITION AND PROGRESS

(All experiments except those conducted at the Arlington Experiment Farm
lyn, Va., are in cooperation with State agricultural experiment statio
other agencies.)

HUMID ATLANTIC COAST AREA (South to North)

GEORGIA

State College of Agriculture, Athens (Cereal Agronomy, R. R. Childs

VIRGINIA

Arlington Experiment Farm, Rosslyn (Small Grain Agronomy, J. W. Tay.
(October 16)

The weather was favorable for the seeding of fall-sown grains, and
field plots and the nurseries were sown at the desired dates. There is
cient moisture at this time to insure germination. Germination of the b
is somewhat spotted owing to the beating rain of September 30, but on th
the stands are up to the average.

Greenhouse operations are under way. The first seeding was made by
ern Wheat Investigations on October 16.

A minimum temperature of 32 degrees was recorded on October 11. No
ing injury has been observed, however, aside from some blackening of the
of the sweet potato leaves.

Arlington Experiment Farm, Rosslyn (Corn Breeding, F. D. Richey)

Arlington Experiment Farm, Rosslyn (Cereal Smuts, V. F. Tapke, Acti
Charge)

Arlington Experiment Farm, Rosslyn (Virus Diseases, H. H. McKinney)

NEW YORK

Cornell University Agricultural Experiment Station, Ithaca (Cereal
H. H. Love) (W. T. Craig)

HUMID MISSISSIPPI VALLEY AREA (South to North)

LOUISIANA

Rice Experiment Station, Crowley (Rice Agronomy, J. M. Jenkins) (October 11

The weather in September was ideal for field operations. Most of the nursery and increase plots were harvested, as well as many of the other plots. The indications are that yields will be better in many instances than previously expected.

The main portion of the rice crop of southwestern Louisiana was harvested by the end of September, and a large portion was threshed.

The soybean crop in many of the commercial fields will be a total failure from the standpoint of seed production on account of the destructive feeding of the Velvet Bean Caterpillar (Anticarsia gemmatiles). This insect was erroneously referred to as "grass worm" in the report for the Courier of September 10.

The late maturing varieties of soybeans, Otootan and Goshen, were first attacked. They were beginning to flower, and as the caterpillar ate all the buds and leaves there is no chance of a crop being produced before frost. The varieties Biloxi and Barchet, which were further advanced when attacked, will produce a fair crop, as the caterpillar attacked them last and pupated before beginning on the young pods and stems. A third brood appeared late in September on the young foliage of Otootan and Goshen. The caterpillars are few in number, however, and are feeding very little.

Most of the soybeans in the variety test rows will produce a normal crop, as these were saved by dusting with sodium fluosilicate.

Dr. E. C. Tullis, agent in the cooperative rice-disease investigations conducted at Fayetteville, Ark., was a Station visitor from September 19 to 21.

Agricultural Experiment Station, Baton Rouge (Corn Breeding, H. F. Stoneberg

TENNESSEE

Agricultural Experiment Station, Knoxville (Corn Breeding, L. S. Mayer)

MISSOURI

Agricultural Experiment Station, Columbia (Cereal Agronomy, L. J. Stadler)

OHIO

Ohio State University, Columbus (Corn Breeding, L. R. Jorgenson)

IOWA

Agricultural Experiment Station, Ames (Oat Breeding, L. C. Burnett)

Agricultural Experiment Station, Ames (Corn Breeding, M. T. Jenkins)

Agricultural Experiment Station, Ames (Crown Rust of Oats, S. M. Dietz)

ILLINOIS

Funk Bros. Seed Co., Bloomington (Corn Root, Stalk and Ear Rots, J. R. Holbert)

INDIANA

Purdue University Agricultural Experiment Station, LaFayette (Corn Rots and Metallic Poisoning, J. F. Trost, Acting in Charge)

Purdue University Agricultural Experiment Station, LaFayette (Leaf Rust E. B. Mains)

WISCONSIN

Agricultural Experiment Station, Madison (Wheat Scab, J. G. Dickson)

MINNESOTA

Agricultural Experiment Station, University Farm, St. Paul (Wheat Breed E. R. Ausemus)

Agricultural Experiment Station, University Farm, St. Paul (Stem Rust, E. C. Stakman)

Agricultural Experiment Station, University Farm, St. Paul (Flax Rust, H. A. Rodenhiser)

GREAT PLAINS AREA (South to North)

OKLAHOMA

Woodward Field Station, Woodward (Grain Sorghum and Broomcorn, J. B. Sieglinger)

KANSAS

Agricultural Experiment Station, Manhattan (Cereal Breeding, J. H. Parker)

Agricultural Experiment Station, Manhattan (Corn Breeding, A. M. Brunson)

Agricultural Experiment Station, Manhattan (Wheat Foot Rost, Hurley Fellows

Agricultural Experiment Station, Manhattan (Wheat Leaf Rust, C. O. Johnston

Fort Hays Branch Experiment Station, Hays (Cereal Agronomy, A. F. Swanson)

NEBRASKA

North Platte Substation, North Platte (Cereal Agronomy, N. E. Jodon)
(October 16)

The first killing frost occurred on the night of October 10, when the temperature fell to 28 degrees F. The weather has been unusually warm since.

The inbred strains of corn grown in the crossing blocks have been harvested On the table land, about 70 crosses with sufficient grain to plant at least one 1/100-acre plot were obtained. In the crossing block under irrigation, 39 crosses and reciprocals, together with enough seed for testing, were obtained.

. The uniform and the irrigated smut nurseries were seeded October 10. The temperature since that date has not been favorable to the development of bunt.

F_2 seed of seven crosses involving smut-resistant strains were space-plante to permit a study of segregation for smut resistance. A number of H44-Minhardi F_4 lines also were seeded in the smut nursery.

The corn varieties will be harvested within a few days.

WYOMING

Sheridan Field Station, Sheridan (Office of Dry-Land Agriculture) (R. S. Towle) (October 11)

The following yields were obtained from the spring and winter wheat varieties grown in plot experiments at Sheridan in 1929

Spring Wheat

Hard Red Spring	C. I. No.	Yield (Bu. per acre)
Reward	8182	26.2
Ceres	6900	24.7
Kota x Marquis 1656.84	8004	24.4
Kota	6248	22.2
Reliance	7370	22.0
Garnet	8181	22.0
Supreme	8026	21.6
Marquis	3641	21.1
Marquillo	6887	19.6
Hope	8178	16.9
Durum		
Kubanka	1440	18.9
Mondak	7287	18.2
Nodak	6519	18.0
Mindum	5296	18.0
Akrona	6831	16.9

Winter Wheat

Hard Red Winter		
Nebraska No. 6	6249	33.6
Oro	8220	32.2
Hays No. 2	6686	31.8
Montana No. 36	5549	31.3
Karmont	6700	31.3
Turkey	1571	31.3
Kharkof	1442	30.9
Regal	7364	29.1
Newturk	6935	28.7
Kanred	5146	28.2
Beloglina	1543	28.0
Sherman	4430	26.5

SOUTH DAKOTA

U. S. Cereal Field Experiments, Redfield (Wheat Improvement, E. S.

NORTH DAKOTA

Dickinson Substation, Dickinson (Cereal Agronomy, R. W. Smith) (O

Mild weather has prevailed most of the time so far this month. Fo
past few days the weather has been like Indian summer. A rainy period
8th to the 10th supplied 0.87 of an inch of rain, which together with t
September, will aid the fall plowing and hasten the growth of fall grai
maximum temperature of 80 degrees was reached on the 5th; the minimum f
first half of the month was 27 degrees on the 12th and 13th.

Varieties and strains of winter grain in plots and nursery, especially
he latter, have made rapid growth since emerging, and the stands obtained are
etter than last fall.

Results obtained from a part of the smut nursery are presented in the fol-
owing tables. The results of a 3-year test of seeding smut-inoculated varie-
ies of hard spring wheat are shown, arranged in order of apparent susceptibil-
ty to the smut used. Other varieties and hybrids not shown here also were
ested. Many of these and other varieties were tested in 1926, but the percent-
ges of smut were lower than in the subsequent three years. So far Turkey x
lorence (G334) is the only variety showing no smut during the four years tested,
nd Ulka No. 1 has shown the highest percentage of bunt. Strains of Hope x
ka No. 1 are being tested for inheritance of resistance to bunt. The data
btained this year are not yet assembled.

The results obtained this year with the date-of-seeding test with sowing
unt-inoculated seed of five varieties of spring wheat also are shown. In gen-
ral, the results agree with those obtained the previous three years, the percentages of bunt decreasing as the date of seeding advanced. This apparently
is due to warmer soil conditions in the later seedings and to a shortening of
the period of infection. Soil thermograph records were obtained and soil-
moisture determinations were made to obtain information regarding the possible
factors influencing the percentage of smut.

Annual and average percentages of bunt obtained from certain varieties of
spring wheat grown in the smut nursery from bunt-inoculated seed on the Dickinson Substation during the period from 1927 to 1929[1]

Variety	Percentage of bunt			
	1927	1928	1929	Average
Turkey x Florence G334	0	0	0	0
Hope	T	1	0	0.3
Kota x Kanred B2-1 .7	T	0	3	1
Axminster	7	5	14	9
Quality	15	12	8	12
Marquillo	20	7	6	11
Renfrew	16	14	16	15
Reliance	22	24	6	17
Marquis	21	24	27	24
Garnet	26	31	15	24
Red Fife	24	26	24	25
Haynes Bluestem	32	25	34	30
Preston	35	24	37	32
"Hurdsfield"	17	42	45	35
Supreme	21	46	45	37
Power	30	41	44	38
Reward	36	61	34	44
Marquis x Kota 1656.84	51	53	42	49
Ceres	51	63	59	58
Kota	55	74	52	60
Ulka No. 1	84	77	84	82

[1] Many other varieties and hybrids have been tested for bunt resistance
but the results are not given here.

Percentages of bunt infection obtained from a date-of-seeding experiment with 5 varieties of spring wheat sown at 10-day intervals with bunt inoculated seed on the Dickinson Substation in 1929[1]

Date of Seeding	No. of days seeding to emergence	Percentage of bunt					
		Hope	Quality	Marquis	Kota	Ulka No.1	Average
April 13	15	0.5	10	17	60	86	35
April 22	15	0.5	8	12	70	87	36
May 1	14	2.5	3	9	36	66	23
May 11	7	0	0	4	20	53	15
May 21	7	0	0.8	4	17	39	12
June 1	7	0	0	0	13	37	10
June 11	5	0	0	0	0	8	1.6
June 21[2]	5	0	0	0	0	3	0.6
July 1[2]	5	0	0	0	0	0	0
Average		0.4	2.4	5.1	24	42	15

1/
   The smut used was Tilletia levis obtained originally from Kota wheat at Dickinson.

2/
   Heads produced from this seeding were not mature enough to determine accurately whether any smut was present.

Northern Great Plains Field Station, Mandan (Cereal Agronomy, V. C. Hubbard)

Northern Great Plains Field Station, Mandan (Flax Breeding, J. C. Brinsmade, Jr.) (October 16)

During the first half of October we have enjoyed Indian Summer weather except for a short rainy period. The maximum temperature was 83 degrees on October 5, and the minimum 32 degrees on October 7. Light frost has been noted nearly every night in low places bordering the rivers, but freezing temperatures were not recorded except on October 7.

The total precipitation for this period was 1.22 inches, all of which was recorded on the four days, October 8 to 11, inclusive.

The remaining flax varietal and date-and-rate-of-seeding-and-tillage plots have been threshed, and the seed has been cleaned. The average yields are presented in the following tables:

Average acre yields of 20 flax varieties grown in triplicate 50th-acre plots at Mandan, N. Dak., in 1929

Variety	C. I. No.	Yield, 1929 (Bu. per acre)
Bison	389	5.0
Redwing	320	4.9
Sib 206	473	4.6
Hybrid 19 x 112 Selection	385	4.5
Hybrid 19 x 112 Selection	478	4.5
Winona	481	4.4
Selection 167-254	475	4.3
Selection 8-17	485	4.2
Hybrid 167 x 179 Selection	476	4.2
Selection C. I. 119	474	4.2
N. D. R. 52 (N. D. 3080)	275	4.1
Rio (Long 79)	289	4.1
Linota Selection	482	4.1
Linota	244	4.0
N. D. R. 114	13	4.0
N. D. 40013	241	4.0
Slope	274	3.9
Buda	326	3.7
Chippewa	178	3.7
Commercial Argentine	488	3.4

Average acre yields in the date-and-rate-of-seeding-and-tillage experiment with flax at Mandan, N. D., in 1929, and annual average yields for the four years 1926 to 1929, inclusive

Date of Seeding	Tillage treatment [1]	Average yield (Bu. per acre)	
		1929	1926-1929
April 20	DDH 4-20	4.1	4.7
May 1	DD 4-20, DDH 5-1	7.1	4.4
May 11	DD 4-20, 5-1, DDH 5-11	6.0	6.1
May 20	DD 4-20, 5-1, 5-11, DDH 5-20	4.4	5.2
May 31	DD 4-20, 5-1, 5-11, 5-20, DDH 5-31	3.6	4.0
June 10	DD 4-20, 5-1, 5-11, 5-20, 5-31, DDH 6-10	3.6	3.1
May 20	PDHPk 5-20	3.5	3.6
May 31	PDHPk 5-31	2.8	3.7
June 10	PDHPk 6-10	1.4	1.9
Rate of Seeding [2]			
16 pounds		4.0	3.9
24 pounds		5.5	5.0
32 pounds		4.9	4.9

[1]
    DD=double disk, H=harrow, D=pack with disk, Pk=pack with cultipacker.
[2]
    Average of six plots sown at six dates indicated above.

Bison flax produced the highest average yield in the triplicated triple-row nursery as well as in the varietal plots.

Early spring rains followed by drought, and cool weather in May, which delayed the development of weeds, doubtless account for the higher yield of the flax sown on May 1. The stand and consequently the yield of flax sown on April 20 were reduced by freezing temperatures early in May.

Yields of flax harvested at intervals after ripening indicate considerable loss of seed from shattering in some varieties and hardly any loss in others. Significant varietal differences in percentage of loss after ripening are evident.

Agricultural Experiment Station, State College Station, Fargo (Flax Diseases, L. W. Boyle)

Williston Substation, Williston (E. G. Schollander) (October 12)

Yields of spring wheat varieties grown in triplicate plots on summer fallow at Williston in 1929

Variety	C. I. No.	Yield (Bu. per acre)
Hard Red Spring		
Ceres	6900	28.1
Reward	8182	26.8
Garnet	8181	26.5
Ruby	6047	26.4
Kota x Marquis 1656.84	8004	26.4
Supreme	8026	26.2
Kota x Marquis 1656.85	8385	26.1
Marquis-Mitchell	----	25.8
Marquis	3641	24.8
Reliance	7370	24.7
Kota	5878	24.6
Marquillo	6887	22.9
Renfrew	8194	21.0
Volga	----	19.8
Hope	8178	18.8
Montana King	8878	18.1
N. D. R. 209	----	17.6
White		
Quality	6607	23.7
Durum		
Monad	3320	20.5
Nodak	6519	19.9
Kubanka	1440	19.5
Mindum	5296	18.2

Langdon Substation, Langdon (Wheat Improvement, G. S. Smith)

MONTANA

Judith Basin Branch Station, Moccasin (Cereal Agronomy, B. B. Bayles)

WESTERN BASIN AND COAST AREAS (North to West and South)

IDAHO

Aberdeen Substation, Aberdeen (Cereal Agronomy, L. L. Davis)

Agricultural Experiment Station, Moscow (Stripe Rust, C. W. Hungerford)

WASHINGTON

Agricultural Experiment Station, Pullman (Cereal Breeding, E. F. Gaines)

Agricultural Experiment Station, Pullman (Stinking Smuts of Wheat, H.H.Flor)

OREGON

Sherman County Branch Station, Moro (Cereal Agronomy, D. E. Stephens)

CALIFORNIA

Biggs Rice Field Station, Biggs (Rice Agronomy, J. W. Jones)

University Farm, Davis (Cereal Agronomy, G. A. Wiebe)

Agricultural Experiment Station, Berkeley (Cereal Smuts, F. N. Briggs)

BARBERRY ERADICATION PROGRESS

OHIO

Ohio State University, College of Agriculture, Columbus, J. W. Baringer

INDIANA

Purdue University College of Agriculture, LaFayette, W. E. Leer [October 22

Mr. C. H. Miller, a former barberry field man in Indiana, now employed as a salesman with Swift & Co. in northern Indiana, has reported 31 leads on the location of barberry bushes in his territory in the past four months. Mr. Miller has had six summers' experience as a barberry agent, and these leads are no doubt all authentic. It is planned to have two field men investigate as many of the leads of barberry locations this fall as time will permit.

Mr. McCoy began his educational activities in southern Indiana on October 7. It is planned to continue the activities there so long as the roads remain in good condition. Fortunately, in central Indiana all roads remain passable during the entire year, and work can be done there throughout the winter months. In southern and northern Indiana, not all the roads are passable in winter.

MICHIGAN

Agricultural College, East Lansing, W. F. Reddy

WISCONSIN

Department of Agriculture, State Capitol Annex, Madison, R. M. Caldwell (October 14)

Most of the barberry-eradication field activities in Wisconsin were terminated the last week in September. At that time the intensive survey of Rock County still was incomplete, approximately three townships needing to be surveyed. Only small heavily infested areas in Dane County were covered this summer. The survey in the Black Earth area of escaped bushes still was confined to heavily infested territory, although in some places areas were reached which had relatively few bushes. It seems probable that the greater portion of the heavily infested region has been surveyed, and that next season more rapid progress may be expected in the Black Earth area.

A total of 46,472 bushes and seedlings was destroyed in the State this
ear. The largest number was found in Dane County. However, an area of
scaped bushes was discovered in Rock County and completely surveyed, 5,491
ushes and seedlings being destroyed. More than 85 tons of salt were used in
radication this season.

Stem rust in the southern part of the State was much more severe than it
as last season. The greatest loss was sustained by the oat crop, which is
xtensively grown in Wisconsin. The following estimates represent stem-rust
osses in Wisconsin for 1929:

```
            Oats - - - - - - - 6.7 per cent
            Barley - - - - - - 2.3   Do
            Rye  - - - - - - - trace
            Spring wheat - - - 8.3 per cent
            Winter wheat - - - trace.
```

The attempt to estimate the loss in oats was complicated by a severe epi-
emic of crown rust which undoubtedly caused heavy losses in the same region
here stem rust was abundant. These two rusts may be held largely responsible
or the generally light oat crop in the southern counties.

ILLINOIS

Box 72, Post Office Building, Urbana, R. W. Bills

IOWA

Iowa State College, Ames, P. W. Rohrbaugh

MINNESOTA

Agricultural Experiment Station, University Farm, St. Paul, L. W. Melander

NEBRASKA

College of Agriculture, University Farm, Lincoln, B. F. Dittus, Acting in
Charge

SOUTH DAKOTA

College of Agriculture, Brookings, R. O. Bulger

NORTH DAKOTA

Agricultural Extension Division, State College Station, Fargo, G

MONTANA

State College of Agriculture, Bozeman, W. L. Popham

WYOMING

College of Agriculture, University of Wyoming, Laramie, W. L. Po

COLORADO

Agricultural College, Ft. Collins, E. A. Lungren

C E R E A L   C O U R I E R

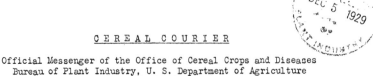

Official Messenger of the Office of Cereal Crops and Diseases
Bureau of Plant Industry, U. S. Department of Agriculture
(NOT FOR PUBLICATION)

Vol. 21   No. 27
October 31, 1929
Personnel (Oct. 21-31) and General Issue

PERSONNEL ITEMS

Mr. Colburn C. Fifield, associate baking technologist in cooperative baking
investigations with the Grain Division of the Bureau of Agricultural Economics,
was authorized to go on October 31 to New York City and Jersey City to study
the manufacture of alimentary pastes and macaroni and to study tests applied to
soft wheat flours used in the manufacture of biscuits and crackers. Mr. Fifield
will be away about five days.

Dr. J. R. Holbert, senior agronomist in charge of the cereal-disease investigations conducted in cooperation with Funk Bros. Seed Co., of Bloomington,
Ill., and the Illinois Agricultural Experiment Station, wrote on October 12 of
spending three hours looking over corn fields from the air. He was accompanied
by Mr. Bills, agricultural editor of the Bloomington Pantagraph, who took a picture from the aeroplane, showing the field refrigeration chambers and the incu-
bation tent constructed by Mr. P. E. Hoppe, of Madison, Wis. Dr. Holbert was
not entirely satisfied with the picture but believes that it offers interesting
suggestions for the possibility of getting better aeroplane views next season.
Dr. Holbert says: "It was a real treat and, needless to say, a thrill."

Mr. M. A. McCall, principal agronomist in charge of cereal agronomy, returned to Washington on October 28 from a month's trip in the West in the interests of cooperative cereal investigations.

VISITORS

Mr. G. T. French, Chief Botanist and State Entomologist, State Depar
of Agriculture and Immigration, Richmond, Va·, was an Office visitor on O
31. `. Mr. French was especially interested in getting information on th
identification of Fulghum and Red Rustproof oats from grain samples.

Dr. R. J. Garber, Head of the Department of Agronomy and Genetics of
University of West Virginia, was an Office visitor on October 26.

Dr. C. G. Woodbury, of the Research Department of the National Canne
Association, with headquarters at Washington, D. C., called at the Office
October 29.

MANUSCRIPTS AND PUBLICATIONS

62 A manuscript entitled "A Method for the Determination of Uronic Acids," by Allan D. Dickson, Henry Otterson, and Karl Paul Link, was approved October 29 for publication in the Journal of the American Society of Agronomy.

63 A manuscript entitled "Nuclear Divisions in the Pollen Mother-Cells of Triticum, Aegilops, and Secale, and Their Hybrids," by A. E. Longley and W. J. Sando, was submitted on August 22 for publication in the Journal of Agricultural Research.

Galley proof of Technical Bulletin 143 entitled "Field Studies on the Rust Resistance of Oat Varieties," by M. N. Levine, E. C. Stakman, and T. R. Stanton, was read on October 24.

The manuscript entitled "Wheat Production in America," by C. R. Ball, appears in the Encyclopedia Britannica 23: 563-564. 14th ed. 1929.

The article entitled "The Value of Physiologic-Form Surveys in the Study of the Epidemiology of Stem Rust," by E. C. Stakman, M. N. Levine, and J. M. Wallace, appears in Phytopathology 19 (10): 951-959, figs. 1-2. October, 1929. (Cooperative investigations between the Office of Cereal Crops and Diseases and the Minnesota Agricultural Experiment Station.)

CHICAGO MEETINGS
November 11-15, 1929

The Land-Grant Colleges and affiliated societies will meet in Chicago during the week beginning Monday, November 11.

The corn improvement conference held under the auspices of the Corn Improvement Committee under the Purnell Act will be held on November 13. Mr. F. D. Richey is secretary of the Committee.

The American Society of Agronomy will meet at the Stevens Hotel, Chicago, on November 14 and 15. Mr. M. A. McCall will discuss the relationship of the United States Department of Agriculture and the State experiment stations in cooperative programs.

Dr. C. R. Ball expects to be in attendance at the meetings during the week and while there to confer with Station directors and agronomists.

C E R E A L   C O U R I E R

Official Messenger of the Office of Cereal Crops and Diseases
Bureau of Plant Industry, U. S. Department of Agriculture
(NOT FOR PUBLICATION)

Vol. 21   No. 28
November 10, 1929
Personnel (Nov. 1-10) and Field Station (Oct. 16-31) Issue

NOTICE

Beginning in December the Cereal Courier will appear on the 15th and last days of the month until April, 1930. Contributors of news items will please continue to send their notes on the 15th and last days of each month.

PERSONNEL ITEMS

Dr. C. R. Ball, principal agronomist in charge, left Washington on November 11 for Chicago to attend the meetings of the Land-Grant College Association and the American Society of Agronomy to be held the week of November 11. Dr. Ball will confer with officials of State agricultural experiment stations and field employees of the Office who may be in attendance at these meetings regarding cooperative cereal investigations.

Mr. J. Allen Clark, senior agronomist in charge of western wheat investigations, has been authorized to attend the meetings of the American Society of Agronomy at Chicago on November 14 and 15. Mr. Clark is chairman of the Sub-Committee on Wheat Registration of the Society and will present the annual report of this Sub-Committee at the business session.

Mr. L. L. Davis, junior agronomist in charge of the cooperative cereal experiments at the Aberdeen (Idaho) Substation, has been authorized to go to the Kansas Agricultural Experiment Station for the winter months to make an additional study of genetic material that was sown before he left Manhattan early in 1929 to take up the work at Aberdeen. Mr. Davis also will complete a statistical study of the protein and milling and baking data from the wheats grown in the cereal nursery at Manhattan. He will remain at Manhattan until March 10, 1930.

Mr. M. A. McCall, principal agronomist in charge of cereal-agronomy investigations, will leave Washington on November 13 to attend the meetings of the
American Society of Agronomy on November 14 and 15. Mr. McCall will confer
with officials of the State agricultural experiment stations and field employees
of the Office who may be in attendance at the meetings. Mr. McCall is scheduled
to present a paper entitled "The Function of the U. S. Department of Agriculture
in the State Program of Agronomic Research" before the Society on November 14.

Mr. M. T. Meyers, field assistant in corn-borer research at Wooster and
Bono, Ohio, came to Washington on November 4 to prepare a manuscript on the
results of the cooperative corn-borer experiments. Mr. Meyers left Washington
on November 9.

Mr. F. D. Richey, senior agronomist in charge of corn investigations, left
Washington on November 11 for a field trip. While in Chicago he will attend on
November 13 the meeting of the Corn Improvement Committee established by the
agricultural experiment stations of the Corn Belt under the Purnell Act. He
also will attend the meetings of the American Society of Agronomy on November
14 and 15. Mr. Richey also will confer with officials of the University of
Chicago regarding physiologic experiments with corn.

Mr. Richey's trip will include stops in Ohio, Iowa, Nebraska, Kansas,
Missouri, and Wisconsin, where he will confer with cooperating officials about
corn investigations.

Mr. John F. Trost, associate pathologist in the cooperative cereal-disease
investigations conducted at the Purdue University Agricultural Experiment Station, has been authorized to attend;at his own expense, on November 13, the
meeting of the Corn Improvement Committee established by the agricultural experiment stations of the Corn Belt under the Purnell Act, as well as the meetings of
the American Society of Agronomy to be held on November 14 and 15.

VISITORS

Mr. Edward C. Johnson, Director of the Washington Agricultural Experiment
Station, Pullman, Wash., was an Office visitor on November 4 and 9.

Dr. Alexander McTaggart, Senior Plant Introduction Officer, Council for
Scientific Industrial Research, Canberra, Australia, was an Office caller on
November 5 and interviewed several members of the Office staff.

Mr. S. G. Ujansky, Professor of Agricultural Economy, of the Scientific
Research Institute of Agricultural Economy, Moscow, U. S. S. R., was in the
Office on November 6 to confer with various project leaders with special refer-
ence to economic aspects of the cereal crops.

MANUSCRIPTS AND PUBLICATIONS

64 A manuscript entitled "Chromosome Number and the Mutation Rate in Avena and Triticum," by L. J. Stadler, was approved on November 1 for submittal to the Proceedings of the National Academy of Sciences.

65 A manuscript entitled "Apparatus and Method for Obtaining Sterile Filtrates of Biological Fluids," by Emery R. Ranker, was submitted on November 6 for publication in the Journal of Agricultural Research.

66 A manuscript entitled "Determining the Date of Silking in Experiments with Corn," by Marion T. Meyers, was approved on November 7 for submittal to the Journal of the American Society of Agronomy.

Page proof of Farmers' Bulletin 1611 entitled "Oats in the Western Half of the United States," by T. R. Stanton and F. A. Coffman, was read on November 7.

Second page proof of Tech. Bul. 96 entitled "Yields of Barley in the United States and Canada, 1922-1926," by H. V. Harlan, L. H. Newman, and Mary L. Martin was read on November 4.

The article entitled "Mosaic Diseases in the Canary Islands, West Africa, and Gibraltar," by H. H. McKinney, appears in the Journal of Agricultural Research 39 (8): 557-573, figs. 1-21. October 15, 1929.

U. S. Dept. Agr. Tech. Bul. 133 entitled "Flax Cropping in Mixture with Wheat, Oats, and Barley," by A. C. Arny, T. E. Stoa, Clyde McKee, and A. C. Dillman, was received from the Government Printing Office on November 11, bearing date of September, 1929. (In cooperation with the agricultural experiment stations of Minnesota, North Dakota, Montana, South Dakota, Wisconsin, and Ohio.)

The article entitled "Review of the Literature on Pollination, Hour of Blooming, and Natural Crossing in Rice," by Jenkin W. Jones, has been published in multigraphed form. 13 p. 1929

FIELD STATION CONDITION AND PROGRESS

(All experiments except those conducted at the Arlington Experiment Farm, Ro
Va., are in cooperation with State agricultural experiment stations or oth
agencies.)

HUMID ATLANTIC COAST AREA (South to North)

GEORGIA

State College of Agriculture, Athens (Cereal Agronomy, R. R. Childs)
(November 5)

Owing to unfavorable weather conditions there has been some delay in so
winter grains on the Station farm. However, most of the oats were sown abou
October 15. They have emerged with excellent stands.

VIRGINIA

Arlington Experiment Farm, Rosslyn (Small Grain Agronomy, J. W. Taylor)

Arlington Experiment Farm, Rosslyn (Corn Breeding, F. D. Richey)

Arlington Experiment Farm, Rosslyn (Cereal Smuts, V. F. Tapke, Acting i
Charge)

Arlington Experiment Farm, Rosslyn (Virus Diseases, H. H. McKinney)

NEW YORK

Cornell University Agricultural Experiment Station, Ithaca (Cereal Bre
H. H. Love) (W. T. Craig)

HUMID MISSISSIPPI VALLEY AREA (South to North)

LOUISIANA

Rice Experiment Station, Crowley (Rice Agronomy, J. M. Jenkins)

Agricultural Experiment Station, Baton Rouge (Corn Breeding, H.F.Stone

TENNESSEE

Agricultural Experiment Station, Knoxville (Corn Breeding, L. S. Mayer)

MISSOURI

Agricultural Experiment Station, Columbia (Cereal Agronomy, L. J. Stadler)

OHIO

Ohio State University, Columbus (Corn Breeding, L. R. Jorgenson)

IOWA

Agricultural Experiment Station, Ames (Oat Breeding, L. C. Burnett)

Agricultural Experiment Station, Ames (Corn Breeding, M. T. Jenkins)

Agricultural Experiment Station, Ames (Crown Rust of Oats, H. C. Murphy)

ILLINOIS

Funk Bros. Seed Co., Bloomington (Corn Root, Stalk and Ear Rots, J. R. Holbert)

INDIANA

Purdue University Agricultural Experiment Station, LaFayette (Corn Rots and Metallic Poisoning, J. F. Trost, Acting in Charge)

Purdue University Agricultural Experiment Station, LaFayette (Leaf Rusts, E. B. Mains)

WISCONSIN

Agricultural Experiment Station, Madison (Wheat Scab, J. G. Dickson)

MINNESOTA

Southwest Experiment Station, Waseca (R. E. Hodgson and H. K. Wilson) (October 29)

Yields obtained from spring-wheat varieties grown in triplicate plot experiments at Waseca in 1929.

Class and Variety	C.I.No.	Minn.No.	Nursery No.
Hard Red Spring			
Marquis	3641	1239	---
Double Cross	10005	2305	II-21-47.
Kota x Marquis	8385	2298	1656.85
Do	6898	2224	1656
Double Cross	10003	2303	II-21-28
Ceres	6900	2223	---
Double Cross	10002	2302	II-21-7
Marquillo	6887	2202	II-15-44
Reliance	7370	2308	---
Marquis x Emmer	8177	2301	H-44
Kota x Marquis	8004	2244	1656.84
Double Cross	10004	2304	II-21-42
Hope	8178	2297	---
Reward	8182	2204	---
Supreme	8026	2309	---
Durum			
Mindum	5296	470	---
Mindum x Pentad	10007	2307	II-19-198
Kubanka	1440	2310	---
Nodak	6519	2311	---
Mindum x Pentad	10006	2306	II-19-227

Agricultural Experiment Station, University Farm, St. Paul
E. R. Ausemus)

Agricultural Experiment Station, University Farm; St. Paul
(October 29)

Yields obtained from spring wheat varieties grown in tripli
ments at St. Paul, in 1929

Class and Variety	C.I.No.	Minn.No.	Nursery No.
Hard Red Spring			
Reliance	7370	2308	---
Marquillo	6887	2202	II-15-44
Marquis x Emmer	8177	2301	H-44
Marquis	3641	1239	---
Kota x Marquis	8385	2298	1656.85
Double Cross	10005	2305	II-21-47
Ceres	6900	2223	---
Supreme	8026	2309	---
Double Cross	10004	2304	II-21-42
Do	10002	2302	II-21-7
Kota x Marquis	6898	2224	1656
Do	8004	2244	1656.84
Double Cross	10003	2303	II-21-28
Hope	8178	2297	---
Reward	8182	2204	---
Haynes Bluestem	2874	169	---

Class and Variety (cont'd)	C.I.No.	Minn.No.	Nursery No.	Yield (Bu. per acre)
Durum				
Mindum x Pentad	10006	2306	II-19-227	30.6
Do	10007	2307	II-19-198	30.0
Mindum	5296	470	---	29.6
Nodak	6519	2311	---	29.4
Kubanka	1440	2310	---	25.8

Agricultural Experiment Station, University Farm, St. Paul (Stem Rust, E. C. Stakman)

Agricultural Experiment Station, University Farm, St. Paul (Flax Rust, H. A. Rodenhiser)

West Central Experiment Station, Morris (R. O. Bridgford and H. K. Wilson) (October 29)

Yields obtained from spring wheat varieties grown in triplicate plots at Morris in 1929

Class and Variety	C.I.No.	Minn.No.	Nursery No.	Yield (Bu. per acre)
Hard Red Spring				
Marquis x Emmer	8177	2301	H-44	27.7
Double Cross	10002	2302	II-21-7	25.1
Hope	8178	2297	----	24.3
Double Cross	10003	2303	II-21-28	24.2
Do	10004	2304	II-21-42	23.8
Reliance	7370	2308	----	23.3
Kota x Marquis	8385	2298	1656.85	23.2
Double Cross	10005	2305	II-21-47	22.9
Kota x Marquis	6898	2224	1656	21.7
Marquillo	6887	2202	II-15-44	21.3
Kota x Marquis	8004	2244	1656.84	20.3
Ceres	6900	2223	----	19.7
Reward	8182	2204	----	19.5
Marquis	3641	1239	----	19.0
Supreme	8026	2309	----	16.3
Durum				
Mindum	5296	470	----	28.6
Nodak	6519	2311	----	26.2
Mindum x Pentad	10006	2306	II-19-227	25.5
Do	10007	2307	II-19-198	24.8
Kubanka	1440	2310	----	24.3

Northwest School and Station, Crookston (R. S. Dunham and H. K. Wilson) (October 29)

Yields obtained from spring wheat varieties grown in triplicate plots at Crookston in 1929.

Class and Variety	C.I.No.	Minn.No.	Nursery No.	Yield (Bu. per acre)
Hard Red Spring				
Double Cross	10005	2305	II-21-47	34.2
Do	10003	2303	II-21-28	33.3
Do	10004	2304	II-21-42	32.8
Kota x Marquis	8385	2298	1656.85	32.7
Double Cross	10002	2302	II-21-7	29.6
Kota x Marquis	6898	2224	1656	29.4
Marquis x Emmer	8177	2301	H-44	29.2
Ceres	6900	2223	----	28.6
Kota x Marquis	8004	2224	1656.84	28.1
Reliance	7370	2308	----	27.1
Hope	8178	2297	----	26.3
Reward	8182	2204	----	25.4
Marquillo	6887	2202	----	21.6
Marquis	3641	1239	----	20.5
Supreme	8026	2309	----	15.0
Durum				
Mindum x Pentad	10006	2306	II-19-227	35.1
Mindum	5296	470	----	32.6
Nodak	6519	2311	----	31.6
Kubanka	1440	2310	----	30.4
Mindum x Pentad	10007	2307	II-19-198	29.0

GREAT PLAINS AREA (South to North)

OKLAHOMA

<u>Woodward Field Station, Woodward</u> (Grain Sorghum and Broomcorn, J. B. Sieglinger) (November 2)

The first killing frost occurred on the night of October 30. Most crops were harvested, though a few had been delayed by summer drought and did not ripen.

The sorghum yields will be around average, but those of broomcorn will be below average.

The weather conditions this fall have been ideal for wheat and that sown during September has nearly covered the ground.

The minimum temperature for October was 29 degrees on the 31st; the maximum was 85 degrees on the 6th. The precipitation for the month was 1.84 inches recorded on 14 days.

KANSAS

<u>Agricultural Experiment Station, Manhattan</u> (Cereal Breeding, J. H. Parker)

<u>Agricultural Experiment Station, Manhattan</u> (Corn Breeding, A. M. Brunson) (November 2)

More than twice the usual precipitation was recorded in October, the rainfall on 10 days totaling 5.07 inches as compared to a normal of 2.18 inches. The maximum temperature was 88 degrees on the 16th and the minimum 31 degrees on the 25th. The mean temperature for the month was 58.1 degrees as compared with a normal mean of 56.1 degrees. A light frost occurred on the 21st and the first killing frost on the 25th. The average date of first killing frost at Manhattan is October 9.

The late maturity of the corn crop and the rains in October have delayed considerably the harvesting of experimental corn plots. Under these conditions, the unusually late first killing frost helped to minimize possible seed injury. Corn in this section is turning out somewhat better than expected, although the crop will amount to only about three-fourths of the average production.

Wheat has made an unusually rank fall growth, and many fields have been pastured for two weeks or more. Reports from some localities indicate that Hessian fly may be serious this year.

<u>Agricultural Experiment Station, Manhattan</u> (Wheat Foot Rots, Hurley Fellows

<u>Agricultural Experiment Station, Manhattan</u> (Wheat Leaf Rust, C. O. Johnston (November 1)

The weather in October was very favorable for the growth of winter wheat in most parts of the southern Great Plains. Considerable rain fell over the entire area and no severe killing frosts occurred except in the western part. As a result winter wheat has made a very rank growth; in fact, too rank a growth for this season of the year.

The writer made a trip to southern Kansas late in September to sow a leaf-rust nursery at Harper. Even at that early date many farmers were complaining of the large acreage of volunteer wheat. The light, chaffy crop of last spring resulted in much seed being scattered on the ground by the combines. This seed began germinating with the fall rains and in many cases the farmers let it remain for next year's crop instead of sowing. In general, however, such stands are unsatisfactory because of their lack of uniformity.

The large amount of volunteer wheat and the rank growth of early-sown wheat coupled with the rainy, rather warm, fall weather, have resulted in a very heavy fall infection of leaf rust over much of this area. Considerable stem rust also is present. Many fields are beginning to turn yellow, due to rust infection, and farmers are becoming alarmed. They fear the weakened plants will not surviv the winter. If the temperature declines gradually, however, the wheat plants will continue for some time to put out new leaves, while rust infection will rapidly decrease. Should severe weather come on suddenly, many plants now weakened by rust probably would be killed.

A large leaf-rust nursery has been sown here at Manhattan. This includes 218 pure lines, 50 standard varieties, 61 introductions, 225 hybrid selections in advanced generations, and the uniform leaf-rust sowing of 99 selections. All of these were sown in 5-foot rows. In addition, there are 343 new head selections from promising varieties and hybrids, 6,000 spaced F_2 and F_3 plants, and 67 rows of hybrids in bulk sowings from which head selections will be made. Counting check rows and miscellaneous sowings not mentioned above, the nursery contains a total of 1,551 rows.

Uniform leaf-rust nurseries have been sown at Beeville, College Station, Denton, and Amarillo, Texas; Stillwater and Woodward, Okla.; Harper, Hays, Colby and Manhattan, Kans.; and Lincoln, Nebr.

Fort Hays Branch Experiment Station, Hays (Cereal Agronomy, A. F. Swanson)

NEBRASKA

North Platte Substation, North Platte (Cereal Agronomy, N. E. Jodon) (October 31)

There have been recorded 1.14 inches of precipitation from October 28 to October 31, ending with snow during the last two days.

Corn varieties have been harvested and sorghum varieties have been threshed. The 1928 and 1929 sorghum yields are given in the following table which shows the average of duplicated 6/100 acre-plots. The 1928 crop was threshed in the spring of 1929.

Average acre yield of grain-sorghum varieties grown in duplicated 6/100th-acre plots at the North Platte Substation, North Platte, Nebr., in 1928 and 1929.

Variety	Yield (Bu. per acre)	
	1928	1929
Milo	12.6	16.0
Feterita	9.4	20.1
Yellow kafir	---	23.4
Club kafir	---	19.4
Pink kafir	12.8	8.7
Dawn kafir	11.1	18.6
Sunrise	11.5	16.1
Modoc	---	18.7
Dwarf Freed	---	11.3
Dwarf Straightneck	---	17.5[a]
Dwarf milo	---	11.6[a]
Hegari	10.1	---

[a] Duplicate 1/100th-acre plots.

SOUTH DAKOTA

U. S. Cereal Field Experiments, Redfield (Wheat Improvement, E. S. cFadden) (October 29)

The following yields were obtained from the plot experiments with spring heat at Redfield in 1929

Class and Variety	C. I. No.	Yield (Bu. per acre)
Hard Red Spring		
Ceres	6900	10.4
Reward	8182	9.9
Kota x Marquis 1656.85	8385	9.8
Supreme	8026	9.6
Ruby	6047	9.3
Progress	6902	9.2
Kota x Marquis 1656.84	8004	9.2
Marquillo	6887	8.7
Marvel	8876	8.1
Preston	3081	7.7
Reliance	7370	7.2
Kota	5878	6.9
Marquis	3641	6.9
Hope	8178	6.3
Power	3697	5.3
Haynes Bluestem	2874	3.8
White		
Quality	6607	11.2
Durum		
Acme	5284	6.6
Mindum	5296	6.3
Pierson	4163	6.3
Nodak	6519	6.2
Akrona	6881	5.9
Kubanka	1440	5.6

Belle Fourche Experiment Farm, Newell (Beyer Aune) (October 29)

Yields obtained from spring-wheat varieties grown in duplicate plots at Newell in 1929

Experiment, class, and variety	C. I. No.	Yield (Bu. per acre)
Irrigated Land		
Hard Red Spring		
Reliance	7370	42.2
Ceres	6900	41.9
Marquillo	6887	37.2
Marquis	3641	35.3
Hope	8178	33.1
Supreme	8026	32.2
Reward	8182	30.6

Experiment, Class, and Variety	C. I. No.	Yield (Bu. per acre)
Irrigated Land (cont'd)		
Durum		
Nodak	6519	42.8
Mindum	5296	37.5
Kubanka	1440	34.2
Dry Land		
Hard Red Spring		
Ceres	6900	31.4
Marquis	3641	26.9
Durum		
Kubanka	1440	31.7

NORTH DAKOTA

Northern Great Plains Field Station, Mandan (Cereal Agronomy, V. C. Hubbard)

Northern Great Plains Field Station, Mandan (Flax Breeding, J. C. Brinsmade, Jr.) (November 2)

Cloudy weather with some rain and snow during the last half of October has interfered with harvesting flax in the determination of after-ripening loss. About four inches of snow fell during the last four days of October. Drifting of this snow greatly impeded traffic on the roads of the Field Station for some time. The snow is melting rapidly to-day, but in protected locations it still covers the ground to a depth of several inches.

The maximum temperature for the last half of October was 79 degrees on October 17; minimum, 26 degrees on October 23. The precipitation was 0.59 of an inch.

Yields of the 25 highest yielding varieties of flax grown in triple 17-foot rows in triplicate on uninfested soil, and yields of the same varieties grown on flax-sick soil are presented in the following table:

Yields of the 25 highest yielding varieties of flax grown in triple 17-foot rows in triplicate on uninfested soil, and yields of the same varieties grown or flax-sick soil at Mandan, N. Dak., in 1929

Variety	C. I. No.	Yield (Bu. per acre)	
		Uninfested soil	Flax-sick soil
Bison	389	7.6	6.4
Damont	3	7.3	.1*
Hybrid 11-2-59-1	---	6.9	5.0
Hybrid 167 x 179	476	6.4	4.2
Hybrid 160 x 179	---	6.3	5.0
Reserve	19	6.2	T *
Newland	188	6.0	0 *
Argentine E.	---	5.9	.9*
Argentine F.	---	5.3	1.1*
Linota	244	5.1	6.3
Linota Selection A	482	5.0	5.7

Variety (Cont'd)	C. I. No.	Yield (Bu. per acre)	
		Uninfested soil	Flax-sick soil
Buda Selection	---	5.0	6.5
N. D. R. 114	13	4.9	6.2
Redwing	320	4.8	6.7
Linota Selection B	485	4.7	6.3
Buda N. D. R. 119	326	4.7	4.5
Hyb. 10-3-52-5	---	4.7	3.0
Commercial Argentine	488	4.7	.6*
Winona	481	4.6	5.0
N. D. R. 52 Selection	275	4.6	7.0
Buda Selection	---	4.6	3.0
Rio (L. 79, Argentine)	280	4.5	4.1
Ottawa White Flower	24	4.4	3.7*
Chippewa	178	4.4	5.7
Hyb. 24 x 160 x 19	---	4.4	6.3

Note. All varieties were grown on flax-sick soil in single 17-foot rows, except those indicated by an asterisk (*). The latter were either known to be susceptible, or had not previously been tested for wilt-resistance, and were therefore grown separate from the others in 5-foot rows in triplicate. Varieties grown in single 17-foot rows were all known to be wilt-resistant.

The three strains of commercial Argentine flax, which are grown locally to a limited extent, are very susceptible to wilt, whereas the improved variety, Rio, C. I. 280, is highly wilt resistant.

Dickinson Substation, Dickinson (Cereal Agronomy, R. W. Smith) (November 1)

Mild weather prevailed in October up until the last few days, when blustery weather was followed by rain and snow. The snow is melting to-day and the ground is nearly bare again. The coldest temperature recorded so far was 22 degrees on the 24th, and the warmest for the month was 87 degrees on the 17th. The total precipitation for the month was 1.40 inches or about 0.60 of an inch above normal. The excess moisture falling in September and October has been very beneficial to the winter grain which is in better condition at the substation at this time than for several years. Fall plowing has been aided by the fall rains and more than the usual amount has been done in this district, which usually has not done a great deal of fall plowing.

During the past two weeks a series of agricultural economic conferences has been held in the Slope region of North Dakota. Two-day meetings were held at Mandan, Carson, New England, Beach, and Dickinson. The meetings were conducted by extension specialists from the North Dakota Agricultural College and county agents in cooperation with farmers and farm women. At each conference several committees were formed, each to consider the problems and practices relating to one phase of farming and then to make recommendations for adoption as a part of the extension program.

Yields obtained in varietal tests and the results of different tillage methods obtained at this and other substations in the district were studied as a basis of discussion and recommendation in the various conferences. The meetings showed the interest in dairying and diversified farming in the eastern part of the Slope region and a tendency toward grain farming and the growing of cash crops in the western part. Reports showed a decreased acreage of oats and an increase in barley and flax. The acreage of wheat has increased in certain localities where combines are most numerous.

Agricultural Experiment Station, State College Station, Fargo (Flax Diseases, L. W. Boyle)

Langdon Substation, Langdon (Wheat Improvement, G. S. Smith)

MONTANA

Judith Basin Branch Station, Moccasin (Cereal Agronomy, B. B. Bayles)

WESTERN BASIN AND COAST AREAS (North to West and South)

IDAHO

Aberdeen Substation, Aberdeen (Cereal Agronomy, L. L. Davis)

Agricultural Experiment Station, Moscow (Stripe Rust, O. W. Hungerford)

WASHINGTON

Agricultural Experiment Station, Pullman (Cereal Breeding, E. F. Gaines)

Agricultural Experiment Station, Pullman (Stinking Smuts of Wheat, H.H.Flor)

OREGON

Sherman County Branch Station, Moro (Cereal Agronomy, D. E. Stephens) (October 24)

The drought continues in eastern Oregon. There was no precipitation of consequence in September or October and farmers have begun seeding winter wheat in dry ground. Considerable fallow ground probably will be left for seeding in the spring.

The following tables present the results obtained this year in the cereal varietal experiments on the Pendleton Field Station of the Office of Dry-Land Agriculture. In the winter wheat nursery, 41 varieties were grown. Yields are reported only for the 15 highest and for a few other varieties commercially grown in the Pacific Northwest.

Yields of winter-wheat varieties grown in triplicated three-row blocks
after fallow at the Pendleton Field Station in 1929

Variety	C.I.No.	Nursery No.	Yield (Bu. per acre)
Fortyfold x Federation	8247	----	48.2
Fortyfold Sel. 29	----	----	45.6
Fortyfold x Federation	----	980	45.3
Hard Federation x Hussar	----	1011	43.9
Federation	4734	----	43.8
Fortyfold x Hybrid 128	----	942	43.5
Hard Federation x Martin	----	995	43.1
Arcadian x Hard Federation	----	977	42.7
Fortyfold x Hard Federation	----	964	42.5
Kanred x Marquis	----	Kans. 214214	42.4
Fortyfold x Hard Federation	----	965	42.0
Fortyfold x Hybrid 128	----	945	41.7
Hybrid 128 x Fortyfold	----	1997A4-3-2-2	41.7
Blackhull	6251	----	41.0
Argentine	1569-2	----	40.3
Triplet	5408	----	39.0
Hybrid 128	4512	----	36.4
Ridit	6703	----	36.6
Kanred	5146	----	36.1
Albit	8275	----	32.1

Yields of winter-wheat varieties grown in triplicated 1/20-acre plots afte
fallow on the Pendleton Field Station in 1929

Variety	C.I.No.	Nursery No.	Yield (Bu. per acre)
Fortyfold x Federation	8247	----	43.9
Federation	4734	----	42.1
Jenkin	----	----	39.2
Arcadian x Hard Federation	----	1992A4-4-6-1	37.8
Jenkin Selection 160	----	----	36.9
Hybrid 128	4512	----	36.8
Hybrid 128 x Fortyfold	----	1997A4-3-2-2	36.0
Arco	8246	----	35.5
Albit	8275	----	35.2

Yields of winter-wheat varieties grown in single 2-acre plots after fallow
on the Pendleton Field Station in 1929

Variety	C.I.No.	Nursery No.	Yield (Bu. per acre)
Fortyfold x Federation	8247	----	44.8
Fortyfold Sel. 43	----	----	40.6
Fortyfold Sel. 54	----	----	37.9
Arco	8246	----	36.3
Arcadian x Hard Federation	----	1992A4-4-6-1	35.4
Hybrid 128 x Fortyfold	----	1997A4-3-2-2	35.1
Albit	8275	----	28.8

Yields of spring-wheat varieties grown in triplicated 1/20-acre plots after fallow on the Pendleton Field Station in 1929

Variety	C. I. No.	Yield (Bu. per acre)
Federation	4734	44.7
Onas	6221	44.6
Baart	1697	39.1
White Federation	4981	38.6
Hard Federation Sel. 82	----	38.6
Baart x Federation	8254	37.4

Yields of spring barley varieties grown in triplicated 1/20-acre plots after fallow on the Pendleton Field Station in 1929

Variety	C. I. No.	Yield (Bu. per acre)
Trebi	936	73.4
Arequipa	1256	70.6
Peruvian Sel. 1	----	63.2
Meloy	4656	57.8

Yields of oat varieties grown in triplicated 1/20-acre plots after fall on the Pendleton Field Station in 1929

Variety	C. I. No.	Yield (Bu. per acre)
Markton	2053	92.7
Three Grain	1950	89.1

CALIFORNIA

Biggs Rice Field Station, Biggs (Rice Agronomy, J. W. Jones) (Octobe

The weather in October has been ideal for moving the rice crop, and I that 85 per cent of the crop is now threshed and in the warehouses. We ha had only one shower this month and the temperatures have been higher than : mal.

University Farm, Davis (Cereal Agronomy, G. A. Wiebe)

Agricultural Experiment Station, Berkeley (Cereal Smuts, F. N. Briggs

BARBERRY ERADICATION PROGRESS

OHIO

Ohio State University, College of Agriculture, Columbus, J. W. Baringer
October 31)

The weather of the greater portion of October was favorable for field sur-
ey. Seven agents were kept on second survey in Harrison, Randolph, and Butler
ownships of Montgomery County during the month. They finished the work in
andolph and Butler townships. Five of these seven field men resigned on Octo-
er 31. The other two agents will continue during November in Harrison Town-
hip, which embraces a large part of the city of Dayton and its suburbs to the
orth. It now appears that the second survey of Montgomery County will be about
alf completed by the end of the 1929 field season.

In that part of rural Montgomery County which so far has been covered by
econd survey more locations are being recorded than were found the first time,
ut the situation in respect to number of locations is just the reverse as far
s city locations are concerned.

A start has been made on the compilation and summarization of data for the
1929 annual progress report of barberry eradication in Ohio.

INDIANA

Purdue University College of Agriculture, LaFayette, W. E. Leer (October 31

A barberry demonstration was placed in the convention headquarters of the
Izaak Walton League of Indiana for the period of its annual convention at
LaFayette on October 10 and 11. About 200 delegates from all over the State
attended this convention. The State Department of Conservation had a demonstration at this convention, showing the various phases of its work. The principal
feature of its demonstration was the fish of Indiana.

The survey activities in Montgomery County were discontinued October 31.
Slightly less than 50 per cent of the county was intensively surveyed in 1929.

For the remainder of the season two field men will investigate the reports
of barberry locations in various parts of the State. If weather permits, they
probably will work until some time in December.

MICHIGAN

Agricultural College, East Lansing, W. F. Reddy

WISCONSIN

Department of Agriculture, State Capitol Annex, Madison, R. M. Caldwell

ILLINOIS

Box 72, Post Office Building, Urbana, R. W. Bills (October 23)

Field operations will be suspended at the end of the month. Twelve and one-fourth counties in the south end of the State remain unsurveyed. Six known barberry plantings in those remaining counties were destroyed this month. The second survey of Jo Daviess County was completed in October.

Plans are being made for conducting educational activities in northern Illinois schools during the winter months.

(November 7)

All field operations in barberry eradication were brought to a close on October 31. During the course of the first survey of 10 southern Illinois Counties, 180 bushes were found and destroyed.

The second survey of Jo Daviess County was completed after spending three seasons there. This county is one of the hilliest in northern Illinois and has a large acreage of woodland which has made the intensive survey very slow. In this county 18,867 barberries were found on first survey and 13,590 on second survey.

IOWA

Iowa State College, Ames, P. W. Rohrbaugh

MINNESOTA

Agricultural Experiment Station, University Farm, St. Paul, L. W. Melander (October 24)

In order to complete the survey of Hennepin County this year all of our activities are concentrated on that county. At present conditions are ideal for survey. Most of the trees and underbrush have lost their leaves making it easy to find barberries. In the township in which the survey is now being conducted scattered bushes are being found with frequent regularity. It is not uncommon to find one or two isolated escaped bushes in a single big woodlot. A recheck of many of these failed to locate additional bushes. In many cases the former location of planted bushes was several miles from these escaped bushes.

On Monday, October 21, the survey of the Fort Snelling Military Reservaion was started. The authorities at the Fort detailed six men to do this under he supervision of one of the regular barberry field men. The Reservation conists of approximately seven square miles situated at the junction of the Minneota and the Mississippi rivers. The river banks and flats will be rather dificult to survey. Therefore, the assistance of a detail of soldiers will mean considerable saving to us.

On September 20 the State Leader talked to the teacher institute of McLeod ounty at Glencoe. Teaching plans and file boxes were presented to each of 80 eachers at this institute. It is planned to do the same thing in Rice and akota counties. It is probable that second survey will be started in the latter wo counties next year. Therefore, it is planned to have the rural students cquainted with the relation of common barberry to black stem rust before the econd survey begins.

NEBRASKA

College of Agriculture, University Farm, Lincoln, B. F. Dittus, Acting in harge

SOUTH DAKOTA

College of Agriculture, Brookings, R. O. Bulger

NORTH DAKOTA

Agricultural Extension Division, State College Station, Fargo, G. C. Mayouo (October 11)

The survey activities of 1929 were practically closed on September 28. In this season's survey more than 500 bushes and seedlings were found. This number represents some very important barberry locations in North Dakota. An interesting feature of the survey this year was the fact that again, as in last year and previous years, bushes were found in areas where outstanding local rust epidemics occurred.

In September, County fair demonstrations were held at Ashley, McIntosh County, and Ellendale, Dickey County, in a district of the State where the rust situation of this year points quite directly to local sources of infection. The outstanding demonstration of the season took place near Larson, Burke County September 18, when farmers and business men of that community were shown a rust spread from barberries to grasses. Those in attend~~e were much interested in this field demonstration, which, according to their statements, clearly demonstrated to them the relationship between barberries and stem rust. Besides the local people there were several visitors from outside the county, who came a considerable distance to see this demonstration. Newspapers gave it some very good publicity.

In addition to the talks at the demonstrations, there were talks before
community club meetings and a Rotary Club luncheon at Fargo. Since September
24 literature files furnished by The Conference for the Prevention of Grain
Rust, of Minneapolis, and materials for class room study, including lesson
plans, bulletins, circulars, specimens, plates, etc., have been distributed
to the rural teachers through demonstration meetings held in Cass, Dickey, and
LaMoure counties. Through the courtesy of the State Superintendent of Public
Instruction this office was permitted to take part in these programs, which
afforded an economical opportunity to make personal contact with teachers and
county superintendents who manifested much interest in the short barberry talk
and the educational materials.

MONTANA

State College of Agriculture, Bozeman, W. L. Popham

WYOMING

College of Agriculture, University of Wyoming, Laramie, W. L. Popham

COLORADO

Agricultural College, Ft. Collins, E. A. Lungren

C E R E A L   C O U R I E R

Official Messenger of the Office of Cereal Crops and Diseases
Bureau of Plant Industry, U. S. Department of Agriculture
(NOT FOR PUBLICATION)

Vol. 21   November 20, 1929   No. 29
        Personnel (Nov. 11-20) and Field Station (Nov. 1-15) issue

----

PERSONNEL ITEMS

Dr. C. R. Ball, principal agronomist in charge, returned to Washington
on November 20. In the course of the various meetings at Chicago conferences
were had with many of the Station directors and agronomists with whom this
Office is engaged in present or projected cooperative activities. The Land-
Grant College Association committee on experiment station organization and
policy, under the chairmanship of Director James T. Jardine, of Oregon, and
the joint committee of the Association and the U. S. Department of Agriculture on projects and correlation of research, of which Director F. B. Mumford,
of Missouri, is chairman, both reiterated the advanced stands taken last year
on the subject of cooperation, including the matter of regional problems and
the desirability for inter-Station cooperation by the States comprising such
regions.

In Minnesota a discussion was had on the progress of our activities in
rust epidemiology and barberry eradication, and in Iowa similar conferences
were held on barberry eradication and on crown rust of oats

The generally good autumn weather has enabled effective work in barberry
eradication to be continued later than usual in the fall.

Mr. N. E. Jodon, junior agronomist in charge of the cooperative cereal
experiments conducted at the North Platte Substation, North Platte, Nebr.,
has been authorized to go to Lincoln, Nebr., to spend the winter months at
the University of Nebraska. Mr. Jodon will consult with officials of the
Nebraska Agricultural Experiment Station regarding plans for future experiments and will conduct certain lines of investigation in the greenhouses and
review agronomic literature in the University library, besides preparing his
annual report of the work at North Platte.

Mr. Jodon's address until March 10, 1930, will be Department of Agronomy,
College of Agriculture, Lincoln, Nebr.

Mr. M. A. McCall, principal agronomist in charge of cereal agronomy,
returned on November 18 from Chicago, where he presented a paper before the
American Society of Agronomy.

Mr. J. Milford Raeder, who for several years has been agent in the stripe-rust investigations conducted in cooperation with the Idaho Agricultural Experiment Station at Moscow, resigned his position on September 15. Mr. Raeder will engage in graduate study at the University of California.

Mr. R. G. Shands, agent in cooperative investigations of barley scab conducted at Madison, Wis., has been authorized to go to Chicago to conduct barley-scab demonstrations at the National Hay and Grain Show to be held during the week of November 29.

Miss Stephanie Shiman, assistant clerk-stenographer in the Washington office since September 1, 1922, resigned her position on November 15 Miss Shiman left for California. Miss Mary A. Kelly has been appointed to succeed Miss Shiman.

Mr. D. E. Stephens, superintendent of the Sherman County Branch Station, Moro, Oregon, will be in Corvallis, Oregon, for the winter months to use the library and other facilities of the Oregon Agricultural Experiment Station, and to prepare his annual report of the investigations at Moro. Mr. Stephens' address until further notice will be 2727 Jackson Street, Corvallis, Oregon.

MANUSCRIPTS AND PUBLICATIONS

The following ten abstracts were approved on November 14 for submittal to Phytopathology:

67 Further Studies on Cold Resistance and Susceptibility in Corn, by J. R. Holbert and W. L. Burlison.

68 Progress Report on Barley and Wheat Scab, by J. G. Dickson, R. G. Shands, P. E. Hoppe, Helen Johann, and E. B. Mains.

69 Report upon Scab-Resistant Cereal Varieties, by R. G. Shands, P E. Hoppe, and E. B. Mains.

70 Report upon the Emetic Substances in Gibberella-Infected Barley, by A. D. Dickson, K. P. Link, B. H. Roche, and J. G. Dickson.

71 Feeding Scab-Infected Barley, by B. H. Roche, G. Bohstedt, and J. G. Dickson.

72 Inheritance of Resistance to Puccinia coronata avenae p. f. III, by S M. Dietz and H. C. Murphy.

73 Further Studies on Physiologic Specialization in Sphacelotheca sorghi (Link) Clinton, by L. E. Melchers, G. H. Ficke, and C. O. Johnston.

74 Physiologic Specialization in Puccinia coronata avenae, by H. C. Murphy.

75 Physiologic Specialization in Phlyctaena linicola Speg., by H. A. Rodenhiser.

76 Factors Affecting the Development of the Aecial Stage of Puccinia graminis, by R. U. Cotter.

77 An article entitled "Registration of Improved Wheat Varieties, IV," by J. A. Clark, J. H. Parker, and L. R. Waldron, was approved on November 18 for submittal to the Journal of the American Society of Agronomy.

78 An article entitled "Registration of Varieties and Strains of Oats, IV," by T. R. Stanton, E. F. Gaines, and H. H. Love, was approved on November 18 for submittal to the Journal of the American Society of Agronomy.

79 A manuscript entitled "Broomcorn Growing and Handling," by John H. Martin and R. S. Washburn, was submitted on November 20 for publication in the Farmers' Bulletin series.

Iowa Agricultural Experiment Station Bul. 265 entitled "High Yielding Strains and Varieties of Corn for Iowa," by H. D. Hughes, Joe L. Robinson and A. A. Bryan, has been received, bearing date of July, 1929. (The third author is assistant agronomist of this Office)

Technical Bulletin 131 entitled "Spacing and Date-of-Seeding Experiments with Grain Sorghums," by <u>John H. Martin</u> and <u>John B. Sieglinger</u>, assisted by <u>A. F. Swanson, D. R. Burnham, H. J. Clemmer, E. H. Coles, F. E. Keating</u>, and <u>W. M. Osborn</u>, was received from the Government Printing Office on November 16, bearing date of November, 1929. (Cooperation with the Kansas Agricultural Experiment Station.)

An article entitled "Effect of Smut Infection on the Yield of Selfed Lines and F_1 Crosses in Maize," by <u>L. R. Jorgenson</u>, appears in the Journal of the American Society of Agronomy 21(11): 1109-1112. November, 1929. ("This study is a part of the general program of corn breeding conducted cooperatively by the Department of Agronomy, Ohio Agricultural Experiment Station, the Department of Farm Crops, Ohio State University, and the Bureau of Plant Industry.")

FIELD STATION CONDITION AND PROGRESS

(All experiments except those conducted at the Arlington Experiment Farm, Rosslyn, Va., are in cooperation with State agricultural experiment stations or other agencies.)

HUMID ATLANTIC COAST AREA (South to North)

GEORGIA

State College of Agriculture, Athens (Cereal Agronomy, R. R. Childs)

VIRGINIA

Arlington Experiment Farm, Rosslyn (Small Grain Agronomy, J. T. Taylor)

Arlington Experiment Farm, Rosslyn (Corn Breeding, F. D. Richey)

Arlington Experiment Farm, Rosslyn (Cereal Smuts, V. F. Tapke, Acting in Charge)

Arlington Experiment Farm, Rosslyn (Virus Diseases, H. H. McKinney)

NEW YORK

Cornell University Agricultural Experiment Station, Ithaca (Cereal Breeding, H. H. Love) (W. T. Craig)

HUMID MISSISSIPPI VALLEY AREA (South to North)

LOUISIANA

Rice Experiment Station, Crowley (Rice Agronomy, J. M. Jenkins)

Agricultural Experiment Station, Baton Rouge (Corn Breeding, H. F. Stoneberg)

TENNESSEE

Agricultural Experiment Station, Knoxville (Corn Breeding, L. S. Mayer)

MISSOURI

Agricultural Experiment Station, Columbia (Cereal Agronomy, L. J. Stadler

OHIO

Ohio State University, Columbus (Corn Breeding, L. R. Jorgenson)

IOWA

Agricultural Experiment Station, Ames (Oat Breeding, L. C. Burnett)

Agricultural Experiment Station, Ames (Corn Breeding, M. T. Jenkins)

Agricultural Experiment Station, Ames (Crown Rust of Oats, H. C. Murphy)

ILLINOIS

Funk Bros. Seed Co., Bloomington (Corn Root, Stalk and Ear Rots, J. R. Holbert)

INDIANA

Purdue University Agricultural Experiment Station, LaFayette (Corn Rots and Metallic Poisoning, J. F. Trost, Acting in Charge)

Purdue University Agricultural Experiment Station, LaFayette (Leaf Rusts, E. B. Mains)

WISCONSIN

Agricultural Experiment Station, Madison (Wheat Scab, J. G. Dickson)

MINNESOTA

Agricultural Experiment Station, University Farm, St. Paul (Wheat Breeding, E. R. Ausemus)

Agricultural Experiment Station, University Farm, St. Paul (Stem Rust, E. C. Stakman)

Agricultural Experiment Station, University Farm, St. Paul (Flax Rust, H. A. Rodenhiser)

GREAT PLAINS AREA (South to North)

OKLAHOMA

Woodward Field Station, Woodward (Grain Sorghum and Broomcorn, J. B. Sieglinger)

KANSAS

Rest Experiment Field (Wilson County) I. K. Landon (Nov. 15)

Through the courtesy of the Kansas Agricultural Experiment Station, Mr.
I. K. Landon, in charge of Southeastern Kansas Experiment Fields, has reported
the yields of flax varieties grown in triplicate plots in 1929.

Yields of flax varieties on the Rest Experiment Field (Wilson County)
Kansas in 1929.

Variety	C. I. No.	Yield (Bu. per acre)
N. D. R 114	13	9.9
Argentine (Commercial)	488	9.0
Redwing	320	8.9
Southwestern (local)	---	7.9
Rio (L. 79)	280	7.7
Linota	244	7.7
Bison	389	7.5
Damont	3	5.3

Flax wilt reduced the yield of the susceptible variety Damont, and pasmo
was quite prevalent in the Commercial Argentine and Rio varieties. A thin
stand and considerable lodging probably reduced the yield of the Bison variety.

Agricultural Experiment Station, Manhattan (Cereal Breeding, J. H.
Parker)

Agricultural Experiment Station, Manhattan (Corn Breeding, A. M. Brunson)

Agricultural Experiment Station, Manhattan (Wheat Foot Rots, Hurley
Fellows)

Agricultural Experiment Station, Manhattan (Wheat Leaf Rust, C. O.
Johnston)

Fort Hays Branch Experiment Station, Hays (Cereal Agronomy, A. F.
Swanson)

NEBRASKA

North Platte Substation, North Platte (Cereal Agronomy, N. E. Jodon)

SOUTH DAKOTA

Agricultural Experiment Station, Brookings (K. H. Klages) (Nov. 8)

Yields obtained from spring-wheat varieties grown in triplicated plot experiments at Brookings, in 1929.

Class and Variety	C. I. NO.	Yield (Bu. per acre)
Durum		
Kubanka, S. D. 75-3-15	---	41.7
Nodak	6519	38.9
Mindum	5296	36.1
Acme	5284	34.2
Arnautka	4064	33.3
Monad	3320	31.1
Kubanka	1440	27.5
Hard Red Spring		
Kota x Marquis 1656.84	8004	35.0
Hope	8178	28.6
Ceres	6900	28.0
Reliance	7370	27.9
Reward	8182	27.0
Marquillo	6887	26.9
Garnet	8181	26.7
Kota	5878	23.3
Prelude	4323	21.7
Marquis	3641	20.3
Supreme	8026	15.6
White		
Quality	6607	26.9

Highmore Substation, Highmore (K. H. Klages and S. W. Sussex) (Nov. 8)

Yields obtained from spring-wheat varieties grown in triplicated plot experiments at Highmore in 1929.

Class and Variety	C. I. No.	Yield (Bu. per acre)
White		
Quality	6607	18.9
Hard Red Spring		
Reward	8182	17.4
Kota x Marquis 1656.84	8004	17.2
Supreme	8026	17.2
Ceres	6900	16.8
Marquillo	6887	16.7
Marquis	3641	15.2
Reliance	7370	15.0
Preston	3081	14.0
Hope	8178	12.7
Kota	5878	12.6
Garnet	8181	12.1

Class and Variety	C. I. No.	Yield (Bu. per acre)
Hard Red Spring (cont'd)		
Power	3697	8.3
Haynes Bluestem	2874	8.2
Durum		
Kubanka	1440	15.3
Mindum	5296	13.8
Algerian	3310	13.3
Kahla	6252	13.4
Acme	5284	13.3
Arnautka	4064	12.6
Nodak	6519	11.4

U. S. Cereal Field Experiments, Redfield (Wheat Improvement, E. S. McFadden)

Eureka Substation, Eureka (K. H. Klages and Walter Schonbrod) (Nov. 8)

Yields obtained from varieties of spring wheat grown in plot experiments at Eureka in 1929.

Class and Variety	C. I. No.	Yield (Bu. per acre)
Durum		
Nodak	6519	20.3
Kubanka	1440	19.1
Mindum	5296	16.4
Hard Red Spring		
Reliance	7370	16.1
Marquillo	6887	15.3
Hope	3173	13.6
Ceres	6900	12.8
Marquis	3641	12.5
Reward	8182	12.2
Supreme	8026	10.0

NORTH DAKOTA

Northern Great Plains Field Station, Mandan (Cereal Agronomy, V. C. Hubbard)

Northern Great Plains Field Station, Mandan (Flax Breeding, J. C. Brinsmade, Jr.)

Dickinson Substation, Dickinson (Cereal Agronomy, R. W. Smith) (Nov. 13)

A light snow fell the first week of November and remained for several days before melting. Since then the ground has been bare. Comparatively mild weather prevailed last week. The maximum temperature was 60 degrees on the 11th, and the minimum 13 degrees on the 12th and 13th.

Winter grain in plots and nursery reached a height of about three inches before growth was terminated by cold weather. Germination of this grain had been delayed by the dry condition of the soil.

Owing to the light yields obtained this year only a limited quantity of grain of the different varieties will be available for sending out from this station after reserving seed for sowing in 1930. This is especially true of the wheat varieties, as two samples of each variety have been reserved for milling and baking experiments.

Progress is being made on the annual report of cereal experiments at the Substation.

Agricultural Experiment Station, State College Station, Fargo (Flax Diseases, L. W. Boyle)

Langdon Substation, Langdon (Wheat Improvement, G. S Smith)

MONTANA

Agricultural Experiment Station, Bozeman (J. E. Norton) (Nov. 12)

The following yields were obtained from winter-wheat varieties grown at Bozeman in 1929.

Variety	C. I. No.	Montana No.	Winter Survival. (per cent)	Yield (Bu. per acre)
Triplicated 1/40-acre plots				
Montana No. 36	5549	36	91.7	60.0
Superhard	8054	45	81.7	56.5
Newturk	6935	3	95.0	55.8
Karmont	6700	7	88.3	53.6
Kharkof	1583	3	90.0	50.7
Oro	8220	68	93.3	50.4
Jones Fife	4162	16	93.3	49.8
Turkey	1558	4	86.7	49.3
Ridit	6703	38	95.0	49.3
Kanred	5146	2	91.7	46.7
Albit	8275	44	93.3	37.8
Triplicated 1/120-acre plots				
Minhardi x Minturki	8034	73	100.0	73.3
Turkey x Minturki (N. N. 487)	---	56	100.0	62.0
Turkey x Florence	---	82	100.0	58.7
Regal	7364	69	96.7	58.0
Cooperatorka	8861	49	95.0	58.0
Nebraska No. 60	6250	5	88.3	57.3
Minturki x Bel.-Buff.	8033	64	100.0	56.7
Berkeley Rock	8272	25	88.3	56.7
Iowa 1946	6934	8	95.0	56.0

Judith Basin Branch Station, Moccasin (Cereal Agronomy, B B. Bayles)

North Montana Branch Station, Havre (M A. Bell) (Nov. 13)

The following yields were obtained from winter-wheat varieties grown on fallow at Havre in 1929.

Variety	C. I. No.	Winter survival (per cent)	Yield (Bu. per acre)
	Duplicated 1/23-acre plots		
Turkey x Minessa	8028	60	16.1
Turkey	1558	38	15.3
Kanred	5146	38	13.8
Kharkof	1583	30	13.6
Karmont	6700	14	13.2
Kanred x Minhardi	8031	40	12.1
Oro	8220	20	9.2
	Single 1/23-acre plots		
Montana No. 36	5549	30	18.4
Kanred x Buffum 17	8030	60	13.0
Newturk	6935	50	11.5
Minhardi	5149	60	11.5
Ashkof	6630	40	6.5
Regal	7364	10	4.6

WESTERN BASIN AND COAST AREAS (North to West and South)

IDAHO

Aberdeen Substation, Aberdeen (Cereal Agronomy, L. L. Davis)

Agricultural Experiment Station, Moscow (Stripe Rust, C. W. Hungerford)

WASHINGTON

Agricultural Experiment Station, Pullman (Cereal Breeding, E. F. Gaines)

Agricultural Experiment Station, Pullman (Stinking Smuts of Wheat, H. H. Flor)

OREGON

Sherman County Branch Station, Moro (Cereal Agronomy, D. E. Stephens)

CALIFORNIA

Biggs Rice Field Station, Biggs (Rice Agronomy, J. W. Jones) (Nov. 8)

Practically all, if not all, the California rice crop is now threshed and in the warehouses. We have had no rain to date except for one light shower of 0.23 of an inch in October. Rice yields on commercial fields were much better than expected before the harvest began.

University Farm, Davis (Cereal Agronomy, G. A. Wiebe)

Agricultural Experiment Station, Berkeley (Cereal Smuts, F. N. Briggs)

BARBERRY ERADICATION PROGRESS

OHIO

Ohio State University, College of Agriculture, Columbus, J. W. Baringer

INDIANA

Purdue University, College of Agriculture, LaFayette, W. E. Leer (Nov. 15

Since November 1, 77 barberry bushes on 29 properties have been found and destroyed as a result of leads received from various sources. It is planned to have two men continue to investigate leads as long as weather will permit.

The educational work in the high schools, which is being conducted by Mr. McCoy, is progressing nicely. All of the high schools in six counties have been visited so far this fall. The reports received indicate much interest among the students.

The county agents of Cass and Bartholomew counties have asked that the educational work in the grade schools in these counties be repeated this year. The first grade-school program in Cass County was conducted in 1926, and the first program in Bartholomew County was conducted in 1927. The interest on the part of the county agricultural agents regarding educational work is extremely gratifying.

The major part of the State Leader's time now is being devoted to the preparation of the annual report.

MICHIGAN

Agricultural College, East Lansing, W. F. Reddy

WISCONSIN

Department of Agriculture, State Capitol Annex, Madison, R. M. Caldwell

ILLINOIS

Box 72, Post Office Building, Urbana, R. W. Bills

IOWA

Iowa State College, Ames, P. W. Rohrbaugh

MINNESOTA

Agricultural Experiment Station, University Farm, St. Paul, L. W. Melander

NEBRASKA

College of Agriculture, University Farm, Lincoln, B. F. Dittus, Acting in Charge

SOUTH DAKOTA

College of Agriculture, Brookings, R. O. Bulger

NORTH DAKOTA

Agricultural Extension Division, State College Station, Fargo, G. C. Mayoue

MONTANA

State College of Agriculture, Bozeman, W. L. Popham

WYOMING

College of Agriculture, University of Wyoming, Laramie, W. L. Popham

COLORADO

Agricultural College, Ft. Collins, E. A. Lungren

C E R E A L   C O U R I E R

Official Messenger of the Office of Cereal Crops and Diseases
Bureau of Plant Industry, U. S. Department of Agriculture
(NOT FOR PUBLICATION)

Vol. 21   No. 30
November 30,1929
Personnel (Nov. 21-30) and General Issue

PERSONNEL ITEMS

Dr. J. R. Holbert, senior agronomist in charge of the cereal-disease investigations conducted in cooperation with the Funk Bros. Seed Co., of Bloomington, Ill., and the Illinois Agricultural Experiment Station, has been authorized to attend the meetings of the International Crop Improvement Association to be held at Chicago December 4 and 5 and to read a paper on corn breeding.

and

Dr L. F. Randolph, associate cytologist in the cytological morphological studies of corn conducted cooperatively with the department of agronomy of Cornell University, has been authorized to go to the University of Missouri, Columbia, Mo., to make a cytological study of the corn material coming from Dr. L. J. Stadler's X-ray investigations.

Mr. F D Richey, senior agronomist in charge of corn investigations, has been authorized to attend the meetings of the International Crop Improvement Association to be held at Chicago December 4 and 5.

Mr. Hugo Stoneberg, assistant agronomist in the cooperative corn investigations at Baton Rouge, La., has been authorized to come to Washington to confer with members of the Office regarding the progress of cooperative corn investigations in Louisiana and to prepare reports of his investigations.

VISITORS

Prof. C. B. Hutchison, director of the Giannini Foundation of Agr cultural Economics, and associate director of research at the Californ Agricultural Experiment Station, University of California, was in the Office on November 27 for a conference on cooperative experiments with cereals, including rice, in California.

Dr. L. R. Jones, professor of plant pathology in the University of Wisconsin, was an Office visitor on November 18 and 19.

M. Jean Larivière, 143 Rue de Longchamp, Paris, France, who is a large land operator near Rosario, Argentina, was an Office visitor on November 21 to obtain information on the production of corn. M. Lariv also is interested in the utilization of fiber from seed flax, and afte interviewing Mr. Dillman he was taken to the Office of Fiber Plants to obtain further information.

MANUSCRIPTS AND PUBLICATIONS

80 A manuscript entitled "Relation between the Vigor of the Corn Plant and Its Susceptibility to Smut (Ustilago zeae)," by C. H. Kyle, was submitted on November 23 for publication in the Journal of Agricultural Research.

81 A manuscript entitled "Nutrition as a Factor Influencing the Expression of the Reaction of Corn to Smut Infection," by E. R. Ranker, was submitted on November 29 for publication in the Journal of Agricultural Research.

82 An article entitled "Methods for the Quantitative Extraction and Separation of the Plastid Pigments of Tobacco," by Paul D. Peterson, was approved on November 30 for submittal to Plant Physiology.

Galley proof of article entitled "Observations on Tassels of Teosinte Malformed by Sclerospora," by W. H. Weston, Jr., and J. H. Craigie, for publication in the Journal of Agricultural Research, as read on November 14.

Galley proof of article entitled "Relation of Stomatal Behavior to Stem-Rust Resistance in Wheat," by Helen Hart, for publication in the Journal of Agricultural Research, was read on November 26.

Galley proof of article entitled "Registration of Varieties and Strains of Oats, IV," by T. R. Stanton, E. F. Gaines, and H. H. Love, for publication in the Journal of the American Society of Agronomy, was read on November 29.

Galley proof of article entitled "Registration of Improved Wheat Varieties, IV," by J. A. Clark, J. H. Parker, and L. R. Waldron, for publication in the Journal of the American Society of Agronomy, was read on November 30.

Technical Bulletin 96 entitled "Yields of Barley in the United States and Canada, 1922-1926," by H. V. Harlan, L. H. Newman, and Mary L. Martini, was received on November 22, bearing date of November, 1929. (Cooperation between the Office of Cereal Crops and Diseases and the Dominion of Canada Experimental Farms)

Farmers' Bulletin 1607 entitled "The Nematode Disease of Wheat and Rye," by R W. Leukel, was received on November 26, bearing date of November, 1929.

The article entitled "Correlation Studies with Inbred and Crossbred Strains of Maize," by Merle T. Jenkins, appears in the Journal of Agricultural Research 39(9): 677-721. November 1, 1929. (Cooperation between the Office of Cereal Crops and Diseases and the Iowa Agricultural Experiment Station.)

AMERICAN SOCIETY OF AGRONOMY

Officers, 1929-1930

President. Dr. W. P. Kelley, Professor of Agricultural Chemistry, California College of Agriculture and Agricultural Chemist, California Agricultural Experiment Station. (Address: Riverside, Calif.)

1st Vice President. Dean and Director William W. Burr, Nebraska College of Agriculture and Experiment Station.

2d Vice President. Dr. Arthur B. Beaumont, Head of the Department of Agronomy, Massachusetts Agricultural College and Experiment Station.

3d Vice President. Dr. Selman A. Waksman, Microbiologist of the New Jersey College of Agriculture and Experiment Stations.

4th Vice President. Dr. George Stewart, Professor of Agronomy, Agricultural College of Utah and Agronomist, Utah Agricultural Experiment Station.

Secretary-Treasurer. Dr. Percy E. Brown, Professor of Soils and Chief Soil Chemist and Bacteriologist, Iowa State College and Experiment Station.

Editor. Prof. James D. Luckett, Editor, New York State Experiment Station, Geneva, N. Y.

_____

Three members were made Fellows of the American Society of Agronomy at the meetings held in Chicago November 14 and 15:

Dr. E. F. Gaines, Associate Professor of Farm Crops, State College of Washington and Cerealist, Washington Agricultural Experiment Station, Pullman, Wash.

Dr. H. L. Shantz, President of the University of Arizona, Tucson, Ariz.

Prof. W. L. Slate, Director of the Storrs Agricultural Experiment Station, Storrs, Conn.

AMERICAN ASSOCIATION FOR THE ADVANCEMENT OF SCIENCE
AND AFFILIATED SOCIETIES

December 27, 1929, to January 2, 1930

A number of the members of the Office of Cereal Crops and Diseases are planning to read papers before societies participating in the 86th annual meeting of the American Association for the Advancement of Science to be held in Des Moines, Ia., December 27, 1929, to January 2, 1930.

Ten papers by members of the Office are to be presented before the meeting of the American Phytopathological Society. Abstracts of these papers were listed in the Cereal Courier 21(29): 414. November 20, 1929.

CANADA THISTLE

C E R E A L   C O U R I E R

Official Messenger of the Office of Cereal Crops and Diseases
Bureau of Plant Industry, U S. Department of Agriculture
(NOT FOR PUBLICATION)

Vol. 21   December 15, 1929   No. 31
        Personnel (Dec. 1-15) and Field Station (Nov. 16-30) Issue

----

PERSONNEL ITEMS

Mr. Jenkin W. Jones, superintendent of the Biggs Rice Field Station, Biggs, Calif., is en route to Washington, D. C., to confer with administrative officers regarding plans for future rice investigations and to prepare manuscripts and use facilities of the Department library. Mr. Jones is making stops at points in Texas, Louisiana, Arkansas, and Missouri in the interests of cooperative rice investigations.

Mr. F. D. Richey, senior agronomist in charge of corn investigations, returned to Washington on December 5 on completion of travel in the Corn Belt. He also attended the Purnell Corn Conference and the meetings of the American Society of Agronomy (November 13 to 15) and the International Crop Improvement Association (December 4) all held in Chicago.

Mr. Glen H. Stringfield was appointed agent, effective December 10, in the cooperative corn investigations in Ohio.

MANUSCRIPTS AND PUBLICATIONS

83 A manuscript entitled "Chemical Seed Treatments for Sorghums," by A. F. Swanson and R. E. Getty, was approved on December 2 for submittal to the Journal of the American Society of Agronomy.

84 A manuscript entitled "Some Growth Curves of Barley Kernels," by Mary L Martini, H. V. Harlan, and Merritt N Pope, was approved on December 7 for submittal to Plant Physiology.

85 A manuscript entitled "A Useful Holder for Plot Stake Labels," by A. F. Swanson, was approved on December 11 for submittal to the Journal of the American Society of Agronomy.

Galley proof of article entitled "The Weedishness of Wild Oats," by H. V. Harlan, for publication in the Journal of Heredity, was read on December 10.

Page proof of Technical Bulletin 143 entitled "Field Studies on the Rust Resistance of Oat Varieties," by M. N. Levine, E. C. Stakman, and T R. Stanton, was read on December 11.

----

86 An abstract entitled "Hybridization and Mutation in Puccinia graminis," by E. C. Stakman, M. N. Levine, and R. U. Cotter, was approved on November 15 for submittal to Phytopathology.

DEPARTMENT OF AGRICULTURE
OFFICE OF THE SECRETARY
WASHINGTON, D. C.

Nov. 25, 1929

MEMORANDUM NO. 591

Executive Order No. 5221 of November 11, 1929, is as follows:

Limitation on non-official employment of officers
or Employees of the American Government.

It is hereby ordered that no officer or employee
in the executive branch of the United States Government,
regardless of whether he is on annual leave or leave
without pay, shall be employed with or without remuneration by any foreign government, corporation, partnership,
or individual that is in competition with American industry.

In view of the necessity of individual interpretation of this

order with respect to cases within its scope arising in the Department,

it is directed that hereafter no employee of the Department, whether in

a duty status, on annual leave, or on leave without pay, shall accept

employment with or without remuneration from any foreign government,

corporation, partnership, or individual, without the prior authoriza-

tion of the Secretary.

R. W. Dunlap
Acting Secretary.

UNITED STATES DEPARTMENT OF AGRICULTURE
DIRECTOR OF PERSONNEL AND BUSINESS ADMINISTRATION
WASHINGTON

November 25, 1929.

P. D. A. Circular No. 139

Procurement of Tents and Tentage
Through the Office of the Superintendent
Of Prisons of the Department of Justice.

This Department is advised that the Department of Justice is
now in a position to accept orders for such tents and tentage as may
be required in future by our several bureaus. Accordingly, all such
orders will hereafter be placed direct with the Superintendent of
Prisons, Department of Justice, Washington, D. C., instead of
requesting quotations on same from the commercial market. Require-
ments should be anticipated as far in advance as practicable to
permit a reasonable time for manufacture and satisfactory delivery.
In cases where the Department of Justice is unable to make a
satisfactory delivery it will promptly advise the bureau concerned and authorize it to effect the procurement through proposals
from the commercial market. Telephone inquiries for information
in connection with specific orders may be made of Mr. J. S. Barrows,
Superintendent of Prisons, Department of Justice, Washington, D. C.
Any difficulty which may be encountered in the application of the
new procedure should be referred to the Division of Purchase, Sales
and Traffic.

W. W. Stockberger

Director.

UNITED STATES DEPARTMENT OF AGRICULTURE
BUREAU OF PLANT INDUSTRY
WASHINGTON

OFFICE OF CHIEF OF BUREAU
B. P. I. MEMO. 467

December 10, 1929.

MEMORANDUM FOR HEADS OF OFFICES

Gentlemen:

We have been notified by the Office of Information that from now on the printing requisitions on which the proof is held in the Bureau longer than thirty days will be canceled by the Government Printing Office. Because of the great volume of work it now handles, the Government Printing Office has found it necessary to make this ruling so that its material will not be tied up too long a time on any one job.

All authors should be notified of this action, especially those in the field, so that proof which has to be submitted to them for reading will be immediately handled and returned. It is requested that you cooperate with the Bureau Office of Publications to the fullest extent so that all of our proof may be handled promptly.

Very truly yours,

Wm. A. Taylor
Chief of Bureau.

FIELD STATION CONDITION AND PROGRESS

(All experiments except those conducted at the Arlington Experiment Farm,
Rosslyn, Va., are in cooperation with State agricultural experiment stations or other agencies.)

HUMID ATLANTIC COAST AREA (South to North)

GEORGIA

State College of Agriculture, Athens (Cereal Agronomy, R. R. Childs)

VIRGINIA

Arlington Experiment Farm, Rosslyn (Small Grain Agronomy, J. W. Taylo

Arlington Experiment Farm, Rosslyn (Corn Breeding, F. D. Richey)

Arlington Experiment Farm, Rosslyn (Cereal Smuts, V. F. Tapke, Acting
in Charge)

Arlington Experiment Farm, Rosslyn (Virus Diseases, H. H. McKinney)

NEW YORK

Cornell University Agricultural Experiment Station, Ithaca (Cereal
Breeding, W. T. Craig) (Dec. 6)

The tests of oats and barley for the past season are of doubtful
value because of a very wet spring followed by dry weather.

The wheat test was fairly good, but owing to the mild winter in
New York State some of the best winter-resistant sorts did not show up
as well as in other years. The new wheat hybrid 1243α1-14-3 (Valley x
St. Louis Grand Prize) outyielded the check Forward by only one bushel.
In spite of this we believe the new hybrid of value because of its winter
hardiness.

In comparison with the red-kerneled wheat selections the white-kerneled sorts are still low in yield, but we are continuing our efforts to obtain a good soft, white-kerneled winter wheat to meet the demand for this type in New York.

The rod rows of wheat are starting into the winter in find condition. The following summary indicates the nature of the test this year.

Ten-Row Test	76 red-kerneled sorts 60 white-kerneled sorts
Five-Row Test	27 red-kerneled sorts (17 of these have Aegilops as one parent) 149 white-kerneled sorts (116 of these from cross Rye x Honor x Honor - 27 of these have mostly hairy necks - 11 with no smooth necks found in rows observed)
Two-Row Test	74 red-kerneled sorts (1 Honor x Rye x Honor) 128 white-kerneled sorts (126 from cross Honor x Rye x Honor - 30 of these with hairy necks - 26 with no smooth necks found in rows observed)
Single-Row Test	20 red-kerneled sorts 178 white-kerneled sorts (51 from cross Honor x Rye x Honor, many with hairy neck),
Total Sorts Tested	197 red-kerneled 515 white kerneled

In addition to the sorts tested in rod rows, 2,400 head selections from Junior No. 6 were sown. These were carefully selected heads of this variety from various sources in the State; they are being tested to obtain a soft white wheat of this type.

In the head-row test are included also 100 hybrid selections, and 567 Chinese wheats grown last year at Sacaton and sent to Ithaca by Dr. Leighty. This makes a total of 3,779 sorts under test.

Dr. H. H. Love returned to Ithaca on November 19. Dr. Love has spent the past eight months at the University of Nanking, Nanking, China, in connection with the plant-improvement program for China.

HUMID MISSISSIPPI VALLEY AREA (South to North)

LOUISIANA

Rice Experiment Station, Crowley (Rice Agronomy, J. M. Jenkins)(Dec. 3)

Weather conditions in November were very unfavorable for all kinds of field work. Rain fell on 14 days, resulting in a total precipitation of 14.92 inches. This is the heaviest rainfall that has ever been recorded at this Station for the month of November. The 19-year average for November, not including this year, is 3.84 inches. The temperature for this month was somewhat higher than for November, 1928. The first ice of the season occurred on the 30th. The minimum temperature for this date was 28 degrees F. Last year the first ice was recorded on November 21.

There was just enough good weather during the month to permit the completion of threshing operations. The latter part of the month was devoted mainly to recleaning seed rice for sale and for use on the Station next year.

The American Rice Growers' Cooperative Association announced on November 21 that there were 136,545 sacks (190 pounds each) of rough Fortuna rice in first hands in Louisiana and Texas.

Mr. W. M. Cooper, of the Guantanomo Sugar Co., Guantanomo, Cuba, was a visitor at the Station in November.

Agricultural Experiment Station, Baton Rouge (Corn Breeding, H. F. Stoneberg)

TENNESSEE

Agricultural Experiment Station, Knoxville (Corn Breeding, L. S. Mayer)

MISSOURI

Agricultural Experiment Station, Columbia (Cereal Agronomy, L. J. Stadler

OHIO

Ohio State University, Columbus (Corn Breeding, L. R. Jorgenson)

IOWA

Agricultural Experiment Station, Ames (Oat Breeding, L. C. Burnett)

Agricultural Experiment Station, Ames (Corn Breeding, L. T. Jenkins)

Agricultural Experiment Station, Ames (Crown Rust of Oats, H. C. Murphy)

ILLINOIS

Funk Bros. Seed Co., Bloomington (Corn Root, Stalk and Ear Rots, J. R. Holbert)

INDIANA

Purdue University Agricultural Experiment Station, LaFayette (Corn Rots and Metallic Poisoning, J. F. Trost, Acting in Charge)

Purdue University Agricultural Experiment Station, LaFayette (Leaf Rusts, E. B. Mains)

WISCONSIN

Agricultural Experiment Station, Madison (Wheat Scab, J. G. Dickson)

MINNESOTA

Agricultural Experiment Station, University Farm, St. Paul (Wheat Breeding, E. R. Ausemus)

Agricultural Experiment Station, University Farm, St. Paul (Stem Rust, E. C. Stakman)

Agricultural Experiment Station, University Farm, St. Paul (Flax Rust, H. A. Rodenhiser)

GREAT PLAINS AREA (South to North)

OKLAHOMA

Woodward Field Station, Woodward (Grain Sorghum and Broomcorn, J. B. Sieglinger)

KANSAS

Agricultural Experiment Station, Manhattan (Cereal Breeding, J. H. Parker)

Agricultural Experiment Station, Manhattan (Corn Breeding, A. M. Brunson)

Agricultural Experiment Station, Manhattan (Wheat Foot Rots, Hurley Fellows)

Agricultural Experiment Station, Manhattan (Wheat Leaf Rust, C. O. Johnston)

Fort Hays Branch Experiment Station, Hays (Cereal Agronomy, A. F. Swanson)

NEBRASKA

North Platte Substation, North Platte (Cereal Agronomy, N. E. Jodon

SOUTH DAKOTA

U. S. Cereal Field Experiments, Redfield (Wheat Improvement, E. S. McFadden)

NORTH DAKOTA

Northern Great Plains Field Station, Mandan (Cereal Agronomy, V. C. Hubbard)

Northern Great Plains Field Station, Mandan (Flax Breeding, J. C. Brinsmade, Jr.)

Dickinson Substation, Dickinson (Cereal Agronomy, R. W. Smith)(Nov. 30)

During the past 10 days the temperatures have been below normal most of the time, and some snow has fallen nearly every day. The total precipitation for the month is only slightly above normal, however, and the total depth of snow on the ground at one time has been only about three inches. The maximum temperature for the month was 60 degrees on the 11th, and the minimum 13 degrees below zero on the 21st.

The total precipitation for the year 1929 to date has been approximately 15.50 inches, which is very nearly the normal annual precipitation for this substation. Another month of normal precipitation would make the total for 1929 about 0.40 of an inch above normal. The very light crop was caused by a deficiency of rainfall in June and July.

Winter grain is beginning to receive some protection from the snow, although the ground was almost bare at the time of the 13-below-zero weather.

Yield of flax varieties grown in triplicate plots at Dickinson, N. Dak., in 1929.

Variety	C. I. No.	Yield (Bu. per acre)
N. D. 40034	491	7.5
Linota	244	6.1
N. D. 40046	492	5.7
Newland	188	5.6
Rio	280	5.4
Buda	326	5.2
Bison	389	4.8
Hybrid 19 x 112	383	4.8
Redwing	320	4.2
Sel. of Buda	474	3.9
N. D. R. 114	439	3.2
N. D. R. 52	490	2.6
Sib. 206	473	4.7[1]

Agricultural Experiment Station, State College Station, Fargo (Flax Diseases, L. W. Boyle)

[1] One plot only

Langdon Substation, Langdon (Wheat Improvement, G. S. Smith)

MONTANA

Judith Basin Branch Station, Moccasin (Cereal Agronomy, B. B. Bayles)

WESTERN BASIN AND COAST AREAS (North to West and South)

IDAHO

Aberdeen Substation, Aberdeen (Cereal Agronomy, L. L. Davis)

Agricultural Experiment Station, Moscow (Stripe Rust, C. W. Hungerford)

WASHINGTON

Agricultural Experiment Station, Pullman (Cereal Breeding, E. F. Gaines)

Agricultural Experiment Station, Pullman (Stinking Smuts of Wheat, H. H. Flor)

OREGON

Sherman County Branch Station, Moro (Cereal Agronomy, D. E. Stephens)

CALIFORNIA

Biggs Rice Field Station, Biggs (Rice Agronomy, J. W. Jones) (Dec. 8)

There is some rain today, and it looks as if the prolonged drought is to end.

University Farm, Davis (Cereal Agronomy, G. A. Wiebe)

Agricultural Experiment Station, Berkeley (Cereal Smuts, F. N. Briggs)

BARBERRY ERADICATION PROGRESS

OHIO

Ohio State University, College of Agriculture, Columbus, J. W. Baringer (Nov. 30)

All but two of the field agents in barberry eradication in Ohio, resigned on October 31. In November five per cent of Montgomery County was covered by second survey and considerable resurvey was done in the county in connection with the second-survey operations. Field operations for the season are being discontinued today.

The compilation of location records and cost data and the preparation of maps and discussion for the 1929 annual report of barberry-eradication activities in Ohio are now in progress. It is hoped that the first copies of this report will be completed before Christmas. As soon as the annual report is finished immediate attention will be given to the completion of plans and the preparation of materials for the winter publicity and education program.

INDIANA

Purdue University College of Agriculture, LaFayette, W. E. Leer

MICHIGAN

Agricultural College, East Lansing, W. F. Reddy

WISCONSIN

Department of Agriculture, State Capitol Annex, Madison, R. M. Caldwell

ILLINOIS

Box 72, Post Office Building, Urbana, R. W. Bills

IOWA

Iowa State College, Ames, P. W. Rohrbaugh

MINNESOTA

Agricultural Experiment Station, University Farm, St. Paul, L. W. Melander.

NEBRASKA

College of Agriculture, University Farm, Lincoln, B. F. Dittus, Acting in Charge

SOUTH DAKOTA

College of Agriculture, Brookings, R. O. Bulger

NORTH DAKOTA

Agricultural Extension Division, State College Station, Fargo, G. C. Mayoue.

MONTANA

State College of Agriculture, Bozeman, W. L. Popham

WYOMING

College of Agriculture, University of Wyoming, Laramie, W. L. Popham

COLORADO

Agricultural College, Ft. Collins, E. A. Lungren

CEREAL COURIER

Official Messenger of the Office of Cereal Crops and Diseases
Bureau of Plant Industry, U S. Department of Agriculture
(NOT FOR PUBLICATION)

Vol. 21   No. 32

December 31, 1929
Personnel (Dec. 16-31) and General Issue

PERSONNEL ITEMS

Dr. Carleton R. Ball, notice of whose resignation has been
announced, closes a long and productive service in the United States
Department of Agriculture. A graduate of Iowa State College (B. S.
1896, M. S. 1899, D. Sc. (Hon.) 1920), Dr. Ball was appointed in June,
1899, as assistant agrostologist in the then U. S. Division of Agros-
tology. From that date until June, 1906, he was engaged in the study
of grasses and forage crops in the humid eastern half of the United
States, both North and South. During this period Dr Ball started
the Department's first agronomic field experiments (1900), made a
survey of forage resources of the Southern States (1901-1902), conducted experiments with grasses and forage plants in the South,
including the beginning of cooperation with State agricultural experiment stations (1903), and continued taxonomic and ecologic studies of
North American willows, which made possible, then and later, the determination of hundreds of specimens collected as browse plants for the
U. S. Forest Service and the Bureau of Biological Survey. Dr. Ball's
studies of the willows have been continued in connection with other
duties, and he is recognized as the American authority on this difficult
family.

In June, 1906, Dr. Ball was appointed agronomist in charge of
grain-sorghum and broomcorn investigations in the then Office of Grain
Investigations, which in 1912 became the Office of Cereal Investigations.
He conducted extensive pioneer studies and experiments with grain sorghums
and broomcorn in the southern Great Plains and in the Pacific Southwest.

He developed dwarf and early, drought-escaping and drought-resisting
kafirs, milos, feteritas, and broomcorns suitable as cash and feed
crops. He worked out better methods of growing, harvesting, storing,
and utilizing these important crops. He also discovered the sorghum
midge as the cause of sterility in sorghums, and worked out the seed-
ing-date method of control.

Dr. Ball was acting cerealist in charge from June 16, 1912, to
June 15, 1913, during the absence of Mr. M. A. Carleton, cerealist,
who was granted a year's furlough to undertake investigations for the
Pennsylvania Chestnut Blight Commission.

In 1914 Dr. Ball became agronomist in charge of western wheat
investigations. In this assignment he assembled the material and
initiated the extensive and important studies resulting in Department
Bulletin 1074, "The Classification of American Wheat Varieties," a
classic in its field. He outlined and conducted extensive field experiments covering the entire western United States, and performed an outstanding service to the American agricultural experiment stations in
bringing about standardization and accuracy in varietal experimentation.
His assembling and summarizing of Federal, State, and Canadian varietal
data also pointed the way for another extremely useful and valuable service by the Department.

Appointed in 1918 to head the Office (in 1926 designated Cereal
Crops and Diseases), he was successively cerealist, senior agronomist,
and principal agronomist in charge. In this capacity he welded the
Office into an effective research organization, reaching into almost
every part of the United States, and producing 80 to 90 scientific
publications a year. Extensive and productive cereal pathology studies
were initiated and developed into an important part of the program. The
important barberry-eradication campaign, covering the 13 north-central
states, was organized and developed as a crop-protection service of the
Office. The former Office of Corn Investigations, of the Bureau of
Plant Industry, was put under Dr. Ball's direction in 1919 and developed
into an important and productive unit. The annual appropriations increased from $136,000 in 1918 to $850,000 in 1930, with some $90,000
additional in the pending appropriation bill.

As an administrator, Dr. Ball particularly emphasized cooperation
in research between the Department and the State agricultural experiment
stations. He organized the Office field program on the basis of cooperation with the State stations, and also encouraged cooperation with other
units in the Department. Recognizing the respectively different major
responsibilities of the Department and the State experiment stations, he
organized the Office program on a regional basis, emphasizing the obligation for Department research to supplement and to correlate the regional
programs of groups of State stations rather than to duplicate their activities.

Dr. Ball always encouraged the broadening of both agronomic and pathologic projects to include fundamental research in genetics, plant physiology, and biochemistry, and emphasized the necessity for better trained personnel. Much of the best work done by the Office of Cereal Crops and Diseases can be traced to his encouragement of workers to take additional training. Dr. Ball devoted a great deal of his own time to helping others present their data in a clearer, more logical, and better written form. He himself is the author of more than a hundred papers, dealing with scientific studies, the preparation and editing of scientific papers, scientific terminology, and cooperation in scientific research.

Dr. Ball always has been an indefatigable and tireless worker, carrying in addition to official duties an important part in societies and organizations serviceable to agronomic work. He is a charter member of the American Society of Agronomy, which he has served as Secretary and President. In appreciation of his service to American agriculture he was elected a Fellow of the Society in 1925. He was editor of its Proceedings and Journal from 1910 to 1914. He now holds membership on its editorial board. He also is a member of the editorial board of Plant Physiology. He is Editor of Agronomy for Biological Abstracts.

Dr. L. R. Jorgenson, assistant agronomist and agent in the corn-breeding investigations cooperative with the Ohio Agricultural Experiment Station and the Ohio State University, came to Washington on December 18. He and Mr. Geo. F. Sprague graded canned sweet corn representing 207 different F_1 crosses between self-fertilized lines of the narrow-grain Evergreen variety. Dr. Jorgenson also conferred with members of the Office staff regarding results of the 1929 corn-breeding experiments at Columbus, Ohio, cooperative with the Ohio Agricultural Experiment Station and the Ohio State University. He left for Columbus on December 21.

Mr. Bascom M. King, agent in charge of rice investigations conducted at Elsberry, Mo., in cooperation with the Missouri Agricultural Experiment Station, came to Washington on December 23 to confer with administrative officers regarding plans for continued cooperation at Elsberry and to use the facilities of the Department library. Mr. King will be in Washington about 30 days.

VISITORS

Mr. J. R. Hooker, formerly scientific aid in western wheat investigations, was an Office visitor on December 26. Mr. Hooker is engaged in the practice of law in Youngstown, Ohio.

MANUSCRIPTS AND PUBLICATIONS

_87_ A manuscript entitled "An Inheritance Study of the Distribution of Vitamin A in Maize. III. Vitamin A Content in Relation to Yellow Endosperm," by <u>Sigfred M. Hauge</u> and <u>John F. Trost</u>, was approved on December 20 for submittal to the Journal of Biological Chemistry.

_88_ A manuscript entitled "Wheat Take-All Symptoms Compared with Injuries Caused by Chinch Bugs," by <u>Hurley Fellows</u>, was submitted on December 26 for publication as a Department Circular.

Galley proof of article entitled "Earliness in F_1 Barley Hybrids," by <u>H. V. Harlan</u> and <u>Mary L. Martini</u>, for publication in the Journal of Heredity, was read on December 16.

Galley proof of article entitled "Hygroscopic Moisture of Flaxseed and Wheat and Its Relation to Combine Harvesting," by <u>A. C. Dillman</u>, was read on December 16.

Galley proof of article entitled "Tenuous Kafir Plants," by <u>John</u> B. Sieglinger, for publication in the Journal of Heredity, was read on December 31.

The abstract entitled "Heterothallism in <u>Puccinia graminis</u>," by <u>R. F. Allen</u>, appears in Phytopathology 19(12): 1146-1147. December, 1929. (Cooperation between the Office of Cereal Crops and Diseases and the California Agricultural Experiment Station.)

The article entitled "Registration of Improved Wheat Varieties, IV," by <u>J. Allen Clark, J. H. Parker</u>, and <u>L. R. Waldron</u>, appears in the Journal of the American Society of Agronomy 21(12): 1172-1174. December, 1929.

The article entitled "The Cereal Rusts and Their Control," by <u>H. B. Humphrey</u>, appears in Scientific Agriculture [Canada] 10(4): 225-231. December, 1929.

The article entitled "Registration of Varieties and Strains of Oats, IV," by <u>T. R. Stanton, E. F. Gaines</u>, and <u>H. H. Love</u>, appears in the Journal of the American Society of Agronomy 21(12): 1175-1180. December, 1929.

The article entitled "Observations on Tassels of Teosinte Malformed by Sclerospora," by William H. Weston, Jr., and J. H. Craigie, appears in the Journal of Agricultural Research 39(11): 817-836, figs. 1-4. December 1, 1929. (Both authors were formerly members of the staff of the Office of Cereal Crops and Diseases.)

Articles for 1929 Yearbook

Slight changes have been made in the titles of the five articles submitted by this Office last summer for the 1929 Yearbook of the Department of Agriculture. The titles as approved on December 16 are as follows:

45 Harvesting Flax with Combine Succeeds in Northern Great Plains, by A. C. Dillman.

47 Oats of Fulghum Variety Win Place in Southern States, by T. R. Stanton and F. A. Coffman.

48 Black Stem Rust of Cereals Has More Than 60 Physiologic Forms, by M. N. Levine and E. C. Stakman.

49 Wheat Protected from Black Stem Rust by Dusting with Sulphur, by E. C. Stakman and Lee H. Person, Jr.

51 Barley Scab Effectively Controlled by Rotations and Clean Fall Plowing, by James G. Dickson.

Lightning Source UK Ltd.
Milton Keynes UK
UKHW010711051218
333473UK00012B/653/P